NIGHT FIGHTERS

Stories from the Flyers of Canada's
All-Weather Fighter Force

CF-100 PILOTS—PATH TO GLORY

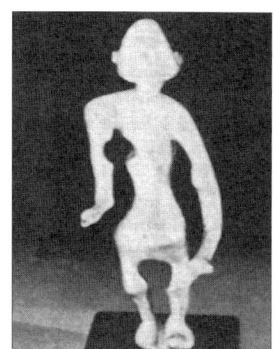

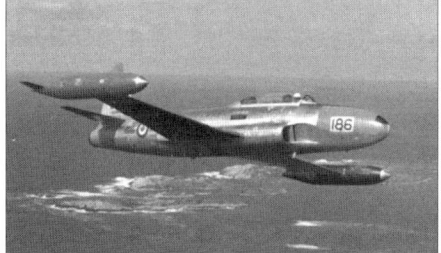

The Pilot

Pointed head to check flap jack
Single eye for manual rocket firing
Built-in headset to eliminate inner helmet
Jutting chin to prevent oxygen leak
Offset head to facilitate reaching blind
Curved spine to fit seat
Bucket-bottom for bucket seat
Indentation under right arm for hard hat
Short right forearm to reach cockpit lights
Long left arm to reach Yaw Damper trim
Strong right biceps to close HP cocks
Strong fingers left hand to check brake pucks
Hole in forefinger to check "press to test" lights
Bowlegged to reach seat "D" ring

CF-100 NAVIGATORS — PATH TO GLORY

The Navigator

Too modest to remain up on pedestal
Permanent hunch back to suit occupation
Built-in headset to eliminate inner helmet
Built-in canopy cleaver for ejection
Right thigh flattened for knee pad
Ball point pen built into index finger
Pencil built into right elbow for Emergency U/C lowering
Long left toe to operate mute switch from stirrups
Flat circular face to fit scope
Scope etched on face to continue on memory if radar fails
Extra eyes, high on side of head to visually check target break.

(*From* The Roundel – *late 50's. submitted by Ray Griffiths*)

VOODOO PILOTS — PATH TO GLORY

VOODOO NAVIGATORS — PATH TO GLORY

Flying Officer John C. Eggenberger, while serving with 445 Sqn., 1960.

Bob Merrick, when he was instructing on F-4Cs at Luke AFB, Glendale, Arizona.

Doug Munro, while serving with 407 Squadron before starting his AW(F) career.

NIGHT FIGHTERS

Stories from the Flyers of Canada's All-Weather Fighter Force

CANADA AND EUROPE
1953 TO 1984

COMPILED AND EDITED BY

JOHN EGGENBERGER   **BOB MERRICK**   **DOUG MUNRO**

GSPH

> Note:
> The opinions expressed in this book
> are not necessarily those of the editors.

GENERAL STORE PUBLISHING HOUSE
499 O'Brien Road, Box 415
Renfrew, Ontario, Canada K7V 4A6
Telephone (613) 432-7697 or 1-800-465-6072
www.gsph.com

ISBN 978-1-926962-21-4

Copyright © All Weather Fighter Association 2011
www.allwxfighters.ca

Design and composition: Magdalene Carson
Printed by Custom Printers of Renfrew Ltd., Renfrew, Ontario
Printed and bound in Canada

No part of this book may be reproduced, stored in a retrieval system or transmitted in any form or by any means, without the prior written permission of the publisher or, in case of photocopying or other reprographic copying, a licence from Access Copyright (Canadian Copyright Licensing Agency), 1 Yonge Street, Suite 1900, Toronto, Ontario, M5E 1E5.

Library and Archives Canada Cataloguing in Publication

    Night fighters : stories from the flyers of Canada's all-weather fighter force : Canada and Europe, 1953 to 1984 / compiled and edited by John Eggenberger, Bob Merrick, Doug Munro.

ISBN 978-1-926962-21-4

    1. Canada. Royal Canadian Air Force--Airmen--Anecdotes. 2. Canada--Armed Forces--Airmen--Anecdotes. 3. Cold War--Aerial operations, Canadian--Anecdotes. 4. Cold War--Biography--Anecdotes. 5. All-weather fighter planes--Canada--History--20th century--Anecdotes. 6. Air defenses--Canada--History--20th century--Anecdotes. I. Eggenberger, John, 1933- II. Merrick, Bob, 1933- III. Munro, Doug, 1933-

UG635.C2N54 2011   358.40097109'045   C2011-904705-5

The AWF memorial cairn was dedicated at the then RCAF Memorial Museum, 8 Wing, Trenton, on September 14, 2002. The monument commemorates the 127 men who lost their lives in aircraft accidents while flying on CF–100 or CF–101 units. One hundred and three were killed in CF–100s, fourteen were killed in CF–101s, nine in T–33s, and one in an Expeditor. This book is dedicated to our many friends and colleagues who gave their lives for their country. We will remember them.

(See Appendix for a complete list of the names inscribed
on the AWF Memorial Cairn.)

IN MEMORIAM

These Contributors are no longer with us.

Lee Evans

Gerry Gagne

Jim Gregory

Hank Hemming

Tom Lambrick

D'Arcy LeDrew

Gord Letcher

George Rawson

Vic Rushton

Contents

Foreword *Joe Schultz*	xiii
Acknowledgements	xv
Introduction *Doug Munro*	xvi

PART ONE : THE CF–100 YEARS

How night-fighters became all-weather fighters *Bill Sterne*	1
The CF–100: Some orientation *Author Unknown*	3
Clunks remembered *Doug Munro*	3
Why in the world . . . ? *Bob Merrick*	6
That final B–25 check at Winnipeg *Gerry Walker*	8
On getting married *John Eggenberger*	10
In the beginning, it was different *Tony Gunter–Smith*	12
A day at the OTU *Ivan Ransom*	13
Emergency? *Hank Hemming*	14
If the glove fits! *Pat Parker*	14
Kelowna air show, 1955 *Gerry Gagne*	14
Another Kelowna air show, 1956 *Pat Parker*	15
How high the Clunk? *Bob Merrick*	16
Bagotville tales *Ian "Nip" Cumming*	18
Hijinks with Jerry Frewen *Hank Sands*	19
The "Professionals" *John Eggenberger*	22
The Air Div mess dinner *Bob Grandmaison*	25
Bon mot *John Eggenberger*	27
Stants *Lee Evans*	27
Middleton magic *Alex Saunders*	27
Musings of an AI navigator *Les Taylor*	28
More ho-hum? *Les Taylor*	29
Aerial buffoonery I *Doug Munro*	30
The 414 All-Weather Fighter Squadron, RCAF North Bay, Ontario, 1959–61 *Greg Stevens*	32
The making of a fighter pilot *Terry Thompson*	33
Operational training *John Jackaman*	37
"Chuck" Harris . . . flak attracter *Tom Lambrick*	53
Aerial buffoonery II *Doug Munro*	56
Failed briefing *Doug Munro*	57
NFB tale *Bruce Montgomery*	58
A 413 Squadron BG tale *D'Arcy LeDrew*	58
Master bus(t) *Robert "Pup Tent" Grandmaison*	59
Abort at BG *David Leigh*	59
An air test? *Bob McKendry*	60
CB and me! *Bob McKendry*	61
Basic nav training *Pete Armour*	64
Two OTU tales *John Angus MacDonald*	65
"Two out of four ain't bad for a Clunk crew" *Scott Maclagan*	65
SARAH *Pete Armour*	68
Sorfleet/Wood *Author Unknown*	68
Stray voltage *Doug Munro and Doug Stuart*	68
That first posting . . . *Bob Merrick*	69
Thunder Bay near-miss *Lloyd Olafson*	71
Ottawa bits *Bob Hyslop*	71
Ottawa blackout *Bob Hyslop*	72
No-notice exercise! *Don Carney*	72
More Bagotville tales *Author Unknown*	73
Quebec carnival *Don Carney*	73
A 409 ejection *Gerry Gagne*	73
Bagotville ejection *Gerry Gagne*	74
Vertigo *Gerry Gagne*	74
A 409 scramble *Gerry Gagne*	74
A 414 Squadron emergency *John A. MacDonald*	75
Nimble Bat 419 Sqn *John A. MacDonald*	76
Per Ardua Ad Ridiculum *Ron Hayman*	76
Red alert *Gord Letcher*	77
Big black bogey *Robert "Jock" MacDonald*	79
Sorfleet ejection *Lee Evans*	80
Not your run-of-the-mill live scramble *KO Simonson*	80
"2" Wing tale *Nick Nicholson*	81
Robbie tales *Robbie Robinson*	82
Speed brakes . . . Speed brakes . . . GO! *Turbo Tarling*	83
Scramble! *Turbo Tarling*	84
The Mosquito . . . *Bob Merrick*	84
Scramble scramble *Greg Stevens*	86
A 409 Squadron mayday *Pat Parker*	88
QQ's EWU Det . . . *Bob Merrick*	88
With my scarf fluttering in the breeze . . . *Vic Rushton*	90

PART TWO : ODD JOBS

The Totem Times Various	92
Where have all the leaders gone? *Doug Munro*	100
Aerial buffoonery *Doug Munro*	103
A 423 Squadron tale Part One *Gil Desbecquets*	106
A 423 Squadron tale Part Two *Bob "Pup Tent" Grandmaison*	106
A 423 Squadron tale Part Three *Larry Clark*	107
Vietnam *Don Carney*	108
More Vietnam *Alex Saunders*	109
Fishing derby—North Bay *John A. MacDonald*	110
For he's a jolly good fellow *Gil Desbecquets*	110
The amateurs *John Eggenberger and Bill Gladders*	112
Montreal's finest *Bill Gladders*	114
Vietnam incidents *Ernie Poole*	116
Peacekeepers, eh? *Lynn Wagar*	116
Exchange excitement *Alex Saunders*	119
Sea survival—Deci style *Doug Munro*	120
Sardinia days *Al Chapman*	122
Naylor's farewell *Gary Naylor*	123
Chatham daze *Gary Naylor*	123
447 SAM Squadron *Bob Merrick*	124
Squadron picnic *John Wheeler*	128
Blue Four *Author Unknown*	128

PART THREE : THE CF–101 IN CANADIAN SKIES

Bob Merrick 130

PART FOUR : SUPERSONIC YEARS

Creating the Voodoo *Bob Merrick*	150
425 CF–101 Squadron formation *Les Taylor*	151
Bagtown follies *Doug Brown*	151
A tribute to Eric "Thumper" Matheson *Larry Lott*	153
Bear intercept *John "Bosco" Haazen*	154
Maple flag—1979 *John "Bosco" Haazen*	155
RAF cross country *John Wheeler, RAF exchange navigator, 416 Sqn*	156
Scramble *John Wheeler*	157
My first scramble *Jim Gregory*	158
W/C J D "Red" Sommerville, DSO, DFC *Doug Munro*	159
The Ukrainian aerobatic team *Doug Munro*	159
"C'mon, ice cream!" *Kent Smerdon*	160
I remember him well *Doug Munro*	161
Cold Shaft *Jack Partington*	163
The keys *Pete Armour*	169
Buzzer . . . Stream . . . Evasive . . . What else might he do? *Bob Merrick*	169
Col. Pat and the cable *Pete Armour*	170
Brodeur # 1 *Don Brodeur*	171
Don Parker's AFC *Author Unknown*	172
George Rawson's memories *George Rawson*	173
A trip to Colorado *Jim Gregory*	175
So young—so innocent *Jim Gregory*	176
Heading south *Ron Egli*	178
Queen's colours *Author Unknown*	179
Rendezvous over the Miramichi *Les Hare*	180
SARAH II *Ron Egli*	181
Pre-OTU training *Pete Armour*	182
Snyder stories *Lloyd Snyder*	183
More *Totem Times* Various Authors	185
You just have to ask the right questions . . . *Bob Merrick*	187
Gear down and locked? *Keith Bottoms*	188
Up and down do make a difference in a J–57 *Doug Munro and Bob Merrick*	190
Chatham scramble *Don Harrington*	196
425 tales *Don McCaul*	198
The magic duct tape *Bill Gladders*	201
A piece of cake *Doug Munro*	201
Identify one radar anomaly *Bob Merrick*	202
Hawk 1 tour *George Herbert*	202
One-nighter *Turbo Tarling*	204
The ghost plane episode *Turbo Tarling*	205
Topless Voodoo *John Cucheran*	205
Luke Air Force Day *Doug Munro*	206

PART FIVE : THE 1981 WARLOCKS FROM 425 SQUADRON

Jim Gregory 208

Appendix	211
Glossary	213
About the Editors	215

Foreword
Joe Schultz

I am pleased to have been asked to contribute the foreword to a book that presents stories of our post-war "night-fighters," as we were called in WW II.

By and large, the stories in this book are irreverent and "tongue in cheek." Some are a little frivolous, but these stories are told by fliers who were among the world's best. They carried on the attitudes and values generated by their WW II forbears who flew Mosquitos and Beaufighters with 406, 409, 410, and 418 squadrons during the war.

When on a scramble, the Cold War aircrew were deadly serious, and our potential enemies knew this. When their Bears neared our turf, they did so very carefully. In this regard, in the pages that follow, please note the "up close and personal" photos taken by the CF–101s of the then Soviet Union's long-range bombers. These pictures are a first-rate testament that our post-war all-weather fighter crews are worthy carriers of the Canadian night fighters' torches.

To set the stage for a good read, here are a few recollections. As WW II ended in 1945, Canada's military acted very quickly to release its troops and reduce its operational capability, especially in the field of fighter-type operations.

However, even as this tremendous reduction was taking place, plans were being made to create a semblance of an air defence force, using the DH Vampire, a jet-powered, day-fighter aircraft. As rumour then had it, these aircraft were promised and delivered by England in return for the equipment and stores that we left behind after the return of all Canadian forces after WW II.

These first plans resulted in the formation of an Air Defence Group in RCAF HQ in Ottawa, which later moved to join No. 1 (F) Operational Training Unit at St. Hubert, P.Q., in early 1948. During late 1948, the first post-war all-weather (Fighter) OTU was formed and began training at the station. This was the beginning of our post-war air defence system.

During this time of organizational turmoil, more plans were made to add Canadian-built all-weather fighter aircraft to Air Defence Group. The aircraft were to be designed and built by a subsidiary of England's A.V. Roe, at a facility in Canada. This aircraft was the Mk.III version, equipped with the APG–33 intercept radar and eight 50 calibre machine guns; 445 Squadron was the first to employ this aircraft, which entered into squadron service in 1953.

Later, the Mk.IVA and B retained the 50 calibre machine guns and included the APG–40 radar intercept system along with fifty-eight folding fin air-to-air rockets (FFAAR). Still later, the Mk.V retained the rockets but lost the guns as a weight-saving measure. These and other modifications to the Mk.V enabled it to get to very high altitudes; it was limited by regulation to 45,000 feet, but the rumour mill still contends that it could often get more than another 5,000 or so higher.

In my opinion, the Mk.III was prematurely pushed out of the factory doors and its reputation was tarnished by a "rush job" of poor workmanship, with ill-designed and badly placed switches and valves and a few duals produced without fuel control units, to mention but a few of the glaring deficiencies. The latter deficiency was especially difficult to deal with, because the fuel flow that got to the engines was directly connected to the throttles. Even the gentlest hand on the throttles could produce compressor stalls and engine blowouts.

Also, in my opinion, the combination of the APG–40 intercept radar with the fifty-eight 2.75-inch FFAARs was much less effective in shooting down enemy aircraft than the APG–40 and the eight machine

"An Airfield in England, Dec. 13, 1943. Rayne Denis Schultz, a 20-year-old RCAF flying officer from Bashaw, Alta., who along with his navigator destroyed three of the four German bombers shot down over Britain Friday night, is a modest fellow and so is his navigator, F.O. Vernon Williams, 24, of 132 Cavell avenue, Hamilton, Ont. . . ."

(CP Cable)

guns would have been. I never did see a whole lot of evidence that the enemy aircraft would fly straight and level through a football field-sized chunk of airspace infested with fifty-eight 2.75-inch FFAARs. Enough said in this regard.

To backtrack a little bit. In 1952, No. 3 AW(F) OTU was established at North Bay, Ontario, thanks to the hard work of many, but especially that of S/L (later G/C) Bob Bayliss, a wartime Nav/RO on 410 Squadron. To help organize this OTU, the Royal Air Force loaned W/C (later AVM) E.D. Crew. He and an experienced team of WW II aircrew accepted the first Mk.III in the fall of 1952, and we started to expand to enable us to meet our air defence responsibilities.

By 1958, we had thirteen CF–100 squadrons in service: nine in Canada, two in France, and two in West Germany.

After the fall of the Arrow, it was clear that the proposed further marks of the CF–100 Mk.V could not meet the challenge of new Soviet intentions. As a result, in 1960, an agreement was signed with the USAF for the RCAF to receive sixty-six F–101s. Initial training for aircrew and ground crew was conducted at several USAF bases, such as Hamilton AFB, near San Francisco, where I had the honour to be the commanding officer of the Canadian contingent.

From this first select group was the team that came home to RCAF Station Namao, Alta., to set up the Voodoo OTU. For the first transition group, I took the position that while were called an OTU, we were simply training already experienced aircrew to fly a new (and supersonic) aircraft. This training outlook was very profitable, because the trainees were not treated as OTU "newbies," but as equals. As a result, our CF–101 aircrew transited extremely rapidly from knowing how to use one aircraft to another without serious incident.

Now we were once again back on the NORAD "A" team, and the excellence of our aircrew and groundcrew kept us there until 1984, when the CF–101s were replaced by the current CF–18. They, too, are an "A" team . . . and still occasionally chasing the same damned Bears!

In closing, I have always been, and still am, extremely proud to have been one of a very professional post-war team of flyers, from the start-up wth the CF–100 Canuck to near the finish of operations with the CF–101 Voodoo in October 1984.

Per Ardua ad Astra

Acknowledgements

A book such as this is not the product of a small group of people. Rather it is the result of many people putting their thoughts together to describe an era when it seemed that our country could come under devastating aerial attack. Many answered the call to join the RCAF and, later, the Canadian Forces. Now some of the old vets have put their thoughts on paper. We won't name them all here, but you can find the names in the Table of Contents and in the bylines at the start of each story. We are most grateful for their literary efforts.

Some of the articles had previously been published elsewhere, and we are indebted to those who gave their permission to use the stories in this book. They include Larry Milberry (*CANAV* Books), Bill March (*Journal of the Canadian Aviation Historical Society*), Tim Dube (*Observair*, Ottawa Chapter, Canadian Aviation Historical Society), Vic Johnson (*AirForce* magazine), and the CFB Comox *Totem Times*.

We also extend sincere thanks to Col. (Ret'd) Joe Schultz, a former "night fighter" who established an outstanding combat record in WW II. Then, he went on to help Canada introduce the Vampire, the CF–100, and the CF–101 to new generations of "night fighters" who followed in his footsteps in the postwar years. Bill Sterne was one of those who benefited from Joe's experience, and we are grateful that he agreed to share his memories.

And last, but not least, we must thank Jane Karchmar. "Jane Karchmar?" you ask. "What squadron was she on?" Well, she wasn't on any of them. But she was the one who read all the stories, corrected all the English, and sought answers to all of her questions. The result? A literate, readable book that can be read, understood, and appreciated by those who never spent a single minute in any aircraft cockpit.

To all of those listed above, we, John Eggenberger, Bob Merrick, and Doug Munro, tender our heartfelt thanks for a wonderful job. Your efforts will help tell the all-weather fighter story that loomed large in Canada's air defence in the years following WW II and the Cold War. We hope you enjoy the book made possible made by all their efforts.

Introduction
Doug Munro

From 1954 to 1983, the RCAF/CAF had a significant number of all-weather fighter squadrons. Canada's first all-weather fighter was the Avro CF–100 Canuck (a.k.a. "Clunk"). At its peak in the late 1950s and early '60s, there were thirteen squadrons: 409 at Comox, B.C.; 410 and 428 at Ottawa; 413 and 432 at Bagotville, P.Q.; 414 and 433 at North Bay; 416 and 423 at St. Hubert, P.Q.; and four squadrons in the Air Division—419 at Baden Soellingen and 440 at Zweibrucken in Germany, 423 at Grostenquin, and 445 at Marville in France. Each squadron had eighteen aircraft skillfully manned by thirty aircrews.

In 1961/62 the Clunk was retired from all-weather fighter service. Coincidentally, the RCAF purchased sixty-six slightly used CF–101 Voodoos from the USAF. After a series of squadron, air frame, and aircrew shuffles, a new iteration of Air Defence Command emerged: the AWF Order of Battle found 409 at Comox, 416 at Chatham, N.B., and 425 and 410 (the Voodoo OTU) squadrons at Bagotville. The Voodoo squadrons were equipped with twelve aircraft and twenty-plus crews.

This book does not pretend to be a history of Air Defence Command or the All-Weather Fighter world. Larry Milberry has already written an excellent history of the Clunk years, the Avro CF–100, CANAV books.

Some months ago, any and all former all-weather pilots and navigators were invited to provide John and me with their favourite experiences while serving on an all-weather squadron. A number of submissions, while not directly related to squadron life, were too interesting or unique to omit or discard. (Unfortunately, a small handful of tales were lost due to a computer problem.) There are as many styles as writers. Furthermore, there are some instances where two or more contributors have submitted the same basic remembrances. We have tried to present a viable composite.

John Eggenberger solicited contributions and prepared the initial layout of the book. Bob Merrick edited the text. Doug Munro assisted John with the story gathering and Bob with the editing. The ranks of the contributors have been omitted lest we promote the un-promoted or, worse, fail to recognize one's proper rank.

With one exception, accidents where fatalities resulted have been omitted. The aim is to enlighten and amuse, not criticize or accuse.

As the literary masterpieces poured in, it soon became readily apparent that, during the 1950s and into the 1960s, junior officers (and, for that matter, senior officers) played as hard as they worked—and they worked very hard indeed. One might notice that with some exceptions, squadron commanders—in the early years all veterans from WW II—cut their juniors a remarkable amount of slack when "disciplining" them for an astonishing array of creative behaviour; behaviour which, in the current Air Force, would probably result in stern punishment!

PART ONE

THE CF–100 YEARS

How night-fighters became all-weather fighters

Bill Sterne

I consider it an honour to provide some introductory words to this long-awaited book. I decided to trace some early experiences that will illustrate the links joining the night-fighters of WWII with the all-weather fighters of the Cold War. It was truly an experience of a lifetime.

Without telling anyone, I hopped on my motorcycle and rode to Victoria from my home in Sydney, stopping en route to tell a friend, Ev Mackay, of my intention. He said, "Just a minute," swept his desktop items onto the floor, and came along with me. It never occurred to us that we might not be accepted.

Shortly after, off we went to the Officer Selection School, where to my surprise I was told that I would be trained as a navigator at RCAF Station Winnipeg. Ev was selected for pilot training.

Peter Hans was our course director at the nav school, and to his great credit, he got almost all of us through. Upon completion of our training, several Canadian trainees were posted to RCAF Station Sea Island, where there were about twenty-one navigators for the one serviceable Canso on standby. No one told us that we were holding there for subsequent training on the newfangled CF–100s.

Fortunately, the wait was short, and we ended up

A trio of CF–100 Mk.III's prowl the northern skies.

at RCAF Station North Bay on Course Five, just behind Joe Schultz, a seasoned night-fighter pilot who had joined the OTU staff. He and others with wartime experience were there to guide the rookies who would go on into the all-weather business.

On completion of the B–25 phase, we crewed up with our pilots for CF–100 training. Our pilots were to receive ten hours' flying in the aircraft before taking their navs airborne. But when they promptly wrote off two of the very scarce aircraft available, this requirement was cut to five hours.

There was ample time to discuss our somewhat glacial progress through this new course. We decided that a posting to Transport Command would give us desirable — and marketable — experience, should we fail to obtain permanent commissions at the end of our short-service commissions.

OTU staff members couldn't help but overhear such discussions. At briefing one morning, Major

(USAF) Eisler said that the OTU staff would assist any trainees who decided to go that route. He asked how many people were so inclined. Mine was the only hand raised.

Very shortly after, I was summoned to W/C (RAF) Crew's office. He asked, "What's all this I hear about your not liking the CF–100, Sterne?" I explained my case, and he responded,

"I see. You joined the RCAF to do what you wanted." After some additional harsh words, he dismissed me, I having assured him I would finish the course. He said, "You'll like it, you know." I had been well and truly set up.

The following weekend, my pilot, John Sorfleet, borrowed a C–45 for a weekend jaunt to Centralia, his previous station. After an interesting trip, we landed and promptly left the runway at a forty-five-degree angle. Nevertheless, he deftly negotiated us through the maze of runway and taxi lights and came to an abrupt halt perfectly in line with the other aircraft on the apron.

Having watched that feat, the duty tower controller said, "In a bit of a hurry to shut down, aren't you, John?"

John answered "Roger," and shut down.

Upon John's exit, the waiting airman said, "Oh, it's you, sir."

This episode set the stage for an exciting time at the OTU, and an equally exciting time at RCAF Station Bagotville, where we were finally posted to 440 Squadron.

We were a green bunch with lots to learn. However, several Sabre pilots who had just completed their tour in Europe and some newbies direct from Chatham arrived at BG to form 431 Squadron. They soon taught us to fly the CF–100 like a fighter. They also took great delight in taking off in formation in lousy weather when we were grounded. With no wing or engine de-icing, and a canopy that regularly fogged over, restricting visibility, it was no contest.

By the time we took part in Exercise Checkpoint, we were a confident, highly motivated group. At BG, I came to realize the dedication and concern of our ground crew. After just one short, but memorable, year, John and I returned to YB; he to the OTU, and me to 419 Squadron.

Right from the start, I enjoyed flying with my new pilot, F/L G. F. "Hammy" Hammond. As well, 419 Squadron was a fun place to be. This was especially true after the arrival of W/C E. G. (Irish) Ireland. We did everything we could to follow his lead and we enjoyed every minute of it. We were overjoyed when we were selected to conduct harlequin tactics development, which was a way to control many fighters with fewer controllers, as might become necessary while combatting mass bombing raids. And, we were delighted when we received the Steinhardt Trophy, given annually to the best squadron in Air Defence Command.

Our deployment to Mount Hope for live fire training provided another opportunity to show just how enthusiastic our ground crew were. When the target flags were dropped, they rushed to see how many holes had been made in the target and they were delighted when "their" aircraft scored well.

Little by little, we were learning from our combat-hardened forbears. While still on 419, Frank Black and I joined two crews at RCAF Station St. Hubert, where we were to determine the fuel consumption of the first three CF–100 Mk.IVB aircraft off the production line. On completion of this task, we flew these aircraft overseas as part of Random 12, to deliver them to the RAF for evaluation at RAF West Raynham. On landing at Prestwick, one of our number ran off the runway, as a result of Maxaret antiskid brake problems. We promptly headed for the bar.

G/C Crew and other members of his evaluation team, who had flown there to escort us the rest of the way, joined us. On seeing me, he asked, "How are you liking the CF–100 these days, Sterne?"

"Very much, sir," I replied.

His retort was, "I thought you would." End of conversation.

While at West Raynham, Frank asked G/C Crew if he "might be permitted to fly the Meteor."

Crew's response was, "Go ahead."

Frank's next question was, "Should I take a staff nav, or should I use my own?"

The response was, "Oh, Christ, use your own." That flight in an NF–11 was truly memorable.

While still on 419 Squadron, I had gotten married, and a short notice posting to the OTU, which was now at RCAF Station Cold Lake, was another "experience of a lifetime," one shared by many "pioneers" at this new station. But it was in Cold Lake that I was able to take my all-weather fighter experience, gleaned from so many battle-tested colleagues, and pass it along to a new generation of all-weather fighters. Although there were many challenging and exciting postings yet to come, I still look back at the lengthy interlude serving as a bridge between the night-fighters of WWII and the all-weather fighters of the Cold War. I know that *Per Ardua Ad Astra* is trite, but it seems fitting to use it here. It was truly a marvellous experience.

The CF–100: Some orientation

Author Unknown

The first full production-standard CF–100, the Mk.III, flew for the first time in October 1952, powered by 2,948-kg (6,500-lb)-thrust Orenda 9's, and entered service the next year armed with eight 0.5-in (12.7-mm) Colt-Browning machine guns in a retractable ventral tray. This armament was supplemented in the Mk.IVA by wing-tip pods of 2.75-in (70-mm) folding-fin air-to-air rockets after the fashion adopted by the United States Air Force in the Northrop F–89 Scorpion. The Mk.IVA also introduced an improved version of radar in the form of the Hughes APG–40 and a collision-course interception computer.

Increased power (Orenda 11s of 3,230-kg [7,275-lb] thrust) came with the Mk.IVB Canuck, which, with the IVA, became the most-produced version of this pioneering, all-weather fighter—a total of 510 were built. Development, however, was not continued, and the Mk.V, with all rocket armament, flew for the first time in 1955. For better performance at high altitude, 1.06-m (3 ft 6 in) untapered sections were added to each wing tip, and the tailplane area was also slightly increased. This in fact raised the combat ceiling by 1,219 m (4,000 ft). Larger wing-tip rocket pods were also fitted to the Mk.V, which became the only model to be exported; commencing in December 1957, fifty-three ex-Canadian air force models were sold to the Belgian air force. United States security regulations prohibited further exports, as some U.S. equipment was fitted.

With its then quite advanced fire-control system, the CF–100 was an obvious candidate for missile armament, and the proposed Mk.VI was to have mounted Sparrow II missiles and be powered by afterburning Orenda 11IR engines.

Clunks remembered

Doug Munro

In the late 1940s, engineers at A.V. Roe (Canada) (Avro) built the CF–100 all-weather fighter. Many of the CF–100's creators were Brits: world leaders and justifiably renowned for producing ugly aircraft with cockpits designed by descendants of Procrustes. Procrustes, you will no doubt recall, was the legendary Greek innkeeper who invented a bed that fit all guests: If the visitor was too short, he was stretched a bit; if too tall, a few inches were lopped off. Legend has it that Avro's chief design engineer, Sir Arthur Higgledy-Piggledy, suffered from chronic bedwetting.

Clunk cockpits were classics. In the front office, the flight instruments were randomly positioned using two major premises. First, where would the pilot least likely look for a given dial? And second, where could an instrument be most inconveniently located? A rapid cross-check frequently caused severe whiplash. Indeed, the Mk.III was ready for the first test flight when the pilot discovered that the compass was hidden behind the control column. Rather than reposition the compass somewhere near the other flight instruments, the boffins bent the upper portion of the control column—which looked for all the world like the handle of an oversized baseball bat—thirty degrees to starboard. First the good news: the pilot could now see the compass. Now the bad news: pilots susceptible to vertigo (or, if you prefer, the "leans") and navigators whimpering softly in the back seat enjoyed a series of unusual positions and some truly memorable moments.

If Avro's design engineers disliked pilots, they *hated* navigators. The rear cockpit was perfect, provided the occupant was four foot, eight inches tall, weighed less than one hundred pounds, and had very short legs. Another desirable physical asset was very long and exceptionally strong arms. Trials using orangutans were abandoned when the apes refused to run the radar unless the pilots agreed to be nice to them or at least to share their bananas.

Some twit had positioned the emergency undercarriage-lowering button on the aft starboard firewall. The only way most back-seaters could exert enough pressure on the button to lower the gear was to unstrap, stand up (a physical impossibility), turn around, kneel on the ejection seat, and push! Should one be fortunate enough to be kneeling on a Martin Baker when it fired, he immediately acquired all the physical characteristics of an ideal navigator (i.e., four feet eight inches tall, short legs, etc.).

The Martin Baker ejection seat was one part of the Clunk that usually worked very efficiently. The seat was a particular favourite of orthopaedic surgeons everywhere: a by-product of an ejection was often a compression fracture of the spine. The seat was foolproof, but unfortunately not idiot-proof. Consequently, aircrew occasionally joined the Caterpillar Club—awarded to survivors of an ejection—while minding their own business.

Norm Grondin and Dave Saunders were on a routine air test out of RCAF Station Bagotville, Quebec, when, during negative "G" trials, Norm suddenly found himself hanging in his parachute straps with a fully deployed canopy over his head. During installation, the safety systems technician had failed to anchor the seat to the aircraft. Subjected to negative "G" forces, the seat rode up its rails, the lanyard pulled, the drogue gun fired, blasting through the canopy, followed shortly thereafter by the seat, the chute, and Norm.

On September 25, 1958, on a mission out of Marville, France, F/O Rudy Willhauk, with F/O Bill Peitri at the throttle, found himself with an unexpected 400-knot wind in his face. During the Board of Inquiry, Rudy encountered wall-to-wall skeptics when he testified that he hadn't ejected just for the hell of it. Fortunately, his ejection seat was later recovered with both ejection handles safely stowed. Cancel one court martial.

A non-ejection incident that qualifies for Ripley's *Believe It or Not* involves a young enlisted airman at RCAF Station St. Hubert, Quebec. He climbed into the cockpit of a CF–100 parked in a hangar, sat on a Martin Baker, and pulled the ejection handle. Nothing! Not to be thwarted, he tried another seat. Nothing!

Some days nothing goes right. Frustrated and visibly annoyed, he stomped into his supervisor's office and declared: "None of the ejection seats work!" He was correct: a panic inspection revealed that, during a recent modification, a triangular shear pin had been installed backward. In an emergency, none of the seats in any of the station's thirty-six CF–100s would have worked.

The cockpit architect had nothing on the Rube Goldberg clone who created the fuel system. It was possible, through careful switch selection, to cross-feed the fuel in such a manner that both engines would flame out more or less simultaneously from fuel starvation. At least two CF–100 crews, both with bags of fuel on board, reaffirmed Murphy's Law. One crew force landed downwind at RCAF Station Uplands, and the other crew ejected five miles back on final at RCAF Station Bagotville. This latter crew enjoyed the experience so much they subsequently bailed out near Zweibrucken, Germany. The request to the city fathers to rename Zweibrucken "Zweiejections," in honour of their double bail-out, met with a resounding *"Nein."*

The Clunk's fifty-eight 2.75-inch "Floundering Fin" rockets, although never fired in anger, terrorized generations of aircrews, armourers, and unscheduled targets. All fifty-eight rockets firing in a salvo were a pretty spectacular sight, particularly if you chanced to be on the receiving end. The rockets, allegedly cousins of the ejection seats, occasionally fired on their own. A gremlin called "stray voltage" was the usual, although not the sole, cause. Struck by lightning while in the circuit at RCAF Station Comox, F/Os Vede Gilchrist and Johnny Mack logged 409 Squadron's only CF–100 "air to mud" sortie by blowing the roof off of the station fire hall.

Armourers, while performing stray voltage checks, bagged some gophers (Comox again), hangar doors, a truck, and very nearly a rapidly ageing wing commander who was taxiing to the ramp when

"It's unknown—you handle it. I'll go back and get help."

a salvo bracketed his Clunk (North Bay). Never one to let minor annoyances fluster him, the WingCo pressed his mike button and said, "You missed."

The pilot had at his disposal three switches that purported to control the cockpits' air conditioners and heating/cooling systems. In fact, the switches were there for the sole purpose of giving the pilot something relatively harmless to play with; nothing controlled these systems. Much of the time, regardless of switch positions, both cockpits were either sauna hot or igloo cold. Jettisoning the canopy brought instant relief from the terminal sweats but guaranteed frostbite and chilblains. On-board campfires were discouraged, as was running on the spot.

Notwithstanding these and other minor irritants, such as oleo legs that tended to shear at awkward moments; wings that folded if too much "G" was pulled; chronic false fire warning lights; a faulty hydraulic system on earlier Marks that led to control seizures; and an airframe that was no match for the engines, the Clunk was easy to fly, had reasonable range, and there was room on board for two sets of golf clubs. Could anyone ask for more?

Why in the world . . .?
Bob Merrick

"Why in the world would you want to fly in those silly CF–100s?" The speaker was an older man—possibly approaching thirty. He had distinguished himself as a long-range navigator on Noisy Stars during the Korean War, flying many missions to Japan—and to virtually everywhere else in the world—and was at the time an instructor in the RCAF's Number 2 Air Observer School at RCAF Station Winnipeg. (We didn't have a Number 1 Air Observer School; we just numbered them that way to confuse the enemy.)

His audience included about half a dozen flight cadets who were partway through the basic navigation course offered at the school. They were immersed in "dead" reckoning, magnetism, compasses, maps and charts, electronic theory, astral navigation, flight plans, logs, and similar arcane lore designed to teach them the rudiments of their craft.

They had recently reached the point where they were allowed to practise that craft in the school's mighty C–45 Bugsmashers. But they hadn't reached the point where they had to submit a preference for which navigation specialty they wished to adopt. It was, consequently, an important topic of conversation among the cadets, some of whom had yet to decide.

The students and the instructor had just attended a movie in the station theatre and were indulging in a post-movie treat of whatever was cheapest on the station snack bar's menu. The instructor had begun his query by asking the students which specialty—long-range navigation, radio, or airborne interception—the students would prefer. He seemed astonished that many in the group were spring-loaded to the airborne interception position.

Before anyone could answer, he continued: "Jet fighters are just a passing fancy. Before you know it, they'll have come and gone. If you guys are looking for careers, you'll be out of jobs. You'll have to be retrained, then start over again, and where will you stand on the promotion ladder? And, if you get out at the end of your short-service commission, there isn't an airline in the world that will hire you. Also, and, I don't like to harp on this, what happens in that community? Did you count the number of funerals they go to?[1]

"No," he said; "if you're wise you'll do what I did and go the long-range route. You'll travel the world in nice, reliable[2] piston aircraft, and you'll be learning—and using—a practical skill." So saying, he finished his coffee, swept up his change, and departed, perhaps to memorize more star charts, leaving several suddenly thoughtful young men to ponder the long-term wisdom of his words.

So why in the world *did* they want to fly in "those silly CF–100s"? And why, apart from hearing-conservation purposes, would they eschew the North Star? For me, the answers to those questions were chiselled in cement a week or two later. The Air Nav School, which in those days had lots of airplanes, used to send motivational visits to various operational bases, so that student navs could see the considerable differences between the "spit and polish" environment favoured by Training Command units and the more relaxed atmosphere found in the real world.

Our course's turn for one of these jollies saw us "slip the surly bonds" in an all-metal, flush-riveted, subsonic Douglas Racer bound for RCAF Station St. Hubert, at that time the headquarters of Air Defence Command and, of more immediate interest, 423 and 425 AW(F) squadrons. Somehow, we had been assigned a SAR Dak, one with the big bubble window

---

1   Ed. note: The death toll on AW(F) Squadrons between 1951 and 1984 eventually reached 127, with most of the fatalities occurring in the earlier years, when many air forces had similar difficulties.

2   Ed. note: For just how "reliable" they were, read Laurence Motiuk's superb work, *Thunderbirds for Peace,* which describes 426 Squadron's North Star years.

designed for SAR spotters, so the journey to RCAF Station North Bay, our midpoint stop, was fascinating for those who hadn't done much previous flying.

Similarly, the leg to HU showed a view of Canada that few of us had ever seen, particularly when, as was the practice in those far-off days, the pilot cancelled IFR not too far east of Ottawa and did his own individualistic bit of tour guiding past the fabled bazaars of Montreal.

On our arrival in St. Hubert, it was immediately obvious that 423 squadron had drawn the short straw, as they were assigned the lovely weekend job of showing these rubbernecking cadets all the wonders of the Air Defence world. One of those wonders was, of course, Montreal, which was full of cathedrals, Christian Science reading rooms, universities, and other attractions. So we were told.

Scheduling imprecisions made it impossible to actually visit any of those places, but there were other attractions on the agenda, most of which featured music, dim lighting, and unusual options for remaining, as the current phrase has it, hydrated. These cultural activities occupied a major portion of Friday evening and, if memory serves, some of Saturday's smaller hours.

One feature of air defence life back then was, apparently, an early start to the day. And it was a good start. The squadron had gone to considerable effort to produce a show that, well, demonstrated just where 423 and its sister squadrons fitted into the overall scheme of things. Squadron life? I've forgotten just how they scheduled their alerts and organized their simulator and flying programs, but it seemed reasonable.

They were honest about the fact that the work week was usually much longer than the forty-hour work week then in vogue elsewhere and said, essentially, "like it or lump it." They took air defence seriously, regarded the Soviet long-range force as a credible threat, and were upfront about stating that those who wanted in to the air defence world had better be prepared to take it as seriously as they did.

There was a visit to the flight simulator, which nicely replicated the CF–100's cockpits but didn't much replicate the aircraft's responses to various control inputs, nor the radar picture a navigator might expect to see. Still, in those days it was a considerable step up from what was available elsewhere and it certainly helped prepare many young crews for service on active air defence squadrons.

Then, it was on to the big event. What was that? For those who wanted it, there was a flight in a CF–100. Did I want it? Only so bad that I could taste it! My host, F/O Arn Dagenais, set about outfitting me with the things one needs to clamber into a CF–100. Then, there was a cram course on what to do if an emergency struck, followed by instructions on what to touch and what not to touch.

Once he declared me fit for flight, he introduced me to my pilot for the day: S/L R.A.B. Ellis, a WW II vet who was, like so many vets in those years, providing sound leadership and tutoring for those coming along behind him. The contributions of these vets, apart from occasional mention in many of Larry Milberry's superb books, have never been adequately recognized. He asked if I had done any flying other than the few Bugsmasher trips accrued thus far on the basic nav course.

"Yes," I said, "there was some time in a Cessna 140, when I was working on, but never quite getting, a pilot licence; and I had a friend who owned — consecutively, not concurrently — a Tiger Moth and a Cornell and I flew with him occasionally, but it probably added up to less than thirty hours."

"Hmm," said Ellis. "Were you able to do any aerobatics in any of that?"

"Yes," I said, "and they were fun."

"Well," he said, "we'll see what we can do." With

that, we went out to the aircraft. It was, of course, the standard Mk.IV—the one with no flight controls in the back seat. That's where Arn strapped me in. There was much to-ing and fro-ing with the ground crew who were assisting with the start-up procedures, and before long, we were ready to roll.

After brief chats with the tower, Ellis expertly threaded his way through the taxiway maze, and soon we reached the end of the runway, where he did a few last-minute checks before seeking, and getting, takeoff clearance.

"All set back there?" he asked.

"All set," I replied.

The two mighty Orendas quickly reached max power or, at least, the max power that was allowed while they were attached to a CF–100. Quickly, the air speed built to nose wheel liftoff speed. Then, almost immediately it seemed, the aircraft jumped off the ground and climbed at an alarmingly steep angle. Although the details of the trip are now lost in the mists of time, we climbed to 20,000 feet or so while I tried to make sense of the radar presentation. Then Ellis did a few steep turns that, to someone just barely getting used to the Wichita Vibrator (no, not *that* kind of vibrator; they're strait-laced out there in Kansas) seemed pretty intrepid.

"How about some aeros?" asked Ellis.

"You bet," I said. (I think the actual phraseology was "Yes, sir," which was about the only thing that flight cadets were allowed to say to squadron leaders.)

"We'll start with some rolls," he said, almost as if he were a waiter serving dinner in a tony restaurant. And we did 360-degree rolls, four- and eight-pointer rolls before shifting to loops, and then going back into the steep turns. Then, there were more climbs and more descents as Ellis attempted to duplicate what it might be like to hassle with a bomber flown by a pilot who didn't have a strong death wish. It was wonderful!

The only problem was that it was too short. All too soon, we were back on initial at St. Hubert, where we did one closed pattern off the original approach followed by a smooth, full-stop landing. There is no question that, with that flight, I was well and truly hooked. S/L Ellis had, unwittingly, perhaps, given me a superb introduction to what turned out to be a long, satisfying time in the "silly little CF–100" business, which eventually took me to the CF–100, CF–101, and the F–4C.

But, you know, that long-ago instructor was right: The CF–100s and CF–101s were a passing fancy. A mere thirty years later, they were gone. And so were the piston engine airliners, along with all the long-range navigators who were leaving the service for an assured career with the airlines.

And so, sadly, was I. Compulsory retirement age caught up to me at the same time it caught up to the CF–101, and the AI navigator specialty went out of business at pretty much the same time as I did.

But to answer that long-ago instructor's question, "Why do you want to fly in those silly CF–100s?"

"Because it seemed at the time that it was exceptionally important to our survival, and it was . . . well, the most fun you could have with your clothes on."

That final B–25 check at Winnipeg

Gerry Walker

"Starboard . . . harder . . . hold. Ease. Throttle right back . . . Ease . . . steady . . . hold speed . . . Target 15 port, 15 high, min range, speed synch." With that, the captain of B–25 Mitchell #5213 confirmed position, eased the throttles up, broke starboard, and headed home to RCAF Station Winnipeg. For me, it meant AI Training Mission 15 was "in the bag." Man, I was really starting to enjoy this AI stuff and was no longer honking when I disembarked from those smelly Mitchells.

My course mates were doing equally well—Wardstrom, Sears, Desmarais, McKendry, Hamilton, Grondin—what a group. It was like living with the Keystone Kops. At times it seemed we were training for the Olympic Beer Drinking Team. Two more missions to go, then final check ride and "Wings" parade on Friday 15th of August 1958. No sweat!

Then dark clouds began forming: I barely passed Ex 16, and then busted 17; the re-ride was dicey but I squeaked through. Then, on the final check, I screwed up royally! My recheck was scheduled for Thursday afternoon prior to Friday's "Wings" parade . . . the "pressure cooker" was sure starting to hiss.

I reviewed the flight schedule and found that F/O Gallow would be my pilot, F/L "Chuck" Vaessen, DFC and WW II "ace," would do the check, and F/L Douglas from AFHQ would tag along in order to "observe." I was the only student aboard. My heart skipped a beat as I absorbed the fact that a WWII ace would be checking me, while a rep from "God" in Ottawa would watch. I did not know Douglas, but I was somewhat comforted that F/L Chuck was a low-key, cool, and helpful operator with a reputation as a firm, but fair, examiner. Nevertheless, how can a pimply-faced twenty-year-old flight cadet impress an "ace" and "God"? The pressure relief valve was now rockin' and hissin'.

We rolled out on zero nine zero, ready to conduct my third and final ID run. The first two were shaky but might rate as a "pass" *if* I did well on this last set-up. I was shaking in my boots! I detected the target, called "Judy" then "Buster," and the manoeuvring and commentary began.

With every turn, one had to ease back or forward on the hand control in order to keep the target spotlighted on the APG 33 scope. No lock-ons or space stabilization of the antenna with this beast—it was all "manual." Similarly, one had to constantly press the "C" scan button to determine target elevation. F/O Dick Fabbro had finally driven this requirement through my thick skull a few missions ago, but I still had not really learned to pay attention to what it indicated!

As we closed with the target, things seemed to be okay. I had cut-off, rollout should be at close range, and I figured speed was under control.

We steadied out on target heading, and the azimuth displacement was bang-on.

Speed?—Oh-oh, way too hot—"Throttle right back." It then dawned on me to look at the "C" scan—Keerist, we were way too low! I had better do something quick, since we were almost down to min range.

Frantic, I recalled a Brevity Code command I had never used before (or since)—in fact I had never heard anyone use it—not even at the bar. "NOSE UP." It was as if F/O Gallow had been waiting years to hear this command. He immediately responded by ham-fisting the yoke back into his lap. The nose came up, up, and up, while the Mitchell groaned, screeched, and sounded like every rivet would pop. The only thing that was silent were the engines, still at idle.

I had never experienced three G's before, and my beak was now fully mashed to the "B" scope. Vaessen was also trying to disengage from the "repeater" scope. Douglas, who had been standing behind us, one hand on each of our seats and one foot cocked on a support bracket, vanished! Scared witless, what with the airframe screaming and my face glued to the scope, I shouted, "Level off! Hold speed!"

Gallow rejoiced and slammed the control column forward while firewalling the throttles. The engines roared, the rivets reseated, and F/L Douglas reappeared, albeit flying forward through the air, only to crumple aft of the bomb bay. He should have worn a flying suit rather than his dress uniform, since it now looked wrinkled and stained.

Doing my best to sound casual, I called, "Bogey 15 port, 15 high speed synch."

Gingerly, I looked to my right, seeking reassurance from F/L Vaessen. Silence.

Finally he said, "Skipper, let's take 'er home." RTB was conducted with complete radio silence, no chit-chat, nothing except for the landing clearance to Stephenson Field.

Dutifully walking to the right and slightly behind Vaessen, I entered the blister. Thankfully, I hadn't barfed on the tarmac, despite feeling queasy. I had no idea where Douglas was, but I figured he was likely rearranging his uniform (AFHQ types were like that). Vaessen motioned for me to stay put as he slowly continued down the corridor and turned into his office/locker room. He was gone for an eternity.

Sweat was pouring off me and it was not because of the August heat: my hands were trembling. I visualized being in the Orderly Room tomorrow morn, getting my train ticket to hometown Brantford. Maybe my girlfriend Karen would be happy!

Finally, F/L Vaessen reappeared and slowly, with head lowered, he approached, occasionally shaking his head. *(I'm done.)* When he spoke, he said something like this:

"Cadet, do you know what you did? You're lucky the pilot had the target in sight. Ever hear of flight safety?" Then, after a pause, he said, "I must admit that was quick thinking—trading speed for altitude—and though somewhat against my better judgment I'm going to pass you, *Keerist* be careful; you'll be on jets next!"

I almost collapsed, and considered planting a kiss on Chuck's cheek, but decided not to push my luck.

Walking out of the hangar, I felt the weight of the world had been lifted from my shoulders. Additionally, I realized I was as dry as a camel's fart! I rushed to the cadets' mess and upon entering the "snake pit," found my course mates already slurping beer. They feigned complete disinterest as to whether I had passed or failed and continued prattling on about tomorrow's parade, girls, sex, drinkin, sex, drinkin—you get the drift. Deep down, I knew they cared and no doubt had been secretly worrying about me all day.

This was reinforced when I bellied up to the bar and ordered a round. Suddenly, I was getting comments from all angles: "Way to go, Gerr!" "Knew you could do it!" etc. When I bellied up for another round, their encouraging, caring comments became boisterous. With that kind of support, I decided to continue my generous ways, even though it was costing me twenty cents a glass. What the hell, I had never bought anyone a drink before (or since), and my pockets felt deep. This continued for a goodly time, when suddenly the camel's fart became wet! With that warning, I decided to shut 'er down.

After all, who would want to hmm, soil their pants during Wings Parade?

On getting married
John Eggenberger

For those of us that "crewed-up" during the CF–100 era, never to be forgotten is the "meet and marriage" ceremony with one's pilot or one's navigator (whichever shoe fitted). This event was tension-laden because we didn't know exactly what would happen—we all were kind of like the young lady waiting for a call that would assure a "date" for the prom, hoping that the call would be from one who was wanted and wishing that the undesirables would not call.

Essentially, the event was more of a "group-grope" than a preprogrammed, well-executed ceremony. It was not choreographed so that a preordained pairing occurred. Instead, we all gathered in the mess at the appointed hour and with beer in hand started to circulate to see what was available. Eyeballs darted here and there, pairings obviously starting to be made. However it happened, eventually (took about ten to fifteen minutes) the pairings were complete and the "marriage" ceremony then conducted by the CO of the OTU. After which we all retired to the bar to celebrate—or not. Although we didn't really "get it" at the time, this pairing was intended to last for the duration of the OTU and the Sqn tour that followed. Obviously, if one or the other got a dud, the crew didn't do well. If both pilot *and* nav were duds, watch out. You get the idea.

I was lucky to crew with Charlie Leake—both of us from the "backwoods." And I had the great luck to find that Charlie already had five years or so of dandy flying in his logbook. The choice I got was good, good, good! But for Nav Bruce Durnan, his choice turned out to be not so good. After the pairing, we, of 3 OTU course 33 then progressed through the "Mitchell Bomber" phase, the CF–100 Mk.III phase, and then to the CF–100 Mk.IVA phase. A real fighter, with eight 50-caliber machine guns—and twenty-nine FFARs in pods on each wing tip (we didn't fly at the OTU with them on, but we could have). This was the "real thing."

So far as we knew, there was no indication that Bruce had troubles on the horizon; the pilot that he had crewed up with was a WW II fighter pilot with a very good track record, which continued at the OTU.

It was during a set of night exercises in mid-January 1957 that Bruce experienced the toughest time imaginable. Charlie and I were waiting for our turn to fly on a later mission set. In the ops room, the radio was always tuned to the flight frequency to help out as needed. Whilst sitting with our fingers up our noses, out of nowhere came, "Mayday Mayday." The tension racked up out of sight, and we learned that the canopy of Bruce's aircraft had been jettisoned, and both of Bruce's arms were flapping outside the cockpit in the frozen air—and from the R/T exchange with the pilot, we knew they were about fifteen minutes from landing.

We learned afterward that the event went something like this. The pilot had experienced anoxia and had become unconscious. When the aircraft started to descend rather rapidly (not in the preplanned flight profile), Bruce started yelling into the intercom, with no response. Eventually, Bruce became convinced that he had to eject. And he went through the routine: first jettison the canopy, then pull the eject handle.

At this point it is important to understand that the Mk.IVA did not have a windscreen in front of the navigator situated to deflect the wind, and the ejection handle for the Martin-Baker was located above and behind the ejection seat occupant's head. After the canopy was gone, Bruce reached up to grip the ejection handle; over the side went one arm, and he then tried with the other arm. Out it went, too. And there he was—helpless.

Mere seconds after the failed attempt to eject, the pilot, having recovered from the anoxic state and recognizing the problem, regained control of the aircraft. He reduced speed so that Bruce wouldn't experience so much arm flapping, but the price paid was that the duration that his arms were out in the freezing January air was extended. In the ops room, we could listen to what was going on, and it was a very difficult experience to hear it happening. It seemed to take forever for them to land, and when they did and it became known that Bruce was alive, we all sighed with relief. Later, we found out that Bruce lost some fingers and fingertips on both hands, but was not otherwise harmed.

In a little lighter vein, of course the show must go on. So after Bruce had been taken to the hospital, out our flight trundled (all bundled up) into the cold January midnight air, we climbed into our trusty steeds and proceeded to start up—going to do some serious "O Dark O" head-bumping practice.[3] Charlie, being a good-hearted soul, kept on chatting me up

---

3 This refers to a night mission devoted to practising intercepts between two CF-100 aircraft; it was a stratagem used when there were no other targets in the system.

"Gotcha!" Tony Gunter–Smith zeroes in on an RCAF photo Mitchell (B–25).

through the aircraft walk-around and start-up routine, thinking (correctly) that it would be a good idea to keep me chit-chatting so that I didn't have time to worry. So, after we got our snot-filled O2 masks firmly fixed on our faces and with a live mike, Charlie got one engine going and said, "Well, we got fire in one."

"FIRE!" yelled I — and I was unstrapped and almost out of there before Charlie could holler, "Whoa — Whoa!" which I understood well enough.

In the beginning, it was different

Tony Gunter–Smith[4]

I was posted for instructional duties to #3 All-Weather Operational Training Unit at North Bay in the middle of January 1953, but it was not until March 11 that I got my hands on the CF–100. Peter Needham (RAF exchange, killed as a passenger in a Canberra, shortly after returning to England) came in that afternoon and asked, "Would you like to fly the CF–100?" Silly question!

---

4 Gunter–Smith was an RAF exchange officer, borrowed from the Brits to help us set up our all-weather program.

Canuck #122 (one of the original Mk.IIIs) was waiting on the flight line; up to that time, we did not have any dual aircraft, so I jumped in and flew off into the wide blue yonder. Standing Orders said, "No vertical manouevres until seven hours on type." However, I had many hours on Vampires, Meteors, Canberras, T–33s and Sabres, so I ignored the order and carried out a loop.

As I approached the top of the loop, the left engine fire warning light came on. I completed the loop and could not see any signs of fire behind me, but nevertheless shut down the engine. I returned to base and carried out a single-engine landing. (No choice!) It turned out to have been a spurious warning.

Later, at dinner in the mess, other instructors asked, "How does it compare with landing with two engines?"

I answered, "I don't know. I haven't landed with two yet." I then discovered that I was the first pilot at the OTU to make a single-engine landing in the CF–100.

On August 20 came the grand "unveiling" of the new (?) CF–100 to the Canadian press from coast to coast. I was detailed to give a solo aerobatic display (in CF–100 #163, my favourite aircraft for aerobatic flying) following the formation display by the newly formed 445 Squadron.

My show started on takeoff. (Not after, as it states in *A Tradition of Excellence*, a splendid book by LCol Dan Dempsey.) As I lifted off the runway and selected "undercarriage up," I carried out a roll at minimum flying speed. The undercarriage was up and the roll completed before the end of the runway. I didn't forewarn anyone that I was going to do this, for obvious reasons. So, none of the press shot photos of the roll!

This was the first time I had done this (although I had done it several times in a Meteor . . . a lighter aircraft), and it was the last time, as at every air show in which I performed, the pilot's briefing started with, "The CF–100 will NOT, repeat NOT, do a roll on takeoff! That is an order." I believe that I am the only pilot to have performed the manoeuvre in the CF–100. It certainly impressed the press and the other pilots, staff, and students who were watching.

A tragic story (one of many) . . . An instructor took a CF–100 up for night circuit with a corporal in the back seat. On landing, the aircraft veered off the runway. For some reason, the pilot left both engines running, called out to the tower, "Help me, tower!" and crashed into a line of B–25 Mitchells, fully fuelled for the next day's flying. The undercarriage collapsed, and he went right under one Mitchell, and, of course, burst into flames. Both crew members were killed.

Then a remarkable act of heroism occurred. The base doctor climbed on top of the fuselage — with water being sprayed over him to try to keep the flames away — and extricated both occupants. Meanwhile, a quick-thinking sergeant threw a chain around the Mitchell's tail and, with a tractor, dragged the Mitchell back away from the other aircraft in the line, thereby preventing a mass conflagration.

One day at North Bay, on the first day of pickerel fishing, flying was cancelled due to inclement weather. The students trundled off to class. Most of the OTU staff made a beeline for Lake Nipissing and hired every fishing boat available. We'd been on the lake but a short time when the weather dramatically improved.

A short time later, Joe Schultz, the OTU's chief flying instructor, nearly blasted us out of the water with a very low pass, clearly encouraging us to return to base. We all gave him the "V" sign and went on fishing . . . for a while, Joe was not amused.

On New Year's Eve 1953, I arranged an evening/midnight party in my married quarter for staff friends and their wives. That afternoon, one of the staff was flying when he had an engine failure. The base weather was awful. However, instead of diverting to the alternate — Toronto, which was clear — the pilot decided to return to base. The aircraft crashed, and both crew members were killed. I called W/C JRD "Bob" Braham, and asked if I should cancel the party. Bob said, "Certainly not."

Notwithstanding the recent tragedy, the party was proceeding at a reasonable pace, when Denny Dennis, a particularly close friend of the dead pilot, had somehow acquired a large jar of medicinal alcohol from the sick bay and surreptitiously emptied same into the punch bowl. Midnight came and went unnoticed.

A day at the OTU

Ivan Ransom

Cold Lake. 8 Sep 1959.

Morning flight. LCC (a Lead Collision Course mission). Aborted at 35,000 feet, pilot had anoxia. +35 min.

Afternoon flight. LCC. Aborted. Smoke from the radar in the rear seat. 1+00hrs.

Evening flight. A cross-country. We were the last aircraft of the mission. On climb out, Al felt a rumble under his feet. He advised the pilot. A red nose wheel light showing. Popped the speed brakes. Coincidental noise of something breaking in nose wheel area. Flew past the tower. The tower confirmed nose wheel "swaying in the breeze." All aircraft recalled. We burnt off fuel. Fire trucks out, ambulance, PMQs empty to see the display. CO arrives. No foam.

Long approach, crash drill reviewed with tower, knees knocking made more noise than the nose wheel. Smooth touchdown on main wheels . . . hold the nose up, feet on binders, nice straight line down the middle of the runway. Canopy coming back, SPARKS LIKE THE FOURTH OF JULY. Grind to a halt, engines cut, onto the wing and run like hell . . . oops! forgot to disconnect oxygen.

The CO was impressed. "Beautiful sight, well done!" Extends cigarette to crew. LAC snatches it out of his hand and lectures on danger of fuel leaks. Breakage caused by mechanical failure. No pilot error. Elapsed 1+10.

At least the flights are getting longer. Great day in Clunkville.

Emergency?
Hank Hemming

When I served on Clunks at North Bay between 1956 and 1958, we were sitting around the alert room and idly listening to the tower/airplane chatter. We heard Roger Lacroix declare an emergency and we all came very alert, wondering what the problem was. So did the tower, but, to our dismay, Roger refused to disclose it. At any rate, we followed the aircraft, which had been given priority landing clearance, and were all quite concerned. Tower had cleared all but one aircraft from the circuit and was trying to get it out of the way when Roger came on again and said never mind, cancel the emergency, and thanks for your assistance.

We were quite perplexed at this but later discovered the nature of his emergency. An Aviation Maxim: Never mix a Martin Baker ejection seat with a gastrointestinal disorder.

If the glove fits!
Pat Parker

An intrepid navigator with 409 Sqn during the late '50s performed a feat of great agility during a cross-country trip with his officer commanding (in those days the "boss" of a squadron was titled "officer commanding," or OC for short). The OC, W/C Terry Evans, had to head east on important business and needed a navigator to run the back seat of his CF–100. Our six-foot-tall heroic navigator was chosen at the last minute, and soon the aircraft was heading east over the snow-covered mountains. All seemed to be going well during the trip when the nav suddenly had an undeniable urge to defecate. He proceeded to undo the seat and parachute straps, climbed out of his winter flying suit, and performed the delicate manoeuvre while crouched on the seat. Not having any suitable container, he used his leather elastic-wrist glove in which to make the relieving deposit. By this time, both the OC and our hero were on 100 percent oxygen, with the OC wondering, "Brown, what the hell are you doing back there?" Upon landing at Portage, "The Glove" was consigned to the garbage can with suitable pomp and ceremony.

I have often felt that this acrobatic feat deserved a medal!

Kelowna air show, 1955
Gerry Gagne

In the summer of 1955, 409 Squadron flew out of the RCAF Sea Island side of Vancouver International Airport while the main runway at Comox was being resurfaced. Being single, Bob Pomerleau and I were selected for very enjoyable weekend duty: a CF–100 air show at the Kelowna Regatta, Sunday, August 12.

Normally this mission would have been a piece of cake—weather in the Okanagan Valley is generally excellent. However, on this day, the weather forecast called for low ceilings throughout the interior. Undaunted, we kicked the tires, lit the fires, launched, and headed for Kelowna. Upon arrival overhead Kelowna, we, with great skill and cunning, descended below cloud.

At 1400 hours, we arrived at centre stage over Kelowna. The lake was jammed with boats of all shapes and sizes; the crowd was one of the largest ever for this event. Now to provide them with an air show they would remember!

First a Cuban Eight to determine the cloud base and then the rest of the show: a maximum-rate 360-degree turn, a slow pass with everything hanging (gear down, full flaps, landing light extended, and so on), a stall turn, a loop, an eight-point roll, an Immelmann, gliding rolls, a twenty-second inverted run till out of sight, and finally a Mach .85 high-speed pass. In the moist and turbulent air the Clunk was, on several occasions, engulfed in ghostly shock waves.

Approaching centre stage, Bob blurted out that he could see a piece of blue sky directly above that could afford a quick exit. Impulsively I yanked the CF–100 on its tail and shoved the throttles fully forward. This bit of good luck provided a fitting finale to an impeccable air show! However, this homesick angel lost most of his elation as 12,000 feet went by. Oh well! We soared above most of the surrounding mountain peaks, known in our trade as cumulo-granite. We eased past 15,000 feet, as the clouds tightened their noose around our craft. Well past the point of no return at 18,000, patience and the airspeed were wearing thin. Heavy breathing from the back seat confirmed that Bob was monitoring his TAS meter diligently. As the Clunk crawled past 20,000, a brighter glimmer of light came from the end of the tunnel. The Clunk finally emerged briefly in the glorious sunshine at 21,200 feet with nothing on the airspeed dial but the maker's name. Alas, the only recourse was to re-enter cloud inverted. In such dire straits, smoothness on the controls is of the essence, unless one wants to spin and entertain the Regatta with a horrendous splash.

Flying inverted was my forte, but doing so in cloud seemed less than glamorous. The Clunk decided to fly past the stall, roll upright, climb above cloud, and smartly head for base. After the adrenalin subsided, we returned to base and terra firma. Hilarity prevailed, but the lesson learned was never forgotten.

Postscript: Gerry was no stranger to solo air shows. While flying Sabres in Europe, he performed at the Paris International Air Show in July 1953 and at Nice, Cannes, and Clermont in September. In June 1955, he came within an ace of giving the 409 OC a heart attack when he concluded a spectacular show in a T–33 by landing off a loop.

Another Kelowna air show, 1956

Pat Parker

On March 8, 1956, in A/C 18399, Cudgel 16 set out on a cross-country to Penticton, Prince George, with a return to Comox. After a low approach and overshoot at Penticton, we carried on down the lake at about 100 feet at a high-power setting so Mac could give me a running tour of Peachland, Summerland, etc. We were thinking of trying to see if the date of the Kelowna Regatta was painted on the Aquatic grandstand, and sure enough, it was. After taking in all the sights in downtown Kelowna, with Mac even pointing out the window at where he used to work, we did a vertical pull-up to 10,000 feet. Just then, the Penticton radio called for our altitude, which we could truthfully report as 10,000 feet, as we were at the top of our loop. Then we plunged down the other side of the loop to fifty feet off the beach. After a few more passes, the announcer on Radio Station CKOV was completely drowned out by a strange noise. When we finally could hear the announcer again, he was saying, "We don't know why the planes are here, but everyone should go out and watch them."

After flying between the two ferries, we headed off to shoot the Greenacres Ranch on the North Thompson River, where Mac's girlfriend was visiting. After shooting an "almost landing" on the ranch house roof, Cudgel 16 headed back to Comox.

At the regatta that summer, Mac and I were both interviewed a number of times about low-flying aircraft that beat up the town and stampeded the fruit packing plant. We were quite amazed that anyone we knew would do such a thing and suggested that a local trainee pilot in a Harvard could be the culprit. Perhaps the true story is still a mystery.

How high the Clunk?[5]

Bob Merrick

In the early days of the Cold War, when air defenders had to worry solely about manned bombers, determining the height of those bombers was sometimes difficult. One day in the heyday of the crew concept, I was flying with Garth Parks, who not only was not my regular pilot, but was from the other flight, so it was an unusual occasion to start with. For whatever reason, we had recovered at RCAF Station Uplands, probably to fill some square regarding staying current in landing at alternate airports.[6] The plan was to have lunch, then return to RCAF Station Bagotville, where we were based with 432 AW(F) Squadron.

Start-up, taxi, and takeoff were all unremarkable. Shortly after we launched, Ottawa departure asked us to contact Crystal, the radar site at RCAF Station Lac St. Denis. We did so and learned that someone in the air defence hierarchy was trying to provide entertainment for a gaggle of Mk.IV CF–100s and their crews who were en route to overseas bases and were stalled in BG (identifier for RCAF Station Bagotville) by wholly unsuitable weather farther down the line.

Knowing that the devil finds work for idle hands, higher authority decreed that our solo Mk.V CF–100, complete with rocket pods carrying twenty-nine Mickey — oops, make that Mighty — Mouse rockets per side would be an ideal simulated bomber to keep the visitors active and out of the bar. They passed the word down the line to see if we would be amenable to a bombing route. Would we? You bet! Parky quickly had the aircraft on the heading proposed by the controller, a heading that would eventually get us into the chunk of sky controlled by Scabbard, the radar site at RCAF Station Mont Apica, Quebec, which would control the fighters.

Through the various control agencies, we learned that the "fighter sanctuary" would be at 30,000 feet. Thus, our target run could be done at any altitude save that, so that if everything turned to corn flakes we would not have a metal-to-metal meeting of the worst kind.

The devil did indeed find work for idle hands. Ours. Parky said, "This is the high-altitude version, isn't it?"

I said, "Roger that."

"Hmm," said Parky, "how high will it really go?" Well, I didn't know. "Shouldn't we find out?" he asked.

"A great idea," I said. Parky smoothly applied the power to attain the best climb speed, and we left 35,000 feet for an unknown destination.

We knew that the Mk.V CF–100 we were in operated quite well at 45,000 feet, as our squadron commander, the redoubtable W/C Bob Braham, insisted that all our practice intercepts be done between 40,000 and 45,000 feet, or below 10,000 feet, where the radar turned molehills into brightly lit mountains, greatly complicating life for the back seaters

---

5   Reprinted with permission from Tim Dube, *Observair*.
6   Crews on those days had to complete a host of requirements and their progress in doing so was tracked on a big board filled in with grease pencil when the crew returned from a mission.

by totally obscuring any bombers that might be lurking down there. Above 45 M (45,000 feet)? Well, we didn't really know how the aircraft might perform, and we primly rationalized the whole venture by saying — to ourselves — that interceptor crews should be fully aware of aircraft performance in all areas of the flight envelope.

Soon we were handed over to Scabbard and we hastened to assure them that our armament was safe — they tended to worry about that — and that we were not in the fighter sanctuary. We were, in fact, far from it. The fighters were airborne, and we listened as they streaked in to "destroy" us. They were told that we were at 35,000 feet. As they came closer, we could see them . . . far below us. The trusty Clunk had surpassed 50,000 feet and was still struggling upward. The fighters were turned onto their attack vectors. We watched as they swept by some 20,000 feet below, and we listened as they reported "No Joy," meaning they had seen neither hide nor hair of us.

There was a brief pause as the controller repositioned his chicks, who then swooped by on another futile pass. Suddenly, the controller had an idea. "Rhino 14 [I think that was Parky's number], say 'altitude.'"

"Altitude," was the response.

"No," said the controller, "I want to know how high you are."

"Neither one of us has had a drink in over twenty-four hours," we said.

"What height are you flying at?" asked the controller, now speaking through what seemed to be tightly clenched teeth.

"Perhaps you should ask your height finder," we suggested, trying to be helpful.

There was a lengthy pause. Then, "The height finder is u/s. It shows you at 55,000 feet."

"Fancy that," we said. "What makes you think it's u/s?"

"The CF–100 can't get that high," he said firmly.

"Well, this one can," was our response, "because that's where we are."

"What are you doing up there?" asked the controller.

"Oh, about .85," was the somewhat flippant response.

It can't be said that we were still truly flying. Parky had about one knot between V stall and V Max P (that is, he had very little margin between the velocity at which the aircraft would stall and the velocity it should never exceed). If the mark of a fighter or interceptor is the ability to point the nose anywhere the pilot wants to point it any time he or she wants to point it there, we were most assuredly neither a fighter nor a credible bomber. Our altitude at the time was fluctuating between about 54,500 and 54,600 with almost no ability to turn and no ability to climb any higher.

Now that the jig was up, Parky gingerly eased us down to an altitude where European-bound CF–100s could play games with us. As they were Mk.IVs, complete with full tip-tanks, we had to go a long way down to be "shot" at, exhibiting a degree of co-operation unlikely to be offered by any Soviet bomber.

Were there repercussions? Not that I recall. We didn't noise it about too widely, and neither, apparently, did the controller, nor the European-bound crews. One or two people asked what we would have done had the canopy blown off, and I don't remember that we had any ready answers, but after that afternoon, we had a good idea of just how high the Clunk would go, and how useful it would be when it got there. Fortunately, that was one chink in our armour that the Soviets never exploited, probably because, despite the supposed omnipotence of their designers, they couldn't fly that high either.

Bagotville tales
Ian "Nip" Cumming

When we won the two Steinhardts, W/C Allison had a sign erected at the end of the runway, near the "run up" area, saying, "413 Sqn - Home of the Steinhardt Trophy." That pissed off W/C Braham, CO of 432 Sqn, and he used to turn his CF–100's tail to it and blow it down on a regular basis. When Braham and his nav, S/L John Boby, ejected, I was in the air and closest to the bailout area. Scabbard Control vectored me to the area to look for signs of life. Almost immediately I found Boby hanging in a tree and reported his position. He was recovered in good shape. There was no sign of W/C Braham for a number of days until a woodsman or hunter found him wandering in a daze . . . He was in pretty bad shape but recovered fully.

Braham was an old and very successful night fighter from WW II. He used to fly around at night with his nav lights off. I looked out one night, and he was flying formation on my right wing. I never even had a clue he was there.

More memories! I was talking with my wife, Evie, over dinner and asked how we ever found out that her cousin had crashed in the North Atlantic with G/C Ralph Ashman, CO, RCAF Station Bagotville. G/C Ashman told me the story.

It happened during WW II. They were flying off Newfoundland in winter in a Digby bomber, when they developed engine trouble. They assumed they were dead—under-cast fog below them and the cold Atlantic awaiting them. They said their goodbyes and went into a slow descent until they ditched in Zero-Zero (zero ceiling, zero visibility) weather. They scrambled out onto a wing only to find a startled Newfoundland dory-man handling codfish right next to them. He said, "Can I give you a lift?" They stepped off the wing right into his dory and never even got wet! Talk about lucky.

Mighty Mouse rockets seek their destination, wherever that might be!

Speaking of G/C Ashman ("I'll kill you, I'll kill you dead!" was his favourite phrase): We were having a big base alert one day, and security was at max. I was sitting outside our hangar on alert and pretty near my airplane when G/C Ashman drove out to my A/C in his staff car. He proceeded to walk around the plane like he was doing a walk around. I was watching his performance with much interest when he marched right over to me and said, "I just blew up your airplane, mister."

I said: "Why would you want to do a thing like that, sir? We need those airplanes!"

He said: "I could have been an enemy agent, and you didn't even try and stop me!"

I said: "Well, sir, I knew it was you, and in any case I don't think an enemy agent would drive up in your staff car."

He said as he stomped off: "God damn it, Cumming . . . I'll kill you . . . I'll kill you dead." He was a funny guy, although I don't think he meant to be.

Two more stories immediately come to mind. Both involve my navigator Gord Mitchell (now deceased), who was a great guy and a super navigator. We served with 413 Sqn in Bagotville from 1958–1960. One night when Gordie and I were standing alert, we got a live scramble. Gordie had gone across the hangar to go to the bathroom and was there when the scramble bell rang. I went to the door leading to the hangar to make sure he had heard the bell and was coming. I saw Gordie hustling across the hangar floor. His flying suit was still down around his ankles, and he was trying to wipe his ass with a wad of paper as he made his way toward the Alert bird. Unfortunately, he kept dropping new feces as he ran, which kept the show going all the way across the hangar floor. I was laughing so hard I could barely make it to the airplane. As a matter of fact, I think he beat me to our respective cockpits. But in the end we did get airborne, and Canada's first line of defence saved the day again!

The second story is from one night when I was on the ground doing my job as flight commander, and Gord was flying with another pilot. Prior to landing, they declared an emergency because their nose wheel wouldn't extend. I went out to see the landing as the "crash trucks" stood by. The landing went well, with a shower of sparks as the nose touched the runway and the a/c came to a stop. There was no fire or smoke, but as the crew rolled back the canopy to wait for a ladder, the fire crew raised their foam cannon and levelled it at the aircrew. Gordie stood up waving his arms and shouting, "No! No!" Before he could get out another "No," they were drenched in foam and stood like two snowmen as the fire crew proceeded to fill the cockpit and douse the whole a/c in foam. A little foam around the nose probably would have sufficed.

Hijinks with Jerry Frewen
Hank Sands

On June 2, 1959, W/C Hal Bridges, OC of 409 AW(F) Squadron, Comox, B.C., ushered us into his office, sat us down, shuffled some papers on his desk, slowly looked up, and said, "Hank, you and Jerry have been accused of using your flights into the States to smuggle vodka into British Columbia." We were both struck dumb, but Jerry gave me that special Irish look of his, and mumbled something indistinguishable like, "Hank, what the hell have you done now?"

Jerry Frewen, an already experienced navigator, and I, a very inexperienced pilot, crewed up in good old Cold Lake, Alberta, along with everyone else destined to fly the Avro CF–100 (also nicknamed the "Lead Sled" and the "Clunk"). It was the last Canadian jet fighter ever built that would proudly patrol Canadian skies during the Cold War, or for that matter any war. Oh . . . there was a plane called the Avro Arrow. Can't remember what happened to it. I think it just had the misfortune of being designed and built when there was a shortage of scrap metal.

Much against Jerry's wishes, I got married while training in Cold Lake, which I think doomed us to stay in Canada. Everyone else on our course was sent overseas. But Jerry and I were at least rewarded with a three-year tour in Comox, which, unless you like snow and cold, is the only decent air force base in Canada.

The day after our Cold Lake graduation, we all shipped out to our destinations in a hurry. I believe it had something to do with some alterations we made to the officers' mess during the party the night before. Somehow the sacred, personally signed King's and Queen's pictures that hung proudly in the shirt-and-tie-only part of the mess ended up in the snake pit. The rustic pictures of First Nations people that had hung proudly in the snake pit (where we could have a beer dressed like bums) ended up displayed upstairs in place of the King and Queen. They deserved their moment of glory. I think Jerry had something to do with that. We also ate all the goldfish swimming in the pool. I might have had something to do with that. The OC was not amused. Yep, next day we got outta there fast.

Once settled in Comox, we became outwardly known as being the shortest crew on squadron, and inwardly known for having the highest number of 100 percent kills on film (which of course we couldn't tell anyone, as it was classified). We also held the record for attending the most TGIFs. Jerry was famous for verbal-wrestling the highest-ranking officer unlucky enough to be bellying up to the bar, and I was famous for spending most of the time on the phone, lying to my wife about when I would get home.

Our everyday flying routine in Comox was pretty laid-back in summer, but winter was a different ball game. We were an all-weather fighter squadron, which meant we should be flying in all kinds of weather, day and night. We rarely missed a day's flying. Bad weather would be defined as just a little above Zero-Zero, and good weather as one-fourth-mile visibility with a 100-foot ceiling. Once airborne, we would coax the Clunk up and out of the cloud, often around 42,000 feet. And there we played at trying to kill one another while freezing our butts off. Avro's priority in building this fighter wasn't crew comfort. Actually, when I think about it, I don't know what their priorities were.

It was the height of the Cold War, and it was no joke. Even though our silly weapons system was the equivalent of taking on a grizzly bear with skeet shot, we all put body and soul into it. There wasn't the manpower to be on alert status twenty-four hours a day, so we slept at night. The alarm that woke us meant going from a deep sleep to airborne in five minutes. Just because we never had a live bullet fired at us in anger doesn't mean we didn't know fear.

Let's return to W/C Bridges' office. Not only was he an excellent commander, he was also a very wise man. Even before we entered his office, he'd figured that we weren't smugglers. We could buy vodka on the base in the mess anytime. If we'd wanted to bootleg it (and who did?), we sure didn't need to bring it in from the States. However, vodka was indeed illegal in British Columbia. Some B.C. liquor control board dingaling decided that since vodka is colourless and relatively odourless, it should be outlawed.

So how did we end up in this mess? Turns out that on one of my visits to my father in Victoria, I not only took him a bottle of vodka (from the mess, of course), but I told him the story of how the Maritime boys in Greenwood, Nova Scotia, were bringing in whole tankfulls of rum from their training flights to Jamaica. We all thought it was funny at the time, but it was true, and they did get caught at it. Don't bother asking how, but that bottle of vodka and the story somehow got passed on to a Mountie who lived in my dad's apartment building, who in turn passed it on to the liquor control board and customs people, and next thing we knew, Jerry and I were vodka smugglers. Maybe I was a little tipsy when I told my father these flyboy stories, but I will never figure out how smuggling rum in Greenwood turned into smuggling vodka into British Columbia.

"Okay," said the wing commander, "here's what we're going to do. Tomorrow you're going to head down to McChord AFB, pick up some cigarettes and candy, and come back here. And don't tell anyone about this, ever." Next day, Jerry and I flew to McChord, picked up some cigarettes and candy, and some toys for my kids, and returned to Comox.

The biggest crowd of cloak-and-dagger types I've ever seen greeted us. They stripped that poor old CF–100 right down to her underwear, and guess what? They never found an ounce of vodka.

The second break in our boring routine happened on a night flight. It was a three-fighters-on-one exercise, and Jerry and I were selected as target. That meant that we would take off fifteen minutes ahead of everyone else. To say the weather was iffy would be an exaggeration, but you could see *most* of the runway, and the fog was almost clear of the canopy.

So off we went into the not-so-sky-blue yonder. In my years of flying, I've seen it a hundred times. The first airplane off churns up the 100-percent-humidly air and you have blotto. And that's exactly what happened to us. Our three buddies chickened out. Since we no longer had a home to go to, we decided it was time to get on the radio and look for an alternate.

It didn't take us long to find out that all of the West Coast was socked in, and Calgary was a little too far for the fuel we had on board. Besides, who wants to go to Calgary?

Vancouver Control advised us that the only base open was a SAC (Strategic Air Command) base close to Spokane, Washington. So we pointed the old Clunk in that direction. Party time! we thought.

Trouble was that back then our fighters were still using the antiquated VHF frequencies and the Americans used UHF. All the American control towers had one VHF channel, the good old 121.5-year-old emergency channel. In theory they were supposed to keep this channel up and running, but in fact most of the time they simply turned it off, or down too low to notice. In any case, we couldn't raise them.

We had two choices open to us. Bail out before they shot us down or bloody well just go in and land before they shot us down. We both decided that bailing out was not the best plan, but we sure did consider it. You should understand that back then, SAC were the boys who carried the atomic bombs around the world on a twenty-four-hour basis. To put it simply, they had no sense of humour.

The movie *Dr. Strangelove* was not a comedy to us back then. To give you an idea just how lacking in humour they were, let me repeat a story told to a group of us in the bar by Flight Lieutenant John Reynolds while I was on course at Cold Lake. He'd been on an exchange program with SAC in the States, flying their big jets. General Curtis Lemay, the SAC commander at the time, called John into his of-

"Well, so far, so good—that should be Deci right there. I wonder where the airport is."

fice after he did a wheels-up on the runway with a B–47, and the way John put it, "He picked up a colt .45 off the desk, pointed it at my head, and pulled the trigger. There was the loudest click I've ever heard. I was scared shitless." So what happened? we all asked. "Well, Curtis glared at me and said, 'If you ever wreck another one of my airplanes, this gun will be loaded.'"

John was shipped back to Canada in a big hurry and probably spent his air force life in Cold Lake.

With thoughts like this dancing in our heads, Jerry and I forged ahead with a dicey ADF let-down,[7] finally broke out of the gloom, and landed on the first runway we saw. I can only imagine the look of shock on the tower controller's face when an airplane suddenly appeared out of nowhere, unannounced and totally unknown, and landed at one of the most secure airports in the United States.

Since we didn't know what to do or where to go, I turned off the runway and simply shut down. Within seconds, jeeps, tanks, and any number of

---

7 An automatic direction-finding let-down was used by a CF–100 returning home on a mission by following transmissions from a home beacon.

dangerous weapons were pointed at us. "Show your ID," a loudspeaker blared. Both Jerry and I had nothing on us but our dog tags. My biggest fear was that my very outspoken Irish navigator just might get us shot, by telling the guy with the loudspeaker what an idiot he was. I think it was the CF–100 that saved us. After all it did have a big Canadian flag painted on it. And it sure didn't look dangerous. We weren't strip-searched, handcuffed, or thrown in jail, but were held in an empty room for quite a while.

When they finally figured out who we were, they shipped us off to the officers' club.

We didn't have a penny between us. I can't remember if we just drank water (no, Jerry would never do that). We must have bummed a few beers off the SAC boys, or maybe we sold some parts of the CF–100. Whatever the case, we did indeed party a little with these strange guys before going to bed.

The next day, after much fiddling and fumbling, they managed to fuel us up and get us started (no easy task) and happily sent us back to Canada with a special gift—a bottle of vodka each. Yikes!

Editor's note: The F/L Reynold's tale has also been attributed to W/C "Smokey" Drake. Allegedly, when CL warned "Smokey" that "the next time the gun will be loaded," Smokey responded, "It had better be!"

The "Professionals"

John Eggenberger

Live rocket firing operations for CF–100 Sqns in the Air Division called for (at least twice per year) the "whole squadron" (not including our French "ops room" cleaner, whose nose was always out of joint because he could not go along) to fly down to Decimomannu Air Base, located near Cagliari on the Isle of Sardinia. Our ground crew were flown down by North Star and our equipment by one of those two-engined, fixed-undercarriage, nose-opening, high-winged follies that we bought from the Brits—the mighty Bristol Freighter.

The Base infrastructure at Deci was owned by the Italians, with the operations being divvied up between us three warrior nations: Canadians, Germans, and Italians. At Deci, there was a Canadian CO to sort us out (make sure we did things right), and he had control of the "Canadian operation." There were similar folk for the Germans and Italians. Our CO had his own ATC people and an operations/administration staff. Also under his umbrella was a barrack building for us, in which over the years there had been developed a small room for a "snake pit," used for after-flight libations and such-like. The Deci Base officers' mess being quite far away (for us, anyway), and while the base mess was nominally one-third ours, the other occupants didn't really want us there because we upset their tranquil lives with our parlour games, etc. We took our meals in a combined mess that was open pretty much all the time.

To the west of Deci (over the ocean, obviously) was a live firing range that was used by us Canadians, the German air force, and, of course, the Italian folks. The idea was to fly the whole Sqn—eighteen aircraft, including the "Hangar Queen"—to Deci in one big gaggle, land, and then have each crew do a few live shoots and any extra shoots that might be needed to make sure that the a/c fired in correctly. After all this "work," we were to fly home, feeling very good that we could indeed shoot something out of the air (if we were real lucky). This operation usually took a couple of weeks or so to complete.

So, at 0800 on the morning of April 17, 1962, 445 Sqn being all briefed up, we were prepared to trudge out to our steeds and be off to do warrior stuff. Included in our kit were several jugs of liquid refreshments from the Base BX. Usually these were stuffed in the back seat, there being some concern that having this precious cargo loaded in the machine-gun rack, or behind the battery, neither of which were pressurized, might lead to the loss of this invaluable cargo by leakage. I don't know if this was so or not, but we didn't risk finding out.

One hiccup (maybe two): the met briefing supplied the information that the weather at Deci was 2,000 and two (I think). But, because the main runway was under repair, we had to use the taxi-way for flight operations; and also because there was no GCA available (not really needed in that sunny clime, but who knows). We were ordered not to depart Marville unless we had 5,000 and five at Deci. Departing Marville at 0800 would have let us get our Deci ops briefing done that day, and then live firing could begin the following morning. But we waited—and waited, until our CO (on the advice of the met man who thought that we "might" have these limits by the time we got there) opined that we could go.

No wimps were we. We were professionals.

We departed at 1050 hrs and arrived at Deci two hours later. The weather had not changed one whit, but we, being very very good at what we do, had no trouble breaking cloud over Deci and we all landed successfully.

Clearly, the weather was going to remain as it was, and it was forecast to be the same for at least two days, according to the met man. So, we off-loaded our kit and cargo and trudged off to the barracks, settled in, and commenced games of poker (for the high rollers), bridge (for the intellectuals), and gin rummy (for the less blessed with brain power). Aided by the liquid refreshments, these games became more and more interesting. Of note, the poker games used money of all sorts—Marks, Francs, Pounds, $US, Lire (big stuff, that), IOUs, whatever. While in the Air Div, we had become fairly adept at doing the mental arithmetic so that we could do the "exchange" (based upon the $US) as we called or raised for a pot with whatever money we had stored up for this major event. As the liquid refreshments diminished, so did the workings of our brains. Inevitably, the players became more and more sure that their competitors were "not playing the game properly," nor were they "ante-ing up" fairly. You get the image, think I.

One thing led to another, and before morning struck, we had consumed almost all of our liquid refreshments for the whole shoot—quite a task in itself. During this evening/night, several of the more inventive of us prepared for the morning—knowing full well that we would not be flying; the met man told us so. Among other things, constructed was a towering pile of empty beer cans (looked like the Eiffel Tower) near the barrack entrance doorway. The tower was designed to collapse upon the entrance of the first unsuspecting soul who would first open the door. Also, several rooms were rearranged so that the occupant, upon arising, would find himself in strange surroundings. Others had the furniture dismantled and put together such that it would come apart at the slightest touch. An ingenious and energetic bunch, you must admit.

But what would you expect . . . we were professionals.

Morning came—bright and sunny, clear and a million. The CO of the Deci Base arrived at the briefing room to welcome us, "sort us out," and bless the occasion. Nobody home; the briefing room was completely empty of air warriors.

The CO of Deci and his adjutant marched over to the barracks. Upon opening the door (the Deci CO through the door first, of course), crash bang! down came the tower. Not to be distracted, the Deci CO stomped over the fallen tower (it really was a beautiful thing to see before it fell) and opened the door of one of the rooms. Unfortunately, he chose a room that had had the furniture dismantled and reassembled so as to fall apart when touched (even ever so slightly)—and sure enough, he did, and it did.

In the next room he opened, he found a completely naked, intrepid, nav-type air warrior sprawled on a bed. He and the room smelled real good. The CO of Deci marched over to the bed, grabbed a foot, yanked it, and shouted, "Get up! There is flying to do!"

Responded the air warrior: "Go shit in your hat!"—then turned over and let go a long, rippling fart.

That did it. Out the CO of Deci stomped, followed by his adj. The base commander of Marville was immediately advised of what a bunch of assholes he had on his AWF Sqn. The commander Air Div was advised, and was also astonished (so to speak). That day, the base commander Marville and his Wing-co Flying flew down in a T–33—and sorted us all out. We did not fly on the 18th. Considerable eye-avoidance activity ensued, waiting for all the shoes to drop. One of the shoes was that our little snake pit was closed up.

We could just suffer and use the combined mess facilities, where we were not wanted by the Germans and Italians—and where we really didn't want to go. That was real punishment.

We flew on the 19th—did a super job, all of us trying our best to recover our first-class image. Unfortunately, we didn't get all the flying done on the 20th, so we had to stay over the weekend and fly on the 23rd and 24th.

Friday the 20th was a little boring; went down to Cagliari—not a lot on the go there. So on Saturday afternoon, a few of the more bored of us decided to attend the combined officers' mess to check things out. Finding out what we already knew, the mess was as still as a forest without wind. As well, the hard booze being very expensive there, we were relegated to drinking a particularly vile, greenish-yellow, cheap Italian wine. One did not have to drink a lot of this stuff to get a buzz, and we slurped up a fair amount in a relatively short time.

Thinking that we would improve our image by showing our fellow air warriors from Germany and Italy the finer points of mess-man-ship, we proceeded to demonstrate "Bummy Ball," "Where are you, Moriarty," "Bomb-run," and so on. To our amazement, these demonstrations were not well received, and we were escorted back to our barracks by the Italian military police. They are not as kind a folk as are our MPs, and more than our feelings were hurt.

Later on, some of our more aggressive folk thought that it was the Germans that told on us (we found out later that this was not so) and got us turfed from the mess, so it was "get-even time." To this end, into several of the beer cans were placed some small pieces of gravel (rattled real good), and as the German barracks was not too far away, around four in the morning those more aggressive amongst us crept out . . . got close . . . hollered, "Mortar! Mortar!" and threw the cans up against the German barrack, making a most considerable and satisfactory racket, which got the Germans out of bed in a most irate mood. But the folks who did this ought not to have shouted, "Mortar, mortar." There being no nearby U.S. air warriors to blame, we Canadians got nabbed (maybe we weren't as smart as we thought we were).

So the 23rd and 24th passed peaceably enough; but (fortunately) on the evening of the 24th, the dregs of some liquid refreshment were located, and the poker, bridge, and gin rummy games resumed. Knowing that we didn't have any more "get out of jail" cards left in the kitty, most of us spent a rather subdued evening. Some didn't—but they were wise enough to stay inside.

On departure home day, the 25th, the met man said that the weather for Marville wasn't all that good, but no matter—we had lost all faith in those folks anyway. We were "good to go." A little foul weather at home just didn't count as trouble. So we lined up all eighteen on the taxi way for a formation takeoff (kind of). The idea was to form up in one big gaggle to transit to Marville—then, before descending, form up in four boxes of four with two trailing, and thence descend in impeccable and beautiful formation, thereafter doing up a magnificent flypast for the Sabre folk to admire—and, more important, alert our wives that we were home, with duffel bags full of dirty laundry and eyes as big as saucers, etc.

In a cloud of flying dirt and gravel (FOD was unknown in those days), off we took; so long, Deci. The plan was to do a 360 overhead so that all could get in the gaggle as we did the transit to Marville. However, one of our happy homeward-bound crews failed to check the undercarriage downlocks and had to land and get them out. I understand that this crew still blame each other for failing to do this vital check. They never did catch up, even though they really tried (so they say).

The transit went just fine. As we approached the descent point, our CO called up Yellowjack, our much-admired (no kidding) GCI radar controller for descent clearance. The CO was told to go to Marville Tower for letdown clearance. And so he did, but as briefed, we all stayed on Yellowjack. We all understood that the CO was to come back from Yellowjack and tell us all "what frequency to go to, etc." and—as we all skimmed the tops of the cloud waiting for further instructions, all in nice and tight formation (Al Chapman and I were on the CO's starboard wing)—eagle-eyed, I saw the CO's speedbrakes start to lift. I shouted to Al, "SPEED-BRAKES!" But Al saw them start to rise microseconds before I did, and he "quick like a bunny" popped the brakes and somehow stayed in formation just as we dipped into the clouds. Jacques St. Cyr and Gil Heon were in the box, and Jacques was able to keep his steed in place, as did Tom Lambrick flying on the CO's port wing. The other three boxes weren't so lucky; the reaction time available didn't allow for good station keeping (oh, yeah). As a result, the rest—all over the place.

The CO had not come back from Yellowjack to call the brakes.

Most of the variety of recriminations were kept within the confines of the cockpits (thank goodness), but idiot, numbskull, twit, your mother wears army boots, etc., were heard from a few brave souls. In due course, we all emerged from the cloud base in reasonably good shape, within eyeball reach of each other (more or less), boxes reformed. Our CO gathered his flock together again—we rejoined in the big gaggle somehow—and did our impressive flypast, and it was a dandy (really).

After all, we were professionals.

The Air Div mess dinner

Bob Grandmaison

It was a day in late November 1962.

The day started with me showing up at the mess for lunch. One of the Sabre squadrons was hitting the bar pretty good. I had nothing to do, so I decided to join them. By four in the afternoon, I was reminded that I was attending the mess dinner that evening, so I headed off for a shower.

On return to the mess for cocktails, I distinctly remember at one point that Al Reimer, a USAF general, the station CO, and myself were having a little chat when one of the junior American officers came to the general pleading his case to return to the States. The general pointed out to this officer that he, the general, had left a very lucrative job behind to take up his current position and that this young officer should just get back to drinking with his new Canadian friends. I think it was this moment in time that made him my friend for life.

Time passed. If you remember the seating arrangements at mess dinners, it was normally male, female, male, etc., with a member of the opposite sex across the table from you. During the meal, I was trying to drum up some support to sing "For He's a Jolly Good Fellow," but to no avail. Prior to the speeches, I had gone up to the head table and offered a drink (from a very impressive brandy snifter) to the station CO and his guest. The station CO suggested I come back in a few minutes (I have forgotten precisely the time he mentioned but something like ten or twenty minutes). That was a mistake on his part. With the cunning of a drunk wearing a stopwatch, I was back at the table at precisely the appointed time.

When the speeches started, I doubt very much if I could actually hear them because I was still trying to drum up support for my song. Unfortunately, it was at the moment that the base commander stated, ". . . and our guest tonight is . . . the commander of the aircraft that dropped the bomb on Nagasaki," that I decided to go it alone.

Shortly afterwards, the duty officer, much to my surprise and indignation, escorted me out of the mess (my flight commander, Choda Belval, had suggested to the duty officer that my night was finished). Like a fool, I decided to go over to the schoolies (teachers at the on-base schools) and tell my tale of woe.

The next day, even though it was my day off, I had an appointment to meet with Choda. After a lengthy sermon, I was awarded one month's squadron duty ops and was told to go in and see the squadron OC, W/C Buzza. By the time he was through with me, I had sunk so low that I needed a chainsaw to cut my way through the carpet in his office to exit. His parting words included "release" and "scoot over to the station CO for your next interview." At this moment I figured my goose was cooked. The flight commander gave me one month's duty ops, the squadron OC threatened release, and I assumed the station CO would execute release proceedings.

I knocked on his door and was invited in. It seemed that I stood at attention for a long time, but likely that was the fear factor. After an eternity, he looked up from his desk and told me to hang up my coat and hat. During the one-way chat, he pointed out to me that he could have been in shit himself because the air commodore from Metz was also at the dinner and did not take lightly the antics of junior officers. However, General Sweeney had stated he'd had a great time and in fact brought up my name. That probably saved my ass. As I was reaching up to grab my hat and coat, I heard the station CO start to speak again. At this point, I thought my own bomb was going to drop and I was on my way back to Canada. However, his words were: "Did you break that glass last night?" "No," I replied. "Good," he said. "We may need it for the next party." Note: The cognac glass mentioned was a five litre glass so it went a long way. When it was passed around the dinner that night, it served quite a few people but made it back to me without damage.

P.S. from Larry Clark

Robert: I believe the date is out a year—it should be 1961, when I was still on Squadron. I attended the aforementioned mess dinner, which I could not have done in 1962. Furthermore, it was Aug–Sept '61 when we had the build-up in aircrew, due mainly to the heightened Cold War tensions (Berlin Wall). If memory serves me correctly, I was sitting at the centre table facing your direction. It seems to me it caused a bit of a huddle (after the momentary hush) at the head table before the word went out. The correct spelling of his name is Sweeney (Charles W.); his other claim to fame appears to have been that he became a brigadier general in 1956, and at the time was the youngest man in the air force to reach that rank. *Quaerimus et Petimus.*

Bon mot
John Eggenberger

RCAF 1 Air Division was head and shoulders above all other NATO air forces during the 1950s and '60s. Its doctrine was clear: *beat the other guy*! To do so called for individual initiative, which was expected—indeed, demanded. Often (always?) personal initiative in the RCAF was irreverent and ironic. It took a special leader to tolerate and encourage behaviour from his subordinates that to others would smack of impertinence. The rare leader who was terminally thin-skinned was no leader at all. The following cameo involves an air navigator who displayed all sorts of individual initiative, at the same time displaying an uncanny ability to say the right thing at the right time.

In the early '60s, the CF–100's days in the Air Division were numbered. The four Clunk squadrons had been removed from the Order of Battle, and crews no longer pulled alert. Nonetheless, the squadrons maintained a high level of proficiency. They continued to fly all manner of airborne intercept missions; 445 Sqn, based at Marville, France, was one of these. One such mission was a high-level "twin threat" profile flown on a seldom-experienced CAFB day, on October 9, 1962.

Al Ehman and I were in the lead aircraft. The GUF (guy up front) of the other Clunk was a "very experienced pilot, well-known for his sometimes ham-fisted aggressiveness"; the GIB (guy in back) was Al Wardstrom. The intercept was scheduled to be conducted at 45,000 feet—rarefied air where the Mk.IVB CF–100 was far from nimble.

During the first run, #2 initiated a particularly aggressive forty-five-degree turn away from Lead, which promptly put the aircraft into an inverted spin. With an almost full fuel load at angels 44 (or so),[8] this was definitely not a good thing to have happen. Noticing the aircraft going around and around upside down, Al Ehman called on the radio, "Are you okay?"

The pilot responded, "Yes, we're okay," which prompted the following GIB retort on the R/T from Al Wardstrom: "Speak for yourself, asshole."

Stants
Lee Evans

"Dutch" Stants, coming in for a landing, decided for some unfathomable reason to touch down at the very *beginning* of the runway. There was a one-to-two-foot lip that he hit, tearing off the right wheel. He went around again and brought it in with the one wheel down, thereby really putting the aircraft out of commission. W/C MacWilliams said, "It may be that your sole purpose in life is simply to serve as a warning to other pilots."

Middleton magic
Alex Saunders

My pilot was W/C Warren (Mid) Middleton. In addition to being his navigator, I was also the 425 Squadron adjutant. We had a rather rocky start, as I recall. He had gone through his dual on the Mk.III, and the time arrived for pilots and navs to team up. Mid apparently wanted to fly with an F/L navigator and he apparently suggested to the OTU staff that he would like to try one of the F/L's first; that turned out to be me. Again, I was to have some GCI exposure on that flight. It was my first time in a CF–100, let alone a fighter of any kind. I was enjoying the

---

8   This was the code word for the height the fighter was supposed to adopt; in this case, 44,000 feet.

ride as he did some pilot stuff and then it was time to come under GCI control for a practice set-up and intercept. It was not a good afternoon.

That was nearly fifty years ago, so the details are hazy. What I do recall was that things were not working out for the GCI, which raised the W/C's frustration level higher and higher. Maybe I was just a little thick, but my reaction was "Okay, a SNAFU of some kind somewhere, but we'll get sorted out." All of a sudden, the aircraft went into (for me) a violent series of rolls, both continuous and "flick," to the tune of an oath from the front seat: "F***!"—"F***!"—"F***!" Then I looked up to see if the "BAIL OUT" light was on . . .

"What the hell has happened?" I asked (yelled, actually).

All he said was, "Christ, I am so goddamned pissed off!" I shut up as we arrived into the circuit and landed.

As we pulled up and shut down, the ground crew placed the ladder. I was out of the cockpit like I had lived there all my life. I told the ground crew to clear out—get away from the aircraft! Mid came down the ladder, and I spun him around and let him have it. "*You're* pissed off! That was my first goddamned trip in one of these things and you let your frustration scare the shit out of me! The airmen can't hear what I am saying to you but they sure as hell would see it if I did what I *want* to do—flatten you on your arse. Don't bloody well tell me that you are a W/C and I shouldn't talk to you this way—screw you!"

He just stood there looking at me for a moment and then a grin spread across his face and he put his hand on my shoulder and said, "I think we should go and have a beer—several beers—okay?"

I think I said something like, "Okay—but watch it, eh?"

From then on, we had three fine years together.

Musings of an AI navigator
Les Taylor

I started the CF–100 OTU at Cold Lake in June 1956. It was my introduction to the vagaries of jet flying. Our course was the largest to date—twenty-six or twenty-seven crews, prompted by a change in intake frequency. We had our usual ups and downs, including the normal radar malfunctions.

One Friday night was particularly harrowing while we were doing LCCs (beam attacks) and the radar was not good. At the last minute, a collision course was detected, and a port break was called. As we passed underneath, I saw the port wing tip light of the target, and my pilot said, "Well, we missed you."

The response was, "Yes, by twenty f***ing feet!"
GCI: "How close?"
"Twenty feet."
GCI: "Enough for tonight—I'll meet you at the bar with the beer!"

On another occasion, we had barely taken off for our exercise when the weather clamped in and we were ordered into the stack for recovery at 35,000 feet. Alternates had also clamped. I don't recall what the other crews had in fuel, but I think the ground crew dipped our tanks at about fifty gallons.

Crew fatalities in the All-Weather world seemed to be high at the time. Before leaving Cold Lake, I shared my room with a new pilot whose crew were killed there within two weeks. Our course suffered its first loss several months later—a crew from St. Hubert.

Besides bridge, characters were the relief from the long hours of boredom holding alert. All squadrons had them, and at 428 in the mid-fifties we had our share. The nav who persuaded his pilot that the big station wagon was a good buy, as they could save money on motel bills! Or the pilot who was changing his driver's licence from the prairies to Ontario; he was having difficulty with the testing officer about his coordination. When he responded to the inquiry of his occupation that he was a "jet pilot," said licence was granted.

New crews were subjected to gentle hazing. TV in hangars was snowy, and the best seats were in the front. Old nav to pilot: "I guess no one briefed the sprogs that the front seats are reserved for the old boys." The new crew dutifully moved to the back. Several weeks later, the new crew inquired of the flight commander how long it would be before *they* could sit in the front row. Shrewd boss, "You've been speaking to Kuzyk,[9] haven't you." The same navigator asked a beautiful young schoolteacher (and hard to get) to let him know when she became pregnant, as he "wanted to see the three wise men come over the hill."

The Uplands Base commander often initiated practice scrambles—particularly if he had to be up early to greet VIPs. In early 1958, while we were on mandatory alert for weather, we were scrambled "hot" (armed). We were #1 and I could not see our #2's rudder! Tower confirmed that the scramble was a go, so we took off. On switching to GCI, they did not seem to know what was happening or what we were doing airborne. We stooged around for a few minutes, sorting things out. GCI eventually came back to inform us that the CO had scrambled us. As alternates were not good, and remembering the accidental discharge of the full load of 2.75 inch rockets at Comox, we declined to "bump heads" and recovered. "Muss" met us to say that he had not checked the weather, and the airman in Ops had not told him. (In those days, when Muss said JUMP, you only asked how high on the way up.) He didn't even have coffee

---

9   This was an individual who had an unusual way of using the English language.

A CF–100 "resting."

ready. Just another day.

Actually, I liked G/C Mussels. He did have some odd ideas—like trying to have thirty-six CF–100s fly line abreast on Air Force Day and climb to hit the contrail level simultaneously. Did not work, as he had forgotten about turns!

Another Sunday morning—early—he roused a group of the single chaps from recovery mode to work on the curling club with him. It was a snowy, blowy, miserably cold morning. However, with the direction of an NCO who knew what he was doing, we placed a lot of the sheet metal siding. It was about one-fifteen when we quit, and it was too late for mess lunch (and for us to change into eating dress), so Muss took us all home for his wife, Jean, to cook bacon and eggs for us.

More ho-hum?

Les Taylor

In late 1958, 428 and 410 Squadrons were tasked to provide crews at Harmon AFB in Stephenville,

Newfoundland, while the USAF converted from F–89 Scorpions to F–102s. At that time, the CF–100 performed better than the local CGI were used to. Hence we were often scrambled early to intercept inbound airliners from Europe; Air France always seemed to be off track. One morning, we were SCRAMBLED — hot — at around five a.m. and had two other scrambles before one p.m. Our replacements were also scrambled in the intervals. Beavers and Ansons at 500 feet were a challenge!

There was an RCN ship in the harbour, and our resident wit engaged its CO in conversation at the bar. "Is that your boat in the Bay?" inquired the intrepid navigator.

RCN type, haughtily, "That's a ship, not a boat."

"I see. Checking fishing licences late this year, eh?"

At which the RCN type stomped to the end of the bar. Shortly thereafter, our Wingco arrived for pre-dinner libations, and seeing the RCN type drinking in solitary splendour, proceeded to welcome him. "Good evening," says Wingco. "I'm the senior RCAF officer on base. Can I be of assistance?"

The response was, "Oh, they are yours, are they?" and the RCN type removed himself from the area, handkerchief still up his sleeve.

"What happened here?" asked our Wingco in puzzlement.

"Oh, he was just speaking to Kuzyk," was the response.

This same wit had an aversion to water, which was strange for a Prairie boy, and we joked that he wore two Mae Wests in wet weather. Several days later, that crew experienced a double engine flame-out over the bay. The pilot advised him, "No engines, John — prepare to bail out."

"You better get them going, or I won't speak to you again," flatly stated the nav.

Aerial buffoonery I
Doug Munro

"Cudgel Three, Comox Tower: The local weather is one hundred feet overcast, visibility one-eighth of a mile in fog and rain, your alternate airport is Vancouver International, and you're cleared as follows—"

A ninety-mile diversion is not brain surgery. Cudgel Three, with a long-in-the-tooth squadron leader at the throttle and a very senior flight lieutenant navigator navigating up a storm, headed for CYVR (the then ICAO identifier for Vancouver, B.C.).

After a superlative jet range approach, they broke cloud at fifteen hundred feet, cancelled Instrument Flight Rules, and called the control tower five miles back for a straight-in on Runway 08. Tower responded: "We don't have you visual, but you're number one and cleared to land." Old Eagle Eye, with the runway visual, dumped the gear and flaps and with great skill and cunning stuck the Clunk on the approach end button. "Jesus, this runway looks awfully short." The driver jumped on the binders and shuddered to a halt with a couple of feet of the runway remaining.

"Skipper, where the hell are we? I've a right to know — I'm the navigator."

"Beats me, but it isn't Vancouver. Let's get out of here."

A one-eighty, full power, and airborne again. "Skipper, I think that's Vancouver on our port side." Five minutes later, the intrepid birdmen parked at RCAF Station Sea Island. The first landing? As Maxwell Smart would say, they "just missed by *that* much." They had landed on a 3,000-foot runway at Boundary Bay, an airport that had been closed for nine or ten years. Fortuitously, the runway they chose did not have a row of telephone poles down its centre line like the other runway did. Leaders like that are hard to find.

A Bagotville-to-St. Hubert diversion shouldn't be too challenging, either! A 432 Squadron crew, part of a mass diversion when RCAF Bagotville was enjoying one of its periodic power failures, reaffirmed the premise that it is just as beneficial to be lucky as it is to be talented. After wandering in a southwesterly direction for some time, all the while reminiscing nostalgically about last night's adventures in beautiful downtown Chicoutimi, the crew belatedly attempted to contact the St. Hubert Tower on VHF. Nothing! The radio compass was working—they'd been closely monitoring a Country and Western station—but had no joy with the St. Hubert non-directional beacon or the radio range. And they were rapidly getting a scosh shy on fuel.

They couldn't stay at 35,000 feet forever, and besides, "You can't hit what you can't see," so down they went. They were reluctant to declare an emergency (experts don't have emergencies), nor did they have any idea whom to call. Passing 15,000 feet, an airliner was spotted climbing out of the undercast.

Airplane! Climbing! Must be an airport nearby . . .

Down they plunged through 10,000 feet of the fluffy stuff. Visual at last, what to their wondering eyes should appear but your basic airport, complete with a hard-surface runway. The old "waggle your wings, lower the gear, and look forlorn" routine brought a green light from the tower. Large letters on the operations building made them both feel warm and cuddly: "Welcome to Wilkes Barre, Pa." Another walking "A" category accident escaped to fly another day.

How does one fly non-stop from Lakehead to Bagotville in a Tutor? With great difficulty and a 300-knot tailwind, that is how! In the mid-1970s, a young pipeline instructor from CFB Moose Jaw, with an awestruck student on board, attempted the impossible. His pre-flight planning was cursory at best. To impress the student and show him "how real fighter pilots" flight plan, he elected to kick the tires, light the fires, get airborne, and head east.

A 425 Squadron VooDoo crew, airborne over Lac St. Jean, overheard a Tutor unsuccessfully attempting to contact Bagotville Tower. "Bandit 30, KN07, can we be of assistance?"

"KN07, Bandit 30, I'm approximately fifty nautical miles northwest of Bagotville. My TACAN is unserviceable, I'm running low on fuel, and I can't raise Bagotville Tower." The Tutor crew hadn't run out of airspeed but they'd clearly run out of ideas.

"Bandit 30, what's the weather like in your area?"

"KN07, solid undercast."

The VooDoo crew were fifty miles west of Bagotville, and the weather was clear as the proverbial bell. "Bandit 30, we don't know where you are, but you're not fifty nautical miles west of Bagotville. Dial in Channel 84 on your TACAN."

"Roger, the TACAN's working now; we're on the 045 radial of that station at sixty nautical miles."

"Now try Channel 42."

"That one works, too. We're on the 260 radial at 105 nautical."

"Bandit 30, return Channel 84—that's Val–d'Or. Home on the station, call Val–d'Or Tower and divert."

"But we don't have a clearance." A great time to choose to be professional ("I ran out of fuel but at least I had a proper clearance").

"Bandit 30, we'll advise Montreal Centre, and Val–d'Or will give you a clearance."

The Tutor landed safely at Val–d'Or. When demonstrating how real fighter pilots flight plan, the High Level chart the instructor was using was folded over, thereby omitting some 275 miles from his calculations. No one is perfect!

Even competent aircrew occasionally suffer from periodic attacks of terminal stupidity. F/Os P.T.W. and JK were on a night leg from Lakehead to RCAF Uplands, Ottawa, Ontario, after a two-week stint at RCAF Station Cold Lake, Alberta. JK, relaxing after randoming 2.75-inch rockets over large tracts of Northern Alberta, spearheading a run on the officers' mess beer supply, and proposing nightly to a startling variety of Base schoolteachers, suggested a wee wager to his front office.

JK: "Engine Room, Bridge: I'll bet you a beer we'll arrive over the Upland non-directional beacon within ten seconds of my estimated time of arrival [ETA]."

T: "You are on."

JK: "Fine. Give me revolutions for four hundred and twenty knots." (JK really talked like that!)

JK provided an ETA, they synchronized their watches, and started to home on the Uplands beacon. The Ottawa weather forecast was reasonable: five thousand feet overcast and very dark. Lo and behold, on ETA plus five seconds, their radio compass needle swung through 180 degrees (station passage), and down they went. When they broke cloud, no Ottawa; indeed, no civilization—just the occasional light here and there. Following a brief exchange of inter-cockpit pleasantries, JK's little grey cells began to function. He really turned the radio compass selection switch to the compass position, they homed on Uplands, eventually obtained a visual on Ottawa, cancelled IFR, and landed.

As the Clunk taxied to the ramp, P.T.W. promised JK that once he'd ripped his arm off and beaten him over the head with it, he would send his remains to his next of kin. Discretion being the better part of valour, JK unstrapped, rolled back the canopy, evacuated the rear seat, and perched on the starboard wing tip. As the CF–100 squealed to a halt in front of the 428 Squadron hangar, JK hit the deck a-runnin' and vanished for forty-eight hours—which allowed P.T.W.'s blood pressure to return to a measurable level.

As you may have guessed, they hadn't homed on the NDB; JK had control of the radio compass needle and "simulated" station passage with the left/right switch.

Past, present, and future budgetary constraints have and will sadly limit aircrew's ability to terrify and amaze; but if enough aviators are provided with enough aircraft and fuel, anything can, and invariably will, happen.

The 414 All-Weather Fighter Squadron, RCAF North Bay, Ontario, 1959–61

Greg Stevens

The brain and nerve centre of any Canadian all-weather fighter squadron is the operations room (OPs), its walls lined with operational and tactical displays. Late one November evening, the duty ops officer answered a telephone similar in size and shape to five or six other telephones in front of him except for its bright red colour. Seconds passed while he listened carefully to the commands. Then he pressed a solitary red button. Twice.

A mile from OPs, sited near the button of a two-mile-long runway, the first siren wailed in the 10-Minute Alert hangars, blaring throughout aircraft bays and the briefing room, lounge, and sleeping quarters, alerting the on-duty ground and air crews that a scramble was being called. Chairs clattered to the floor, cups flew into the air, and cigarettes dropped half-crushed. As the ground crew raced out to the hangars to open doors and turn on the aircraft starting generators, the second wail sounded.

The aircrew, two pilots, and two radar observers completed the buckling of their leg straps, without which they might lose their feet during an ejection, zipped their flight boots up, and within thirty seconds had scrambled up their aircraft ladders into their cockpits. Half a minute later, the connections between men and machines were completed, parachutes, dinghies, shoulder stress, lap baits, leg straps, oxygen, radios, and ejection seats armed. With a nod between pilots and ground crew, ladders and wheel chocks were pulled away, circuit breakers checked, intercom and radios checked between crews and aircraft, and canopies closed. The "All Clear" signals flashed.

Click, click, click, kawumph, whoosh! and one Orenda jet turbine fired, followed by a second roar, and a third, and a fourth, as two CF–100 Canuck fighters came alive. The second "Clunk," as CF–100 crews affectionately called their weapons carriers, checked in. "I'm ready!"

"Roger Two; One here, North Bay Tower, Halfback Ten with one, ready to roll!"

"Roger Ten, cleared for immediate takeoff, runway twenty-seven, winds westerly at ten knots, cleared for departure heading 265 degrees, climb to angels thirty-five, call channel six at angels five. Good hunting!"

Two silver and black interceptors, each armed with fifty-eight 2.75" rockets, moved forward, in unison from their hangars and, with throttles pushed to their forward detents, accelerated directly onto the runway ahead. A mile or so later, they lifted together into the dark skies, where they soon punched into the clouds.

In total time elapsed, from the pressing of the red button to airborne, less than five minutes had ticked by. You may have been awakened by their noisy departure, but during the Cold War you were able to roll over safely to sleep again.

The making of a fighter pilot
Terry Thompson

It was one of those dull days on the Prairies. The kind of a day where you can't see the sun, but from a T–33 jet trainer at 30,000 feet, you can see one hundred miles to the horizon. A thick layer of high cirrus blanketed the whole of southern Manitoba, and we were nearing the end of our gunnery school training at RCAF Stn MacDonald.

I had just landed, following what was to be my last gunnery sortie from that base. My logbook reads: "July 14th 1954—Flag Live, four plane, 30 percent." Not a bad score when one considers that 10 percent was about the average for most of us at this stage of our training. I hesitate to add that this was the only above-average score I was to achieve during the course.

After signing in, I was told to report to the flight commander, who advised me to pack my bags, as I was to leave immediately for 3 All-Weather Fighter Operational Training Unit at RCAF Station North Bay, Ontario. Four of us had been selected for operational training on the mighty CF–100 Canuck and we were to become all-weather pilots in the defence of North America. We departed together for our new home at 3 AW (F) OTU, otherwise known as the Witches' Squadron. The OTU crest was a black witch riding her broom into a full orange moon. North Bay was a fine station, recently designated as a key NORAD base and a temporary training centre for CF–100 aircrew. New messes, new single quarters, new hangars, and new administrative facilities gave us all a sense of pride and a keen desire to get on with our training.

The instructing staff were mostly all seasoned veterans of WW II and many had seen combat up close and personal. We, of course, were in awe of these heroes who had "been there" and we clung to their every word and gesture. Our small group was part of the second course to complete advanced flying training on the T–33 and we all had close to 100 hours on the T–Bird.

It didn't take us long to discover that each of us had more time on type than the whole instructing staff put together. In fact, during my training at Advanced Flying School (AFS) in Portage, I had accumulated around twenty-five hours more on the T–Bird than my classmates. Unfortunately, I *was* deemed to be a slow learner. Somehow I had been cursed with a sickly instructor during the pre-solo stage of my T–33 training.

This gentleman, whom I will call Flying Officer Grump, showed up on the flight line three or four times a week—if I was lucky. It seemed that every time I was fine-tuned for the solo check, F/O Grump would take sick, and after a couple of long days sitting on the ground, I would have to start all over again. This had a very depressing effect on me; and worse, in the eyes of my mates, I was marching down CT (cease training) alley.

Finally, one day, a swashbuckling, youngish instructor strode into the flight room, and seeing me sitting gloomily in the corner, shouted, "Thompson, why the hell aren't you in the air?" I stammered that I hadn't yet passed the solo check. Most of my coursemates had flown solo at around five hours, and there I was with eight hours on type and not yet qualified to fly solo. After a brief examination of my flying records, F/O Roy Windover introduced himself, and I was told to get ready to fly.

In my insecure state, I wasn't sure whether he meant off the end of his flying boot, or actually in an aircraft. With only a hurried—but safe—briefing, we completed our pre-flight checks and were airborne. "Take me to 20,000 feet," said my fearless instructor. Once level, I was told to "burn off the tip tanks," and then, "show me your sequence."

Well, I had heard others talk about their sequences, but with my rather chequered beginning, I had not had the opportunity to practise a consecutive sequence of aerobatics nor had I been shown any of the finer points of developing one. F/O Windover, I discovered, had a very gruff approach on terra firma but, once in the air, he inspired confidence in me and we began to get along amicably. "Show me your sequence," he said once again, as I completed a loop.

Not to admit I didn't know what I was doing, I put together a roll each way and then a loop followed by a lazy eight. "Show me a vertical eight," was the next instruction from the back seat. Once again I was in the dark, as I had never before completed one of these manoeuvres in a T–33. However, relying on second-hand information gleaned from bar conversations, I proceeded with macho confidence, entering the bottom of my vertical eight at 10,000 feet and 350 knots.

All went smoothly at first and as I approached the top of the second loop I thought I had it made. Airspeed a bit low—100 knots and decreasing rapidly—but no sweat. That's when all hell broke loose. The nose of the aircraft pitched upward followed by a snap roll and then a set of unrecognizable and uncontrollable gyrations. I made several attempts to recover but I didn't really know what I was recovering *from*. After a few seconds when nothing seemed to work, I took my hands and feet off the controls, and to my amazement, after a few more flips, the aircraft entered an upright spin, which I did recognize; my subsequent recovery was uneventful. However, I felt certain that the peculiar gyrations at the top of my vertical eight had scotched my chances of ever becoming a fighter pilot.

"Take me back to base," was all I heard from the back seat, and I headed straight home, calling for a fighter break and landing. Since I expected this to be my last trip in the T–Bird, I was pleased that my circuit and landing had been by the book. I completed the post-landing check as I taxied in. I knew that all fighter pilots did that. I pulled off the high-pressure fuel cock as I turned into the line (all fighter pilots did that too) and came to a stop with the nosewheel precisely where the marshaller indicated he wanted it.

We dismounted and walked wordlessly into the servicing shack. I stood quietly while F/O Windover signed in. As he completed the paperwork, he turned to me and said, "You'd better grab a quick coffee puke, because you're going solo." Needless to say, I was surprised and overjoyed but I had no time to celebrate.

As we debriefed over coffee, I was told that the reason for the bizarre manoeuvre at the top of my vertical eight was due to that fact that I had entered the base of the first loop at too high an altitude, which did not allow me to sustain sufficient airspeed over the top to complete the tight sequence. "But what was that thing at the top of the vertical eight?" I asked.

"Well, I don't rightly know," he evaded sheepishly, "but your recovery technique was flawless."

That was the only answer I had until several years later, when a test pilot at Cold Lake, Alberta, experienced strange aircraft behaviour during a routine test flight in a T–33. A test program was immediately embarked upon that identified my unique vertical eight experience, which thereafter was described as a "tumble" and went into the history books as a now-recognizable manoeuvre. My simple recovery procedure was verified and is now an official recovery technique.

I never encountered the tumble again after my initial experience, but had I done so, I would have had the recovery down pat. Furthermore, all of my vertical eight manoeuvres since were entered at a much lower altitude. My training thankfully began to accelerate and, as the course wore on, I found that each time an instructor walked through the student lounge and found me sitting idle, I would be sent off into the air for yet another solo practice. My logbook was getting fairly fat even at this stage of my training.

Back at North Bay, I was introduced to the mighty "Clunk" or CF–100 Mk.III, an imposing monster that had been jerry-rigged with dual controls and a baseball bat handle for a stick in the rear cockpit. After a few months, both cockpits were modified by canting the stick off fifteen degrees to the right so that one could read the instrument panel. This was deemed to be important in an all-weather / night-fighter aircraft, and after the dual aircraft were modified, they went on to modify all succeeding marks.

The first day of the OTU course was called the wedding day. Equal numbers of pilots and AI (wartime talk for "airborne indicator") navigators were dumped into a room together and told to get on with it. "It" being: Each pilot and navigator had to find each other and form a crew before met briefing the next day. There were a few introductory classes during the first day together, and by late afternoon there were a few "courtships" in progress.

Two or three hours after the bar opened at 1700 hours, the ritual had reached frenetic proportions as pilots and navigators careened around the room in search of like-minded souls. I am sure that nowadays there are more scientific ways of matching pilots and navigators and making them into proficient all-weather fighter crews. But this somewhat inhuman means was effective, and many pilot/navigator relationships are still intact to this day. They were "best man" at each other's weddings; some were godfathers to each other's children; and in some instances, their progeny intermarried, thus extending the relationship over two generations. In many cases they became family.

Not all initial pairings were successful, and mine was one that didn't work. Either I had a bad effect on navigators, or I was just too independent for the process. After three attempts at crewing up—each time with a navigator who was unable to complete the training satisfactorily—I went on to complete the course with staff navigators.

This was a slow process, I discovered, as my navigator was whoever happened to be available whenever I was scheduled. Primary and secondary duties being what they were on the OTU, my meagre needs for operational training were accorded a very low priority. To ensure that I didn't get bored sitting around, I was checked out on the C–45 Expeditor, or the "Bug Smasher" as it was fondly called. I became part of the target force and flew many a sortie alone, day or night, fair weather or foul, flying target for the B–25 Mitchell AI trainers.

My C–45 experience was followed by a check-out on the B–25, a WW II twin-engine bomber made famous by Jimmy Doolittle in his carrier-borne attacks on Japan. By the time I graduated from the CF–100 OTU course, I was checked out and current on the T–33, the CF–100, the B–25, and the C–45.

On completion of my final night sortie, marking the end of my OTU training, I idled over to the bar for a quiet beer. To my surprise, there was one helluva party in progress, one of those wild celebrations that had started for no apparent reason and continued on for as long as there were people standing and the bar remained open. The CO, W/C Bob Braham, turned to me as I approached the bar and asked, "Wotcher, cock?"

I guessed that it meant, "How are you?" and I replied, "Fine, sir," as I tried to ease in the direction of company more in keeping with my own modest rank level.

Before I could move away, the Wingco, who was bare from the waist up and wearing a shirt collar and tie around his neck with shirt cuffs around each wrist, asked with great dignity, "I say, cock, how'd you like to stay on at the OTU as an instructor?"

I was momentarily speechless and without much hesitation stammered that I would be delighted to become a genuine "Witch." For a fighter pilot to stay on as an instructor was heresy, but I had good reason to be pleased with this possibility and was told to report to his office at 0800 hrs the following morning.

Once again my confidence failed me and, as I turned out bright and early for my appointment fully pressed and spit-polished, I was sure that the Wingco had completely forgotten what he had asked me the night before. What if he were to ask me why I was there? What the hell would I say? As I walked into the Adj's outer office, all I heard was, "Thompson, get your ass in here!" The Wingco barely acknowledged my presence as he snatched up the phone on his desk and called someone at Air Defence Headquarters in St. Hubert, Quebec.

A brief conversation ensued which seemed a bit one-sided. It went something like, "Thompson is staying here on staff. Get the paperwork done," and that was that. But what a windfall! Pipeline pilots like myself were being trained all around me and, with their navigators, were streaming through to their assigned operational squadrons, some of which had yet to take delivery of their shiny new CF–100 Mk.IV aircraft.

The graduating CF–100 squadron pilots, once established at their various units across Canada, maintained their currency by flying anything they could get their hands on, but mostly it was a small fleet of two or three T–33s assigned to each base that provided for their interim flying needs.

Conversely, I was in pilot's heaven, as there were four types on the base and I was checked out on all of them. It couldn't have been better training for a green young pilot and while I picked up a few bad habits from some of the old war-timers, my basic and advanced training at Penhold, Alberta, and Portage la Prairie provided me with a solid reference point.

They were great days at 3 AW (F) OTU at North Bay. Up at first light, met briefing and into the air; finish flying in time for supper in the mess; and after a few beers, to bed; to start all over again the next day. Weekends were dull, and most of us volunteered to fly anything anywhere, just to be in the air. We were expected to fly cross-country missions on weekends, and there were always a half-dozen aircraft away from Friday night to Sunday night. Whitehorse, Vancouver, Gander, and all points in between were on the agenda. We flew to any airfield in Canada and some in the U.S. that had the appropriate servicing facilities for our aircraft. Our inventory of T–33, C–45, and B–25 aircraft never had a chance to cool down.

We didn't take the CF–100 on away trips very often because of its unique servicing requirements. But we more than made up for it on the other types. Training was stepped up and the course sizes were increased to feed the demands of the operational squadrons that were beginning to receive their inventory of brand-new CF–100s at an ever-increasing rate.

We turned out operational all-weather fighter crews who were trained to carry out lights-out intercepts at night and in all weather. In the process, we learned about jet engines and high-speed aerodynamics as we went along. As technical problems were encountered, they were corrected. If procedures were found wanting, they were modified. Our flight safety record by today's standards was abysmal, but we were learning as we went along. We sharpened the learning curve, found faults, shortfalls, and danger areas that were recorded and rectified. Our knowledge of jet operations improved exponentially as we gained knowledge from experience. In today's parlance, we were "pushing the edges of the envelope."

The OTU's existence at North Bay was to be short-lived, and as my first winter of all-weather flying over the dark expanses of Northern Ontario came to a close, a whole new era was to open as the "Witches" began preparations to move to RCAF Stn Cold Lake. But that is another story.

This passage was taken from Warriors and the Battle Within, *written by Terry Thompson and published by Trafford Publishers. It is reproduced herein with the author's permission.*

Operational training
John Jackaman

RCAF Cold Lake was a newly constructed air force station designed to accommodate the new jet fighters of the era. On arrival, we went through the usual arrival procedures and were given rooms in the brand-new and very modern officers' quarters. We each had a room to ourselves that was large and well furnished. Nearby were common washrooms with baths and showers, all very modern and clean. It was obvious we were not going to be uncomfortable during our stay at "Cool Pool." The officers' mess building was located at the top of a circle of officers' quarters. It, too, was luxurious and of the standard modern design of all officers' messes of that era. Although the buildings were constructed in a basic style, they were often very different inside. As messes matured and became wealthy from profits from the bar and monthly subscriptions, income was set aside for decorating projects and the purchase of better furniture than that which is normally issued by the government. The messes' non-public funds were administered by the Mess Committee, and large-scale projects authorized by the membership at General Mess Meetings. Many officers' messes were quite old and inside they reflected the efforts of generations of officers to improve the overall decor and furnishings. Some were particularly luxurious and had dining rooms furnished with carved solid oak chairs and tables, reflecting the regimental affiliations and unit histories.

Cold Lake continues to be a highly operational base. It has Canada's largest and busiest fighter wing and enjoys an almost unrestricted 1.17 million-hectare weapons range equipped with state-of-the-art threats and targets designed for today's high-speed, computer-equipped fighter aircraft. It is a far cry from the Cold Lake of my day.

The first few weeks of the OTU were spent flying the T–33 and brushing up our instrument flying. Our instrument ratings had to be renewed before we would be allowed to fly the latest all-weather jet fighter, the CF–100 Canuck. As I examined my logbook, I noted with interest that my instrument-flying trips were interspersed with weekend trips to Edmonton in the C–45 Expeditor. Once again, I survived my instrument rating test and soon after, I received a unit check-out on the T–33 so I could fly that aircraft solo. Up to that point, all my OTU missions had been dual flights in the back under the hood, flying instruments. It was great to get up into the front seat again and look out! It was at this point that the navigators arrived. These young men were going to fly in the rear seat of our CF–100s and work the radar and weapons control systems. It was expected that we would get together, crew up, and become individual teams.

The arrival of the navigators straight from their training in Winnipeg was not what one could call "inspiring." They had not flown jets at that point in their training and were, I suspect, nervous. It did not help for them to see a number of wrecked CF–100s at the end of the runways as they drove into the base in their military bus. The CF–100 was very new and was going through the normal teething problems of any aircraft brought into service for the first time. The powered controls using hydraulics were one of the more prevalent problems. The seals and hydraulic jacks tended to leak, and often we would report to our aircraft to find it sitting in a pool of pink hydraulic fluid. We would then reluctantly return to report that it was unserviceable; and the technicians would be back to renewing seals again. It required the introduction of seals that would better respond to the rigors of the enormous temperature changes normal for Canadian winters and high-altitude flight.

At breakfast on the first day after the arrival of the navigators, the first person I saw was my friend Ron from RCAF London days. I must have called his bluff—or he meant what he had said all those months before about knowing where to look for a navigator in the future. Anyway, we hit it off at once, and I suspect we were the first couple to crew-up or "get married." It turned out to be a successful teaming up and one that lasted for four years of exciting all-weather fighter operations. It was the start of a friendship that lasts to this day. Once we were posted away from flying duties after our squadron tour, we were never again to serve together. We were briefly on course together when I received a check-out in the CF–101 Voodoo fighter for test pilot duties in November 1963. I remember it was while I was on this course that President Kennedy was assassinated.

Ron was subsequently appointed commanding officer of a CF–101 fighter squadron, a "first" for a navigator. He continued to enjoy a most successful military career, retiring a year after me with the rank of brigadier general. In November of 1979, while Ron was a colonel and base commander of CFB Ottawa, we had one final flight together. At my request, he joined me on a helicopter flight from St. Hubert to Ottawa. It was during this flight that I completed my 5,000th hour as a pilot. It seemed very fitting that I shared this moment with the one person who had flown more hours with me than anyone else. Ron's first trip with me was in a T–33. I took him up on his first jet familiarization flight. I think he enjoyed it, but on the final approach, he threw up. Fortunately, in our subsequent first CF–100 flight, he had no troubles, despite loops and rolls and other aerobatics.

The initial CF–100 flying was completed in the dual Mk.III model. It was slightly different from the Mk.IVA we were to fly during our tactical flying. The CF–100 was Canadian designed, with the Orenda engines. The cockpit design followed the British concept. British fighters and bombers were designed for bomb and weapons loads. Where to put the crew who were to fly them appears to have been an afterthought. As a result, cockpits were cramped and poorly laid out. The CF–100 was no exception. The control stick in the rear cockpit of the Mk.III dual-controlled training aircraft was a wooden baseball bat, which, instead of being centred, had to be tilted to one side so you could see the instruments. The instruments were scattered all over and were not in any logical sequence. When we subsequently flew the CF–101, an American-designed aircraft, the cockpit seemed to be enormous.

The C–130 transport aircraft is another great example of the roominess and comfort of an American flight deck. Even during the war, the famous B–29 was pressurized and roomy when compared to the British Lancaster. Group Captain Cheshire VC, a famous bomber pilot of WW II who flew in the B–29 when it dropped an atomic bomb on Japan, commented on the comfort unheard of in the British Bomber Command aircraft. At five feet eight, I appeared to be the right size for fighter aircraft. Ron, who is a six-footer, found himself very restricted in the back of the CF–100. Other larger pilots had to squeeze into the cockpit.

Ron and I, full of enthusiasm, were both eager to get on with the course. It was a challenge, as we were entering a new era of all-weather fighting. The airborne radar had improved considerably since the war years, and a computerized weapons control system had been designed to produce a more effective method of attack. The CF–100 had machine guns in a belly pack, but its primary weapons were rockets loaded in pods set on the tip of each wing.

There were two main tactical manoeuvres to learn and train for. One was an initial identification run, and the other a ninety-degree beam attack run. The Ground Control Intercept Controller would pick up an unknown target on his radar and scramble a pair of aircraft to intercept. As soon as the target came into range of the fighter's radar, the navigator would take over the intercept. One aircraft would stay in a position to make an attack, while the other would proceed to intercept the aircraft. The technique used would be for the navigator—or Air Interception (AI) Nav as he was known officially—to talk his pilot into a series of turns and altitude changes to bring the aircraft up behind the unknown aircraft on a similar course. The ideal position would be a few feet below and off to one side so that the pilot could see the target visually even in cloud or at night and then close in visually to identify it. At night with a lights-out target, or in thick cloud, the manoeuvring required clear and precise orders from the navigator and very smooth and accurate flying by the pilot. The navigator would use his radar to "see" the target aircraft and provide a constant brief of its position relative to the fighter. It required a great deal of crew co-operation and transfer of information back and forth between the cockpits.

In the event the target was identified as unfriendly or apparently committing a hostile act, the identifying fighter would back off, and the number two fighter would begin a lead collision attack from a ninety-degree angle to the flight of the target. This particular form of attack was rather similar to playing "chicken." The navigator would try to provide directions to his pilot to keep their fighter on a collision course. When the range was reduced to a few miles, the navigator would lock his radar on to the target. The information from the radar and antenna system was fed into a computer that would provide precise steering information to the pilot in the form of circles and a steering dot reproduced on a small radar screen in the front cockpit. The aim of the pilot would be to keep the dot in the circles that would get smaller as the range decreased. In the final stages, a small dash would appear in the centre of the screen. By keeping the dot on the dash, the pilot would be pointing the aircraft at the correct elevation to ensure a hit with the rockets. By this time, the view from the front cockpit would be terrifying, particularly if the target was a giant B–36 or B–52 bomber. The target aircraft would appear to fill the whole of the front windscreen and a collision looked inevitable. Fortunately, the "boffins" had designed things so that the rockets would automatically fire at the correct range and would accelerate ahead of the fighter to hit the bomber, and the fighter would pass safely a few feet behind the target. The miss distance was, I suppose, quite large, but over-controlling by the pilot and evasive manoeuvres by the bomber could cut the distance down and produce some terrifying moments.

Our first trips together as a crew on the CF–100 Mk.IVA were amusing and perhaps gave poor Ron cause to reflect on his choice of pilot. The new Marks of CF–100 had powerful Orenda axial flow engines that produced significant acceleration on takeoff. It was something I was not used to. Holding the aircraft down too long after takeoff and being slow to lift the landing gear caused us a few aborted missions. The nose wheel doors would not retract properly if a certain speed was exceeded, and even if the aircraft was slowed down and a further attempt made, the damage was often done, and the door bent back so it would not pick up the retraction clips. We then enjoyed a few slow-flying sightseeing tours while we burned off fuel, so we could land safely!

As mentioned, the aircraft and its weapons systems had teething troubles, and we spent many hours waiting for aircraft to become serviceable. The navigators and pilots were also provided airborne training in the wartime B–25 Mitchell bomber. It had been equipped with the CF–100 radar and fire control systems and allowed several crews and instructors to train at the same time in a slower aircraft. During our course, one of these aircraft got into trouble, and the pilot ordered everyone to bail out. One of our fellow course members was the last but one to depart the aircraft. The instructor pilot was still on board, and sadly he had left it too late — he crashed with the aircraft. We were very upset about this incident, and it made us all very aware of the dangers of our chosen careers.

Our flying training at Cold Lake continued to go well. Ron and I, both British immigrants, were nicknamed the "Kipper Crew." We were both keen to succeed and took our training very seriously. Unlike some crews, we tended to be very conscious of our errors and discussed each mission thoroughly so we did not make the same mistakes twice. Night flying proved to be fascinating and often intimidating, particularly when practising the lead collision tactic. We took off in pairs and took turns at being target. I was never sure what position I preferred. It took all one's willpower to fly a steady course when being attacked, particularly when it seemed that a collision was imminent! Fortunately, we survived these scary incidents!

During our course, Cold Lake opened its gates to its first Air Force Open House Show. We were 150 miles away from Edmonton, the nearest big city, and much of that distance had to be travelled on gravel roads. The organizers therefore anticipated that only a few thousand folk would show up. They were extremely wrong. Tens of thousands arrived, and there was a lineup to enter the station stretching for miles to the south.

Our visitors' long journey to the station was rewarded by the usual impressive air show and a static display of almost every aircraft in the RCAF and USAF inventory at that time. I remember the air show for perhaps one big reason. One of the OTU instructors, a Brit like myself, put on a low-level aerobatic display in the CF–100 that made the aircraft's capabilities appear much greater than they were. His final manoeuvre was to enter the circuit for the final landing upside-down, do a 180-degree turn to downwind, lower the gear, still upside-down, and then turn right side up on the final approach and land. The famous AV Roe test pilot Zurakowski was another pilot who made the CF–100 performance look impressive. He executed the CF–100's famous cartwheel manoeuvre at the Farnborough Air Show one year. The poor old CF–100 was a heavy old fighter known affectionately as the "Clunk." For its era, it was, indeed, one of the better all-weather fighters; however, it was not too long before even regular jet airliners could outrun the CF–100.

With our operational training complete, it was time to be posted again. This time it was back to Eastern Canada. We had been assigned to 425 All-Weather Fighter Squadron at RCAF St. Hubert just outside of Montreal. This was a famous bomber squadron in the past known as "The Alouettes" for its close connection to French Canada.

425 All-Weather Fighter Squadron

On reflection, I feel that my first operational posting was a formative experience that set the tone and the manner in which I tackled my military duties for the rest of my career. It was an exciting period for the air force. It was at this time that the Cold War was getting into full swing, and Canada's air defence, in conjunction with that of the United States, was expanding and developing. North American Air Defense (NORAD) was the umbrella agreement between Canada and the United States that influenced Canada's air defence system and continues to this day.

Ron and I reported to the squadron very wet behind the ears but keen to establish ourselves as a formidable all-weather fighter crew. I had my usual feeling of uncertainty as to whether I could make the grade and faced the initial check rides and tests with my normal nervousness. The first half-dozen flights were made in the T–33 Silver Star. I received a local check, instrument flight check, and a night-flying familiarization ride before Ron and I went for our first flight on September 30, 1955, in the new operational fighter, the CF–100 Mk.IVA. It was the first of hundreds of flights we made together over the next four years. About a month later, we were certified as having completed the required syllabus and were declared combat ready as laid down in Air Staff Instructions.

The early squadron days were interesting. We subsequently received updated CF–100 Mk.IVBs and completed our tour flying the CF–100 Mk.V. This mark of aircraft had extended wing tips and the belly gun packs removed to provide greater altitude capability. It was during an air show in London, Ontario, that the pilot of a CF–100 Mk.V and his navigator died when he pulled up sharply, causing the extended wing tips to break off. It was a hot, bumpy day, and the gust loads coupled with the high G he pulled were more than the wing structure could stand, and it failed.

There was no question in my mind that I was blessed with the best navigator in the squadron. I know that Ron was disappointed at not being selected for pilot training but he was not one to dwell on what might have been. Instead, he worked at being the best navigator in the business. He was never satisfied with any performance that he felt could have been better. All our missions were followed by analytical examination as to where we went wrong and how we could have done things differently. Broadcast control was particularly challenging to him. He received very limited information on a target's position, and had to work out courses to fly and altitudes to climb to so that we could find the target on our airborne radar without further assistance from the ground.

Later, we were involved in some special trials using a new black box. This black box provided the navigator with a computerized system to assist in plotting target information and providing navigational information to find the target without assistance from ground radar. These tactics became necessary because of the enormous strides made in the electronic jamming of ground and airborne radars and radios. Our efforts at electronic counter-counter measures provided a great challenge, and Ron was an enthusiast in trying out new ideas in this complex aspect of all-weather operations.

Many incidents come to mind to reflect Ron's keen enthusiasm for our job as an all-weather fighter crew. Often when we returned from an air interception mission, I would practise several ground control approaches (GCAs). A ground radar controller would provide me with heading and glide slope information and direct me to a safe landing at weather conditions as low as a 200-foot cloud ceiling and one-half-mile forward visibility. Ron, at this point in our flight, would have completed his job. He could have just relaxed and admired the view as we flew around the airport. Most navigators did just that. Not Ron; instead, he studied his air interception radar and examined the ground returns in detail as I made each of my approaches. It soon became evident to him that some features, such as high-tension cables and certain buildings, including the alert shelters at the end of the runway, were very easily recognizable on his expanded PPI radar screen, despite the distortions. He then noted that he could determine the distance certain key points were from the landing runway and how they should be lined up. In this way, he could direct me from his airborne radar to line me up, even in dense cloud, with the landing runway. He then compared his distance markers with the altitudes I should be at during a normal approach. This then gave him altitude information to assist me during a blind approach. He was able to give me a surveillance approach similar to that given by the GCI controller on the ground. We practised these approaches together, and I was fully prepared to descend under Ron's instructions to at least 300 feet and one-mile visibility, should radio contact with the ground be lost or the ground radar failed. This situation was not unknown in those early days when electronic equipment was not as reliable as it is today with its modern transistors and microchips, etc.

Although I had great admiration for Ron, I was not sure that the feeling was reciprocated. There were times that I probably did not provide him with the feeling of security that I might. It was during my early squadron days that I noted my distance vision, particularly in my left eye, was beginning to be less than perfect. By squinting during annual eye tests, I was able to bluff my way through medicals, but even this ruse was beginning to fail me. Inevitably, I was caught out, but fortunately, as "veteran" aircrew, it was possible to continue flying even if glasses were prescribed. I suppose it makes sense.

Long gone was the open cockpit. By the time a pilot of a modern fighter looks through the combined layers of gunsight glass, several layers of windscreen glass, and a helmet protective visor, an extra layer of glass makes little or no difference. Eventually my new spectacles arrived and included special sets to fit over oxygen masks. I remember coming out of the optician's office in Montreal and comparing my vision with and without glasses. I was horrified. I looked up at tree-covered Mount Royal and instead of seeing a green blur, there were trees with individual leaves! Later, during a subsequent night-flying mission, Ron reported a target on his radar at seventeen miles, and I told him, "Yes, I have a visual on his navigation lights." Ron was amazed, for up to this time I had not seen anything closer than about three miles!

The CF–100 was having its fair share of technical difficulties, and a number of flying accidents took place. More than one hundred aircrew lost their lives in CF–100s during its eleven years of squadron service. I often wonder why some survived and others did not. In many ways, I was a cautious pilot, perhaps very well aware of my limitations, and during my thirty-six years of military flying, I can recall only a few scary moments. In hindsight, I now realize that in those early days the aircraft often flew me, rather than the other way around. Many pilots and aircrew were very ignorant of the aircraft they flew. This became very apparent when the first of the new flight simulators entered into service. Aircrew, now able to be observed under simulated conditions, frequently demonstrated abysmal ignorance of emergency procedures and often compounded what was a relatively simple problem into a serious and life-threatening situation. I will have more to tell on this situation.

There is one incident that comes to mind, one that Ron must have engraved in his memory. (So much so, that he has a painting of a CF–100 in his study that has the aircraft number of the CF–100 in which we had our joint adventure.) It all started innocently enough. During our pre-flight briefings involving several sections of aircraft, we realized that we had not checked off our month "out of boost" landing training. The object of this training was to practise landing our CF–100s with manual controls. Normally, our controls operated by a hydraulic boost system, a sort of power steering. It was possible to lower a lever in the cockpit and go to a straight manual system. As with power steering in an automobile, the loss of the hydraulic assist resulted in heavy aileron and elevator controls, and sometimes both hands were required on the control stick to execute any flight manoeuvres.

On this day, the squadron took off, and later in the day close to dusk, we all returned together, and one after the other declared that we were making "out of boost" landings. A training syllabus requirement, this was an emergency procedure and required larger-than-normal circuits. As a result, we had a number of CF–100s circling around waiting for their turn to make this rather more lengthy landing procedure. When I selected my out of boost condition, all went well until I suddenly found that I could not trim the elevator controls with the electrical trim system. This system operated a little trim tab on the elevator and ailerons to use airflow to hold the elevator or aileron in a specific position without having to hold it in position by brute force. Loss of trim in an "out of boost" situation means aircraft control is very difficult, if not impossible, at some speeds. However, no worries, all I had to do was to select "boost back on." This did not work. I found I could get the elevator boost in, but the aileron control jammed up and the aircraft would go into a slow roll until I disengaged the boost again and manually, using both hands, levelled the wings again. I later found out that popping speed brakes, which would momentarily drop the aircraft hydraulic pressure, might have helped get the ailerons in boost. By this time, I realized I had a big problem and declared an emergency. I found that with both hands pushing the stick forward, I could keep the aircraft in a climb. I then flew north well away from the built-up areas of Montreal and discussed a possible bailout with Ron.

Ron was well aware of the poor success rate of bailouts for navigators. The special extra windscreen for the rear seat and the ejection handle between the legs had not yet been fitted in those early days. Instead, the navigator had to reach up to the ejection handle above his head. In doing so, elbows could be caught in the slipstream, the arms flailing behind, often resulting in dislocated shoulders and making ejection impossible. One navigator in a bailout situation had experienced this situation, but fortunately his pilot realized the problem and managed to bring the aircraft back to a safe landing. Sadly, the navigator had badly frozen hands, resulting in the loss of most of his fingers on both hands. When Ron realized that bailout was imminent, he carefully pulled the ejection handle and face mask down until all it required was a pull of a fraction of an inch to release the pin and fire the ejection seat.

In the meantime, we had reached about 10,000 feet and, looking over the side of the cockpit, we decided that it looked a long way down. I had second thoughts about departing the aircraft. By then my panic had subsided to the point that I could begin to experiment with power settings and speeds. I discovered that it was possible to control the aircraft at the lower landing speeds without elevator trim. By now, though, two red lights indicated that I was down to the last few hundred pounds of fuel; if I didn't get back to the airfield soon, the decision would be taken out of my hands. I set up a glide for base, informing the tower of my intentions. Things settled down, and I could hear Ron saying, "It's okay, Jackie, you can handle it."

It was during our final approach, just minutes from a safe landing, that a squadron confrere tried to formate on me and cut in front in such a way that I thought we would collide. His efforts were made in the hope that he could help in some way. I was not amused and told him, "Fuck off, I've got enough trouble without you." By this time, it was almost dark, but fortunately the final landing was successful, and we taxied in to the line with only three hundred pounds of fuel on one side and nothing registering on the other side.

The station commander met us on the flight line, but before anyone put a ladder up to the aircraft, Ron insisted that I — and only I — put in his ejection seat safety pins. When I saw what little movement would have been required to set the seat away, I was horrified and very gingerly reached across from my front seat to insert the safety pins. It was no wonder that Ron did not want an airman technician to come up without knowing the true situation of the ejection seat system. A minor slip or fumble would have sent Ron to eternity.

The group captain indicated he was pleased to see us and congratulated us on getting back safely. In hindsight, there were many mistakes made by me that day, but there were also some examples of poor leadership that were to play a prominent part in squadron life, not only in 425 Squadron but all other squadrons of the era. As noted previously, a great number of accidents took place, and it was many years later before the air force managed to go through a complete year of flying operations without a single death. Today there are still flying accidents, but checks and balances at all levels of command and control have helped to reduce them significantly. It was a stupid decision to order us all to try "out of boost" landings during the same mission. It was inevitable that we would all become short of fuel as our landing patterns were increasingly extended. It only needed a real emergency to take place to bring everything to a critical situation.

This particular station commander became a role model for Ron and me. The only time we had seen the previous station commander was during inspections of our squadron facilities. It reminded me of my recruit days, as this station commander seemed more concerned about dust and dirt than our operational capability. With the arrival of this latest group captain, there was an immediate change in thrust to our operations. We suddenly found that there were joint operations briefings every day, and the group captain was very much in evidence. On one occasion, during a practice scramble, I was surprised to find the group captain at the top of the ladder helping me with my straps. It was no surprise during our emergency to find the "old man" waiting for our safe arrival right on the flight line.

I rather suspect that the "Kipper Crew," as we were known on our French Canadian Squadron, the Alouettes, was a bit of a favourite with the group captain. He was still a bachelor but subsequently got married during our squadron tour. In many ways, he was a very traditional senior officer who understood his role and the leadership he could offer to a group of young aircrew. He could be a hard taskmaster, and if you goofed, he would let you know all about it in no uncertain terms.

Another ex-Brit on the squadron felt the full force of the G/C's displeasure when he inadvertently lowered the landing gear on a climb-out. The high speed tore parts of the nose wheel landing gear away, and he was unable to get it down and locked. The subsequent landing had to be made without the nose wheel; much of the nose of the aircraft, which included the radar and fire control system, was worn away. In many ways, it was not the pilot's fault, but rather a design fault.

The boffins had managed to design a gyro erect button for the radar antenna system similar to the landing gear down button. To make matters worse, they were placed in the cockpit very close to each other. To a busy pilot flying under instruments and responding to air traffic and ground control instructions, it was easy to react to the navigator's request to erect the gyro by punching the button without looking. Later, when flying the CF–104, I noticed that when one reached out to pull the drag chute handle, it was possible to poke a finger into the "Panic Button" and thereby jettison all external stores, including wing tip fuel tanks. An experienced test pilot, landing just in front of me, did this, and I had to overshoot while they cleared the runway of the discarded equipment. Cockpit design can be critical. Fortunately, with modern flight simulators, many of these design errors can be discovered and corrected before the aircraft goes into full-time service.

The leadership demonstrated by some of the squadron commanders of that era was less than perfect. Most were wartime pilots who had reached their wing commander rank during the war years when survival was a factor rather than inherent leadership capability. There were times when our "gung-ho" squadron commanders put us in critical situations. I remember one who enjoyed having the whole squadron up for a mass formation so he could lead us line astern on a low-level pass across the airfield. Ron and I were often number twelve in a twelve-plane formation. This resulted in being on the end of a long line of aircraft. I either had full power on to catch up, or had everything back to idle with speed brakes so as not to overtake the aircraft in front of me. When the wing commander flew over the airfield at a few hundred feet, the last aircraft were below treetop level—not the safest manoeuvre. Later in my career, I can remember a couple of incidents where I should have remembered these lessons and hope that the young pilots involved have forgiven me.

Another wing commander led two twelve-plane squadrons each in long line astern, flying about a mile abreast of each other on a simulated bombing run on the United States. The plan was to have the lead aircraft and each subsequent aircraft of the two lines of aircraft join up for a close-formation approach and land in pairs at Niagara Air Force Base in New York State. In this way, it would require only twelve recovery approaches and not twenty-four. All went well until the ground control extended the mission, and the two lines of aircraft became separated by one line's pulling ahead of the other so that we were no longer abreast.

This resulted in no one's being able to link up with the briefed partner for the approach. It was at this point that Niagara AFB experienced a total power failure. The formation commander lost control of the situation, and when no leadership or directions were forthcoming, a squadron leader, St. Hubert's operations officer, who was flying within the formation, quietly declared, "Every man for himself!"

I had spotted a CF–100 making a dive for the clouds below, so assuming he knew where he was going, I followed him in an attempt to join up. I yelled to Ron to get him on our airborne radar and provide me with directions so we could follow him when he entered the cloud. Ron, as usual, came through and even found time to give me the safe altitude for the area we were flying in. Fortunately, we broke out at a safe altitude, and sure enough, there was the CF–100 directly in front of me. We followed him around, soon spotted the airfield, and made a final approach with, once again, our low-level fuel warning lights aglow. All around us were other CF–100s, with equally low fuel, declaring emergencies. It was a chaotic situation and one that good, steady leadership in the air could have avoided. The request to extend our mission should have been denied, and the pre-briefed plan followed to the letter. Amusingly enough, one young pilot of our squadron kept his head. Instead of immediately trying to find Niagara Falls AFB, he kept up at altitude, conserved fuel, and when all the panic was over, descended under radar control to a safe recovery—just as had been planned for us all.

There were other amusing incidents. We had experienced a rash of pilots getting confused when taxiing along the taxiways and mistakenly going between the wrong lights and ending up on the grass and stuck in the mud. Our flight commander gave us a very graphic briefing before night flying on just what he would do with any of us who made this sort of mistake. If we were in any way unsure of our position, we were to use our landing lights. Later that night, when we returned from our mission, we observed with great amusement a CF–100 slowly sinking out of sight in the mud between a taxiway and the runway. I chuckled and said to Ron, "Someone is in trouble tonight." On arrival in the squadron lounge, it was even more amusing than we had thought: Our intrepid flight commander was the pilot involved!

They were fun days in many ways, and we often had some good laughs. There were periods when we worked ninety hours a week. We were either flying or on standby. Sure, we could sleep and relax, but we were still at work and liable to find ourselves at 40,000 feet with just a few minutes' warning. There were times when the only contact my wife, Joan, and I had were with small notes left on the kitchen table of our apartment. I would return from work after she had left for her job and then be back at the squadron before she arrived back in the late afternoon. On one occasion, I had returned late after night flying only to be recalled to work in the early hours of the morning. We were subsequently scrambled, and due to awful weather in the Montreal area, were diverted to Wurtsmith AFB in Michigan. To ensure that my wife did not worry, I phoned home collect to let her know where I was. When the operator asked her if she would accept a collect call from John Jackaman she replied, "But he is asleep right beside me." My response to the operator was, "I don't know who *that* John Jackaman is asleep with my wife, but this one is in Wurtsmith." At this point, Joan woke up fully and realized that I was *not* beside her and accepted the call. That's her side of the story, anyway!

By this time, we had a dog called Toby. He sometimes came to work with me. No one seemed to mind. I suspect that it was perhaps a flashback to wartime years and Nigger, the famous dog belonging to Wing Commander Guy Gibson of *The Dam Busters* fame. Toby became very popular after an amusing incident that took place in the crew room. Another pilot had brought his dog and, for some reason or other, it cocked its leg and peed on the carpet. Toby, not to be outdone, went up to a somewhat unpopular squadron leader, who was relaxing in an armchair, and proceeded to pee against his pant leg. The other aircrew present, all of whom were junior officers, were delighted to see this positive demonstration of contempt toward a senior officer. Toby was an instant hero!

During our squadron tour, we spent periods at Cold Lake at the Weapons Practice Unit firing our air-to-air rockets at a towed target. We used special wing tip rocket pods with three rockets in each but were allowed to fire one full load consisting of fifty-eight 2.75 rockets. It was an impressive display, and, with the somewhat erratic flight path of the 2.75 rocket, could also be frightening. There was a fear that the rockets would do a 180-degree turn and attack the fighter rather than the target!

We also flew to various American bases. In those early days, the USAF equivalent fighter was the F–89 Scorpion. This was no match for the CF–100, and we enjoyed showing off our aircraft to our brothers-in-arms to the south. On our big NORAD exercises, we were often called upon to intercept the B–36, B–47, and subsequently the giant B–52. Our first lead collision-type attacks on these huge aircraft were frightening, as they seemed to fill the whole sky in the final stages of the attack. Their radar-controlled machine guns that tracked us so accurately did nothing to inspire confidence that our attacks would be without damage if they had been for real. The CF–100 was designed as a long-range fighter, and I know that the SAC pilots were always surprised to see us stay up with them for long periods of time. The F–89 had to use an afterburner at the higher altitudes and had a limited fuel capacity so usually made just the one pass and returned to base. However, the B–52 could outrun us, as could most of the new jet airliners entering service at that time.

Our cross-country trips took us from one side of Canada to the other. We spent a week at RCAF Station Comox on Vancouver Island flying with 409 AW (F) Squadron. We flew some enjoyable airborne intercept missions and made numerous IFR approaches to Comox in what were minimum weather conditions. It was only when flying during a clear winter day when there was not a cloud in the sky that we realized what we had been doing. The Comox let-down chart instructed us to remain to the right of the on course during approaches. It became very apparent that this restriction was for a very good reason. All around us on the climb out and on the descent were some significant mountains towering up to 6,000 feet and more. We had been flying around the area blissfully unaware that there was so much cumulus-granite in the area. Even by maintaining well right of the "on course," we still felt the mountains were uncomfortably close on the approach.

Our night cross-countries to New York City were always interesting flights. The lights of the city below seemed to stretch for miles, and on our return to the much smaller Montreal, we often wondered if it was indeed Montreal, as it looked so small. In those days, the airspace above 20,000 feet or so was almost completely free of commercial and civilian aviation. As the British Comet, American DC–8, and Boeing 707 came into production, this was to change, and now airspace is rigidly controlled from surface to well over 40,000 feet. In our squadron days, we often roamed very freely about the higher altitudes with only military radars keeping an eye on us. The rigid controls now in effect, as far as airspace is concerned, have taken all the fun and challenge out of flying. In those days, it was possible to get lost—which was indeed a challenge!

One important event took place during this period: I was awarded a permanent commission in the RCAF. PCs were hard to come by in those days, and very few young pilots were offered them. My station commander had often indicated to me that I should purchase a proper mess kit for formal dinners. As a young married officer with two children, I had little extra money, and certainly not enough to buy a formal air force mess kit. I used to respond that if he gave me a PC, I would purchase a mess kit. Well, one morning I was ordered to the station commander's office, where a smiling group captain told me that he wanted to see a confirmed order for a mess kit from my tailor later in the day. This was how I found out that I had been offered the opportunity for a long-term career in the RCAF!

After two years on squadron, we became vulnerable for a posting to ground duties. Fortunately, the introduction of new, sophisticated flight simulators gave Ron and me a new lease on our flying careers, and we remained operational aircrew while at the same time instructing on the CF–100 flight simulator.

Early flight simulator

By 1957, the RCAF had a sizable "order of battle" for its fighter squadrons. There were several Wings of Sabre fighter aircraft in Europe, and in Canada the CF–100 squadrons were located throughout the country from east to west. At St. Hubert, there were two CF–100 squadrons of eighteen aircraft each plus a couple of T–33s for instrument training. In addition, St. Hubert was home to a reserve squadron flying Vampires and the Overseas Ferry Unit (OFU) flying Sabres; 104 Communications Flight, located further down the flight line, housed the Electronics Warfare Squadron flying C–119s. It also supported the C–45 Expeditor transport aircraft and even a couple of Harvard trainers. It was an impressive airport to fly from and at times a busy one. It was a great time for aircrew, and we seem to have had few restrictions on flying hours. It was also obvious that supporting this number of aircraft was an expensive business, and flying costs, in particular training costs, had to be reduced. Technical breakthroughs in electronics were beginning to take place.

For years, part of a pilot's training had taken place in a Link trainer. This was a machine designed to simulate flight. It had a basic cockpit with rudimentary instruments and was mounted on a system of bellows to provide a small amount of pitch and roll that would provide a degree of realism to the pilot as he operated the flight controls. Later models provided a navigation system using radio signals that could be supervised by the instructor observing a horizontal plotting board and a "crab" that moved according to the simulated flight path of the Link trainer. It was basically a simple machine but effective for teaching pilots the basics of instrument flying and radio navigation without reference to the ground. As the technical skills of the electronic engineers developed, it became apparent that flight simulators of much greater capability could be designed. A basic flight simulator of the F–86 was made, and the CF–100 flight simulator, which was known more accurately as an operation flight and tactics trainer (OFTT), soon followed. This simulator not only accurately reproduced the flight envelope of the CF–100 but also provided a simulated radar and weapons system. For the first time it was possible to put a pilot and navigator in the cockpit of the simulator and provide a complete, simulated environment where not only instrument and navigation could be practised, but also all the emergencies likely to be experienced in the CF–100. In addition, the tactical roll of the fighter could be practised. The air-to-air radar system and weapons control system were completely simulated. The navigator could acquire targets and execute either an identification run or a "lead collision attack."

It was fortunate that we were selected to be the first CF–100 flight simulator instructor crew. It delayed the inevitable posting to ground duties. We hoped that our selection was because we were a top crew and considered capable of handling this new responsibility. Unfortunately, it had been the practice to send grounded aircrew to Link trainer or simulator duties. These were not always the best individuals for the job, and their credibility with current aircrew was often suspect. It was with reservations that we accepted our new duties. We were, however, extremely interested in the challenge that had been offered.

We spent two weeks at Canadian Aviation Electronics (CAE) in Montreal. CAE had been awarded the contract for the CF–100 simulator. It was their first attempt at this sort of business, but they were to make a great success of the venture. They are now one of the leading manufacturers of flight simulators in the world. During our two weeks, we worked with the military test pilots who were engaged in the final acceptance of the first production model scheduled to be installed at RCAF St. Hubert. It proved to be a most productive time, and we were soon convinced that this machine could provide an excellent training vehicle for CF–100 pilots. Little did I know that this particular appointment was to lead, many years later, to my appointment as a test pilot for the Central Experimental Proving Establishment (CEPE). I was to spend four years of my subsequent career working at CAE on even more sophisticated flight simulators.

After our return to RCAF St. Hubert, we sat down and devised a flight simulator training program for the squadrons. Later we assisted in the installation of the machine that was housed in a specially constructed and air-conditioned building. The installation required three large rooms. One contained the cockpit, which did not move but was a completely accurate replica of the real thing. All the switches, controls, and instruments worked just as they did in the real aircraft. With the frosted canopy closed, it was not hard to feel that one was actually flying in cloud and not anchored safely to the ground.

The centre room of the three rooms housed the instructors' console, which duplicated all of the aircraft instruments and had two horizontal plotting boards mounted vertically to provide a graphic indication of the simulated aircraft's position throughout the flight. The instructors were able to set up all the relevant radio aids for navigation, provide radar targets, and input emergency situations. Mechanical problems such as hydraulic and fuel pump failures, fire warning lights and other instrument failures could be inserted to provide crews practice in the appropriate emergency procedures.

The final room, much bigger than the other two, was filled with three rows of computer cabinets. These computer cabinets were filled with servomechanisms and amplifiers using antiquated vacuum tubes. The heat these early computers generated required these rooms to be air-conditioned. It is interesting to realize that this old analogue computer that took up so much space could now be reproduced in a suitcase-sized modern computer. The flight simulator program installed in the computer I am using as a word processor has a greater capability than the CF–100 OFFT of my St. Hubert days. Modern flight simulators now include sophisticated motion systems that provide pitch and roll motions and visual displays that are very realistic. Most airline pilots do their entire instrument training and testing in these machines rather than in the actual aircraft. The testing and training are just as effective and at a fraction of the cost of flying an aircraft that is better put to use carrying revenue-earning passengers.

The next two years of our tour proved to be fascinating. We were able to continue to fly with the squadron and maintain our flight proficiency, but best of all we learned a great deal more about our aircraft and its tactical role than we ever could if we had remained just a squadron crew. Our subsequent experiences as instructors on the Flight Simulator were rewarding, amusing, and even perhaps terrifying. It did not take us long to realize that many aircrew had a dismal knowledge of the aircraft in which they flew. As we simulated emergencies, we often watched in horror as pilots compounded their problems with incorrect and often dangerous decisions and inappropriate actions. Many would have lost their lives if they had been actually flying.

The CF–100 with its two engines and two separate fuel control systems for each engine would sometimes experience a double engine failure. It was not long before we, in the simulator, realized how this impossible situation could take place. If we simulated a red warning light to indicate a fuel boost pump failure, the checklist stated, "Select cross feed to the unaffected pump." These cross feed switches were hidden beneath the canopy rail on the left-hand side of the cockpit and difficult to see. Repeatedly, pilots would select cross feed, but to the failed pump. Under these conditions, the engine-driven pumps could not suck enough fuel through the failed boost pump to feed both engines, so they both flamed out! This explained the unexplained double engine failures. Other mistakes by pilots were unforgivable. Some could not even find the handle to switch to manual flight controls when the hydraulic system failed. Other crews failed to identify radio aids and made descents in the wrong areas using improper procedures. Misreading the altimeter by 10,000 feet resulted in several tragic flying accidents. We saw several incidents of this on the flight simulator and we hoped that the error made pilots a lot more careful when checking altimeters when next they flew. A design change of the altimeter subsequently helped to prevent this error. Other design changes, as well as adjustments to emergency procedures, were made, in part, by our experiences learned in the flight simulator training program.

While I tended to concentrate on the pilots and their capabilities, Ron was busy checking navigators and in particular their radar tactics in the air-to-air role. One of our biggest selling jobs was to convince aircrew that the simulator provided a highly accurate reproduction of the CF–100 flight characteristics and weapons control systems. We often received criticism that it did not do this or that in the actual aircraft. We even had our own doubts, but fortunately, as active aircrew, we were able to get in an actual aircraft and duplicate the situation and see with our own eyes just what happened under certain circumstances. One criticism concerning the radar was that when a turn was made toward the target, the radar return would appear to initially move away from the direction of the turn instead of toward it. On a subsequent flight, we discovered that if you rolled into the turn quickly, this, in fact, was the case. In the CF–100 simulator that was not equipped with a motion system, pilots would roll into a turn much quicker than they would in an actual aircraft. The result was the unusual movement of the radar return on the navigator's screen. By jamming the stick hard over and quickly in the actual aircraft, we could duplicate the movement. This was not the most comfortable technique for the poor old navigator trying to keep his face in the radar screen's rubber hood.

I know that my simulator experiences proved to be invaluable later on in my flying career. I learned not to jump to conclusions and to observe the symptoms displayed during aircraft problems more carefully. During one period at St. Hubert, we had a serious problem in the fire control system of the simulator that made it impossible for pilots to keep the steering dot in the centre of the attack circle. The technicians spent hours searching through the schematics of the radar system and testing various amplifiers and servomechanisms. It was not until I noticed the ball of the turn and bank indicator move erratically during turns that it became apparent that the fault was not in radar system but in the flight simulation system. After hours of intense work, the fix took mere minutes to carry out.

It was also very evident from watching hundreds of simulated attacks that the MG2 fire control system had an inherent "S" curve built into the steering program during the final phase of a lead collision attack. It is during this phase that the pilot receives precise steering information from a small scope situated above his instrument panel. The S curve resulted in more turns than necessary, and a fighter attacking a bomber that was as fast or faster than the fighter would end up getting behind on a ninety-degree attack and find itself in a tail chase, missing the attack altogether. Ron and his fellow navigators came up with a new technique that was to attack not from ninety degrees but one hundred degrees from the bomber's track. At the same time, navigators maintained control of the intercept to much later in the attack and worked out a system whereby the pilot would provide backup data on his steering information and the position of the steering dot relative to the steering circle. Without the simulator experiences, it would have taken much longer for the new ideas and changes in procedures to be incorporated on our air defence flying tactics.

Our simulator training days provided many amusing experiences. As instructors, we did our best to make each flight as realistic as possible. It required a great deal of play-acting, including simulating the radio transmissions from the control tower and the ground control intercept units. We also provided accurate and realistic ground control approaches to the runway. In this way, we found that it was not long before the crew under instruction entered into the full spirit of the training. They became so immersed in the "flying" that for all practical purposes they were in a real aircraft and facing real flying and tactical situations.

On one occasion, while in the middle of a training session, the simulator instructor crew from RCAF Station Bagotville, several hundred miles to our northeast, showed up. This presented us with the opportunity of simulating bad weather at St. Hubert and forcing our crew under training to divert to Bagotville. As soon as the crew approached Bagotville, we turned over the simulator to our Bagotville friends, who provided the air traffic control inputs and talked our crew down to a safe landing. In the meantime, Ron and I put up signs that would indicate that the simulator was the Bagotville machine and hid where the training crew could not see us. The crew having made the specific approach procedure to Bagotville and hearing different voices on the radio, found themselves looking at wall signs that would indicate they had arrived in Bagotville. They then entered the instructors' console area to find two Bagotville aircrew, complete with Bagotville squadron flashes, waiting to debrief them! Needless to say, they were impressed with the degree of simulation and we suspect they both wanted to pop outside the building just to confirm that it was indeed a simulation and that they had not been transported to Bagotville!

The flight simulator also proved to be a point of interest to a variety of support people and visitors to the station. We were the subject of a thirty-minute documentary on *Raportage*, a French-language TV station weekly program. The flight surgeon often came to visit and was most interested in the respiratory rates of pilots when executing complex flying manoeuvres. I was reminded of this when flying the CF–104, which has a button on the control column that activates the nose wheel steering but then becomes an extra transmit button when the weight is off the front wheel. Often a pilot would inadvertently keep the button pressed after nose wheel liftoff, with the result that his heavy breathing was broadcasted to the world! A private moment in a pilot's life he would rather not advertise — it destroys the image!

On one occasion, we had a group of military padres undergoing their annual retreat at the station. One day they requested to visit the flight simulator. When they arrived, we had a crew practising intercepts at 40,000 feet. We briefed the visitors, then allowed them to group around the cockpit area, and then opened the cockpit so they could see inside and view the crew at work. The pilot looked up, saw he was surrounded by gentlemen in clerical garb, and without a moment's hesitation said over the intercom that we could all hear, "Good God, I didn't think we were that high!"

While Ron was busy writing papers on tactics, I sat down and wrote an article for the RCAF flight safety magazine, *Flight Comment*, on the CF–100 simulator, which was subsequently published. This effort and my enthusiasm for simulators generally were instrumental in my receiving interesting appointments over the succeeding years. Best of all, it cut short my next ground tour by at least two years. I used this example to other young officers who were upset at receiving postings that, on the surface, were not ideal ones. A flight simulator appointment was not viewed with enthusiasm in those days.

After four years in a flying appointment, it was inevitable that a posting would soon be forthcoming. It was also certain to be a dreaded ground appointment. Fortunately, as I came to the end of my tour at RCAF St. Hubert, I was promoted to the rank of flight lieutenant, which meant that any future job I received would involve a leadership position. It was at this time that the Avro Arrow, Canada's new fighter aircraft, was being test flown, and Ron and I had been selected to be on the evaluation team when the first production models became operational. Unfortunately, it was not to be. Canada's government at the time decided that the new venture was too expensive and ordered all the initial production models destroyed. Sadly, this decision also destroyed Canada's aircraft production industry, and many engineers left for the United States, where they later contributed to the American space program. It was particularly sad for me, as it seemed that although I had been flying jet aircraft for many years, I had yet to fly supersonic. The Arrow with its titanium alloy construction and powerful engines was capable of speeds up to twice the speed of sound. It was an aircraft with technology well in advance of its time.

The posting finally arrived, and both Ron and I found ourselves posted to isolated radar stations. I was off to Parent, 150 miles north of Montreal. Ron was sent to Moisie, located toward the mouth of the St. Lawrence River. Before we could report to our new stations, we had to undergo three months' training on air weapons control. This course was held in the U.S. at Tyndall AFB in Florida, a beautiful location on the coast of the Gulf of Mexico. Another advantage was that accommodations were not provided on the base, so we had to find our own accommodations off the base. In turn, this meant we were given a special temporary duty allowance that was generous enough for me to take my wife and the family with me.

The air weapons control course was interesting. In those days, fighter control was done manually from raw radar returns. The only tools we had were a grease pencil and a thin piece of Perspex on which angles were inscribed to help us provide the correct intercept headings for the fighter aircraft. The radar screens had range lines to provide us with distance information, and the outer rim was marked in degrees. As a target approached, we used our grease pencils to mark its progress on the screen, and after a period of time, depending on how far it had travelled, it was possible to work out its ground speed and track. With the forecast winds for the specific altitude, we were then able to work out the target's heading and airspeed. This had to be done manually using a hand-held circular slide rule.

Having spent hours on the CF–100 simulator providing intercept directions to training aircrew, both Ron and I found that we could think three dimensionally without difficulty. We were also introduced to an early computerized system of interception, but it was cumbersome, and one needed to be a three-armed paperhanger to operate the controls. I controlled one fighter for many trips before I realized that his call sign was Freedom Nine, not Freedom "Nan." No doubt this Southern American pilot also found my London accent somewhat difficult to comprehend at times. I suspect that the instructors found our radio communications rather amusing! Soon, though, our Southern "vacation" ended, and I was on my way to my first but not last ground tour.

"Chuck" Harris ... flak attracter

Tom Lambrick

When I arrived on 445 Squadron in 1958, at Marville, France, the resident wit was a tiny Jewish guy named Chuck Harris. He was famous for his pithy, original sayings, like: "Confucius say pilot who bail out over Paris go in Seine." Atrocious pun, but original. We were both golfers, and one afternoon at the Royal Luxembourg course, I was pondering a shot over a trap to a narrow green. Harris finally said, "Hit the ball, will you!"

I said, "I just want to waft the ball over the trap, because there is no green to hit to."

"So, use your waffle iron," said Chuck, and I spent the next minute giggling uncontrollably.

The first Christmas on squadron, I spent on "alert," which meant that Mo Morris, my navigator, and I, and another CF–100 crew were in our flying suits at the alert shack, ready to fly to the defence of Europe at a moment's notice. The other crew was Chuck Harris and his nav, Arthur Hughesdon, a transplanted Brit. Although Chuck was far senior to me on the squadron, I ended up the lead pilot of the section, for reasons that I can't recall. The single guys held alert on Christmas so the married men could be with their families, and the married fellows reciprocated on New Year's so the single men could get puking drunk.

It was a typical winter's day in northern France, gray and dreary, with a mid-level overcast. By three in the afternoon, I was monumentally bored and decided to call "Yellowjack," our radar interceptor control unit based in Metz, to see if we could fly a practice mission. The officer who answered the phone was skeptical and said he didn't think it would be possible. I asked him to check anyway and went back to playing cards. Ten minutes later, the klaxon horn went off, and Harris and I sprinted for the fighters. In less than five minutes, we lifted off Marville and changed over to Yellowjack control.

"Yellowjack, Horseshoe Section airborne, what do you have for us?"

"Horseshoe Lead, we have nothing. I thought you gentlemen asked for this flight."

"Oh, Roger, Yellowjack, that's correct. How about some practice intercepts?"

"Roger, Horseshoe Section. Lead, come forty-five degrees port to a heading of 090, and Two, come starboard forty-five degrees to heading 180."

We separated and ran a few ninety-degree collision course intercepts. It was easy to see that no one's heart was really in this, so I requested a vector back to Marville and a descent below the undercast. Harris was on my wing as we broke out of the clouds at 5,000 feet near the Belgian border town of Virton, where a large contingent of RCAF pilots lived "on the economy."

"Yellowjack, Horseshoe Section will proceed visually to Marville; thanks for the help."

"Roger, Horseshoe; Yellowjack out."

"Horseshoe Two from Lead, let's welcome Santa to Virton. Tuck it in, and we'll wish the boys Merry Christmas."

Chuck swung into tight formation on my right wing, and I took the section down to a few hundred feet over the church steeple in the square. We were doing about 400 knots and made a hellacious racket at that altitude. Our heading back to base put the Permanent Married Quarters at Longuyon right on the nose, where the majority of the officers and men based at Marville were located, and where I knew our buddies were enjoying a Christmas dinner cooked by their dutiful wives. Maintaining a scant five hundred feet of altitude, we roared over the complex in the gathering dusk. As we made our pass, it dawned on me that the commanding officer of the base lived there, as well as my squadron commander. Oh, well . . .

I QSY'd (changed the radio frequency) the section to Marville Tower and told them we would be making a low pass over the officers' mess. A very hesitant Larry Hines, the chief controller, who had been unexpectedly called out to duty, gave us the okay. I cranked the speed up to close to 500 knots, and stepped Chuck up to a formation position just above my wing. At maximum CF–100 speed, which is just over 500 knots indicated, we ripped across the roof of the mess, making a noise that I was later told spilled a few drinks in the bar. I pulled up into a 90-270 course reversal, and we came back from the opposite direction. I could see that the terrace and parking lot of the officers' mess was now full of gesticulating pilots, pumping their fists in the air. RRRROOOOOARRRR! . . . we loosened a little mortar from the chimney. Hey, this was fun!

"HORSESHOE SECTION, HORSESHOE SECTION!"

An uncharacteristically shrill yell from Larry, in the tower, interrupted my glee.

"Go ahead, Marville Tower."

"HORSESHOE SECTION, RETURN AND LAND IMMEDIATELY! I SAY AGAIN, RETURN AND LAND IMMEDIATELY I SAY AGAIN RETURN AND LAND IMMEDIATELY! THIS IS A DIRECT ORDER FROM THE STATION COMMANDER!"

Oops! I returned to an overhead break, and Chuck and I landed the armed alert birds and taxied to the shack. A somewhat chagrined Harris ambled over to my aircraft from his own and gave me a rueful smile.

"I think we may be in a spot of trouble here," he opined, then grinned and said, "But it was worth it!"

The next day, both crews were summoned to the squadron commander's office. "What in the name of God did you two think you were doing?" our boss, Wing Commander "Red" Sutherland, yelled. "Do you realize you have created an international incident? Do you know that you violated a NATO-wide protocol, a solemn agreement between all the signatory states that no military fighters will fly on Christmas Day? Jesus Christ, the phones are ringing off the hook at headquarters! How goddamned dare you scramble yourselves on Christmas!"

"Sir," I said, "we didn't scramble ourselves! Yellowjack scrambled us! I simply asked if it would be possible to fly, and ten minutes later, they scrambled us. I never heard of any prohibition against flying on Christmas. None of us has. Apparently, it was a mix-up, but we certainly didn't just scramble ourselves . . . sir."

"Red" had turned his namesake colour, a kind of beet-crimson, the veins sticking out of his forehead. This crucifixion had hit a snag. He had been prepared to throw the book at us, but I had introduced an element of doubt, and he would have to get to the bottom of it before he could kick our asses.

He sputtered, "We'll just see about that. Now, talk to me about the low flying. What made you think you could beat up the base like that? Christ, they tell me you nearly blew the mess over!"

I thought I could detect a hint of pride in the way he said that. The CF squadron suffered from terminal insecurity, always on the defensive against the F–86 pilots and their commanders, who derided our straight-winged, 36,000-pound behemoths. The Sabre jocks were insufferable as they muscled their super steeds around the skies of Europe. They were flying the best jet day-fighter ever built, and they knew it. The CF–100, derisively nicknamed "the Clunk" by our swept-wing brethren, was the finest all-weather night fighter in the air, in 1958, but it was still not a VFR day fighter. So, we suffered the slings and arrows of constant abuse. Perhaps this earth-shaking wake-up call delivered over the officers' mess would back the Sabre boys off for a month or two.

"Sir, no excuse, sir. I just got carried away. And I was the lead aircraft, sir. Not Flying Officer Harris's doing at all, sir. He just followed me."

"Balls, Lambrick. You're both in deep shit, here. Now get out of my office. I'll see who called who, and then we will get to the bottom of this mess."

I never heard another word about the incident, and Chuck left for Canada about six months later. However, he got involved in another low-flying scrape, in Gimli, where he was posted as a T–33 instructor. He actually blew a fisherman out of his boat on Lake Winnipegosis. Unfortunately, the guy got Chuck's airplane number as he fell into the water, and at the ensuing board of enquiry, they brought up the Marville Christmas flight, which hurt his case. So, our follies do come back to haunt us, it seems.

Anyway, Chuck was posted back to Canada, travelling in great style. His ship, the *Saxonia*, of the Cunard line, was due to sail from Le Havre at 10:00 a.m. on June 20. We had a great send-off party in the Fifteenth-century Room, which served as our back bar at Marville. This was a castle anteroom, lifted bodily from a medieval fortress, and put back board for board in the officers' mess. In actual fact, the entire room, except for one board, was reassembled in the mess. French law precluded the complete structure's being taken from its original place, and to circumvent the restriction, a single board was left behind. When De Gaulle, with typical French gratitude, threw the Canadians out of France during his reign as dictator, the room was disassembled once again and shipped to the RCAF station at Moose Jaw, Saskatchewan. There it was put back together and used again as a bar. Recently, someone retrieved the missing board from the castle, and a ceremony was held to fit it into place, thus completing a job begun some thirty-five years earlier.

On the morning of the 20th, I flight-planned a trip from Marville, tucked up in the northeast corner of France, to Le Havre, on the coast. The range of the CF–100 was just capable of a flight to the coast in the high-low-high mode. If we climbed immediately to 40,000 feet and did a shallow descent to the coast, we would have about five to ten minutes at sea level before we would have to climb back up to 40,000 feet for the return trip. At eleven o'clock, I lifted off with Mo Morris in the back seat and Roger Thibodeau and his navigator, Graham McCleod, on my wing. I figured to give the ship a few hours to clear port and pick it up as it went to sea.

We flew above the omnipresent 30,000 feet of cloud that is the curse of European weather and let down in a long, gentle, descent as planned. We crossed the coast. The clouds finally gave way at 4,000 feet, and we spotted the city of Le Havre off our left wing. Out in the English Channel, Mo picked up a lone ship at twelve o'clock. I put Roger in step-up formation, echelon right, and began a descent to 500 feet. The angry waves of the sea, a leaden gray, with sea fret tearing off the tops, looked singularly uninviting. Rain squalls came and went, and the visibility varied as we darted in and out of the showers. The ship grew larger and larger in the windscreen, and I let down another 200 feet. Now we were ripping across the ocean, just above the level of the ship's stacks. We were coming at the boat at ninety degrees and flashed over it. I saw the name *Saxonia* on the bow, as we made the pass. The rails were nearly bare of passengers, and I took the formation on a wide, sweeping turn out to sea. This time, we were approaching the ship head-on, and I put Roger farther out to my right.

"Horseshoe Two, I'll take the left side of the boat, you take the right, and we'll go by at the upper deck level."

The beautiful white vessel was arrowing through the rough seas, looking as sleek as a destroyer. We rocketed by the observation deck at about 400 knots, and I saw that crowds had gathered at the railings, waving deliriously. I couldn't pick Chuck out of the mob, but then again, he is pretty small! We both rocked our wings as we passed, and rejoined the formation for our flight home. Our little jaunt out to sea ate into our fuel reserve, and both of our planes were running on fumes when we landed back at base. Once again, I heard no repercussions from the brass, meaning the ship's captain must have been a cool kind of guy. Shortly after this, the Canadian Air Force bought CL–44 passenger prop-jets and ferried all of its personnel back and forth across the Atlantic by air. So ended first-class boat travel for officers.

Chuck and I remain friends to the present day and still play golf. And there are still many times I could use a waffle iron. Failing that, a good giggle.

Aerial buffoonery II
Doug Munro

AVRO built 692 CF–100s. Canada's "finest" didn't wreck them all, but it wasn't from a lack of effort.

Four-o-nine All Weather Fighter Squadron, RCAF Station Comox, B.C., was Air Defence Command's sole squadron in the Royal British Columbian Air Force. Life was bucolic, if not idyllic at 409 — pilots were encouraged to keep a dictionary beside them at all times. This solitude was forever shattered by a CBC camera crew that arrived to film life on a typical CF–100 squadron.

The pièce de resistance was to have been the filming of a "normal" no-notice scramble. In those days, the alert birds were parked in front of 409's hangar and their crews assumed a spring-loaded stance in the squadron ready room — up four flights of stairs and some 150 yards from their aircraft. Unfortunately, the crew selected to demonstrate the scramble possessed a characteristic that ill-suited them for the task at hand. They were rather lacking in physical fitness and both had very short tempers.

The scramble bell rang. The crew leapt from their bunks and dashed for the ready room door.

"Hold it, the cameraman wasn't ready!"

Some forty-five minutes later, after endless "takes" to reposition the camera at every turn, the thoroughly frustrated and exhausted crew finally cleared the front door of the hangar and headed for their aircraft. The navigator, with more élan than good judgement, attempted to leap onto the rear part of the wing. Unfortunately, he jumped a smidgen early, struck the flaps a glancing blow during his descent, and skidded to a halt by the left main gear.

The climax came with merciless swiftness. With both crew members finally buckled in and both engines running, the pilot slammed the throttles, performed a sharp left turn, and stuck his aircraft's left rocket pod through the radar dome of the Number Two alert aircraft.

The chairmen of the accident board recommended that all future accidents be filmed — it makes the investigation so much simpler.

Failed briefing

Doug Munro

Many of you will have heard the expression, "He failed briefing." A four-plane CF–100 formation from RCAF Station Uplands gave a new meaning to this phrase. Once again, the CBC was on the scene: "We had so much success filming a scramble, just think what we can do with a four-plane formation."

The crew of the Number Three aircraft missed the briefing. No big deal, right? Things went just dandy during start-up, takeoff, and climb. A number of standard formation changes were executed with great skill and cunning. And then, The Grand Finale. The flight settled down in a nice, tight, echelon starboard ("This formation flying is a piece of the proverbial"). Lead called for a one-second break. "Break now." Number Three was, as you might have expected, glued to Number Two's right wing. Suddenly, Number Two cranked on ninety degrees of starboard bank and collided with Number Three (they had briefed for a "reverse" break: Four, Three, Two, then One). No matter how carefully a mission is planned, no system is perfect. (P.S., One crew flew home; the other walked.)

Then there was the Airborne Interception (AI) navigator on the CF–100 course at 3 All Weather Operational Training Unit, RCAF Station Cold Lake, Alberta, who single-handedly bagged a Mk.IV Clunk. On a routine day mission, the student navigator noted that a wing tank transfer pump circuit breaker had popped. He pushed it in. It popped. He pushed it in. It popped again. He pushed it in and held it in with his finger. The circuit breaker soon became very warm. He was forced to hold it in with a pencil. Problem solved? On descent, the crew noticed that the wing was on fire. Cancelling a briefed series of touch-and-goes, the crew returned safely to earth. Unfortunately, the fire had an insurmountable head start, and all efforts to extinguish the flames proved futile. Scratch one Clunk.

CF–100 stories are legion. How about the 432 Squadron pilot (thought you were being ignored, didn't you?) who decided to put on an impromptu air show over his girlfriend's cottage at Lake Otis, Quebec. It was a lovely Sunday afternoon, the formal part of the crew's mission was complete, and besides, who would ever know? During one of many passes, the aircraft accidently contacted a power line. The crew declared an emergency and headed for home — RCAF Station Bagotville. The control tower alerted the squadron commander, one Wing Commander J.R.D. "Bob" Braham, DSO and 2 Bars, DFC and 2 Bars, etc.

Bob, as was his wont, was enjoying a couple of sarsaparillas in his backyard. He was less than impressed at being disturbed and when he was not impressed he made no effort to hide his displeasure. Bob was at the bottom of the ladder when his young warriors pulled into the flight line. It was difficult to miss the substantial length of wire that had guillotined the radar nose and lay imbedded in both wing roots. And there was little wrong with the Wingco's eyesight, to which twenty-nine WW II *Luftwaffe* pilots could attest. The ensuing conversation forms an immortal part of the 432 Squadron history.

W/C: "What the hell happened to you?"
F/O: "I think I hit a bird, sir."
W/C: "The son of a bitch must have been sitting on a wire."

NFB tale
Bruce Montgomery

When on squadron at North Bay (433 and 414), I was privileged to take part in a major National Film Board (NFB) movie, *Canada's Air Defence*, in 1957. I won't name the other participants, to protect the innocent. There are some excellent air-to-air shots of CF–100 formations. The cameraman was situated in the tail gunner's position on a 408 photo Lanc, hanging out in the breeze. The movie was shot in North Bay, Cold Lake, and the GCI site at Lac St. Denis. The gorgeous young lady who played the fighter controller at the GCI site was actually a pharmacy flight cadet on summer training at North Bay. I can tell you that the real lady fighter controllers were seriously bent at not being considered pretty enough by the film's director to play their actual job. A final note: the young flight cadet eventually married one of the CF–100 pilots in the film. I met them again at the Ottawa AWFA Reunion in 2002.

(The movie was shown on national TV in 1957 or 1958. You can order a copy of this movie from the NFB by calling 1–800–267–7710 and request the VHS version. Cost is about ten dollars plus shipping.)

A 413 Squadron BG tale
D'Arcy LeDrew

I was on 432 Squadron at Bagotville from July 1957 to September 1961 and have many fond memories of those early days in the all-weather fighter business. One of the more amusing anecdotes of the day involved 413 Squadron commander W/C Bert Allison and A.I. operator F/O Walt Suttie. There seemed to be a penchant in those days to call an unannounced exercise on Friday nights, as most aircrew were at the mess attending "beer call" — as was expected of them. This meant that within a few minutes, they could have a very strong contingent on the flight line, and this was one of the primary points on which we were being measured. The fact that we were all pretty drunk didn't seem to matter much, as the restorative powers of an hour on 100 percent oxygen were universally accepted.

On this particular Friday, S/L Allison did an external, and then climbed into the wrong aircraft. Right behind him, Walt Suttie (who did belong in this aircraft) climbed in to the back seat. They both knew that they were not supposed to be together, but neither one would get out. An airman brought the L14 out to the plane and S/L Allison signed out the plane in which he sat. They fired up, took off immediately, and were vectored west by Scabbard Control. When they were assigned a target, Walt locked onto the "altitude line," and they chased it all the way to North Bay, where they had to land, somewhat red-faced, to refuel.

Master bus(t)
Robert "Pup Tent" Grandmaison

Bill Jones and I had just levelled off at altitude on my first CF–100 night nav trip (third trip in the Clunk). I was mesmerized by a sexy voice from GCI and was likely not paying enough attention to what I was doing. As I listened to her fix information, romantic fantasies were going through my head and I carelessly threw my plastic ruler over to the side. The aircraft became very quiet for about two seconds, until Bill Jones was shouting back at me to "Turn the F-ing master bus back on!" It never happened again.

A mid-century eye test shows a CF–100 squadron at its best. Glenn Emerson and friends.

Abort at BG
David Leigh

One night in 1955, Walt Garner and I launched in a Clunk from BG and proceeded on a night navigation round robin of the beacons to the east. On return to BG, Walt decided to do a couple of touch-and-goes and then land. On an overshoot, an engine hung up. Walt immediately stop-cocked both throttles and landed on RWY 18—which was only +/– 5,000 ft long, as I recall. We coasted to a stop at the south end of the runway and pulled into the GCA area. To our amazement, we had no lights, electricity, etc. The electrical failure had apparently been caused by the APG 40 AI radar, which hadn't been turned off!

What had happened? With the radar operational, it drew so much current that, without the engine generator output, it caused a forty-amp fuse to blow, completely shutting down the a/c's electrical system. We sat there in the dark for about an hour before being rescued. While we waited, we tried every escape concept but nothing worked. Without power, we could not roll back the canopy, nor could we blow the charges. Why didn't we declutch? We almost pulled both T-handles off the frame, but to no avail. TRAPPED!

Twice an airman from GCA came outside and gazed all around, obviously looking for a missing CF–100, but did not see us. Meanwhile, the tower was in a panic because we had vanished without a radio transmission and, of course, they were suspecting the worst. Eventually, GCA personnel found us and called a mule, which towed us into 5 Hangar, the home of ADC's finest—432 Sqn. When we stopped inside the hangar, the ground crew plugged in an energizer, and we just rolled back the canopy—as simple as that! An inspection followed. They discovered the blown master fuse and, in checking the declutch system, found that the cable was routed *under* a structural panel rather than *over* it (or vice-versa). I understand that the wrong routing made the cable too long for the available draw of the T-handle. A special inspection was ordered. It revealed that the canopy systems of about half the fleet were wrongly routed.

An air test?
Bob McKendry

After completing training on the CF–100 at the Operational Training Unit (OTU) at Cold Lake in early 1959, my pilot, F/O Jim Cratchley, and I were fortunate enough to be posted to 4 (F) Wing at Baden Soellingen, Germany. In those days, you "crewed up" and, in principle, flew together during your squadron tour. Having received our posting messages, we both made preparations to take leave prior to our journey to Germany. It was pretty exciting stuff for two young single types, particularly during the days of the Cold War. We then noticed that I was required to report to 419 Squadron some two weeks in advance of my pilot. As we were a crew, we were a bit puzzled about this, but it was not common practice in those days to question the wisdom of the RCAF hierarchy. In addition, I was not at all opposed to arriving in Germany a bit early to sample the local culture, which, at that point in my life, I assumed to be "*gasthauses* and beer." We had been briefed in detail on these aspects by some of the "veterans" at Cold Lake.

I made my way to Germany via North Star and Dakota and dutifully reported on the required date. I was advised that my squadron had departed the day before for Sardinia, Italy, to participate in the annual three-week gunnery and rocket training camp! Of course, no one at the base could tell me why I had been required to arrive on that particular date. I was somewhat disappointed to be left behind by the squadron, but soon made myself comfortable in my new home in Germany.

As I had no squadron responsibilities, the base operations personnel found several "useless duties" for me to perform, so my days were full. On the social side, I immediately began to enjoy life in the officers' mess, as there were, in those days, many single people living on base. In addition, some of the Sabre pilots were kind enough to show me around the area and give me an introduction to the local nightlife.

Life was good!

One day soon after I arrived, I received a call from base operations advising me that a CF–100 was due for a test flight and that a navigator was required. I gathered my flying gear and reported to Wing Maintenance at the appointed time. I met the pilot, F/L Stu Brickenden, a very experienced flyer who had many hours on the CF–100. He had been on 419 Squadron until recently but was now on a ground tour at the base while maintaining his currency on the CF–100. Stu briefed me that this was a "part card" air test, which meant that only certain components of the aircraft required testing. He said the flight should be routine and that there were no special requirements from me, other than to record certain data that he would advise me of at the appropriate time.

I should mention at this time that to say I was "green" in those days would be an understatement of some magnitude. My flying experience to that date had been dedicated to mastering the art of air navigation and, later, the black art of air interception. My pilot had demonstrated some basic aerobatics such as loops and rolls in the CF–100 when we were at Cold Lake, but that was about the extent of my knowledge of non-all-weather manoeuvres in jet fighters.

In any event, we took off and proceeded to do the air test. It was, as Stu promised, a routine flight to that point, and we completed the air test in short order. As we had quite a bit of fuel, he decided to give me a tour of the local area, so we climbed away from the base area.

As we were climbing, I noticed that we began to manoeuvre rather abruptly and that there were a number of Sabre aircraft in close proximity. Stu appeared to be a bit preoccupied with flying at that point, so my initial assumption was that the airspace in Europe was much more crowded than the Canadian skies in which

I had trained! However, I soon gathered from snippets of sentences from the front seat that we had been "attacked" by a section of four Sabres, and that Stu had decided to make their task as challenging as possible. It was my first experience of high "G" manoeuvring and my introduction to aerial dogfighting.

After a little while, he told me that one Sabre pilot was being particularly persistent, but that he had an interesting way to shake him off. I then felt the nose of the aircraft come up abruptly as we began what appeared to be the start of a loop. Things then became a bit confused for me, as I soon found myself looking upward at the earth, and the earth was rotating rapidly. I felt rather uncomfortable with all this, but as the pilot appeared to be a bit too busy for a discussion at that point, I remained silent. After what seemed an eternity, the earth stopped spinning and came back to where I felt it belonged. Without any further discussion, Stu decided it was time to return to base and land, which we did. Later on, when we were changing out of our flying gear, he said to me with what may have been a slightly sheepish tone, "Sorry about that inverted spin, Bob; it was supposed to be a stall."

"No problem," I responded in what I hoped was a casual tone, while thinking at the same time: "So that's what it was!" (The spin was prohibited in the CF–100.) During the following three years on squadron, I learned much more about the game of air combat and air-to-air gunnery. However, I often wondered what that Sabre pilot must have thought as he watched the CF–100 in his gunsight make such an unusual escape manoeuvre!

CB and me!

Bob McKendry

A flight etched indelibly in my memory took place in May 1971 when I was with 414 (EW) Squadron based in Ottawa. I was an experienced CF–100 back-seater, but, as things turned out, that was not much help. I was coming to the end of my tour, and in fact already had my posting message for Syracuse, New York. The squadron was tasked to send two aircraft to MacDill Air Force Base in Tampa, Florida, to participate in a NORAD exercise. I was selected as a crewmember, partly because this would be a nice farewell deployment prior to my leaving the squadron. My pilot for the mission was Captain Ted Benson. Lt. Jim Ritzel was the pilot of the other aircraft; his electronic warfare officer (EWO) was Major Clay Boucher. We deployed to MacDill as planned; however, the exercise was first delayed for twenty-four hours then cancelled because of bad weather—thunderstorms in the exercise area. After spending two pleasant days in Florida while all this went on, we were scheduled to return to Ottawa.

The weather at MacDill was fine on our departure day, but when we went for our weather briefing, we were told to expect cirrus cloud up to 36,000 feet for most of the flight back to Ottawa. We were also advised that there were severe thunderstorms in the area of Charleston, North Carolina, with cumulonimbus cloud reaching to 52,000 feet. On the basis of this information, we decided to file separate flight plans and chose a route that would avoid the thunderstorms. Jim and Clay were to depart first, and we would follow five minutes later. However, when we arrived at our aircraft, we found that the servicing crew had already positioned the engine-starting energizer at our aircraft. This being the case, Ted and I would depart first, a change that had a significant impact on later events.

We departed from MacDill as planned, but shortly after becoming airborne, we received a change in our routing from Jacksonville Centre to avoid areas of thunderstorm activity. This change applied to both aircraft. Ted and I were pleased that the system appeared to be taking care of us. Some minutes later, we levelled off at 37,000 feet, still in cirrus cloud. However, it was fairly thin, and we appeared to be close to the tops. The flight was routine for about the first hour, but we did observe that the cloud was becoming thicker as we headed north. This was not a cause for concern until I later observed that suddenly the inner skin of the aircraft, at least in the rear cockpit, had become coated with thick frost. It was not unusual for frost to appear on the aircraft inner skin, although, in my experience, by no means as quickly or as thickly as had just occurred.

Immediately after this first sign of trouble, we began to experience turbulence, mild at first, but rapidly increasing in intensity. We both felt that we were heading into the centre of a thunderstorm. Ted promptly called Charleston Centre to ask if we were heading into buildups and, if so, for vectors around them. While this was going on, the turbulence was increasing in intensity to the point where he said he was having difficulty controlling the aircraft. Charleston eventually did advise us that we were close to large buildups and gave us a vector to avoid them. Ted turned to the heading specified, but the turbulence seemed to get worse, and the situation was rapidly getting out of control. The aircraft was being buffeted severely, and Ted was having increased difficulty in maintaining control. I noticed that our true airspeed was getting low and mentioned this to him. He had already increased power, but now began a gradual descent. Things then got worse at a rapidly increasing pace. The turbulence was now quite severe, and we were being tossed about in a way that I had never before experienced. It was at this point that Ted decided we would have to eject. The following text, from the September-October 1971 issue of the air force magazine, sets the stage for a rather frightening close-up view of the inside of a thunderstorm.

After my reply, I immediately pulled the overhead handle on my Martin Baker seat and left the aircraft at thirty-one thousand feet. My next sensation was a very strong wind-blast and something hammering me on the face, all the while being tossed around violently in the seat. Wind-blast and oscillations abated shortly, at which time I noticed that my helmet and gloves were missing.

When the seat drogues deployed, I had a relatively smooth but long descent through cloud. At one point I considered using the manual override system to open the chute but decided that the seat was doing a pretty good job by itself. Shortly after this, automatic seat separation occurred, followed by a very smooth chute deployment. When the chute canopy opened, I pressed my stopwatch.

Moments later, a wild ride began. It started with a very strong updraft, exerting what I would estimate to be force of three G's. This carried me up into the hail again and into what seemed to be the centre of the cell. The updraft stopped and I was suspended momentarily while the canopy began to deflate, then I started to drop and swing violently in the chute while being peppered by hailstones. I dropped out of the hail and went into an area of ice fog. There seemed to be no precipitation but everything became rapidly covered with ice. I had to flex my hands often to break the ice from them. Just when things seemed to go more smoothly, I was caught in another updraft and brought into the hail again. The same procedure was followed this time until I was back in the ice fog. I don't know how often I made that trip, but at the time it seemed endless.

During these ascents and descents, there were numerous lightning discharges all around me. The thunder noise associated with this was very sharp and occurred at the same time as the lightning. Once I received a moderate shock that travelled through my entire body—I later learned that the lightning had burned several holes in the chute canopy.

Finally, I dropped into a zone of heavy rain and at last had an indication that I was descending. I knocked the ice from my quick release box and moved it to the unlocked position. Gradually the cloud pattern seemed to change and I broke out about one thousand feet above ground.

The first thing I noticed was an area of grass and tall trees with a paved road directly under me. I was drifting rapidly to the right so I pulled on the left risers. This seemed to slow the drift and I landed in a grassy area right next to some large trees. After landing, I punched my stopwatch again. The elapsed time from chute opening at 15,000 feet to landing was *25* minutes!

When I got sorted out, I undid my chute and walked out to the paved road, a distance of less than 100 yards. About five minutes later, two men came along in a pickup truck and, after an exchange of pleasantries, they took me to the civilian hospital in Beaufort, South Carolina. Later Stu and I were reunited at a nearby military hospital and enjoyed ten days of true "Southern hospitality."

A few postscript notes are in order: First of all, Ted ejected seconds after me and fortunately did *not* get caught up in the centre of the thunderstorm. As a result, he had a smoother descent and landing. In fact, he caused some excitement in the town of Beaufort because he landed in a shopping centre parking lot. Ironically, the shopping centre had set up a mini-fairground in the lot, with amusement rides and other attractions. This led the locals to believe that someone descending in a parachute was part of the show! Ted managed to convince them otherwise and was taken to the military hospital, arriving much before I did.

The aircraft did not fare as well as the two of us, but, under the circumstances, things could not have worked out better. We learned later that after we ejected, the aircraft entered a descending spiral and was actually seen flying very low over base housing at Naval Air Station Beaufort before crashing into the ocean! We were very grateful that there were no injuries to other people as a result of our accident. I had sustained serious injuries to my back from the ejection and from the hard landing caused by the damage to my chute. I was therefore confined to bed by the doctors and fitted with a special back brace. I must say that the U.S. Navy treated us like royalty during our stay. When the doctors there decided we were fit enough to travel, we were both flown by air evacuation to Ottawa by 412 Squadron. When we finally met once again with the crew of the other CF–100, we learned that they had nearly suffered the same fate as us. Clay Boucher said that he experienced severe frosting in the rear cockpit, and in fact his boots froze to the aircraft floor! Jim Ritzel said that he heard Ted's request to Charleston Centre for assistance, and shortly after that, the 1000-cycle tone on guard frequency, generated by an ejection. At the same time, he began to encounter turbulence. Wisely, he made a 180 and obtained clearance to land at a nearby air base.

As to the cause of our misfortune, other than finding ourselves in a place where we should not have been, the Accident Investigation Board concluded that we had lost control because of the severe turbulence associated with the thunderstorm activity. This was not specific enough for our squadron commander, LCol Fern Villeneuve. He initiated a follow-up investigation and came up with what I believe was the true cause of our troubles. One of his primary findings was that the pitot system fitted to the CF–100 was designed in the pre-jet era and its heating element was not capable of coping with the low temperatures common at higher altitudes. As a result, supercooled water, which is a phenomenon associated with thunderstorms, turned to ice after it entered our pitot static system. Consequently, we experienced a gradual and insidious under-reading of our air speed. We were in fact travelling well in excess of our critical mach, and this, no doubt, along with the turbulence, was the root cause of the problem in controlling the aircraft. The Directorate of Flight Safety accepted this finding.

As for me, I did go to Syracuse, although a little later than initially planned. After completion of that tour, I rejoined 414 (EW) Squadron in North Bay and had another four years on Clunks; not a bad way to end the flying days of my military career.

Basic nav training

Pete Armour

New navigators arrived at 3 (AW) OTU with shiny wings and little knowledge of Air Intercept procedures. The flight simulator provided a good basis of the skills they would need. Air sense developed from flying: initially conducted in T–33s.

One trip that provided flying time and broadened their knowledge of intercepts and tactics was a visit to the NORAD site at North Bay. Twenty-second NORAD Region was a "hardened" site buried deep underground in the Cambrian rock. For the navs, it meant planning and navigating from Bagotville to North Bay, a visit to "the Hole," and the return flight the next day. Part of the procedure en route was a diversion from the planned track. This provided the nav with the challenge of "guestimating" a heading to regain the track to North Bay.

Flying Officer Mel Warren, the T–33 flight commander at Bagotville, and I were the pilots who took two of the navs on the trip. We went separately for the sake of the exercise. My fellow did quite well on the whole way there, and, on landing, we were whisked onto a bus to take part in the visit into the bowels of the NORAD facility. The underground visit complete, we arrived in the mess and informally debriefed the navs.

Mel asked how it had gone for us, and I outlined how we had been successful. Mel said his nav had been superb! Never had he seen a performance like it. Following the "diversion from track," which involved some intricate variations in aircraft attitude, Mel declared it was time to set course again for North Bay. Within seconds, the young nav had responded with the correct heading. Mel was suspicious. That heading had turned out to be the *exact* heading required. Mel described his utter delight with the prowess displayed. The nav looked bashfully proud, and after some backslapping, we went up to dinner. Throughout the evening, Mel kept repeating how the young lad had done so very well. After a few more drinks, the new nav blurted out that he had known exactly where they had been. Mel exclaimed he certainly must have known because his heading had been so bang-on.

"No, you don't understand; I mean, I grew up around there and I know all those lakes we were over!"

We thought Mel was going to burst and then he laughed and laughed near to tears. It was a good trip.

Two OTU tales

John Angus MacDonald

There is a lot of history to mull over and events to select that may be worthy to report.

Here is one story. As you are aware, when we were at Cold Lake from April 1956 to the end of June 1956, there were about six schoolteachers that were members of the mess. One evening, a couple of the fellows were in a heated debate as to which one was to take a lady home. A squadron leader sitting at the same table suggested they go outside of the mess and settle the matter. When they left, he promptly escorted the lady home.

And here is another: During the early period of training, on one of our exercises, one engine in the CF–100 began making a constant, loud noise. We shut down the engine, returned to base, and wrote up the fault as descriptively as possible. The following day, we were assigned the same a/c, and upon checking the L–14, we found that a piece of rubber had caused the noise by flapping against the a/c in the wind stream. Needless to say, we were not satisfied with the explanation. Dave requested permission to take a spare a/c. Squadron Leader Allison took the a/c that we were originally assigned and blew an engine on takeoff. Maintenance had a lot of explaining to do on that issue.

"Two out of four ain't bad for a Clunk crew"

Scott Maclagan

Cold Lake—March 18, 1957

It was the morning of March 18, 1957. The weather at Cold Lake was miserable with heavy freezing rain, and all the taxiways and runways were coated with ice. We were in the final week of our OTU Course #35 on the CF–100, and, despite the bad weather, the OTU operations officer thought it would be great practice for all concerned if three crews were to be scrambled to intercept a British V bomber routed over the Pole to a USAF base in the United States.

When the Valiant bomber was picked up at 250 miles north of Cold Lake, the scramble order was given. All three crews raced for their aircraft and started up. Flying Officer Dave Strachan, pilot, and I, F/O Scott Maclagan, navigator, were third in line in aircraft 18249. Number one slid off the taxiway and almost collided with the control tower, while the next aircraft tried to turn too fast, skidded off into the snow, and became stuck.

At this point we were advised the Valiant was at 63,000 feet, 200 miles out. We laughed to ourselves, thinking we would be the heroes of the day if we alone got airborne and intercepted the Valiant.

Power on, takeoff roll, fifty feet in the air, halfway down the runway, and the left engine exploded. Debris came flying through the cabin, and flames engulfed the left wing and engine. Luckily none of the shrapnel hit either of us.

Rather than attempt a bailout at such a low altitude—with ejection seats that required 500 feet for a safe ejection—Dave decided to make a quick turn away from the base and an approach back to the active runway we had just left. He succeeded, but it was an extremely hard landing, with an almost full fuel load, and we were immediately surrounded by fire trucks spraying foam on the burning aircraft. Dave and I escaped from the aircraft and received a somewhat less than heroic ride back to the hangar in a crash truck.

North Bay—September 29, 1958

It was Monday, September 29, 1958, and "Halfback

Nine"; Dave and I were the "First Alert" crew at RCAF Station North Bay. The day was dreary with a heavily overcast sky, a 100-foot ceiling, and quarter-mile visibility. At about ten a.m., we were scrambled by Ops with our CF–100 fully armed, because of recent intrusions into the James Bay area by Russian bombers.

Once airborne, we contacted "Tomboy" control at Falconbridge and were directed to intercept a civilian aircraft in distress near Val–d'Or, Quebec, that had declared an emergency due to low fuel. We flew to Val–d'Or and did a beacon letdown to 500 feet, where the distressed aircraft was declared to be. Tomboy then directed us to the aircraft's position south of Val–d'Or, but we could not see it, even though our two blips had merged on the controller's radar screen.

On our third pass, I tilted the radar upward and finally made contact. Climbing up through the solid overcast, we broke out at 5,000 feet, and there was the Cessna 172 flying above the cloud deck. We pulled alongside with full flaps down, speed brakes out, and gear down, in an attempt to slow down to the Cessna's speed of about 120 knots. We signalled the pilot with hand gestures and finally made intermittent radio contact, transmitting on one channel and receiving on another, while almost stalling as we kept abeam of him.

The Cessna pilot indicated he had less than five minutes' fuel remaining and needed to land. We dove down through the now broken clouds and looked for any spot that he could put down, but found only lakes and dense bush. Checking my knee map, I located the Lac Des Loups beacon and emergency airstrip about twenty-five miles to the north of our position. We climbed back up to the Cessna and guided it to an emergency landing at the airstrip. On final approach, the Cessna's engine sputtered because of low fuel, but kept running long enough to complete the landing.

At that point, we had only 500 pounds of fuel remaining and could not make it back to Val–d'Or. Rather than bail out, we opted for a landing on the Lac Des Loups 3,000-foot runway. It was a nail-biter, given the aircraft's weight with the armed rocket pods, but we got stopped with the nose gear just barely off the end of the runway. We climbed out of the aircraft, de-armed it, and proceeded to the DOT maintenance building at the far end of the strip.

On reaching the building, we were greeted by the local manager, who spoke only broken English. Once inside, we saw the pilot of the Cessna talking on the phone; his passenger, a very glamorous woman, was standing beside him. When the pilot got off the phone, he introduced himself but did not even thank us for saving them.

We then phoned North Bay and advised that we were down safely — we had lost contact with "Tomboy" on our descent — and arranged for a fuel tanker and energizer to be sent so that we could get back to the Bay.

By the time we had completed our call and went back out to talk to the pilot, he was taxiing for takeoff! He had convinced the maintenance staff to fuel his aircraft and was on his way. We learned he was heading for Val–d'Or and quickly called the tower there to advise them of the situation. Upon arrival at Val–d'Or, the pilot was arrested by the RCMP!

It turned out that he had used a false identity and was really the twenty-five-year-old son of a wealthy Montreal family with a total of thirty-five VFR flying hours to his credit. Once over the cloud deck, he had no idea how to operate the navigation equipment on the Cessna and panicked. His passenger was a well-known madam from Montreal visiting her brothels in Val–d'Or and Rouyn–Noranda.

Dave and I spent the night on the maintenance manager's couch while the fuel truck and energizer made their way from Ottawa, some 250 miles to the south. The next morning, we were surprised by a visit from all of the local members of the Ground Observer Corps within a fifty-mile radius of the airstrip. By early afternoon, we had been refuelled and were on our way back to North Bay.

To my knowledge, this is the only documented case of a CF–100 crew saving a civilian aircraft in distress, and the story made headlines in North Bay and apparently across the country. But I am not sure if it was the rescue or the occupation of the Cessna passenger that made it newsworthy . . .

North Bay—March 18, 1958

As the "First Alert" crew, Dave and I were scrambled to intercept an "Unknown" flying at 22,000 feet over Northern Ontario at a speed of 300 knots. "Tomboy" directed us to the target and requested an "ident-run," as they had no idea whose aircraft it was, and it was not "squawking," the appropriate signal required at that time.

We intercepted and identified a USAF KC 97, #2989. When we pulled up alongside, we learned from their hand signals that the aircraft had lost all electrical equipment, including their radios. Furthermore, they had no idea where they were because of the heavy weather we were both in at the time and that they had obviously been in for some time. Using hand signals, we indicated they were to follow us and we guided them down through the weather to a safe landing at Kinross AFB, just outside Sault Ste. Marie, Michigan.

We then returned directly to North Bay.

North Bay—March 27, 1958

Dave and I were scheduled for a night AI exercise with another 414 crew in order to complete our required hours for the month. It was a crystal-clear, cold night with an almost full moon. On start-up, the other aircraft had an engine problem so aborted the mission. By this time, we were almost on the button for takeoff and decided to make it a low-level night navigation trip instead, filing a VFR flight plan with the tower.

Following takeoff, we climbed to 500 feet and followed Highway 11 south, heading for Toronto. Over Orillia, my wife's hometown, we let down to fifty feet, lowered the gear, and with full flaps, speed brakes out, and landing light on, flew down the main street at full power—what a noise that must have been on that cold night!

Retracting the gear and flaps, Dave pulled the aircraft into a nearly vertical climb, heading for Toronto, about sixty air miles to the south. As we passed through 48,000 feet and switched automatically to pressure breathing, I asked Dave what he was up to. His response was: "I want to see how high this bird will really go!" By now we had burned off half of our 8,400 pounds of fuel, and the Mk.V continued to climb, albeit more slowly than before. At 60,000 feet it was still climbing at 500 feet per minute. Dave finally levelled off at 65,000 feet right over top of Toronto, with air traffic control requesting our position and altitude, as they were concerned we were inside the control zone for Malton International.

At that altitude, we could see the curvature of the earth, with Montreal, New York, Boston, Detroit, and Chicago clearly visible due to the beautiful, clear night. The northern lights danced in the northern sky as we started our descent. As Dave put the nose down, the aircraft started to "bunt," as was typical of the Clunk when it exceeded Mach .96. Dave rolled the aircraft on its back and we fell upside-down to the denser air at 42,000, when he righted it and flew back to the Bay.

At age twenty-one we obviously thought we were indestructible and did many crazy things like this altitude attempt that we could never talk about while we were in the service. No one would have believed us! But it did happen in #18484 that night. What I would have given for one of today's camcorders that night! It was truly a night to remember.

SARAH
Pete Armour

SARAH stands for Search and Rescue and Homing. It is designed, once installed in an aircraft, to home on a person who has ejected and has subsequently activated his homing beacon. Once directly over the downed aircrew, SARAH indicates that the search aircraft is passing over the beacon. Successively lower passes are flown until the survivor is pinpointed for pickup.

SARAH training consists of a pilot and navigator conducting a simulated homing on a training beacon. George McAffer and Al Cooper were crewed together. Al had quite a reputation for a sense of humour and quick wit. They had been on a SARAH training flight. They arrived back at the squadron with George grinning his widest grin and Al attempting to match its size. We learned the reason. In the final and finite moments of the homing, Al gave a number of corrections for their homing course: port five degrees—steady—starboard three degrees, and so on. Then Al called sharply, "Port one degree," and George responded, "What? You can't turn one degree. Be realistic."

Al asked, "Well, what CAN you handle?"

"I need at least two or three degrees."

"Okay," Al replied in his most co-operative tone, "turn port three degrees."

"All right, that's more like it," George countered as he turned the aircraft.

"Now starboard TWO," Al delivered in a level but emphatic voice. And, of course, both cockpits convulsed in laughter. That was the end of the run!

Sorfleet/Wood
Author Unknown

On January 19, 1956, Mk.III CF–100 18180 lifted off of Runway 30 at RCAF Station Cold Lake. On board was a student pilot, F/O Wood, about to enjoy his initial dual trip under the watchful eyes of F/L Johnny Sorfleet.

Within nano-minutes of launch, the aircraft's controls seized. F/O Wood immediately ejected, closely followed by John. Wood landed on the south side of the creek that skirts Runway 30 and Johnny came to earth on the north side. The tower van retrieved Wood in gig time. By the time the "rescuers" reached Johnny (who landed within site of the base), he had eaten a substantial portion of his emergency rations and was sending up assorted flares.

Once the crew was safely back at base, the rescuers and the rescued repaired to the officers' mess for a formal debriefing. Johnny succinctly summarized the mission when he advised Wood: "Today we showed you how to perform the takeoff—tomorrow we'll show you a landing!"

Stray voltage
Doug Munro and Doug Stuart

The mighty Clunk was armed with fifty-eight 2.75-inch folding fin (some cynics might argue "floundering fin") unguided rockets—twenty-nine in each of two pods attached to the tips of the main wing. When fired, they departed in a gaggle, nanoseconds apart. Sometimes they were fired intentionally. Sometimes they were fired by accident. And sometimes, they were apparently fired by a Higher Being. The oral records reveal at least five "Oops, real sorry about that" inadvertent launches.

At RCAF Station Bagotville, a Trans-Canada Airline Viscount crew, on close final to Runway 29, were unpleasantly surprised to witness a salvo of rockets flash across their bow. Accidents will happen.

The armourers at RCAF Station North Bay solved the problem of the elements by firing a pod of rockets inside a hangar . . . with the doors closed. The rockets penetrated the door, entered the side window of a snow removal truck, exited the rear window, and sprayed across the ramp with the usual accuracy expected of the Clunk.

The statement of the flight sergeant: "I was working on the right wing of the aircraft when there was a tremendous explosion. I jumped off the left wing and ran out of the hangar."

Board member: "How did you get from the right wing to the left wing?"

Flight sergeant: "Fast."

At RCAF Station Uplands (Ottawa), armourers were conducting a "stray voltage check" on an armed aircraft. Murphy's Law was in charge: some — or all — of fifty-eight rockets departed for points unplanned. Squadron Leader Joe Bodien, the CO of 410 Squadron, happened to be taxiing past the recalcitrant Clunk. Rockets bracketed his aircraft. Unscathed and unperturbed, Joe said: "Piss-poor shot, old man."

A similar incident took place at RCAF Station Comox. It was identical to the Uplands firing with one regrettable difference: the squadron commander was nowhere to be seen. Flying officers Vede Gilchrist and Johnny Mack treated base personnel to the most spectacular firing. They were returning to base, fully armed, from an active air scramble. The runway in use was 29. The crew called three miles back for an overhead break. Standard practice called for a left-hand break, toward the base and base married quarters. Over the middle of the runway, Vede slapped on ninety degrees of bank and turned hard left. Just then, their aircraft was struck by lightning (for all you meteorological buffs, electrical storms at Comox are as rare as virgin births). The upper (right-hand) pod of rockets fired. The aircraft was about 1,200 feet above the ground, pointed directly at #16 hangar — the home of 409 Squadron. At a picture window, a number of their squadron mates were admiring Vede's and John's skill and cunning.

Remarkably, none of the rockets hit the hangar, but they didn't miss everything. A rocket sailed over the hangar and blew a very substantive hole in the roof of the base fire hall. Both fire trucks were peppered with shrapnel, and the hall doors were buckled. Fortunately, it was lunchtime or there would have been casualties — perhaps fatalities.

No other damage ensued. The base armourers faced an insoluble puzzle — how to account for twenty-nine rockets when they only knew where one of them went?

It is remarkable that, in these five potential disasters, there were neither casualties nor fatalities. The 2.75-inch rocket clearly scored very poorly on the Weapons of Mass Destruction Index!

That first posting . . .

Bob Merrick

After about a year and a half of training, which included three months at pre-flight school, a boot camp of sorts at RCAF Station Centralia; nine months or so of learning the rudiments of navigation at No. 2 Air Observer School at RCAF Station Winnipeg; and three months spent acquiring the skills needed to operate the CF–100 at 3 AW(F) OTU at RCAF Station Cold Lake, fledgling navigators and their newly acquired CF–100 pilots faced the long-awaited first posting that would whisk them to a front-line all-weather fighter squadron. Here they would "stand on guard for thee" during the Cold War, when Bulls, Badgers, Bears, Bisons, and other fearsome beasts threatened Canada and Europe.

Where would that posting be? The RCAF then had thirteen CF–100 squadrons; nine were in Canada and the remaining four were either already in Europe or getting ready to go there. The Canadian locations were not half-bad. Comox, of course, was number one for many, as the climate was pretty agreeable, the flying could be challenging, and the coastal lifestyle was laid-back and relaxed. North Bay? That also had its fans. The weather could make the airborne job quite a challenge, but it was a reasonably central location with much to recommend it. Oh yes, there was much to draw people to "the Bay."

Ottawa? Well, in those days, it was a quaint little Ontario town that wasn't too exciting, but was right across the Riviere from Hull, which could be quite exciting, especially for the younger folk who were flooding out of the pilot and navigator training mills. St. Hubert had its fans, too. It was close to Montreal, which, back then, was the nightlife capital of Canada, and many people were eager to be posted there.

Somewhat fewer people sang the praises of Bagotville, as the consensus was that the winters were severe and interminable, and during the short season of poor sledding, the mosquitoes were large and voracious. Besides, it was somewhat isolated, although Quebec City could be reached in about three hours via a somewhat inadequate (in those days) road through Laurentide Park, where the weather was even worse than it was in Bagotville.

In each of these locations, the flying and the air defence life was similar, so there was little to pick and choose there. The leadership varied from unit to unit, but there was really no disaster area — and no nirvana, either. A harsh taskmaster or a "hail fellow, well met" would come and go according to the vagaries of someone's posting plot, so picking a location to work for — or avoid — a particular leader was not a sound long-term plan.

But the big draw was overseas. It was Europe, after all, and likely to be close to the action if WW III came down the pike. And, it was a wonderful opportunity to travel around a historic continent. It was such an attraction that, as I recall, our entire course, noble souls all, opted to defend Europe from the communist threat, leaving Canada to its own devices. We all sat down one afternoon to fill in the requisite forms for use by the personnel wallahs of the day. We handed them in, then sat back to await the ship vouchers that we hoped would arrive in our immediate future.

When we assembled the following morning, we were greeted by W/C E.W. "Big Ed" Smith, a distinguished Bomber Command vet who was then commanding the OTU. He was holding a sheaf of papers: our posting preferences. He looked at the assembled multitude, chuckled a bit, then said something like this:

"Good morning, gentlemen. I've had the opportunity to review your choices, and they are interesting and self-sacrificing indeed. But, I believe it may have escaped your attention that we have nine all-weather squadrons here in Canada, and only four in Europe. What's more, those squadrons in Europe either just got there, are just getting there, or will be there shortly. And there are no plans for any wholesale rotations now or in the near future. I'd be surprised if this course sends more than one crew to Europe. [Ed. note: It sent but one crew, Paul Manson and Norm Freeman. And yes, that's the Paul Manson who later headed the NFA program that got us the CF–18 then went on to become CDS.]

"That means this course will contribute a bunch of crews to Canadian-based squadrons, and if you don't provide some guidance to the people pushers, they will distribute you randomly across the country. I know that some of you have Canadian locations you'd like to go to, and I know that some of you have locations you'd dearly love to avoid. I think that if you give the personnel people some guidance, they'll be able to get you where you want to be, provided it's not Europe.

"I'm going to hand these back so that you can, if you wish, reconsider your choices in light of the fact that European postings will be few and far between over the next few months. You can have a couple of days to think about it, but I'd like to send these off by the weekend."

So saying, he went back to his office, leaving behind him a clutch of pensive crews to ponder just where in Canada they might want to go. My pilot, Don Gregory, had, during his RMC years, spent a summer in Zweibrucken and desperately wanted to return there. Would I agree?

Most certainly I would agree. But, mightn't it be better to say "Europe," rather than Zweibrucken? That way, if there were a vacancy in, say, Marville, we might be considered for it, whereas pinning it down to Zweibrucken might preclude a posting to any other European base.

Well, that seemed like a good idea at the time, so we resubmitted our preference, and sat back to await our European posting, with visions of God only knows what dancing in our heads.

Ere long, the answer came back. But wait, there is a note attached to it. What does the note say? It says, "They speak so much French up in Bagotville that you'll think you're in Europe anyway. Good luck during your tour on 432 Squadron."

Was it a good tour? From a squadron or flying point of view, it was great. Much more important, though, was the fact that there was a Protestant school on base, and the teachers lived in the officers' mess. One of those teachers caught my eye . . . and my heart. Fifty-two years later, she still has both, and we're still together. I still bless the unknown staff officer who decided that we would go to 432 Sqn at Bagotville. It was the best "first posting" that anyone could have wished.

Thunder Bay near-miss
Lloyd Olafson

In May 1959 I was employed with B.A. Oil at Thunder Bay airport, which had just acquired a contract to refuel CF–100 and T–33 jets. On this particular day, I was standing beside Sgt. Guthrie waiting for this particular jet to land—me to refuel the aircraft, and Sgt. Guthrie to conduct a visual inspection, which he performed on all CF–100s that came through Thunder Bay.

The CF–100 made its approach but touched down in the sand short of the concrete runway, which had a four-to-six-inch ledge. The plane bounced over the ledge in a cloud of dust. About fifty feet downrange, it made contact with the runway on its port wheel and port wing tip. It righted itself and made a very rapid deceleration.

Sgt. Guthrie exclaimed, "That was the closest I've seen!" The plane continued around very slowly to its refuelling spot, and two very shaken officers deplaned. The wing tip was bent two to six inches about twenty-four inches back from the tip. The next few days, lots of brass hats surrounded that plane in the hangar.

Ottawa Bits
Bob Hyslop

"Big Ed" Smith was the 428 Sqn boss. We all got a kick out of working next door to the old hardware that were the cause of many ID runs for traffic returning from Dew Line buildup. Joe Bodien, Sqn boss, ex-RAF with prewar background in the Middle East, was heard explaining it this way to some sprogs: "I was doing loops over Baghdad when you were still in dad's bag."

Mussels, Upland's base commander of Korean airlift fame, said when his presence was requested, "I will be there at 1300; at 1301 I will not."

And so it was!

Postscript: One sunny morning, Big Ed arrived in the 428 crew room with a wee smile on his puss. "I see the base commander is flying the Clunk this morning."

"How did you know that, sir?"

"All the navs are hiding in the shithouse."

Ottawa blackout
Bob Hyslop

The gutsy guys who climbed into the back seats of all-weather fighters have carved a permanent niche in my log of memories.

Take, for instance, one disgustingly foul night with high winds, heavy rain, and lightning in all quadrants of the national capital. The Uplands squadrons were placed on alert status. Half the operational personnel were living downtown, but within the hour, almost all crews had been accounted for when, without warning, the entire base of Uplands was thrust into total darkness.

The emergency diesels provided power for the tower and the runways, while in the old wartime hangars, candles and flashlights illuminated the preparations for scrambling. At this moment, through the dim light of the ready room entrance, a voice boomed out, "Who am I crewed with?" Only those close to the doorway would have found Des Larock recognizable. He was soaking wet from head to toe, muddied, bloodied, ripped, torn, scraped, bruised, a basket case, but somehow through the shadows he had found his locker and suited up.

The operation ended early that night, but it wasn't until dawn that we learned Rocky had left a gravel road curve and taken out the main Uplands transformer, then clawed his way from the wreckage and stumbled with little to guide him through the murk to his squadron duties.

No-notice exercise!
Don Carney

My story has to do with the first no-notice exercise called since NORAD was formed in 1957. In view of how attitudes toward alcohol and flight safety have matured since 1957, the story is instructive of the times. NORAD called an exercise on a Friday night about eight-thirty or nine p.m. Really good timing. We were all in a fighting mood by then! Of course we all responded quickly, 413 and 432 Squadrons, to our respective hangars to change, brief, and preflight our aircraft. Not surprisingly, the ground crew folks were in the same mood as the aircrew. Eventually we had our individual aircraft set up and waited for a scramble. I don't recall anyone feeling he was unfit to fly or otherwise indisposed. Nor do I recall that the squadron commander or a flight commander disqualified anyone or themselves.

When the first scramble sounded, the squadron commander and the crew of the second aircraft sprinted to the flight line. The second crew was somewhat behind the speedy CO and when they got to their aircraft, they found it already occupied by the CO and his nav! The conscientious young pilot shouted, "Sir, you're in my airplane!" to which the CO responded, "Get another airplane. I'm not climbing another ladder!" The CO was Bert Allison and the pilot of the other aircraft was Mark Fairley. I don't believe there was ever another Friday night no-notice exercise. All aircraft returned to base in one piece, but perhaps not safely!

More Bagotville tales
Author Unknown

Four-thirteen Squadron formed on May 1, 1957, at Bagotville. In June, the whole squadron went to Cold Lake to fire-in the new aircraft for the first time and for the new aircrew to experience firing rockets for the first time. At the end of the camp, we all ferried our aircraft back to Bagotville via Portage, Thunder Bay, and North Bay. I think we flew in pairs, but in any case, my flight commander, F/L Bob Moir, and his nav, Al Runge, were somewhere behind Gary Flath and me. Bob was older and wiser than us young sprogs and always set a good example. He really helped us to learn the ropes and build our flying confidence, always performing his job in a professional and serious manner.

As the story goes, Bob and Al were somewhere over Lake Superior, with just the radio compass and out of range of any beacons. Bob naturally expected Al to keep track of their progress and to be able to provide him with some idea of where they might be. At some point, he innocently asked Al where they were, to which Al responded: "I don't know where you are, but I'm on page fifty-three of the *Reader's Digest*." Needless to say, Bob was not impressed.

Quebec carnival
Don Carney

During the winter of 1957–58, there were a lot of bachelors in quarters and they couldn't always find enough to keep their fertile minds occupied. They decided the solution might be to see the sights in Quebec City. They enjoyed the city and eventually returned during the Winter Carnival. It seems the boys really got into the spirit of the festival and visited many of the ice sculptures. During the festivities on a Saturday night, they decided it would be a grand idea to see if they could burn down the ice palace! They were intercepted before any serious damage was done, and lost whatever friends they might have had among the organizers of the carnival. They also became acquainted with Quebec City's finest. As I recall, they may have made it back to Bagotville on their own recognizance, being officers and gentlemen. However, on Monday morning they had to explain their creative behaviour to the station commander, G/C Ashman. He did not have the same sense of humour and assigned them several days, perhaps weeks, of Orderly Officer.

A 409 ejection
Gerry Gagne

Flying Officer Len Bolger and his stoic GIB, F/O Ken Parker, were approaching runway 11 at Comox at circuit height after a successful mission. Feeling his oats, upon arriving over the runway, Len yanked the throttles to idle and banked hard left. The sudden "G" force on Len's hand inadvertently pulled the throttles through the stopcock detent, flaming out both engines. Quickly recognizing their dire predicament, Len ordered Ken to eject! Ken immediately pulled the ejection seat handles, which jettisoned the canopy and fired the Martin Baker ejection seat. Ken recalled later that the seat worked exactly as advertised—ejection and seat separation quickly followed by full parachute deployment. Meanwhile, Len managed to relight one engine, and then the other, and returned to land on the runway sans canopy and sans Ken.

When the RCAF crash boat based at the Comox pier reached Ken, he was uninjured, snugly installed in his one-man dinghy and busily waving to a bevy of young ladies who watched him with starry-eyed admiration from Kye Bay Beach.

Bagotville ejection
Gerry Gagne

A similar accident took place at RCAF Bagotville during an AOC's inspection. Pilot Don Mair and nav Claude Filiatreault terminated their air display when high "G" forces flamed out both engines. In this instance, they were unable to relight the Orendas. Both crew members ejected well below the suggested minimum altitude and survived, while suffering leg injuries.

A few hours later when the AOC paid the crew a visit in the base hospital, Claude indicated that he'd not lost his sense of humour when he advised the ADC commander that the crew had gone overboard to provide him with a roaring good show, but he would have to return if he wished to witness one of their renowned, super-smooth landings.

Vertigo
Gerry Gagne

It was a dark and dirty Comox night when we launched on a mutual AI mission with another CF–100 crew. Finally, on top of the main layer of cloud at 33,000, we separated, and the GCI controller set up the first run.

For the first part of the mission, we acted as target, flying between layers of thin, wispy cirrus. It may have been the moon's eerie glow that triggered the ensuing visual phenomena. Suddenly, our CF–100 appeared to be flying upside down, even though the flight instruments indicated that we were flying straight and level.

My gut-wrenching feeling was exacerbated by my navigator (Bob Pomerleau) suddenly yelling, "Gerry, why the hell are you flying upside down?"

A trifle miffed, I responded in my best "You idiot" voice, "Bob, please shut your mouth—for the past few minutes, I've been battling the same sensation. But the engines haven't stopped, so I assume the flight instruments are accurate and we're really right side up!"

Then, as rapidly as they had appeared, the mirage and the moon vanished, and we both resumed breathing.

A 409 scramble
Gerry Gagne

As the alert crew, Bob Pomerleau and I were scrambled after an unknown target tracking SSE along the western edge of Vancouver Island.

This was not uncommon; we had launched many times before on similar missions. In most cases, it involved an Alaska Airways evening flight from Fairbanks to Seattle. In trying to make up precious minutes after a late departure, the pilots bypassed an airway dogleg along the eastern edge of Vancouver Island, thus straying from their flight-planned route by an unacceptable margin and becoming classified as an unknown.

An identification intercept to minimum radar range ensued. The target was acquired visually, and the CF–100 was positioned in close formation with the tail plane of the intruder. Bob had purchased a four-cell flashlight for such occasions and took pleasure illuminating and recording the unknown identification markings. Normally, the sudden beam of light and our flashing navigation lights roused one of the flight attendants, who nervously observed our every move. After passing all pertinent data to the ground radar controller, the Clunk was eased forward to let the airliner pilots know that they had been identified with TLC by an intrepid Night Hawk crew.

But in this instance, the unknown was not behaving according to the usual script. After all, this was a mid-morning intercept, and its track was farther out at sea. Eventually, Bob got a radar contact and directed an identification intercept to minimum range. Shortly thereafter, we were formatting on the right tail boom of a USAF C119 "Packet" transport. Getting the tail number was a cinch. Then we moved smartly forward to salute our Yankee comrades.

But lo and behold, where there should have been two pilots, a flight engineer, a navigator, and a radio officer in the cockpit, there wasn't a soul! Zilch. Nobody. For a better look, we moved the Clunk forward and back, up and down, starboard and port—but to no avail. We tried to peek through the portholes of the cabin but the lights were off, and nothing could be discerned in the darkness. We could only surmise that this transient crew had had a doozer of a party the previous night and had gone to the cabin to sleep off their hangovers. But surely they would have designated someone to monitor the instruments, the navigation, the fuel burn, and the autopilot! However, he too must have succumbed to drowsiness and joined his prone buddies. After a twenty-minute vigil, we were recalled to base.

We later learned that the crew had shaken off their torpor abeam Oregon after several USAF fighter intercepts.

If John Magee in his poem "High Flight" could declare having "touched the face of God," Bob and I can attest verily of an intimate encounter with the Holy Ghost.

A 414 Squadron emergency

John A. MacDonald

Upon arrival in Baden-Baden, Dave Garland and I expected to remain on with 419 Squadron. But, because I was married, it was decided that it would be much easier to have me return to 433 Sqn at North Bay. Dave had the option of staying on 419 Sqn or returning to 433 Squadron. Dave elected to return to 433 Sqn and keep our crew intact. The return to North Bay was by Transport Command North Star.

We were mugged out of 433 Sqn and assigned to 414 Sqn in late August 1957. Most of the flying were normal training flights and Air Defence exercises, with faker forces and SAC aircraft.

On return to base after a night training exercise, on the approach for a landing and at fairly low altitude, approximately 400 feet above the ground, Dave had to take an evasive manoeuvre to avoid a CF–100 using the same runway for takeoff. The avoidance manoeuvre was a sharp turn to the left and down, and as the a/c was at a low altitude to begin with, I attempted to pull out the "D" ring blind but was unable to do so. Fortunately, Dave indicated that he had control, the near miss was avoided, and the a/c was landed safely.

We returned to maintenance to write up the incident in L–14, and as result the a/c was grounded. While the a/c was in the hangar, the Martin-Baker seat was de-armed. Once again, I attempted to remove the blind in normal seating position and was unable to; again, with both feet against the seat facing the ejection handle for the blind, I was unable to remove the ejection blind. It was seized (wedged).

This caused the CF–100 fleet to be grounded until every a/c was checked to ensure that the ejection handle on each Martin-Baker seat was working properly.

The exact date of this incident escapes me at this time, but it was in 1957 when the CF–100s were being refitted with ground-level Martin-Baker ejection seats. To distinguish the 400-foot ejection seat from the ground level seat, the higher-level ejection seat had a red slash painted on it so that it could easily be identified as low or high. In my incident, the seat was the 400-foot version. I was very fortunate that the seat failed to work.

Oxygen failure

Dave was on leave in early February 1958, and I was flying with Art Parker. On February 6, 1958, while climbing to our assigned altitude given by GCI, Art overshot the altitude by a couple of thousand feet. On telling Art that we were above our assigned altitude, his response was incoherent, and I realized he was having problems. I gave the heading to return to base, which he overshot by thirty to forty degrees. I persisted in having him descend to the altitude that did not require oxygen and at the same time I gave headings for the base. We landed safely, and Art was taken to MIR for some medical checks.

Nimble Bat 419 Sqn

John A. MacDonald

The squadron departed North Bay on August 1, 1957, on the first leg of the trip to Baden-Baden, Germany. The first stop was Goose Bay, Labrador. Dave Garland and I were part of a four-plane formation led by F/L Kevin McNulty and his navigator, F/O Jim Wilding. As we approached Seven Islands, Lead began having problems with his flight controls—they became very stiff and difficult to move. With twenty-one crews in the air, there were plenty of suggestions as to how to rectify the problem. One of the suggestions was to de-boost. He did this, with catastrophic results. The CF–100 pitched-up hard right and dived for the ground. Dave Garland and I attempted to follow Lead down. We exceeded the limiting Mach and had to abandon the pursuit when we entered cloud at 20,000 feet. Dave thought he saw a parachute canopy prior to Lead's entering cloud. Sadly, the aircraft crashed, and both crewmembers were killed.

The squadron remained at Goose Bay until August 4, when it departed for Keflavik AFB, Iceland. This leg of the trip took three and a half hours. Our aircraft experienced pressurization failure. We descended to an altitude that didn't require pressure breathing and kept a close check on our fuel and oxygen supply.

The third and final leg, from Keflavik to Baden-Baden, was three and three-quarters hours, and again we lost our pressurization and had to descend. Over the UK, Dave had an attack of the bends and began a slow descent over southeast England to Baden-Baden. About a half hour later, I had a similar problem.

Upon our arrival at Baden-Baden, the squadron was greeted with a splendid reception—the champagne flowed!

Per Ardua Ad Ridiculum

Ron Hayman

The date: July 22, 1960. The place: RCAF Station Uplands, Ottawa, Ontario.

There were two CF–100 squadrons at Uplands—410 "Cougars" and 428 "Ghosts." I was a member of 428. There was also a Headquarters Flight of T–33s and C–45s that enabled AFHQ's armchair jockeys to proficiency fly on cloudless days and pocket their hard-earned flight pay.

The CF–100 "Canuck"—or, as Sabre pilots would call it, "The Clunk"—was unarguably the best all-weather interceptor of its era in all North America and, possibly, the world. The Mk.V that we flew had extended wing tips and could easily reach above 50,000 feet, cruise at .85 Mach, and go forever. The purpose was to defend Canada against the dastardly Russians who were threatening to bomb us into oblivion with their Bears, Badgers, Bisons, and Backfires, coming over the Pole from Stalin land. We seldom saw the four "B"s so had to content ourselves with running intercepts on B–47s and B–52s thoughtfully provided by Strategic Air Command and the odd errant airliner.

To hone our skills further, the PTB (Powers That Be) decided we could profit immeasurably from a mock nuclear attack on Ottawa ("Operation Chess Match Faker"). We were issued dosimeters to measure how soon we would die or become impotent (sadly we had to return them after the event). The scenario involved flying a regular intercept mission, returning to a vaporized Ottawa. Upon engine shutdown, we were instructed to evacuate the aircraft and submit to a hosing down and decontamination by the fire department. The firemen were dressed in radiation suits and used imaginary fire hoses. Immediately thereafter, we had to run for the hangars to reduce our radiation exposure to the absolute minimum.

Overseeing our return and delousing procedure from the control tower was the base commander, G/C "Cam" Mussels. To many, he was considered a martinet—a bit of a Captain Queeg in air force blue. To be fair, Uplands was a show station where diplomats and dignitaries arrived from all over the world to do business in our nation's capital, and Muss got things done! We all thought it a bit excessive when the G/C had flowers delivered and planted, in the middle of winter, along the sidewalk leading from the terminal building just before the arrival of Ambassador So and So.

Such was the scenario when Bob Fisher, a 428 pilot, entered stage left. Having done a tour with the RAF on Meteors and Hunters, Fisher had transferred to the RCAF and ended up in Ottawa. To say he was somewhat different from the rest of us would be most charitable.

As we taxied into the ramp, shut down, evacuated the aircraft, and submitted to the imaginary decontamination procedure, Fisher's finest hour was at hand. While the rest of us raced to the hangars at the high port, Bob strolled nonchalantly across the tarmac, the last by far to arrive "safely."

Mussels, observing Fisher's cakewalk, went ballistic and ordered the duty officer to bring him to the tower immediately. Ushered into the CO's presence, Mussels screamed, "What in *hell* do you think you were doing, mister? You were ordered to *run* for the hangars, not *walk*!

"Well, sir," responded Fisher, "I reasoned that if I ran to the hangars I would breathe harder, thereby inhaling more radiation than if I walked. So I decided it was more profitable for my health to stroll."

Mussels, bug-eyed and apoplectic, yelled "Get that man out of my sight before I *&^%$# . . ."

Red alert

Gord Letcher

Few Canadians, even those with military backgrounds, are aware that an infamous plot hatched in the U.S. was snuffed out by fortuitous circumstances in the sky over Northern British Columbia forty-six years ago.

The story has its beginning in Washington, D.C., where the Armed Forces Appropriations Committee of Congress was trying to cope with the conflicting demands of "who gets what" among the "hawks and doves" in the U.S. Pentagon.

The hawks were led by General Curtis LeMay, the famous commander of Strategic Air Command (SAC). LeMay's contention was that most of the defence budget should be allocated to expanding the jet bomber and intercontinental missile forces under his command. He argued that spending money on the fledgling North American Air Defence Command (NORAD) was futile because the system would not have the capability of detecting, let alone deferring, an attack on the continental United States.

While the debate raged in the U.S., Canada was quietly but quickly building up its commitment to NORAD. In addition to establishing a radar warning system, wartime bomber and fighter squadrons were being reactivated as all-weather fighter squadrons at bases in strategic locations. One of these was 409 (Nighthawk) Sqn, a renowned night fighter unit during WW II. The squadron was reactivated under the command of a wartime member, S/L Frank Haley, in the fall of 1954 at Comox, B.C., a place that LeMay, to his everlasting chagrin, no doubt, never knew existed.

Fast forward to May 5, 1955, a beautiful spring day in the Comox Valley. Despite feverish activity, 409 Sqn was less than halfway to its goal of achieving full combat-ready strength and readiness. On this fateful day, a crew recently graduated from the All-Weather Fighter Operational Training Unit AW (F) OTU at North Bay, Ontario, had just completed an air test on CF–100 18247. As the crew walked from the aircraft toward the hangar to complete the inevitable "paper war" that followed each flight, a harried-looking commanding officer burst from his office door shouting, "Get back in that aircraft, there's a Red Alert!"

Somewhat dismayed, though well-disciplined, the crew quickly scampered back on board the aircraft and watched in amazement as the CO and several NCOs directed the ground crew swarming around the aircraft with ammo, oxygen carts, and a fuel bowser. After what seemed ages but was officially clocked at under five minutes, the aircraft was fired up and heading to the active runway for takeoff. As the aircraft lifted from the runway and commenced a steep turn to port, the control tower transmitted, "Cudgel Seven cleared from tower control, contact Waterfall Control on channel four."

"Waterfall Control, this is Cudgel Seven on channel four, over."

"Cudgel Seven, this is Waterfall Two," yelled a high, excited voice. "This is a Red Alert! Repeat, a Red Alert! Repeat, a Red Alert, over!"

"Roger, Huey [the controller's voice was recognized as belonging to "Huey" Houston, a neighbour in married quarters], this is Cudgel Seven. Cut the commercials and give us directions, over."

The last transmission evidently convinced Huey that the Cudgel crew knew the situation, because he calmly replied, "Cudgel Seven vector three six zero, make angels 35, go Buster, acknowledge." For the uninitiated, this transmission meant, "Take up a compass heading of 360 degrees, climb to 35,000 feet, and fly at maximum continuous cruising speed—about 550 knots."

"Cudgel Seven, Waterfall Control, six bogies twelve o'clock, 350 nautical miles, closing at 1,200 knots."

The next bit of conversation took place between the aircraft crew on intercom. "Terry, what the hell was Huey talking about?"

Terry, being a resourceful fellow, had memorized the various alert stages, taught at the OTU by concocting the following sentence, which he repeated in a hushed voice: "Rape (red) your (yellow) bride (blue) with gusto (green)." Red meaning that an enemy attack is imminent or in progress, and green meaning all clear. As Terry recited the sentence, comprehension dawned on the pilot and he reached down and activated the gun cocking switch. As the breech blocks on the eight .50-calibre machine guns slammed back and forth, arming and cocking the guns, the aircraft shuddered as though it, too, recognized the seriousness of the situation.

The initial closing speed had been estimated at 1,200 knots. This meant that the bogies should appear on the aircraft's radar approximately fifteen minutes after takeoff. Ten minutes had elapsed, and the aircraft, now at the designated altitude and speed, was racing away from all evidence of civilization into a wilderness area as the fuel gauges moved ominously toward zero. Cloud cover obscured all of northern British Columbia, so it was impossible to determine the aircraft's position visually. Somewhere northwest of Prince George, a barely audible transmission was received by Waterfall Control: "Cudgel Seven, bogies twelve o'clock at forty nautical miles, overtake now fifty knots, bogies appear to have reversed course, over."

An urgent consultation took place between the aircraft's crew. To press on would mean overtaking the bogies at about the same time as the aircraft ran out of fuel. But if the speed was reduced to "loiter," minimum cruise speed, and one engine shut down, the aircraft could "anchor" or fly in a circle, for ten minutes and still have enough fuel left to return to base.

After anchoring for ten minutes without radio or radar contact with any agency, the crew decided to return to base at "saunter," the best fuel economy speed. Thirty minutes later, with the fuel gauges reading empty, a straight-in approach was made on Runway 29 and landed safely. The aircraft taxied back to the hangar line. The only person in sight was the aircraft marshaller, all the rest having gone to lunch.

The next day, all the major newspapers on the West Coast of North America ran headlines screaming, "What happened?" and revealed that while Canadians had gone blithely about their daily business in cities such as Vancouver and Victoria unaware that a Red Alert had been declared, U.S. cities from Seattle, Washington, all the way to the Mexican border had been warned, and many people had taken refuge in air raid shelters.

The politicians on both sides of the Canada/U.S. border quickly got into the act, and air defence became everybody's darling. Several months later, it was quietly revealed that the "bogies" had, in fact, been SAC B–47 bombers secretly launched from Alaska with instructions to fly southward until detected and/or intercepted.

Who were the members of the Cudgel Seven crew that ruined SAC's nefarious plan? Two RCAF officers: yours truly, Gordon Letcher, pilot, and Terrance McGale, navigator. Both of us continued our military careers for another twenty years in the RCAF/CF, then retired to pursue other challenges.

When aircraft 18247 was refuelled after the alert, it was revealed that there remained only ten gallons of fuel in its tanks—barely enough fuel to run the engines for another thirty seconds while airborne. The 409 Sqn continued its combat-ready preparations and, at the end of August 1955, despite having only just over half of its planned establishment in aircraft and personnel, passed its combat-ready test and was placed on full-combat-ready status.

General Curtis LeMay continued to serve in the United States Air Force and was honourably retired a decade or so after the Red Alert.[10]

Big black bogey

Robert "Jock" MacDonald

Jim (Andy) Anderson and I were on an air test flying out of 1 Wing, Marville, France, in 1958, armed only with guns. We had finished all the tests and were looking around for some "trade" to bounce when we were vectored on to a bogey. Yellow Jack seemed quite excited, as the unknown was committing a "hostile act" in dropping "chaff." The aircraft was below 6,000 feet, heading straight for Paris and not responding to any communication. We were above 30,000, following vectors and descending at "buster" when I picked up the target at maximum range. The identification pass was perfect except that we (I) got carried away and forgot about an overtake speed 250+ knots. We passed the bogey but kept it in sight in a max rate very high G turn and rolled out behind. The unknown was a B–50 painted all over in black with absolutely no markings, and the bundles of chaff were still puffing out. Andy was reporting all this to Yellow Jack when the bogey spotted us and made straight for the cloud; but we followed, locked

---

10 This article was previously published in *AirForce,* Vol. 25 No. 1, Spring 2001; reprinted with permission.

on at minimum range. After a few minutes, we were told to break off, but I was not going to be deceived by false instructions.

"Authenticate Romeo Romeo," I called and I could almost hear the scuffling around trying to find the codes. It gave us a short time more to tail this strange B–50 before someone realized that we did not have the codes, either. Eventually, someone rather rudely ordered us to break off and RTB (return to base). I think their authentication response was "Foxtrot Oscar."

We never did find out the ownership of that strange and mysterious aircraft, but speculation has it as belonging to the CIA, as it landed at a USAF base outside Paris.

Unfortunately, Andy died very young in 1970, not long after he retired, so he can't expand or embellish my tale of almost firing the Clunk's .5 Brownings in anger and saving the world from WW III.

Sorfleet ejection

Lee Evans

The CF–100 was also known as the B–99 (almost a hundred). It had more monikers than any other aircraft I flew.

At Cold Lake, my deputy in the Instrument and Conversion Flight took a new student up on his first CF flight. He put the student in the front seat, which was his first mistake. To bolster the lad's confidence in the aircraft, Johnny shut down the starboard engine and, after a few manoeuvres, attempted to relight. No luck—not enough amps to get it going. Unfortunately, this meant lack of use of (and don't quote me on this because my memory flags) flaps and fuel readings.

So Johnny decided to bail out after getting closer to the end of the runway. First the student went out and landed in a tree (unhurt), and then Johnny landed in a snowdrift. In the meantime, the base had been alerted and their helicopter took off with Dr. Ken Running aboard. When it landed near Johnny, Doc Running yelled to him, asking if he was hurt. When the answer was no, the good doctor told Johnny to make his own way to the helicopter. When I saw Johnny in the hospital, all he complained about was, "They didn't give me time to try out the emergency rations."

Not your "run-of-the-mill" live scramble

KO Simonson

It was a blustery, rainy day on August 31, 1959. I was on ten-minute alert with F/O Dave Mitton at 425 AW(F) Sqn, based at St. Hubert, Quebec, when a live scramble order came through. We were airborne well within the ten-minute requirement. Shortly after takeoff, we were switched over to the radar unit controlling us for the intercept of an unknown low-level target southbound in northern Quebec. We were given a northeasterly vector and told to climb to 10,000 feet. We were also told that our target was slow-moving and appeared to be cruising at about that altitude.

As I recall, Dave and I discussed the likelihood of this being a sneak Russian raid and we came to the conclusion that it was probably a C–47 (Dakota) or similar type aircraft that had either wandered off course or had neglected to file a flight plan. In any event, our mission was to intercept this unknown aircraft and to pass its identity to the proper authorities, who in turn would decide what further action, if any, should be taken. As was normal on all live scrambles, we were armed with a pod of twenty-nine rockets on each wing tip and were therefore prepared for any eventuality.

At 10,000 feet, we were in thick cloud and heavy rain. Following radar vectors from our controller and concentrating on getting a radar contact on our intercept radar, as was quite normal under the circumstances, we were not really aware of our exact location. After several more vectors, Dave said he had a contact at a certain bearing and distance, and we told our controller that we would take over the intercept. He acknowledged that our contact was the unknown and we proceeded to close on the target.

All of a sudden, the target started evasive action, turning away from us. We were quite surprised that the target could know we were behind him in the thick cloud and rain; nevertheless, we continued to close, having to slow our aircraft to below 200 knots to avoid closing too fast. We were still quite heavy, as we had not burned a lot of fuel since takeoff, so I had to select some flap to maintain a good degree of control at slow speeds.

Meanwhile, the target kept turning as we approached our minimum range for an identification run. All this time, it was still raining very heavily. At minimum range, our speed was down to around 130 knots, and I had to use a lot of power and flap to maintain good control (I can't remember for sure but I think I also put the undercarriage down). We moved very slowly closer, still no eyeball contact, and we were about to call off the intercept when the target turned again and I picked it up! We were flying loose formation on a Quebecair Fokker Friendship, which, as it turned out, was in a holding pattern over Quebec City! Imagine our surprise; better still, imagine the Quebecair pilot's surprise to suddenly see a CF–100 on his wing in the holding pattern in heavy cloud and rain!

Having identified the target, I decided it was time to get the hell out of there, so I broke off, cleaned up the aircraft, got some airspeed back, and requested vectors and a more comfortable altitude back to St. Hubert. We completed a normal recovery. On landing, I learned that I had been served with an airspace violation by the Department of Transport; the Quebecair pilot got my aircraft number, although I didn't get his!

As was required by QR&O, a summary investigation into the incident was ordered. Several weeks later, I was approached by the investigating officer, who informed me that we had been cleared of any blame and that the radar controller had obviously put us on the wrong target. (The controller was subsequently disciplined.) The investigating officer also told me that Dave and I had been commended by the board for carrying out a successful intercept under extremely adverse conditions.

"2" Wing tale

Nick Nicholson

During the Berlin Crisis of the fall of 1961, 423(AWF) Squadron, based at Grostenquin, France, was augmented by several flight crews from Canadian-based squadrons. One of the navigators who joined us was John Mack. John's reputation had preceded him: He was famous for having unleashed a full rocket pod while on the break for landing at RCAF Comox. I believe only one rocket hit a new fire hall that was scheduled to be occupied for the first time the next day. Unfortunately, that was not to be, as the one rocket effectively demolished the new building. Johnny always mumbled about gremlins and stray voltages.

And now to my story. In the spring of 1962, I was riding back with John in his Austin Healy sports car after having played golf at Vittel. We came up through Gerardmer, and as usual John was driving like the wind. It was early evening, and I recall looking up the road as we started to enter the right-hand turn into the long north-south reverse "S" turn that leads up to the Col de Saverne. I remember thinking that it was a beautiful day and was vaguely aware of a girl up ahead walking along the right-hand side of the road at about the midpoint of the reverse "S."

As John got farther into the right-hand turn, the rear end of the car started to break away, and we entered a screeching four-wheel skid up the left (wrong)-hand side of the road. As unlikely as it might seem, at exactly the same time the Austin Healy was entering the right-hand turn, a DS 19 Citroen was entering from the north end. The driver of the DS 19 was also flying and, as he attempted to turn to the right, the rear end of his car started to lose friction, and he ended up in a screeching four-wheel skid down the right (wrong)-hand side of the road. At exactly the midpoint of the reverse "S" turn, the two cars, on their respective wrong sides of the road, passed nose to nose in a mind-numbing blur.

Gradually, as we reached the northern left-hand turn out of the reverse "S," John managed to wrestle the car under control. He immediately glanced over at me and I at him. As one, we both blurted out exactly the same question: "Geez, did you see that girl?"

Robbie tales

Robbie Robinson

Well, since you encouraged me, I will pass on a few experiences that might be interesting, especially to Clunk crews.

The first happened early in my CF career, and John Sutherland remembers it quite well, I am sure. He was in the back seat!

It involved a faulty flow-control valve, which caused the port engine to refuse to accelerate on overshoot from an intended touch-and-go approach. It was touch, but no go! Hard starboard braking held us straight while I closed and reopened the throttles! But NO acceleration on the faulty engine. We were using the short runway (at Cold Lake) due to wind direction, so there was no option but to abort the overshoot and stand on the brakes. We had moved to port so much that we ran the port wheels off the edge of the runway, where we clipped a drain grid and snapped off the port u/c leg! As we crossed the taxiway at the end of the runway, we lost the second u/c leg! Now we were motoring along on the nose wheel, the tail cone, and the tip tanks! We stopped off on the dirt just short of a big buried boulder that would have taken out the nose wheel, too!

Minimal damage to the a/c, as it turned out, and it was re-flown a short time later. The suspect engine was installed in another airframe and a run-up done by Orenda's tech rep Terry Motorshead. I stood and watched. When he opened the throttle, all we heard was a loud moan and vibrations! Positive proof of why the overshoot failed.

Another unnerving event happened when one tip-tank stopped feeding when still half full. Landed okay with a bit of imbalance. The next time, a few days later, was more traumatic. One tank refused to feed at all, while the other one emptied. (Note: Tips were pressurized with air, and once selected, could NOT be turned off!) So, the tank's tip blow-off was selected to drain the full tank, and would you believe: only the empty tank tip blew! There was over a ton of fuel in the port tank we could not get rid of. So, after doing slow speed control check at a safe altitude, we did a rather high-speed landing, putting the a/c on the runway at 150 kts to avoid loss of control. Directional control was difficult, but we stopped on the runway. We taxied looking like a lame duck! When I reminisced years later with a North Bay crew on CF–100 static display here in London at the air show, they said they were instructed never to try such an unbalanced landing, but to eject! Likely good advice, to be on the safe side!

Years later, while flying with the E.W.U. out of St. Hubert, we were deployed to Bagotville to serve as a faker a/c in a NORAD exercise. There was a huge front approaching, but we did not realize how violent it was. While climbing out through the cloud, we experienced violent lightning, and the whole canopy began flashing with St. Elmo's fire all around the perimeter. Dazzling and rather scary! We were ingesting tons of water into the engines, which had a known problem with shrinkage of the lining of the engine when cooled too much. So, the compressor blades rubbed violently, and the grindings were digested by the turbine section. One crew lost both engines and bailed out over Northern Quebec, the nav landing in a tree, where he hung till dawn, as he had no idea how far above ground he was. Another crew lost one engine, but continued home. We had severe damage to both engines, but they kept going. Sometimes ignorance IS bliss!

So there are a couple of "interesting" experiences from ten years of CF flying. Sure broke up the boredom. I wouldn't have missed the experience for the world. And anyone who bad-mouths the CF–100 is likely an incompetent pilot or never had the old bird come through for him when the chips were down! With nearly 2,400 hours, I feel I can be a good judge! (I once took on a younger pilot flying a T–33 in a tail chase and he was amazed at what the "Clunk" could do! He couldn't lose us!) The dive brakes were far more effective than those on a T–33.

Speed brakes
... speed brakes ... GO!
Turbo Tarling

The T–33 Silver Star and the F–86 Sabre had small speed-brake panels on the bottom and side of the fuselage, respectively, and, to be charitable, they were barely adequate. The CF–100 Canuck, on the other hand, was endowed with massive, serrated-edge speed brakes on the upper and lower surfaces of the wing and they were very impressive and effective.

The speed-brake selector switch, mounted on the forward face of the right-hand throttle lever, was identified as "Drag Flaps" for some strange reason; no one ever called them "drag flaps," they were always called "speed brakes" or "dive brakes." In actual fact, they were spoilers.

The CF–100 was never flown with speed brakes extended during the final turn or approach to the runway because of the high sink rate or premature stall that inevitably resulted. This fact was driven home to us when we began our CF–100 training at RCAF Station Cold Lake, Alberta. Only months before, there had been a tragic fatal accident when a CF–100 crashed on final approach. The cause was improper use of the speed brakes.

On March 25, 1957, I had my first dual flight in the CF–100 with my instructor, Don Lamont. As we got station passage for our radio beacon instrument approach, I eased the nose down, threw out the speed brakes, and promptly left the seat, much to the amusement of Don in the back seat—talk about deceleration! We soon got used to it, but as a courtesy I always gave my navigator a few seconds' warning when the speed brakes were coming out so he could brace himself.

In October 1959, 428 Ghost Squadron participated in Operation Checkerboard at RCAF Station Chatham, New Brunswick, home of the F–86 Operational Training Unit (OTU).

One afternoon, on a day when we were scheduled for night missions, I managed to scrounge a CF–100 to take up a hometown (Toronto) buddy, Flying Officer George Peck, a student on the F–86 OTU.

The trip went well, and George amused himself playing with the radar set, eventually picking up a target. With a little coaching, he got me a lock-on and we attacked and "splashed" an F–86 that had been stooging along without watching for "bandits."

The pilot, an instructor, unaware that he was officially "dead," asked if he could join up for a little formation. As we got closer to the airfield and were preparing to descend, I advised him that our speed brakes were very effective and that he should anticipate them a bit to stay with us. His reply was a nonchalant "Rog" (short for "Roger"), so I called, "Speed brakes . . . speed brakes . . . GO!"

Almost immediately, George began chuckling and described what had happened: the F–86 had wobbled left and right, then went sailing by in a near-vertical bank to miss our wing, its tiny speed brakes frantically clawing the air trying to slow down. I looked over, and sure enough, our Sabre was gone.

Perhaps a touch more anticipation next time, sir?

Scramble!
Turbo Tarling

In September and October 1957, 410 Cougar and 428 Ghost Squadrons in Ottawa were tasked with alert duties at Ernest Harmon Air Force Base, Stephenville, Newfoundland, while the resident USAF 61st FIS (Fighter Interceptor Squadron) replaced their aging F–89 Scorpions with delta-wing F–102 Daggers. I was a new pilot on the Ghost Squadron.

The USAF alert hangars were different from the RCAF ones. The aircrew sleeping quarters were on the second level, above the two aircraft bays; ours were between the bays. When the scramble horn sounded during the night, the pilots and navigators would dress in a matter of seconds, charge down the stairs, dash to their respective aircraft, strap in, start up, and take off.

Officially, we were allowed a maximum of ten minutes from horn to airborne but, as a matter of pride, we always tried to shave this time down, especially since the Americans were watching our performance.

As often happened, the scramble horn went off in the wee hours of the morning, but this particular scramble did not go quite as smoothly as usual. One of the (senior) pilots had been blissfully sleeping on his side when the horn went off and as he struggled out of bed he discovered that his side was completely paralyzed with sleep!

The other aircrew were already dressed and bounding down the stairs as he flopped around the now-deserted room trying to get dressed. By the time he had hobbled down the stairs and over to his CF–100, his navigator was already strapped in and waiting for him.

He clambered up the ladder but halfway up he lost his grip and tumbled back down to the ground. Undaunted, he picked himself up, clambered back up the ladder, lost his grip, and fell back down again. With great determination, he grabbed the ladder and clawed his way to the top, only to have the ladder fall away from the aircraft with him clinging precariously to it! A quick-thinking ground crew grabbed the ladder and managed to push it back to the cockpit.

The pilot tumbled into the cockpit, strapped himself in, started both engines, shoved the throttles forward, and blasted out of the hangar. We wondered what was going through the navigator's mind as they thundered down the runway into the night!

The Mosquito . . .
Bob Merrick

Now that we have fished all the WW II vets into this story with the title, let it be said at once that the Mosquito in question was not one of the plywood pests that so harassed *Reichsmarschall* Goering and others. This was the backwoods pest that continues to harass rural and urban Canadians to this day.

Our story takes place at RCAF Station Bagotville, Quebec, well into the CF–100 era. It was in the days before alert barns were invented. The two alert aircraft, complete with Mighty Mouse rockets capable of inspiring terror in those who fired them—if no one else—sat on the flight line immediately in front of the hangar, a heritage structure that some said dated from WW I.

In this era, when men were men, and women were supposedly glad of it, the crews on 432 Squadron worked twenty-four hours on and twenty-four off. The flight commanders of the day tried for maximum mileage from this arrangement. They always required two crews on alert, but they also had other commitments to honour, or the world as it was then known would cease to exist.

Also in this era, the crews manning the alert aircraft could change several times a day, depending on the vagaries of the flying schedule, the whims of the scheduler, and various other factors that changed with the season or the flight commander's socks.

It was not unusual for a crew to hold alert from 0800 to 1000, fly a trip on the normal schedule, complete a simulator mission, fly a trip on the night schedule, and then spend the rest of the night on alert.

In those days, they were also expected to spend the night awake. Real men worked for twenty-four straight hours and thought nothing of it. But the flight safety *wallahs* also thought nothing—or, at least very little—of it. Gradually, their nagging paid off.

Word came down from on high that henceforth, alert crews would be allowed to spend part of the twenty-four-hour day sleeping while awaiting the clarion call of the klaxon. But where could they sleep? The flying schedule normally ran until about 0200 hours, using nearly all the rooms on the flight line side of the hangar, and often caused commotion verging on pandemonium.

But on the other side of the hangar stood an unused tool crib that could be converted into a bedroom by taking out the shelves and putting in something even more uncomfortable. The carpenters diligently did their thing, and soon the room once filled with used Hawker Hurricane parts boasted four beds and a giant klaxon of the sort now used to back most rock or heavy metal musicians. It made more noise than the aircraft it was supposed to summon into action. There was no phone, as the accountants of the day had it on good authority that the alert crews wouldn't understand phone messages until they had enjoyed a bracing run across the hangar.

On the night in question, it was hot. Really hot. The alert crews putzed around on the squadron side of the hangar for most of the evening but decided to retire at about midnight after watching Earl Cameron put the nightly seal of doom and gloom on the world.

Upon reaching the tool crib-cum-bedroom, they noticed that the temperature was just a smidge under that needed to burn paint off the pipes. So, they opened the miniature window and propped the door open with a large, water-filled fire extinguisher. Then, still attired in flying suits with pockets full of lumpy publications and still wearing their flying boots, they flopped onto the War of 1812 beds and tried to sleep.

The troops from the midnight launch returned, conducted their flurry of post-flight activities, and left the squadron. The roar of the departing MGs and TR–3s subsided and peace returned to the Saguenay Valley. The temperature in the tool crib descended to about 150 degrees F. The alert (?) crews dozed fitfully.

Suddenly, BLAAAAA-A-A-AT! The scramble klaxon sent its message with a force that startled workers in the ALCAN smelter twenty miles away. The lead navigator levitated off his bed and, feet churning at about forty knots, shot out the door. As he went, his hip brushed (brushed, hell—the bruise is still there) the fire extinguisher. The fire extinguisher, shocked by this unprovoked assault, fell over. The door, no longer propped open, snapped shut.

Unfortunately, it snapped shut just as the lead pilot, also now moving at approximately forty knots, reached it. The resulting collision jarred the hangar, but didn't budge the lock that had been put there to protect all those Hurricane parts. The lead pilot rebounded into the bedroom, neatly wiping out the number two pilot, who had been a bit slow off the mark.

With a bellow, the lead pilot regained his feet and launched another assault on the door. His one-handed, one-motion grab and twist was a work of art, as was his triple somersault and one-and-a-half gainer, which he performed when his rapidly churning feet hit the particularly friction-free surface that results when fresh water from a fire extinguisher is added to decades' worth of used Hurricane oil, hydraulic fluid, and whatever else gets spilled on hangar floors over the centuries.

Sadly, there was no one there to witness this classic act, for the lead pilot's first trick on beginning his impromptu air show was to release the door handle. Once again the door snapped shut just in time to derail the number two pilot, who, to make up the lost time, was now moving at about fifty knots.

His subsequent ricochet cut off the number two navigator at the knees. Without pausing to apologize, the number two pilot regained his feet, duplicated the number one pilot's one-handed, one-motion grab of the door handle, and shot out the door, describing approximately the same flight path as that of the lead pilot.

Limping somewhat from the earlier collision, the number two navigator approached the obdurate door somewhat circumspectly, and was rewarded—if that is the word I want—with the spectacle of two pilots floundering about in a receding pool of frictionless fluid that was preventing them from doing much in the way of walking and is probably still responsible for several varieties of mutant fish lurking in obscure corners of the Saguenay River.

Meanwhile, the lead navigator, oblivious to the carnage in his wake, had by now reached the far side of the hangar, visions of marauding Badgers, Bisons, and Bears dancing in his head. The shrill ringing of the ops phone was just barely audible over the noise of the klaxon. He picked up the ops phone, fully expecting to hear that World War III was now playing in the nearby sky. "Scramble instructions," he panted, expecting to hear something really intrepid. And he did.

It was the ops officer. "I'm really sorry, guys. I was swinging at a mosquito and I accidentally knocked the scramble horn off its hook. Oh, well," he concluded, "no harm done."

Little did he know.

Scramble scramble

Greg Stevens

In 1980, in the middle of the Cold War, I was a twenty-five-year-old RCAF combat-ready pilot of an Avro Canuck CF–100 All Weather Twin Jet Interceptor. We were stationed temporarily in Newfoundland while the USAF air and ground crews normally located there were in the southern United States converting to more advanced interceptors. Our home base was at North Bay, Ontario, where I had flown many hundreds of hours of training and identification flights together with my radar observer, Don Frederick, and other members of the Black Knight 414 and Porcupine 433 Squadrons. We relied on air and ground radar, and our defensive weapons were rockets that were primitive by today's standards—a single shot of two-inch rockets, fifty-eight in all, carried in two pods on our wing tips.

On alert duty one early morning, the klaxon sounded. Don and I and the other alert crew were scrambled. As we raced to climb into our ejection seats, buckle in, and fire up our engines and equipment, the radios suddenly confirmed that our mission was a rare hot scramble. Together with our wingmate, we taxied at high speed to the armament shack where ground crew waited to rush out and arm our rockets. This was a first time for us, to be armed, as our many previous scrambles had merely been to identify off-course aircraft believed to be passenger planes or to assist pilots lost or in other emergencies.

On takeoff, to our surprise, we were ordered, despite our armed state, to make an immediate 180 degree turn right over the base and the nearby town, "Climb to Angels 40," and then "Buster!" I thrust the throttles forward to their detents, broke the "witness" wires, and then forced the Orenda engines to overspeed as we went for maximum climb to 40,000 feet.

From our radios we could hear more aircrew being called to duty, other bases scrambling aircraft; the Defence Condition escalated from Green to Yellow. Our ground radar controller told us to head east over the Atlantic, and, as we had reached 38,000 feet, we were now beyond gliding distance back to shore. The engines seemed to develop strange noises and I could hear Don's breathing and my own growing more rapid. We were scanning the sky and our radar screens, and our number two was as busy as we were as we flew in loose formation into the sun and out over the cold, dark blue waters we called The Pond.

Our ground controller informed us the target was now directly ahead, 100 miles, angels 42, and strength six. Holy God, I thought, there are six unknowns! This must be "It." We could hear other targets being tracked from Baffin Island to Bermuda. Our number two aircraft was now turned to a reciprocal heading to stay ahead of the targets and to prepare for an attack run, while Don and I, alone now, were ordered in to identify who and what was out there. Then, at fifty miles and closing fast, the order came to arm. Don in the rear seat pushed in firing circuit breakers, and I turned the Guns/Camera switch to rockets, something we had done only in the simulator before. Now we could have one chance to hit at least one of the enemy—if they didn't blast us first.

At thirty miles apart and lumbering along at 44,000 feet, straining to hold our aircraft, still heavy with fuel, from stalling or buffeting, I could make out a wave of approaching contrails. In the past few moments, Don and I had spoken about our families and friends; the possibility of our rockets' missing and whether we could ram the tail of one of the enemy, ejecting at the last moment; and if still alive, would we ever be found in the waters below? And if one or two of the bombers got through, would they be heading for Boston, New York, or Montreal; and with the bombs they dropped, how many would die?

As I followed Don's directions to bring us into an identification run, I could begin to see individual aircraft. We would be helpless if they had missiles ready to fire on us, but perhaps our number two would avenge us! That was the Plan. That was what the training had been all about. One aircraft sacrificed, one crew lost. As we turned inward and closed on the lead unknown, I could see it was a large, multi-jet bomber, but at a mile away, was it an American B–47 or a Russian Badger or Bear? They seemed oblivious to our approach, but we knew they were tracking us on their radars and could see our contrails leading right to us as we bore in.

Suddenly the radio crackled, "Break off, Halfback 10, break off!" Relief flooded our minds as we dove down and away from the group of six jet bombers, put safe the switches and circuit breakers, and turned toward land, home, families, and friends. They were indeed USAF B–47s, flying from Spain to Florida, and the whole exercise over most of the northeast coast had been a test of NORAD's and our readiness.

We slept well that night, but after the RCAF and this particular mission, the rest of my flying, municipal planning, management, and political career has seemed rather tame.[11]

A 409 Squadron mayday

Pat Parker

The memorable trip for Cudgel 16 was on June 27, 1957, in 18434 when we did an air test. On our walk around, we found the battery down and the flaps disconnected. We went to find a mechanic to remedy the problem. After the problem was rectified, we performed another careful walk around and launched under the guidance of Waterfall and a reserve controller. At about 12,000 feet, we were doing a high-speed run when the port cowling tore off and hit the horizontal stabilizer. We flamed out the engine and went to squawk 4 and were able to get only two squawk 4 radar points before losing the IFF. After the mayday call, the reserve controller panicked and could only say "roger."

The weather was undercast, and we hoped for a heading to base, but the controller must have frozen. We finally told him to "Go get F/L MacKenzie, who would be found in the coffee room, and get him on the scope." We finally took a chance and descended through clouds and headed for QQ. The tower had all the fire trucks out.

Meanwhile, we were finding out whether or not the wheels, flaps, and dive brakes would work, and if the hydro boosters were damaged. About four miles out, we told tower that we should make it; so all the fire trucks were recalled, and we were left on our own. When we touched down, the bottom half of the cowling fell off, and we ran over it.

Both Mac [Boyle] and I were unstrapped and had the canopy back by the halfway point on the runway. We jumped off the wing and let the bird carry on.

New life for an Old Bird.

We sat out on the runway for twenty minutes before a pickup came along picking up pieces of a/c. We scrounged a ride to the hangar. Evidently the cowling was fourteen bolts short due to a fubar[12] by maintenance.

QQ's EWU Det . . .[13]

Bob Merrick

Jamming. If you're a jazz musician, jamming is the stuff of life. If you're a Voodoo scope-wizard, jamming can make your scope light up in interesting ways "you have not dreamed of." Electronic countermeasures (ECM) and electronic counter-countermeasures (ECCM) have played an important role in air warfare since WW II. In the mid-1950s, Canada had an impressive air defence system. Although the daily flying training had much merit, it did little to prepare the CF–100 aircrews and the GCI controllers for the "wizard war" tactics and ruses likely to be used by the Soviet long-range air force.

---

11 "Mosquito" and "Scramble" articles originally published in *AirForce* magazine (April 1994); reprinted with permission.
12 Fouled up beyond all repair.
13 Permission granted by Larry Milberry.

In 1955, the RCAF acted to remedy this deficiency. RCAF Station St. Hubert's 104 KU was tasked to modify some of its Dakotas to dispense chaff and provide radio jamming. In the days before data link, GCI control relied on fast, accurate voice links between controller and aircrew. The Dak crews were readily able to disrupt them. However, the Dak did not carry radar jammers, so 104 KU acquired three C–119G Boxcars to dispense chaff, jam radars, and disrupt communications. These aircraft and their crews served splendidly, but they didn't truly simulate the Soviet force, because they were low and slow, unlike the threat, which was high and (relatively) fast.

Attention then turned to converting surplus CF–100 fighters to electronic warfare "bombers." This proved feasible, and 104 KU started to grow. Air Defence Command recognized that electronic warfare warranted a separate unit, and the Electronic Warfare Unit (EWU) was formed at St. Hubert in 1959. As most of Canada's air defence resources were in eastern Canada, St. Hubert was a reasonably central location for the EWU. But at RCAF Station Comox, 409 Squadron was far from the source of ECM training. In 1962, the EWU set up a small detachment at Comox to train 409's crews. For six years, the detachment provided electronic warfare training and other support to 409 Squadron and 25th NORAD region. Contrary to some published reports, it was never a part of 409 Squadron, but it did work closely with the Nighthawks.

Four crews and three CF–100 aircraft comprised the detachment. Each CF–100 had two chaff dispensers, and usually one Clunk "bomber" had an archaic jammer, wherein each tube was personally signed by Tesla himself. It might have given a CF–100 fighter a few problems, but it was no match for the ECCM features in the CF–101. But by ignoring the "fast-tune" mode on his radar, a 101 back-seater could get a reasonable view of how quickly rudimentary noise jamming could obscure a target.

At low levels, twisting and turning around British Columbia's magnificent mountains, an EWO's skilful use of the jammer, combined with artful use of the chaff dispenser, presented the fighter-gator with a confusing radar picture. The ground clutter from the mountains filled the scope, occasional jamming strobes provided conflicting information, and aptly timed chaff bundles often decoyed CF–101 crews.

The detachment's major shortcoming was that it offered no ECM training for the GCI controllers, either at the radar sites or at the SAGE direction centre at McChord AFB. To remedy this, the EWU sent a Mk.VD Clunk to Comox for one week each month, and it merrily lit up airborne and ground-based scopes all over B.C., provided the jammers stayed serviceable.

The usual flying schedule for 409 Squadron required the EWU detachment to fly three target trips daily: two during the day and one at night. Most of the missions were flown in the Comox military flying area, centred roughly on the majestic Mount Waddington. During these missions, the EW crew acted as target for two or three pairs of fighters launched from Comox at forty-five-minute intervals. The crew in the Clunk used at least all the evasive action permitted by ADC rules; judicious chaff-dropping; and such ploys as blowing the Mae West whistle on the tactical frequency to simulate comm jamming. The jammer, if available, was also used. The objective was to simulate a Soviet bomber crew fighting not for its country, but its life.

The detachment also provided targets for NORAD exercises. During these, the Clunks headed north until they hit that magic point where they became Badgers, Bisons, or Bears. Turning south, they attempted to evade, elude, confuse, and disrupt North American air defences. With luck, the exercise planners provided a route that terminated at Hamilton AFB, just north of San Francisco. Normally, however, the crews returned to Comox. Such exercises occurred every couple of weeks or so, and provided a welcome break from the usual Comox target trips.

The 25th NORAD region regularly evaluated its ground environment, and the detachment supported this program. Twice each week, a CF–100 flew specific routes through the region, checking the radar and radio coverage in remote areas.

Occasionally, the detachment was tasked to work with units of the Royal Canadian Navy off the west coast of Vancouver Island. The nautics wanted something that simulated a missile attack on their ships, which required the Clunk to fly low and fast over the water while looking for the ship. As navigation in the Clunk and navigation on the ship tended to be more art form than science, this occasionally led to low-level "scorch-pasts" of ships that had nothing whatever to do with the RCN.

Initially, the detachment had its own servicing crew but this was quickly gobbled up by the base maintenance organization. Despite this loss of identity, there was no loss of sorties. Throughout its existence, the EWU detachment enjoyed the very finest of ground crew support. The detachment seldom had to borrow one of 409 Squadron's T–Birds to fly a scheduled mission.

Major maintenance of the detachment's aircraft was done by EWU at St. Hubert. When it was time to rotate aircraft, a crew from St. Hubert flew the new aircraft as far as Winnipeg and met the Comox crew bringing the time-expired aircraft east. However, when Expo '67 was on, QQ crews happily took over the ferrying burden. This was reciprocated in the winter, when St. Hubert crews, complete with golf clubs, selflessly volunteered to bring the replacement aircraft all the way to Comox.

Late in 1967, EWU faded into history. The aircraft and crews were still there, but they were called 414 (EW) Squadron, as part of a practice that saw the air force hang squadron numbers on virtually any group of aircraft larger than two. In 1968, 414's QQ detachment fell victim to austerity and it faded into history, leaving behind all those chaff-covered mountains.

With my scarf fluttering in the breeze . . .

Vic Rushton

Not everyone has achieved the fighter pilot's dream of cruising along in an open-cockpit fighter, checkered scarf streaming in the breeze . . . wondering what the hell had just happened. My opportunity to do just that happened fifty years ago, when I was a member of 440 Squadron, flying with my nav, F/O Len Mitchell, in CF–100 #332 on a routine air practice air interception mission out of Zweibrucken, Germany. Len was using his AI radar to keep us in the correct position relative to our lead, and I had just finished a routine scan of the Clunk's somewhat unorthodox, but workable, cockpit layout.

We were at 37,000 feet and we were as "ops normal" as it was possible to get. But not for long. Suddenly, there was what seemed to be a humongous explosion, followed by a prolonged, deafening roar. The cockpit filled with debris. Instinctively, my eyes went to the engine gauges. To my surprise, the two Orendas were purring away just as Avro intended they should. There were no excited warning lights spelling out their message of doom.

But the oxygen system seemed to have gone crazy. For whatever reason, I was having grave difficulty exhaling. And, the intercom system was no longer working. What the hell was going on? It was about then I noted that the canopy had departed on its own independent mission, leaving us with but a few sec-

Last CF–100 OTU Course.
Standing, L-R: Barney Hagen, Unknown, Unknown, Dick Borys, Bill Gladders; kneeling, L-R, Brian Smallman–Tew, Sid Popham, Pete Pellow, Unknown, Unknown, Dick Lidstone.

"Last Post" for the CF-100; the glory days are over!

onds to get down to where oxygen would be the least of our worries.

Rather than exulting in the thrill of open-cockpit flying, I slapped the throttles to idle, popped the boards, and began an immediate, very steep descent, mixed with a left turn that would take us to Marville, where another Clunk squadron lived. It would also take us to the limiting mach, which would make the aircraft do interesting — but controllable — things.

The oxygen content gauge was descending almost as fast as we were, but it seemed that we would be below 10,000 feet before it reached zero. There was a small hole in the clouds. Very soon, we were at 2,000 feet, still without much in the way of intercom or radios. Was Len still aboard? I looked back, and sure enough, the white helmet was still aboard. He was industriously dialling in the Marville beacon to expedite our landing there.

Once in the circuit, we flew by the tower, and the controller responded with green lights and flares. We parked in front of the tower, where the maintenance crews examined the plane and pronounced it fit for a "one-time," low-level flight back to Zwei, escorted by Reg Froom and Jerry Ovington, who had been sent to shepherd us home. But they didn't have their scarves fluttering in the breeze, like the fighter pilots of old. We did.

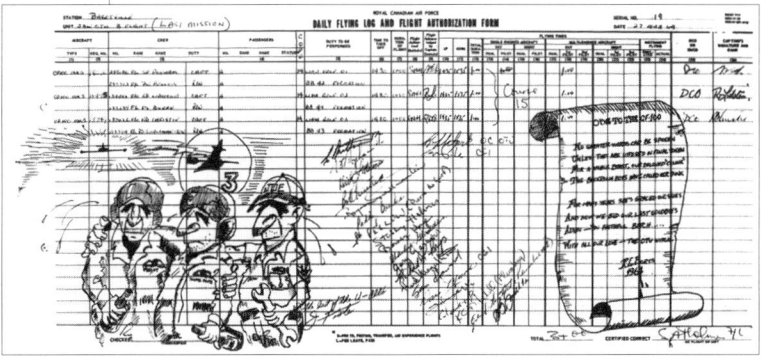

Newbie pilot's logbook for the last flight,
CF–100 OTU, May 1964.

PART TWO
ODD JOBS

The Totem Times[14]
Various Authors

The RCAF/CFB Comox paper (*The Totem Times*) has, for a number of generations, been one of the Canadian military's premier base papers, and 409 Squadron's contribution ("Night Hawk's Nest") was, for approximately twenty-nine years, a major addition to the paper. The quality of the following arbitrary excerpts from "Night Hawk's Nest" columns speaks for itself.

1. Several more crews have escaped from the deep freeze at Beyondville to become inhabitants of the Nest. Ernie Pool, a navigator, who traded in his brain for a set of pilot's wings, and Lynn Wagar, who escaped from ADCHQ, are currently undergoing the tender ministrations of the Olsen and Williams simulator comedy act, along with Erwin Sippert and Hughie Fischer. Fischer, being a transported nautic, does not carry a drag chute in his Voodoo, preferring to rely instead on an anchor.

2. The squadron fund superintendent, Bill Bland, who has oft been accused of financing his household with fund revenue, became the fair-haired boy of the squadron recently when he scrounged a host of Voodoo models from the McDonnell Corporation. It is encouraging to see that McDonnell still feels that it is worthwhile to do PR work in Canada. Maybe there is still hope for the F–4.

3. Carolyn Marie Liddiard arrived early Monday morning, and at 8 lbs. 4 oz. she is almost as big as Gary. Congratulations. **(09/01/69)**

4. Early in February, Beetle MacLeod and Bill Bland will head for Sardinia and the Sea Survival Course. The Department of External Affairs has not as yet issued a statement saying how pleased it is to have such brilliant ambassadors represent the country. Later in the month, Major Morrison and Len Dodd will embark upon the same course. The Department has not commented on this, either, preferring instead to lapse into hysteria. Major Mo says that he is going along to look after Len, which brings to mind the old proverb about sending a wolf to look after a bunch of sheep.

5. Fred Williams is being sent to Winnipeg, where the temperature will further petrify his already atrophied mind. He will take the Advanced Radio Nav Course, and his absence from the squadron will perhaps enable the rest of us to get some flying time. Upon his return he will tell us all about the obliquity of the ecliptic, and how to take a three-star fix from a Voodoo.

6. Brodie Templeton returned from the Weapons Course a couple of weeks ago and because he is

---
14 Published with permission from *The Totem Times*.

now so skilled and brilliant, he is allowed to hold alert. He is also allowed to play defence in front of Stonewall O'Sullivan, which gives Brodie a lot of love.

7. Hugh Fischer's transfer to the West Coast a couple of weeks ago has given him an opportunity to take up a new hobby: Furniture Buying. It is not something that he did very often before, but until the movers burned most of his furniture, he didn't have to, either.

8. Ernie Poole has caused a great deal of unease among the suspicious members of the navigator's union. The shop steward was last seen drawing up a manifesto that, among other things, will forbid him to cluck derisively when some back-seat driver fails to see a super—if such a thing ever happens—and generally prevent him from uttering disparaging remarks about any navigators anywhere.

9. Boom-Boom Little has been given a navigator of his very own, a development which makes Ron think that he should occasionally go flying. However, the nav, Lynn Wagar, has been taken over by Dale Northrup, while his nav, Don Marion, moulders in Staff School, and so Ron is left to rot in the CAC. Maybe next year . . .

10. Speculation of the Week: Right after the French announced that they were selling the Maginot Line, the CDS showed up in Paris for negotiations. Could there be some connection? Will we replace the DEW Line with the Maginot Line? Tune in next week for the next thrilling instalment. **(23/01/69)**

11. Les Putland, who is chronically unable to spell "lieutenant," was promoted to captain, so he will no longer have to do so. There is, however, no guarantee that he can spell that either. Les celebrated the occasion with a wild night in the barn, which seems a magnificent reward.

12. The ex-colonel of the regiment, the old Grey Fox himself, paid a visit to the squadron last week, a fact which so dazzled the troops that most of them appeared in sunglasses the next day. This apparently had something to do with a successful revival meeting during the evening, as most of the celebrants were heard muttering, "Oh my God."

13. Harry Redden astonished everyone by walking in twenty minutes early for an 1100 o'clock briefing the other day. When questioned on this shocking display of punctuality, Harry blushed and said, "Actually, I thought the briefing was at 0700." **(06/02/69)**

14. Last week's Felix Echo exercise was, in stark contrast, a faint echo of what an exercise should be. It featured the maximum number of air and ground crews sitting around for the longest possible time before embarking beyond the minimum possible amount of flying. Gary Liddiard, the resident CAC Genius, was even called upon to invent a couple of targets so that some of the crews would have a chance to fly.

15. The other day, the colonel was complaining about an unsightly heap of paper in one of the offices and he asked the cleaner to remove it. It took the cleaner thirty-five minutes to get to the bottom of the pile, and when he got there, he found Major Sterne, still writing,

16. Paddy O'Sullivan was complaining during one of the recent exercises that he hadn't been allotted a pilot; just Ernie Poole. Ernie readily admitted he might have some defects. "After all," he said, "I've been trying to train O'Sullivan for ten years and he still doesn't know anything."

17 The sports program will take a quantum leap backward this Friday as the pilots tackle the navs in the annual hockey game. Coaches Harry Chapin and Paddy O'Sullivan are both outwardly exuding confidence and prattling on about decisive victory and all that. Inwardly, however, they both feel that no coach has ever been dealt such poor material, and neither one expects to have his contract renewed next year. In fact, neither one *wants* to have his contract renewed next year.

18 Rhiney Koehn is paying a visit to the squadron just now. He returned all fresh and happy from his visit to the continent, was introduced to the crews who have joined the unit during the past six months or so, and even flew a trip or two. Soon, however, he will be gone again, as he is being sent to Charm School in Toronto to pick up some of the couth and culture that he has missed over the years.

19 Vic Rushton is the manufacturer's representative for a new game designed expressly for pilots. It's a one-piece jigsaw puzzle. His only problem is to phrase the instructions in terms so simple that a pilot can understand them.

20 And, this last item: The squadron is taking up a collection to buy a hearing aid for the BAMEO, who lost his hearing while running around the flight line without his ear defenders. Tut-tut. **(20/02/69)**

21 Speaking of the Tac-Eval, it was a great success, apart from Beetle's simulated posthumous DFC. The hack rate was just great, the troops flew safely, and all was well with the world.

22 Above all, the day belonged to the ground crews. The squadron flew a staggering number of sorties during the wartime day, with very few snags. Unserviceabilities that cropped up during the day were always cleared very rapidly. The recovery rate at the end of the exercise was nothing short of miraculous, with all aircraft serviceable in less than one-third the allotted time. All in all, it was a splendid performance by the best ground crew in the Canadian Forces, and they deserve every congratulation for their effort.

23 The big switch is on in CAC. John Emon, Ron Little, and Gary Liddiard have all been paroled back to their flights, while Paddy O'Sullivan, Bob Barr, and Les Putland have been incarcerated in CAC. With that dazzling array of talent, the morning briefings should resemble a poor man's *Laugh-In*, except that Bob Barr can scarcely be called an improvement upon Ruth Buzzi. Come to think of it, Bob Barr can't even be called an improvement on Ron Little.

24 Rumour of the Week: The new gold-encrusted junior officers' caps cannot be worn or stored in aircraft, as batteries for them have a warping effect on compasses. If a senior officer comes aboard, complete with cap, the compass must be swung. **(20/03/69)**

25 Some new bods have arrived to bolster the strength of A Flight. Guy Sullivan, who has been kicking around the system for longer than there has been a system, will eventually take over as nav-dad of A Flight. He is admirably suited for this task, as he has an even longer forehead than the present incumbent, if such a thing is possible. Rudy Witthoeft has also escaped the clutches of Beyondville, and his presence on the flight will enable Bun-Bun to feel senior to someone. Not superior, just senior. **(03/04/69)**

26 Hugh Fischer, the navy's retaliation for the air force unification scheme, has discovered an unbeatable way of getting off the alert schedule. It's called, "Let's just stop in Gimli for half an hour

and stay a week." Works, too, but it drives flight commanders and schedulers mad, or it would do so if it were not their usual state.

27 Anyhow, Hugh eventually returned, and was thrown into solitary confinement in the Q for his troubles. He was also scheduled for the simulator, which he tried to have cancelled as a cruel and unusual punishment, but it didn't work.

28 Don Marion has returned from Staff School and is now running around telling people to be specific, using two-syllable words, and generally acting educated. Sure gets the lights out early at night, though. It must have been a tiring course.

29 The promotion system is not perfect. Word has come through that Bun-Bun will no longer be a balloon, but will be a captain instead. Apparently this was done at the request of the rest of the balloons, who felt that Bun-Bun was giving them a bad name. Congratulations.

30 Another nautic has arrived on the squadron, which is still reeling from the impact of the first one. John Clarke has been sprung from the frozen reaches of Beyondville to take his place on the Nighthawk flight line.

31 For the past couple of years, Pete Armour has been trying to grow a moustache. He has finally been rewarded by a barely discernable shadow on his upper lip, and felt quite good about the whole thing until grumpy old Len Dodd told him to wash his face. **(17/04/69)**

32 The social event of the year occurred last Friday for the Nighthawks when they celebrated family day. All the wives were invited to tour the squadron, and most of them turned up, which vastly improved the drab scenery. Following some spellbinding briefings, the wives were treated to a tour of the simulator, watched a demonstration scramble, and observed all the other things that makes life on an interceptor squadron great.

33 Some of the long-awaited transfers have started to roll in. Len Dodd has been assigned to the Kingdom of the Saguenay, and he will arrive there just in time to write the new Quebec driver's test. In years past, the first question used to be, "What are the three most important parts of the *voiture*? The correct answer was, of course, "The horn, the gas pedal and the St. Christopher medal." Thanks to some interference from Rome, millions of drivers' tests will now have to be scrapped.

34 The superintendent of the links, Bob Sherratt, will also be leaving the confines of the Nest this summer. His brilliant abilities as a golf course designer have come to the attention of higher headquarters, and he will be given a job building a twenty-eight-hole golf course somewhere around North Bay. To drill the holes, he will be allowed to use the warheads from the Bomarcs that opposition politicians keep scrapping.

35 In his spare time, Bob will be working in the personnel shop at North Bay, which came as a shock to many people who didn't even know that one existed. He figures that if he wears his golf shoes to work once a week, he will be able to punch out an entire week's supply of computer cards at once and still have time left for fishing. **(15/05/69)**

36 This week sees the start of formation season, and Nighthawk crews will be practising operating their great fire-breathing steeds in close proximity to one another. Local druggists always know when this is to occur, as there is a marked increase in the number of navigators coming in and asking for tranquilizers or, in extreme cases, blindfolds. It is hoped to get four airplanes going

the same way the same day on Friday to mark a graduation ceremony at Royal Roads.

37 Fresh from its overwhelming success in one practice, the squadron softball team is lurching into yet another season. Henry and Bun-Bun look to be logical contenders for the Rookie of the Year award, and John Larrison will undoubtedly receive some sort of an award for his convincing imitation of a medicine ball. Bill Bland will take the pitching championship easily if he can come up with a pitch that doesn't bounce five times on the way to the plate. In the first game of the season, the Nighthawks waxed a group of high-priced American imports 6 to 5. Scouts for the American and National Leagues were in attendance, but were unavailable for comments, as they were busy being sick. **(25/05/69)**

38 Transfers and their associated mug parties are a large part of the gala Nighthawk social whirl these days. Leonardo De Dodd received his mug at a small gathering recently, and to the stunned incredulity of everyone present, he refrained from hurling any insults whatever, which shows that the age of miracles is not as dormant as the Church would have us believe. At the same gathering, Swede Larsen also received a mug, and he too refrained from hurling any insults, but that isn't even a minor miracle, as he doesn't take off as Command Flight Safety Officer until he gets to North Bay and is not expected to hurl insults until then.

39 The squadron celebrated last Saturday by holding a family day at air force beach. All the crews, their wives, and approximately four million children attended, and who was it that said ping-pong was the most popular indoor sport on the squadron? It was a fun affair indeed, and the organizers are to be commended for thinking it up.

40 After the bash, one prominent anchor-clanker was seen sedately driving his square-back sedan into the QRA, but he managed to go hard astern, or however it is they run their boats, and beat to windward before the gunrunners could get to him. That's what comes of inviting a navy type to an air force beach.

41 Several new bods have reported in lately and are already combat ready, which shows just how far behind this column is. Doug Stuart, who made the jump from back seat to front seat, and his wife, June, arrived about a month or so ago, and Doug Munro, along with his wife, Adele, arrived for his second tour as a Nighthawk. Tats and Pat Sakamoto have also arrived to further complicate the housing market. **(26/06/69).**

42 Major Mo is still accepting plaudits for the rather unusual flypast that he staged over Lewis Park on Dominion Day. The different formation was the result of "Lewis Park is on that side—no, by God, it's on *that* side—hey, by George, there it is right there!" or something of that nature. At any rate, the lead nav, Doug Munro, was heard to say after the trip, "So *that's* where Vancouver Island is. I always wondered."

43 Guy Sullivan has gone to pick up his family, which should ease the strain on T–Bird hours somewhat. He will be moving into the Dodd Estate, while the owner is cementing bicultural relations in Beyondville. A recent message from the St. Jean Baptiste Society said, "We don't mind you opposing the official languages bill, but did you have to oppose it with Dodd?"

44 Ken Driscoll is still working on his combat ready training, which is coming along a lot more quickly now that he is allowed to fly. He says that although flying with all the ropiest pilots on the squadron terrifies him, it is better than putting

up with Clomp-Stomp Goski in the simulator. **(10/07/69)**

45 The Nest and all Hawks send out a big welcome to Captain Pete Dunda, his wife, Susan, and their two children. Pete is our new exchange navigator from the USAF and comes to us from K.I. Sawyer AFB. Even after two days on the base, Pete marvelled at the vast difference in operating procedures between the two air forces. I'm not sure whether it was a compliment or suspicions confirmed. The squadron contingent has returned from Colorado Springs where it was involved in a fly-by in honour of General Reeves, who was retiring. The crew leading the formation was Major Sam Skinner and Bill Bland. The remaining crews were George McAffer and Brodie Templeton; Don Elphick and Lynn Wagar; Bob Olson and Fred Williams; and Dale Northrup and Don Marion. **(07/08/69)**

46 The Hawks must send out a big thank you to Tats and Pat Sakamoto for the tremendous job of decorating the alert truck. Everyone wasn't completely pleased, since both sides were in English.

47 It is indeed unfortunate that space is running out. Unfortunate because I can't relate the story of how Dale Northrup went on leave and managed to leave Marilyn's clothes at home. Perhaps in a later edition . . .

48 COMMENT OF THE WEEK. Harry Redden, who recently returned from his honeymoon, "No, I'm going straight home, but if I really wanted a beer I'd go to the mess." **(04/09/69)**

49 Many exciting exercises have taken place since the last column assailed unwary readers. Only last week, three thrillers burst upon the squadron, and, to paraphrase Churchill (Ebenezer Churchill, the sage of Swayback, Saskatchewan), "Never were so many called in by so few to do so little." Why sit around home watching TV when you can do it just as well at the squadron and watch all those targets take off to boot?

50 Safari Chapin, the terror of wildlife on several continents and a few oceans, managed to bag himself a deer this year, at a cost, had he to buy it at a butcher shop, only less than that of gold. The fowling piece employed by the intrepid Chapin was none other than his trusty 1969 400-calibre Buick, which does an impressive job on a deer. Harry's impressive hack rate followed hard on the heels of some impassioned oratory by the colonel of the regiment, which proves that either Harry sleeps through lectures, or the colonel does not write inspiring speeches.

51 Mice have been reported in the QRA, and ADC's finest lost no time in getting after them. Accompanying the mousetraps were some very explicit instructions for their use, including the suggestion that walnuts be used for bait. This prompted the DAO of the day, Guy Sullivan, to rebel. Said Guy, "As a very senior captain, I get paid peanuts. Why should a mouse get walnuts?" Anyhow, the number of catches logged by the traps has been small. In fact, the only thing caught so far has been Fred Williams, who has occasionally been called a rat but never a mouse. **(18/09/69)**

52 Doug Munro and Guy Sullivan persist with their ground school program, and for those who complain that it isn't needed they have instituted an exam program to prove that it is. While the marks obtained have not always been that good, it is only because Munro and Sullivan are tough markers. We hope.

53 Churnaway Chapin, the poor man's Mario Andretti, is having trouble with his bomb. It seems it came with a lead-lined gas pedal that keeps

it hurtling along several Mach numbers above those recommended by highway engineers.

54 There is the prospect of yet another new car adorning the squadron parking lot. Henry Dielwart, the Nighthawk's Gomer Pyle, is in the market for a set of wheels (no, no, not training wheels) now that he has his driver's licence, and insurance men everywhere are busily adjusting their rates upward because of it. When Henry finally gets his car, we will be advised by Disaster Control.

55 In a frantic attempt to beat the cost of living, John Clark sent his dog out to poach some deer, which is different, by the way, than poaching eggs. The only thing the dog managed to flush out was a game warden, who was not amused by the situation. John is now training the dog to steal grocery bags from unlocked cars.

56 Major Mo, Doug Munro, Doug Stuart, and Pete Dunda went to Hill AFB for a weekend and attempted to join the Mormon Tabernacle Choir. Apparently the choir was not quite ready for three Canadian accents, as well as one incoherent American accent, so they pressed on to Las Vegas, where they preached several sermons on the evils of gambling. They were politely told to take their Socred policies back home.

57 Tom and Laura Murray are still looking for suitable accommodation, which is a difficult thing to find when one has eight children, as Tom and Laura have. The last suitable place, the Riverside Hotel, burned down a couple of years ago. Perhaps they could make the government a suitable offer for the Bonaventure.

58 The Metropolitan Opera Company has signed Bob Barr as a soprano. Their talent scouts were listening out the other night when Bob had a double generator failure, which he announced to the control agency in C above high C. Actually, having all the lights go out like that didn't bother Bob, because, as he said, "Who has their eyes open, anyway?" **(02/10/69)**

59 The pay raise that was announced last week certainly overburdened the phone lines, what with all the wealthy captains and sergeants phoning their stockbrokers, and all the impoverished balloons phoning their friendly loan sharks. The announcement of the pay adjustments came just in time to ensure that Henry Dielwart will spend the next three years barely above the poverty level. It seems that Henry bought himself a car, and while he hasn't told anyone where he bought it, the dealer shouldn't be that hard to find—it's that dealership which has been closed for the past week because the entire staff has been out celebrating. Henry might not have got more money than he expected, but the dealer did.

60 The sartorial star of the March to Misery that was staged on the runway last week just had to be Ankles Kinney, who, in a fit of preparedness, had brought along one pair of gym shorts, one gym sweater, and no running shoes. Consequently, he went rambling down the runway in his gym costume and his winter flying boots, a combination so remarkable that it caused a passing Argus to backfire.

61 It was not the speediest march that has ever been staged down the runway. The Rec Centre staff, which had turned out equipped with the latest in stopwatches and electronic timing devices, soon packed them in and began using the only instrument that really mattered: a calendar.

62 The new quick-release boxes, which were out here on a trial basis, have returned whence they came and no one particularly mourns their

demise. It's too bad that the ingenuity that went into them couldn't instead have been applied to some form of riser release, combined with a tree-lowering device. Variations on an old theme, apparently, pass for improvements these days.

63 Tom Murray has found a place to pitch his tent, or tents. After searching for a lengthy period, he was able to find accommodation for his brood down at Union Bay. To save driving home, he plans to eject over the homestead on his last sortie each day. On Friday nights, many of us might well be advised to adopt such a practice. **(16/10/69)**

64 Bun-Bun the mighty hunter tracked down a deer the other week. Being a true sportsman, Bun wouldn't use anything like a gun, which might give him an unfair advantage. Rather, he used his car, which makes matters a tad more difficult. However, once he gets a deer in his hood ornament, Bun brings him down.

65 Both readers of this column have noted that the arrival of Don Middleton has been kept a secret. Actually, it was played that way. Don was willing to pay good money to keep his name out of such a lowbrow publication, but this week his payment was late. Welcome aboard, Don and Pat. **(30/10/69)**

66 Rhiney Koehn, the OC of Ghost Flight, is back in Comox between TD trips. His next stint of TD has not been announced as yet, but he will undoubtedly be going somewhere soon. He has it all planned that he appears, writes one or two controversial editorials, and disappears before the rockets return.

67 Vern Barker, who traded his hand control for a throttle, has been paroled from Training Command and will be flying T–Birds here for a while before attending the Voodoo course. Also coming to the Rushton–Taylor T–Bird kingdom is Dave McNair, another reformed nav who sold his soul for an extra fifty dollars monthly, and Don Leonard, who comes to us directly from the pipeline. Welcome aboard, guys. It's better to be a target here than almost anywhere else — or so goes the gospel according to Rushton. **(13/11/69)**

68 Tats Sakamoto and Don Kinney have returned from Sardinia, having passed the sea survival course by failing to drown. Henry Dielwart also failed to drown, and was packed off into the woods around Edmonton for his effrontery. Wherever he goes, an automobile finance company man goes with him, so it is hard times for the finance industry these days.

69 In a rare burst of kindness, the squadron commander, concerned about the effect the rising cost of living has been having on his troops, designed a schedule that had them all flying over the supper hour, thereby cutting their cost of living by one-third. It didn't sell, however, and now people living near the base will not have their dinnertime music drowned out by the sound of rampaging Voodoos. It will be difficult indeed to get used to eating three meals a day again. **(27/11/69)**

70 Another exciting Cudgel Caper has faded into history, and the squadron's servicing and maintenance organization did itself real proud. At the end of the day, which wasn't all that late, the squadron had flown the planned number of stories, and there was never any shortage of airplanes. It is a peculiar thing that each year, the exercises stay the same size, and the number of people we have on the flight line decreases. Despite this, the job gets done, and one wonders how? The ground crew make a great number of

sacrifices, as shown by this exchange heard on the flight line: "Hey Warrant, I don't mind having only five minutes for lunch, but—" "Good, good," interrupted the Warrant officer, "then you won't mind having only three minutes for supper." Next year, one supposes, he won't have any lunch at all. At any rate, it was an excellent exercise, made possible by the ground crew who came in at an ungodly hour and stayed around until another ungodly hour and scarcely stopped in between. Well done, gentlemen.

Where have all the leaders gone?

Doug Munro

Long time passing. As a learned judge once said regarding pornography: "I don't know how to describe it but I know it when I see it." Legions of wise men have attempted to define effective leadership. "Leadership is action, not position." (D.H. McGannon) "No man will make a great leader who wants to do it all himself or to get all the credit for doing it." (Andrew Carnegie) "The best executive is the one who has sense enough to pick good men to do what he wants done, and self restraint enough to keep from meddling with them while they do it." (Theodore Roosevelt) "Trust is the emotional glue that binds followers and leaders together." (Warren Bennis and Bert Nanus) "The higher a man climbs, the more his rear is exposed." (Joe Stillwell) "The first method of estimating the intelligence of a ruler is to look at the men he has around him." (Machiavelli) Every Canadian military officer, present, past, or future, fits—or, sadly, fails to fit—these definitions.

It can be argued that for the past twenty years or so the Canadian Forces have, with some rare and welcome exceptions, been bereft of outstanding leaders. Sadly, the motto "Watch your six o'clock" is too often replaced with "Cover your six o'clock." It wasn't always "better in the good old days," but you might wish to judge for yourself!

In the early 1970s, I had the privilege of escorting the National Defense College (NDC) when they made their annual pilgrimage to the centre of the universe—Washington, D.C. The late BGen C.H. "Cam" Mussels was in charge of NDC.

During a Pentagon briefing, General Ryan, Chief of the USAF, addressed the NDC students and staff as follows: "I want to tell you a little story about your leader. During the Korean War, Cam and I were COs of transport squadrons at McChord Air Force Base (W/C Mussels was then CO of 426 Squadron). All units were short of everything, including food, accommodation, and motor transport. Cam solved the latter problem in his usual straightforward fashion. He cornered the young flying officer in charge of the imprest and ordered him to go into Tacoma and buy a bus. The young officer, who quite correctly questioned the propriety of such a purchase, was asked whether or not he recognized a direct order when he heard one. A bus was duly purchased, and, to make matters worse, when they were done with it, they sold it at a profit."

In the late 1950s, "Cam" Mussels was CO of RCAF Station Uplands. One bright and sunny morning, the phone rang in the Base Supply Section. The corporal who answered the phone heard a voice say, "G/C Mussels here." Corporal Gonzplotz, the butt of numerous friendly pranks, was not going to be fooled again. He responded, "AF*** you" and hung up. Two minutes later, his sergeant told him, "Climb into your best blues and report to the base commander's office immediately."

Moving at warp speed, the panic-stricken corporal raced to the barracks, changed uniforms, and skidded to a halt before the CO's secretary. "Have a seat, Corporal." He sat. Some three hours later, the CO's office door opened, the G/C emerged, advised his secretary that he was off to lunch, and departed the fix.15 The corporal continued to sit. At 1330, the CO reappeared and stomped into his office, slamming the door behind him. At 1630, the office door opened once more. Cam headed for the outside world, reached the door, wheeled around, stared at the corporal, said "AF*** you, too," and disappeared into the sunset.

Cam — or, if you prefer, "Muss" — was a regular attendee at Friday night Beer Call. Junior officers, while not actually recruited to tell him how to run his base, were afforded considerable latitude in that regard. On the evening in question, a 428 AW(F) Squadron navigator, one John Kuzyk by name, well into the suds, had his finger firmly buried in the G/C's chest and was studiously advising the base commander of his many personal and professional shortcomings. Early next morning, our hero was fitfully tossing and turning in his bed in the barracks when some sixth sense (there is some question if he had the other five) jolted him awake. Seated by the head of his bed was the G/C, who greeted him with the following question: "You were saying, John?"

In the late 1950s, G/C Bob Miller was posted into RCAF Comox as CO. He was a radio officer who had trained and served during WW II as an air gunner. In the '50s, a non-pilot commanding a flying base was as rare as a virgin birth. His appointment was clearly an error but a most fortuitous one indeed. He spent the better part of two weeks familiarizing himself with his base and its workings. He then called a section head meeting and, legend has it, it went something like this.

Turning to the Station Supply Officer, he advised him that Clothing Stores would be open for issue and return Monday to Friday from 0830 to 1630. They could close one day a month for stock-taking. (Previously, Clothing Stores had been open from 1100 to 1200 two days a week and closed for an extended period of time every week for stock-taking. Issuance of new flying clothing was so restricted that 409 crews habitually drove their Clunks to RCAF Station Cold Lake on a morning mission, traded in their tatty flying suits at Base Supply, ate lunch at the officers' mess, and then flew home.)

The Accounts Section came next. The pay wicket was historically open one day a week, between 1100 and 1200 for payment of travel claims, and the same hours, two days a week, for casual pay parades, travel advances, and the like. The G/C advised Accounts that they would be open five days a week, eight hours a day, for travel advances, casual pay parades, or whatever.

All the other major sections on the base were subjected to a similar briefing. He then told them that they were free to question his instructions but they should bear in mind that if they felt unable to comply, he was certain their replacement could. In a few short days, RCAF Comox was running like the proverbial clock.

In the early '50s, on a mid-winter day, a reasonable facsimile of the following memo appeared on the RCAF Station Greenwood officers' mess notice board. "It has come to my attention that certain of my officers have been taking out my airwomen. It has also come to my attention that they have been picking them up outside the Station gate and dropping them off outside the gate. In future, you will

---

15 "Departed the fix" is a navigational term that means a specific aircraft has now departed the navigational fix to which it has been cleared; in time, it was occasionally expanded to include the movements of a navigator — it was one of those expressions that made one sound like an aviator.

behave like gentlemen—you will pick them up at their barracks and drop them off at their barracks. Signed G/C 'NSA' Base Commander."

Certain squadron commanders demonstrated an abundance of intestinal fortitude which, while it might not have endeared them to their superiors, earned them unswerving loyalty from their squadron members. W/C J.R.D. "Bob" Braham led 432 AW (F) Squadron at RCAF Station Bagotville in the late '50s. One of his pilots, while conducting an external inspection for a routine mission, discovered a loose tip tank cap. He borrowed a screwdriver from one of the ground crew, tightened the cap, and went flying. Unfortunately, one of the tip tanks wouldn't feed, and rather than chance ruining his day by crashing, he jettisoned the tanks, returned home, and landed.

A routine incident report was duly sent to the rocket scientists in Air Defence Command's flight safety shop. Bent on getting to the bottom of this dastardly deed, the FS *wallahs* fired a twenty-question rocket off to 432. The first two questions set the tone of their investigation: "What tool did the pilot use to tighten the tip tank cap? Is it common practice, on your squadron, for the aircrew to do the ground crew's job?" Etc., etc., *ad nauseam*. Your scribe had the pleasure of seeing W/C Braham's response: "The tool he used was a screwdriver. His squadron commander would have done the same thing."

Creative supervision wasn't the exclusive purview of base or squadron commanders. Whether the following qualifies as effective leadership is in the eye of the beholder—or the victim.

One dark and windy night, a 426 Squadron North Star was clawing its noisy way across the North Atlantic. Among the full complement of passengers lurked the then Air Officer Commanding (AOC) of Transport Command. Among his many charming traits was a chronic addiction to contract bridge.

"Bloody boring; let's play bridge." Fortune smiles on the Godly; he quickly located two helpless junior officers who had previously enjoyed a few rubbers with him, but unfortunately none of the other passengers would even admit that they had ever seen a deck of cards. Not one to be easily thwarted, he rumbled into the cockpit, cornered the navigator, who was in the middle of a three-star fix, and demanded, "Do you play bridge?" Not as alert as he might otherwise have been, he confessed that he did.

Back into the passenger compartment swept the air commodore. He quickly located a young flying officer wearing navigator's wings and bellowed, "Get your ass into the cockpit and navigate this aircraft!"

"But sir, I've never been in a North Star before."

"You can take that as an order."

Fortunately, if one heads slightly north of east, there is every chance that he'll eventually hit the UK or, alternatively, the coast of France. The bridge game was a roaring success, and the aircraft landed safely at Prestwick.

On at least one occasion, this very senior officer was on the receiving end of very creative leadership ladled out by a senior flying officer. The AOC was a passenger on one of his C–47s en route to RCAF Station Rockcliffe. The aircraft was on short final when the AOC happened into the cockpit to see how his troops were doing. The aircraft commander, one "Barn Smell" by name (a nickname that reflected his manner of dress rather than any noxious odours he might have emitted), was at the throttle, with a junior pilot in the right-hand seat. As was his habit, a cigarette glowed merrily in his mouth—he smoked everywhere! Recognizing a rule infraction when he saw one, the AOC plucked the cigarette out of Barn Smell's mouth and ground it out on the cabin floor. Barn Smell never dropped a stitch. He overshot, lit another cigarette, turned to the co-pilot and said:

"Keep the passengers in the back." This was undoubtedly a CLM (Career Limiting Move), even in the laissez-faire world of the '50s.

In January 1953, a shiny, new, and very young pilot officer asked to sit in at a nickel/dime poker game in the Greenwood officers' mess. He occupied an empty seat beside and behind a very distinguished-looking W/C. Dame Fortune smiled on the newcomer—he won the next three hands.

    The WingCo turned to the upstart and asked, "What's your name?"

    "Munro, sir."

    "Get out of the @#$%%^ game, Munro."

    Munro got!

If you aspire to lead, you may find the first paragraph of this article helpful. Fear not, for if you aren't successful, there is always a career with Transport Canada—right, Barn Smell?

Aerial buffoonery

Doug Munro

There is nothing even mildly amusing about an aircraft accident or incident involving personal injury or loss of life. However, over the past four decades an amazing variety of RCAF/CAF aircrew have performed injury-free feats of aerial derring-do that would make the most jaded flight safety officer blanch and in the process have provided an endless source of "You'll never guess what old Hot-Shot did!" These numerous occurrences, involving minimum skill and judgment and maximum luck, are connected by a central thread best summarized in a Personal Assessment once written on a young Sabre pilot:

"Flying Officer Gonsplotz is an outstanding officer above 30,000 feet—he should never be allowed to come below."

The following incidents are true; only the names have been changed to protect the guilty.

In the midst of an otherwise dull mess function at RCAF Station Penhold, Alberta, two young Harvard instructors decided to take their dates for a ride in a Harvard. So they did: two in the front seat and two in the back.

Speaking of Harvards, in the early fifties, Training Command had an annoying requirement that Flying Training School (FTS) instructors log a certain amount of "dual" with their colleagues. Two rather creative instructors at RCAF Station Claresholm, Alberta, solved this minor irritant by signing out a Yellow Peril late in the a.m., repairing to the mess for a couple of lunchtime lagers and signing the aircraft back in after lunch. Legend has it that they quietly abandoned this charade when one Flight Cadet J.T. Price (so some of the names have been changed), at his Wings Graduation, advised the schemers that he'd been flying the aircraft for them over the noon hour.

It was a dark and windy night over Lake Superior when a C-45 experienced a complete electrical failure. Occasionally, aircrew have been known to carry a flashlight when night flying, but not this pair of front-office aces. Their lack of planning did not diminish their creative juice. Undiluted panic being the mother of invention, the captain "jury-rigged" a cockpit light by soaking the water-soluble battery from his Mae West in a carton of milk skilfully rescued from one of the ever-present and always delicious box lunches. He completed the trip into RCAF Station Downsview with the cockpit illuminated by the dim light from the Mae West skullcap clamped firmly to his equally dim head.

And how about the ex-WW II staff pilot at 2 Air Navigation School, RCAF Station Winnipeg, who magnanimously consented to take his neighbour, his neighbour's son, and their Labrador retriever—and, of course, the two nav students—on a night navigation detail in his trusty Bug Smasher. All went well (one is tempted to say swimmingly) until both engines quit, more or less simultaneously, over Dafoe, Saskatchewan. The nose tank, perchance? Not this time. Frantic efforts, with the neighbour manning the wobble pump, failed to revive the Pratt & Whitneys. Fortunately, F/L "H Hyphen H" was as skilled as he was careless. By the light of a full moon, "H" performed a flawless forced landing (ditching) in the shallow, muddy waters of Big Quill Lake. After ensuring that his passengers and fellow crew members were clear of the aircraft, he performed one small post-crash task—he reached over and turned on the carburettor heat. As he explained to his mates at Beer Call, "Probably water in the gas—no point in confusing the investigators."

It would be unfair to leave the impression that pilots are the sole authors of accidents and incidents—occasionally they have a little help from their friends.

Within hours of being advised by the then Air Officer Commanding, Maritime Air Command, one Air Commodore Costello, that the first person to "write off" one of MARCOM's new Neptunes was to "head for open water and walk until his hat floats," the inevitable happened. An RCAF Station Greenwood crew on its takeoff roll at Resolute Bay, N.W.T., became prematurely airborne when the aircraft bounced over a culvert located near the midpoint of the gravel runway. The flight engineer, whose reflexes far exceeded his airmanship, raised the undercarriage. Lacking flying speed, the Neptune sank gracefully among the stones and skidded to a halt beside the gas compound. The captain was heard to mutter: "Should I wear my old or my new hat?"

Speaking of MARCOM, a 407 Squadron navigator, during an external inspection prior to a Bombing and Gunnery exercise, spotted what he took to be loose wires hanging from the bomb bay of his Lancaster. Turning to an armament leading aircraftsman standing nearby, Old Sharp Eyes ordered the young airman to "plug in all those loose wires." Mild protests met with that very logical inter-rank conversation stopper: "Count the stripes." The LAC plugged in all the loose wires.

All went reasonably well until the first bombing run. The radio officer dropped a smoke float (the target), and the second navigator selected two bombs for Run Number One. "Turning on, running in, bomb doors open, bombs away." There was an unusual and very loud noise. The Lanc shuddered a bit. "Best take a look in the bomb bay," thought the navigator. Peering through the forward inspection hatch, he was startled to discover that, except for the bomb bay fuel tank, the bomb bay was empty. Missing were six bomb racks and twenty-four practice bombs. Our intrepid navigator had bullied the armourer into hooking up a jettison system that had lain dormant since the days when Hamburg and Cologne were on the aircraft's regular itinerary. Upon departing the aircraft, the bomb racks removed the H2S radar dome, perforated the underside of the fuselage, and bent the tail wheel. The squadron commander was understandably delighted.

In the fifties, many RCAF aircrew were WW II veterans. Many were blithe spirits who constantly followed their own drummer. Some were very skilled; some were not. There was the 407 Squadron Lanc captain who wrote off an aircraft on a lovely, clear, calm morning, landing at Cedar Rapids, Iowa. His fellow crew members, all of whom survived unscathed from the wreckage, will long remember their fearless leader's skill and dexterity. The Lancaster first touched down a quarter of a mile or so short of the runway. It then proceeded to perform a series of spectacular bounces, exacerbated by a ridiculously high initial rate of descent. The height of the bounces increased in reverse proportion to the

Lanc's airspeed. Just as the aircraft was running out of airspeed, and the pilot out of ideas, the main gear departed the fuselage. Heaving a sigh, the gallant old bomber skidded to a halt on the approach end of the Cedar Rapids runway. At the subsequent debriefing, the captain couldn't understand why everyone was surprised because, "Everyone knows I don't have any depth perception." It was later learned that, during the Big Unpleasantness, he'd landed a Halifax short at Gibraltar.

In fairness, many ex-WW II pilots were a treat to fly with; 407 Squadron's F/O Jack Finan was just such a driver. He had great hands. He also recognized and was always prepared to ignore a dumb order when he heard one. In 1954, 407 Squadron was deploying to RCAF Station Torbay, Newfoundland, for Exercise "New Broom II." (I assume this code name has been declassified after forty-plus years. If it hasn't, to quote a fighter pilot friend of mine who sent me a dissertation on the Gulf War, "First, eat this article and then shoot yourself.")

All twelve Lancs arrived in the Torbay circuit more or less simultaneously to discover that the airport was being thrashed to death by the tail end of a still very healthy hurricane. Displaying that innate sense of judgment for which he was justifiably famous, the squadron commander elected to land. A nasty little cross-wind of indeterminate strength was blowing (the anemometer had been torn from the roof of the control tower). Bounce number one took place on the runway, bounce number two in the infield—narrowly avoiding some substantive rocks—and number three back on the runway. And so on and so forth until the aircraft eventually shuddered to a halt. Eleven fascinated crews had witnessed this startling demonstration and all immediately air filed for a variety of alternates. The CO, rather than leaving well enough alone and repairing to the base chapel to give thanks, scuttled up the tower to give his troops the benefit of his vast experience. Jack Finan's crew were ten minutes into their diversion to Gander. The conversation went something like this:

Tower: "865, your CO suggests you land at Torbay."

865: "Negative, tower, we're diverting to Gander."

Tower: "865, your CO is ordering you to land."

865: "Tower, our CO isn't in this aircraft. We're diverting to Gander."

RCAF Station Greenwood contributed more than its share of characters to the Maritime Air Command saga. "Black Doug" McLeod comes immediately to mind, but that is another story or perhaps a book of stories. Flight Lieutenant "X," a skilled 404 Squadron pilot with an unlimited capacity for ingesting Moosehead, was coming to the end of his six-year Short Service Commission. As a "retirement" gift, "X" and his crew were rewarded with yet another all-expense-paid visit to Bermuda. On the homebound journey, their route took them within a few miles of New York City. "X," a bit miffed at having to spend one of his last weeks in the Service so far from his beloved officers' mess snakepit, came up with a grand plan.

F/L "X": "Radio, hop on the key and advise Greenwood that we've lost Number Three engine and we're diverting to Floyd Bennett Naval Air Station."

The crew's bewilderment evaporated when "X" reached over and feathered Number Three. An emergency was declared, followed by an uneventful approach and landing at Floyd Bennett. As the Lanc was pulling into its parking spot, the following dialogue ensued.

Tower: "990, are you from 404 Squadron, Greenwood, Nova Scotia?"

990: "Roger, tower."

Tower: "We've a message from your squadron commander."

990: "Go ahead, tower."

Tower: "Start that Goddamned engine and come home."

And so they did!

The foregoing vignettes are representative of numerous "I learned about flying from that" occurrences that innumerable RCAF/CAF aircrew have enterprisingly, inadvertently, or otherwise performed since Orv and Wilbur first lurched into the blue.

A 423 Squadron tale (Part One)

Gil Desbecquets

Robert G. (a.k.a. Pup Tent) has much better stories about my Volks than I have. For instance, Robert can vouch that a small person (like 6-week-old Brent) can fit neatly—if snugly—behind the backseat of the Volks. Bill Osborne, a telecom type living in 421 barracks, and I tested that possibility one Saturday night as we set out to place said F/O Grandmaison in the newly built Eagle cage in the Sqn wheelhouse. Pup had been partying in the afternoon and would not join us for a party at the mess (at least, being fast asleep as only he could be, he did not answer our invitation).

We carried Bob to the Volks, placed him behind the backseat (I think we had hoped to enlist the assistance of someone else and needed the backseat for other partners), and set out along the perimeter road. Along the way, we realized we were being followed at a distance, possibly by the AFPs, and continued all the way around the perimeter road and back to the mess to let the heat off, thinking to return to the original plan later.

Having joined the party at the mess, Bill and I at one point realized that Pup Tent was still behind the backseat of the Volks and he must be all cramped up. We retrieved him from his uncomfortable position and laid him, still fast asleep in a T-shirt and service-issue blue unmentionables, on the pool table at the back of the mess. He may have been having sweet dreams, because at some point shortly thereafter, we heard a lady on her way to the back parking lot scream at the top of her lungs, "My God, Pup Tent!"

We later heard that his sprint from the back of the mess to the 423 barracks might have been deserving of a gold medal at the Olympics.

Robert had his revenge on New Year's Eve, a few months later, when, thoughtful and generous soul that he is, he was taking a couple of bottles of bubbly to the crews at the Zulu shack shortly after midnight—in my Volks. I'll let him finish the story if he wishes. I was not there to witness what happened; I was at the mess keeping Adrienne sober so she could go to work after the party and be in good shape to admit Robert as a patient at the base hospital.

A 423 Squadron tale (Part Two)

Bob "Pup Tent" Grandmaison

Let the truth be told. Gil did have it correct.

I realized that, as midnight was rapidly approaching at the mess on New Year's Eve and the fact that I was getting there on my own, I should recognize the sacrifice my comrades-in-arms were making to ensure the peace in Europe that particular night.

I picked up a couple of bottles of bubbly and proceeded to the alert hangars to share with my fellow airmen. I know the aircrew did not partake but was not sure if the ground crew had a drink or not. Needless to say, I may have had a dram or two.

As I left the hangar with Gil's mighty Volks, I noticed that it was getting a little slippery. But that was only a challenge for those who feared driving on that dark and wet night.

I made it across the runway, around the ninety-degree bend, and was doing well for about 1,000 feet down the straightaway. Lo and behold, the next thing I know is, the car is heading down the embankment (I've forgotten how far down it was, but I think about six to ten feet). When everything came to rest, I was in the backseat, the engine had stalled, and the key was still on, as I could see the red and green light. The car was also facing 180 degrees from line of flight and sitting on its engine at about a forty-five-degree angle. I still remember today that all I could think of was an engine fire and where I was lying (just about over the engine). I scrambled out (that's a joke) and decided I'd best get to a phone. The closest being back at the alert hangars, I set off.

I told Gil what had happened to his car and proceeded to call the military police. The police showed up and, on the way back to the accident scene, asked me how I felt. I told him I was fine, and he asked if I would mind if we stopped to take measurements, etc. With the cunning of a drunk, I thought this would be an excellent way for me to assist in my defence and prove that extenuating circumstances were ultimately responsible for the unfortunate incident. At one point, he asked me to hold the end of a measuring tape, and as he extended the tape, my arm had to come up and I reacted noisily with pain. At which time, he decided we'd best get to the hospital.

As it turns out, the nurse on duty—either on arrival or the next morning (memory fails me)—was Madam Desbecquets, the mistress of the distressed car. It turns out I had broken my collarbone and ended up missing about six weeks' flying and my remaining leave for the year. When I got back on flying status, for reasons I can't remember, I was unable to take any leave between then and end of March. At my court appearance, it was pointed out to me that I was the first accident of the New Year and was I proud of myself. Humbly, I said "No." I remember Billy Books and others coming to the hospital the day they put on the shoulder collars. I sat backwards on an old metal chair and the doctor pulled by my arms to slip the rings and bandages around the rings. Hurt like hell, and I remember the doc telling those present what they would go through if they were as stupid as I. All in all, not a great moment in my life!

On another occasion, I remember driving around the countryside with Gil and Adrienne when she was expecting. Doctor Gil thought it was an excellent way to induce labour. It's a good thing that car cannot speak.

A 423 Squadron tale (Part Three)

Larry Clark

To give your story more credence, I would have to say that Brent was a very, very large baby at six weeks old. He became quite the seasoned traveller in his backseat domain, although not quite as well seasoned as the a.k.a. that you mentioned appears to have been. Perhaps with PT's aid you could write a book about your Volks. Especially since it seems likely, from your stories, that your Volks had been KTP (known to police). There may be reasons for that! Which reminds me of a couple more stories involving Bugs, one of which involves the police during the Algerian crisis.

Accompanied by Beth, I was driving rather hurriedly from Diffembach to a mess do at GT (Grostenquin). Approaching Hellimer, I observed two gendarmes on the side of the road waving, indicating that I should stop. Now, since I was in a hurry, I used a procedure that had proved successful in the past. I robustly waved back (greeting fashion) and kept speeding along. However, I immediately spotted another police type (armed with a machine gun) step from concealment in front of me, and the brakes of the Volks were burning when I stopped. I was surrounded, chastised, and given a ticket for having a dead tail light. (I ignored it, ended up at the gate to answer for it, and had to pay a doubled fine — three mil.)

On another occasion (I can't recollect where we had been), we were four or five jammed into a Volks; I believe Timber Tom was driving. I think the others were Jack Cadieux and Apps Appleby . . . BM Smith? . . . my memory has failed me here, and maybe Jack or Timber Tom can help out. We had had a bit of a snootful, and that, coupled with the fog, caused us a few problems with map-reading while trying to locate the turnoff for GT (from the Grostenquin to Lixing Road). Instead, we missed a turn and wandered around in some field or other and, despite the fact that there were three navs in the car, we could not find the road. One of us had the bright idea that one would get out of the car (Apps?) and guide the car back to the road. He disappeared into the fog and that was the last we saw of him that night. Somehow TT found the road and eventually GT.

I was asked to report to the guardhouse regarding a speeding offence that had occurred in the previously mentioned location, some two months before. I could barely recall this tiny village but did remember returning a wave to what appeared to be a friendly Polizei. With the citation, claiming that I had been speeding (forwarded to GT AFP), was an affidavit stating that this particular policeman had been trained in determining a car's speed by noting (among other indicators) the sound of a car's motor. Needless to say, we all had a good laugh (yes, meatheads do laugh — they should be writing books), and no fine — whatever amount it was — was ever paid.

Vietnam
Don Carney

Vietnam was one of the first CF unified operations that combined army, navy, and air force personnel. The army guys had been there, done that, lots of times in other places, so we blue suit guys had lots — or should I say, everything — to learn. In that hot climate, you may recall, they dressed us in short, green pants with short-sleeved shirts. The only way you could tell a naval or air force officer from an army officer was by his beret. The navy and air force officers' berets often reminded one of a painter on the Seine or the east bank in Paris. I won't say they suffered us gladly, but they taught me a lot and I appreciated their forbearance.

I was located in the Delta and our region extended from the South China Sea to the Cambodian border. I can't remember many humorous occasions, but I recall one incident that sadly highlights the conditions of war. The U.S. army folks were leaving near the end of March, and we were going to move into their compound. Of course, they had locals doing various jobs for them in the compound, and many were girls.

With the U.S. guys leaving, many of the gals were hoping to link up with the Canadians. The U.S. troops held a party to celebrate their departure and invited the Canadians. I recall standing outside the building that housed the bar, twenty feet from the bank of the Mekong River, talking to someone. I thought I felt something crawling up my thigh and casually attempted to brush it away. It turned out to be the hand of one of the gals! She explained her desperate situation with her U.S. guy leaving and implored me to employ her. Regrettably, I could not provide any assistance because I was the operations officer, not the logistics officer.

Another recollection concerns a certain Canadian colonel. He was slated to be the CO of another region and had two great army majors working for him. They had been in these operations before and naturally could have provided him with a lot of sound advice. Before any of us went to Vietnam we received weapons training and were issued 9mm pistols. The weapons were for unforeseen emergencies. It was policy that we not carry the weapons. In our region, I kept the weapons while the CO kept the ammo and clips.

However, the Canadian colonel of this other region felt that a 9mm was totally inadequate to deal with what he imagined he might have to face. Perhaps I might suggest he had a somewhat apocalyptic view of his job. I choose that word deliberately! Consequently, during the few days we were becoming oriented before going out into the field, he had his boys collecting every conceivable weapon they could lay their hands on. Of course there was no shortage of weapons of any type. The colonel and his collection were a matter of some humour for the rest of us sharing the same quarters, especially since we were there to observe truce violations, not be the *cause* of a violation. He was replaced after a few weeks.

More Vietnam

Alex Saunders

The first group of the ICCS (International Commission for Control and Supervision), a.k.a. "War-Watching" personnel, arrived in Vietnam near the end of January 19, 1973. Their primary duty was to set up a headquarters and organize site teams, while sorting out accommodations in the Stalag compound the four national countries would live in (Canada, Hungary, Indonesia, and Poland—"CHIP"). The accommodation compound was truly akin to a Stalag. The buildings were two storeys high with open screening along the sides, top, and bottom. Access to the upper floor was by an outdoor, one-landing staircase. The Canadian contingent was the most organized and had an additional building for its temporary Operational and Administrative Headquarters.

With some hard work scrubbing, fumigating, and washing down walls, the barracks probably reached their highest level of habitability since Dien Bien Phu. A reminder that this was not a summer camp was evidenced by the sandbagging around the buildings. By "hard work," I mean many of the chaps were working upwards of sixteen-hour days. The food was not great at the outset but soon improved when Canada (alphabetically the first of the CHIPs) took over the first two months of administration for the ICCS enterprise. This included security and food services, amongst functions that the other CHIPs were ill-equipped to manage. The time between the arrival of the first half of the contingent and the arrival of the second half was spent feverishly getting things in order. What the second half would find was vastly different from what the first group faced.

By the day, or rather the night, of the "new boys'" arrival, the work intensity had lessened somewhat. Moreover, our canteen was in full swing . . . well, getting there. What I am trying to say is, there was a supply of liquid libations to be had. The sun had set for some time and we were getting word of the ETA, which kept slipping to later and later. My task as Staff Officer Admin was to be part of the greeting party to direct the tired travellers to their assigned bunks in the two sleeping quarters—building, floor, bunk number, and so on. To pass the time, someone suggested we might as well have a sociable drink—or two!

When the chaps did arrive at around three or five a.m., the members of the greeting party were fairly relaxed. As the weary travellers stepped off the bus, they shuffled around waiting to find out where the hell they could lay their heads. It was a twenty-four-hour flight from Eastern Canada, so solid ground and cozy bed were foremost in their minds.

I have no idea whatever possessed me at that moment. Before anyone could stop me, I was on the balcony of the first barrack block delivering a welcome message with instructions to tell each arrival where he would find his bunk—a simple task, really. However, when I opened my mouth to deliver the welcome and so on, another person had taken over my task: none other than Colonel Klink of Stalag XIII.

"Velcum to our beootiful Stalag, ver you vill be made most comfortable. Pay close attenshun to vat I haf to say! You vill be tolt your place of sleepingk so phay attention!" I went on, reading off the building, floor, and bunk assignments in a fairly sensible manner. I concluded the oration with reinforcing the welcome with words to the effect, "Vhile you are here with the Stalag, you vill enchoy yourselfs as much as is possible. . . pleese understand der only vay oudt of heer is up der chimney! So velcum, but vatch yourselfs."

A ray of sanity returned to me in time to say something in effect, "Okay, enough of that bastard Klink . . . welcome and off to bed. We'll be waiting for you when you awaken to conduct you on a tour of our area here at Tan Son Nhut and show you where you can get some grub." By this time, a snicker had started here and there; fortunately, fatigue had not erased their sense of humour. Off they went to bed. Luckily, I had only a mild sarcastic comment from my boss, Col. Ringma, which I do not recall.

Yielding to impulse can be a little stupid—unless you get lucky and it goes over.

Fishing derby—North Bay

John A. MacDonald

While at North Bay, in the spring there was a squadron fishing party on Lake Nipissing. It was the first day of the fishing season, and the squadron rented boats, with four to a boat. We had a good supply of bait, as well as beer for the day. At noon, we would gather on a small island for a barbeque.

In the morning, I had no catch; in the afternoon, after a healthy supply of beer and sunshine, I dozed off with my line in the water. Dave and other chaps decided to rig a catch for me, so they pulled in my line, fixed a pickerel to it, and tossed it into the lake. With a couple of good jerks on the line, I awoke, thinking I had finally had a bite, and reeled in the pickerel. I was ecstatic and, after removing the fish, I tossed my line into the water and got another bite immediately. I reeled in another good-sized pickerel. It was apparent my luck had changed. The party did not want to tell me about the first catch because I was so overjoyed with my good fortune. Some time later, I was told of the rigged catch!

For he's a jolly good fellow

Gil Desbecquets

A friend of mine used to say that world travel filled a youth's mind but tended to empty his bowels.

When we reached squadron in our teenaged years (many of us were nineteen or twenty), we felt it important to learn the manners of the local populace and the proper etiquette. We quickly learned that it was quite acceptable to eat frogs' legs with your fingers, to wipe your escargot plate clean with a chunk of baguette, and never to ask for a steak tartare medium well done.

Similarly, we discovered that the proper measure for a shot of cognac was to lay the snifter on its side and pour the liquid until it just came to kiss the lip of the glass. T'was just a short skip and a hop for someone's fertile mind to realize that we would not breach etiquette if we were to pour a full bottle of Remy Martin into a large snifter of the type still used today for flower arrangements. It was just the perfect measure.

How to run the DEW Line site, ca. 1959.

PIN (Cape Parry)

How to run the DEW Line, ca. present time.

The large snifter was often used in the same manner and for a similar purpose (to spread joy and promote good fellowship) as our native ancestors used the peace pipe and many of our successors passed a joint of pot around. So be it, and far from us the idea of debating the relative worth of the evolving means of sharing a good time with your friends.

And there were times when developing friendships seemed particularly important. This was the early sixties in Northeast France; this country was fighting its last battles in Algeria; the workforce in the coal mines around 2 Wing was made up, in large part, of Algerians who were understandably wary of any and all pale faces; the rebel French generals in Algeria were threatening to airlift their troops back to France to overthrow the De Gaulle government, and an order was given to the base to shut down flying operations and block the runway with oil barrels and other obstacles. A recently repatriated soldier of the French Foreign Legion had been assassinated at the Gare in Metz, and his comrades had decided that the North Africans living in that city were to pay for his death. Just a little tense!

Just about that time, the East Germans decided to build a wall in Berlin and to make movements more difficult between West Germany and the enclave city. The Yanks responded by calling the Air National Guard to active duty and by reactivating some of the bases they had closed a few years earlier. Thus, the USAF base at Phalsburg, about fifty kilometres SE of Grostenquin became home to two squadrons of F–84s from the Boston area; the aircraft of one squadron sported a shamrock on the tail plane, which seemed a good omen, given the reputation of Irishmen as boozing buddies. They also turned out to be good play pals for Clunk jockeys who could more regularly get another fighter in their gunsight rather than appearing in the gunsight of our Sabre illegitimate brothers.

Having become acquainted in the air (some playful F–84 drivers even went so far as to bounce Clunks in the circuit at Grostenquin), the time came ripe for a social event hosted by the CO of 2 Wing.

Plans were made for a "night landing tournament" and other such games to be held after the mess dinner, where the guest speaker would be the Phalsburg base commander. A good time was had by all during the dinner, the guests being worthy descendants of their Irish ancestors, and a suitable match in wit and imbibing ability for the Canadian hosts.

The time came for the group captain, a big, burly man with a heart of gold, to introduce the guest speaker, an equally big man but of unknown quality of heart at this point. The last paragraph of the introduction went something like this: " . . . and Brigadier General Sweeney was co-pilot on the B–29 that dropped the bomb on Nagasaki," at which point, a young flying officer sitting at the far end of one of the side tables stood up, raised a king-sized snifter of Remy Martin in the direction of the general and intoned, "For he's a jolly good fellow . . ." He did not carry the tune very well, and no one could pick up the key to help him finish it. On the other hand, on a signal from the group captain, a couple of his tablemates picked up the F/O and helped him out of the mess.

The Amateurs

John Eggenberger and Bill Gladders

I flew my last trip on 409 Sqn on January 27, 1960. The trip was with the pilot that I crewed up with in December 1956—Charlie Leake. During that period, I flew nearly 800 hours in the CF–100, almost 700 of these hours with Charlie. But it was time to go—my posting was in and it was to RCAF station Pine [sic].

It may be recalled that this was shortly after the cancellation of the Arrow, and, as all did, I, too, had harboured secret thoughts that Charlie and I would be sent off to the OCU—seeing as how we were so very, very good. But this was not to be, not for anybody; the Arrow cancellation changed things for all of us. Now, RCAF station "PINE" was in my future. The posting message had the "E" added in pencil to PIN, the admin types thinking that there was a spelling mistake and what the message meant was PINE, not PIN. They were wrong. The posting was to PIN. And where was that? I asked; it was Cape Parry, NWT, not easily found on any map, then or now.

Oh, said someone behind the ops desk, I know, that's the DEW Line. And what's *that*? I asked. I was to find out all by myself.

Although this is probably not recalled by many, along with the cancellation of the Arrow, another cataclysmic event occurred. A little before I got my posting to PIN, the Minister of National Defence, Eric Nielsen (brother to Leslie), was chucked into the brig by the USAF at Tuktoyaktuk (Tuk-Tuk to us). The MND had thought he could just "drop in," so had not acquired and filed a Prior Permission flight plan that could only be approved from Paramus, New Jersey, USA. Why should he? thought he; this is Canada, and I am the MND—this is my turf. This information cut no ice with the USAF operating the radar site at Tuk Tuk, and into the brig he went.

Upon getting out of the jug, Eric called up the PM and opined that this sort of thing was not good. The PM agreed and took advantage of a clause in the agreement with the United States that Canada could take operational control whenever it wanted to, but when it did, Canada would have to send up Canadian military operatives to take over from the USAF contingent. There being no excess GCI-trained folks so to do in our inventory, I among others was selected to "go there and do it." The staff on a DEW line main site shifted so as to have a Canadian CO, four RCAF operatives, and one USAF person, instead of the other way around. We were the first RCAF rotation and first junior officer aircrew to go to the DEW Line. (Some of the military commanders were aircrew.)

And so, John Houghton, Bill Gladders, and I became the first of many to spend many happy hours looking for Russians that never came—at least I never saw any. I was very heartened to know that I was not the only one selected for Northern Duty, and I was particularly pleased to find out that we three were to proceed to Streator, Illinois, for a three-day course in how to run the DEW Line, for I knew nothing about the job, nor (as I later found out) did my fellow selectees.

Now serendipity kicks in. We three were destined to meet on a train platform in Chicago, each waiting to catch the train to Streator. Before leaving Canada, each of us had had the wisdom to go to the duty-free and buy a bottle to tide us over. On the train platform, there was considerable steam (that particular train being steam-powered), and through the clouds of steam out emerged Bill and John. I rushed over, and Bill dropped his duty-free bottle on the cement platform; it promptly broke. An omen, thought I. No matter, we were together and felt no longer so lonely.

Also, it must be remembered that we knew naught about GCI other than a visit to a radar station now and then, and being controlled around the sky here and there; in sum, none of us really knew anything about the intricacies of operating a radar site. For whatever reason, that fact didn't seem to bother us.

When we arrived at Streator, we were met by our "handler," a USAF captain, nice fellow—knew lots of stuff. We were RCAF flying officers and therefore junior to this USAF captain who belonged to an organization that thrived on seniority. It was his job to make sure that we learned something and to not let us get into any trouble. So, the first evening there, we had our course-joining party—there not being a mess at the radar site (set up in Streator to practice with/upon)—we had to go downtown to party. Our USAF handler, a little nervous by now, opined that we should get a "bite to eat," go back to the motel, and get a good night's sleep because there was lots to do tomorrow.

Well, that advice didn't sink in too far, but we did have dinner, then a few libations to loosen up. Not too much adventure turned up, so eventually we did get to bed—at about one in the morning. The USAF captain not at all happy. In the morning, we three bounded up fresh as daisies and attended well to what was being offered in the briefings. Not too tough, thought we. This was when the USAF captain found out that not only were we not GCI controllers but were not even going to take the Controller course . . . (The USAF DEWLine ops officers were required to be captains and GCI controllers.)

There had been a mistake in this captain's mind. We were evidently not qualified to watch paint dry (the job of a DEWLine ops officer). Great consternation and phone calls to Washington. There had been no mistake. End of talk of formal course. That evening, we had our mid-course party. It was fairly tame, but this time we had discovered a real good spot to conduct such activities. The next day, we excelled at what they wanted us to do at the radar site, just as if we had been trained for the job. A breeze, thought we.

The last evening of our course, we had our graduation party, at the "real good spot" that we had found (USAF captain was not impressed). Lots of fine people there, all ready to party up. And we did. Along about two in the morning, we were asked to demonstrate the "Arctic Clog Dance." The audience was enthralled. John Houghton did really well, leaping upon a table with feet flashing to stomp out the dance. Not to be outdone, I followed with a display comprised of much more intricate, delicate, and interwoven steps, so much so that I fell off the table and was not permitted to continue. Then Bill did his dance. Now, that was something to behold: He got up there and stomped around, and, being a "little" heavier than John H. or me, the table broke. A series of rousing cheers ensued, and much clapping of hands at our display.

During all this, the USAF captain was pulling at our arms, saying, "We got to go now." (I forgot to mention—we were in uniform, that being the dress we were supposed to wear at all times, I know not why.) Being in considerable distress, the USAF captain said, "If you don't stop right now, there will be severe punitive action taken." (Remember, he outranked us.) And Bill said, "What the hell are you going to do if we don't—send us north?"

Montreal's finest
Bill Gladders

I was one of the first three aircrew flying officers to be posted to the DEW Line. I was sentenced to a year at DYE Main in February 1960. We were to spend four months onsite and then come south for two weeks R and R, another four weeks up north, and two weeks on parole, etc. There were to be no extensions nor time off for good behaviour.

Our predecessors had been older GCI types. On their two weeks out, they went home—or wherever—to see their loved ones. We dumb aircrew had to put in our quarterly flying time. Our fearless leaders hadn't figured out that someone who went north in February would miss a quarter's flying. I had been proficiency flying in mid-June and was granted a three-year extension to my Short Service Commission on the July Permanent Commission list. I was ordered to St. Hubert for a medical. It couldn't wait until September; it had to be done at once. So, in late July, I reported to St. Hubert for the medical and my third quarter's flying. The highlight of the medical was the doctor's harangue at the stupidity of a medical in July when I'd had an extensive isolation medical in February.

This was my first actual experience with "real" proficiency flying. (My second-quarter flying had consisted of dead-heading with 435 [T] Squadron in Namao.) The term "proficiency" implies you are already "proficient." Some of the intrepid drivers on ground tours were proficient in scaring their crew members witless. Flying pay had just been increased from thirty dollars to one hundred dollars per month, which flushed an array of pilots who hadn't touched an aircraft since WW I out of the woodwork to get their not insignificant $300 per quarter.

I spent a few happy hours in the mess with old friends. As I was preparing to leave for Dorval by taxi, I went to the parking lot to retrieve some valuable (unclassified) papers from a colleague's car. Unfortunately, I tripped over a small railing. I extended my arms to cushion my fall and landed on my hands. As the taxi approached the St. Lawrence River, I realized I couldn't move my right arm so I changed my destination from Dorval to the nearest military hospital. It should have been so easy!

As the taxi pulled off the Jack Carter bridge, the exit lanes were blocked by police cars. A policeman opened the taxi's door and told me to get out. His hand on his gun encouraged me to comply. When I asked him what was up, he replied that there had been an attempted bank robbery (they were in vogue in Montreal in that era). My cunning response: "I sure as hell didn't do it in my condition."

He replied: "It was done by a man in his mid-twenties, six feet, 170 pounds, crew cut, wearing a brown suit or uniform and he hurt his arm getting away." The cop could have been reading my ID card. I replied, "Yes, sir," as I raised my arms—well, one arm, anyway.

Crew cuts were very popular in the RCAF at that time, and we travelled in uniform—a strange quirk that military organizations had so the victim could tell the Pension Board that he (or she) was on duty when his (or her) accident happened. The police were charming. They gave me a ride to the hospital in a nice, clean, squad car and were so concerned about my welfare that one cop stayed by my side all the time, even coming into a hospital phone booth with me while I phoned the SDO at ADCHQ to tell him to advise Cape Dyer that I would probably miss my flight north and might be back the following week.

I was entertained in Emergency by a young intern who had me push my arm onto the x-ray table so he could take pictures. He told me he suspected there was something wrong with my arm. I politely asked him how much medical training he had had and commented that it must be hard, though rewarding, work! Then I told him that I had no medical training and I KNEW there was something wrong with my arm. By then it was two in the morning. My policemen friends had lost interest in me and told me I could go. They didn't tell me where to go, and I didn't tell *them* where to go!

Next day, I attended at the camp commandant's office and dictated my story to the Protestant Padre's secretary. A few days later, ADC received an apology from the City of Montreal, but my sad tale was not over.

I had a broken elbow. When they took the cast off at Queen Mary hospital, it hadn't healed properly, so they told me to return on Monday to be admitted. When I reported for admittance, the military staff were a trifle huffy—how was I to know they meant Monday *morning?*

I was assigned to a ward. An army nursing sister pointed to a bed. I told her it was too early to go to bed. She said that was fine—just go when I was tired; a very understanding young woman. They hadn't taken my uniform, so I kept it on. I noticed I was the only one in uniform, and also the only one with a visible injury. I had a shower. The med aide got quite excited when I told him I'd been to have a shower and he asked me not to tell the doctor. He asked for my uniform, and I responded, "When I go to bed."

At about eight p.m., my doctor arrived and conducted an initial interview that went something like this.

"When were you born?"
"How old are you?"
"Where were you born?"
"When did you come to Canada?"
"How old were you then?"
"When did you join the army? [I had an air force uniform on.]
"Do you like the army? [I don't know. I'm not in the army.]"

(Note: This guy was ahead of his time. To him, like everyone else these days, including politicians, anyone in the military is a soldier.)

"Are your parents alive?"
"Were they happy when your father was alive?"
"Have you had any common army diseases? Do you know what I mean by that? [I said, you mean venereal diseases?]
"You know what I'm talking about?"
"Do you like girls?"
"Do you smoke? [No.]
"Do you drink? [Yes.]
"How much? [Probably more than average.]
"What is average? [I don't know.]
"Neither do I."

At this point I asked what this had to do with my broken elbow, and he replied, "Everything is relevant."

After this consultation, I went to the nurse and told her I was in the wrong ward. She humoured me and said: "Oh no, you are in the right ward."

The next morning, I had a chest x-ray and again

told the Matron I was in the wrong ward. She said, "You're F/O Gladders. I've heard about you! Don't worry, you're in the right ward." That afternoon, as I still had my uniform, I walked to the Snowden Tavern for a beer and to see some sane people.

The next day, an old friend of mine, Alex McVicar, came to see me. I said, "Alex, I'm in the wrong ward."

Alex had a great sense of humour and said; "Laddie, I know you are in the wrong ward, and you know you are, but they don't and it's up to them to find out; they get paid for that." (By the way, Alex was an RCAF shrink.)

A couple of hours later, the Matron came to see me and very apologetically said, "F/O Gladders, there's been a dreadful mistake." No kidding!

I went to another ward for two days, got myself discharged, and spent the weekend with a friend of mine, Ed Shibley, who was in the right ward and out on a weekend pass. They never did take my uniform.

Vietnam incidents
Ernie Poole

I was returning four Viet Cong prisoners (they were fifteen, sixteen-year-old kids) to their unit in the jungle just north of Phan Thiet, with my jeep driver and interpreter, Mr. Di. We came upon a North Vietnamese lieutenant who said he would take charge of the prisoners. After completing the paperwork, I complimented him on his command of the English language. He said that he had just graduated from Simon Fraser University in Vancouver.

I said, "What a small world. I was stationed on a fighter squadron just across the chuck on Vancouver Island."

He said, "Oh, you mean 409 Squadron."

When I picked out my jeep at the motor pool in Phan Thiet, it came with Mr. Di. He was a fine gentleman but a terribly dangerous driver. On our first day together, he hit a girl on a bicycle and backed into me. To teach him a lesson, I had him ride in the backseat for a full day while I drove him around. This did little to improve his driving, and for a couple of months it was a constant battle to get him to slow down and drive safely. One morning, he picked me up for our four-mile drive to the airport. I was delighted to see that he finally got my message and was driving like a sane man.

On arrival at the HQ building, I said, "Now that's more like it, Mr. Di. That's how I want you to drive"

Mr. Di said, "Major Poole, I take the jeep to the motor pool—we don't have any brakes."

Peacekeepers, eh?
Lynn Wagar

Canada has had a fairly long history, at least since WW II, of participating in peacekeeping operations in many areas of the globe. Air defenders, along with a few other "volunteers," got to try it on in Vietnam in 1973.

The selection process and the way people were informed were fairly typical of the way the unified force was run in that era. Lieutenant Commander Joe Sosnkowski and I flew to North Bay for an ADC conference. Prior to the meeting, we encountered Major Don Carney, a staff weenie in the Tac Eval shop. He advised us that he had a message that would interest us both. It sure did. After reading a lengthy preamble about Canada's becoming part of an International Commission to observe during the peace accords in Vietnam, I was at the point of asking why he'd given it to us, when we arrived at the list of names. Sure enough, both Joe Sos's and mine were there in startling black on green. Not to worry, said the message, this was just an alert.

Well, after Kissinger made his many more trips to Paris, the accords were signed, and this alert became reality, with all those notified being placed on twenty-four-hour notice for possible departure. Major Ernie Poole, who had originally been selected as an alternate, made the A team when one of the ground pounders at Comox (who shall remain nameless) crapped out. That made 409's contribution about 1 percent of the total force. Not bad, when you consider there are well more than a hundred units in the Canadian Forces. Comox, as a base, had a relatively high number of people selected. I assume the powers that be figured that, being in the West Coast air force, we were the closest to Vietnam—save on transportation costs, etc.

The interim between selection and "doing" was replete with such humdrum activities as getting a depressingly long list of needles, training in such activities as building a "hootch," and, mostly on Friday nights, Ernie and I planning our entrepreneurial Vietnam enterprises—running the "Rent-a-Gurkha" and "Rent-a-Mongoose" concessions. As it turned out, the only live snakes I ever saw in VN were sea snakes in the China Sea off Phu Quoc Island. That restricted my swimming activities to the pool at Tan Son Nhut AB, in spite of the fact that the country has some of the most beautiful beaches in the world.

The Paris Accords were announced in late January of '73, and shortly thereafter, the first contingent of the Military Component of the Canadian Delegation to the International Commission of Control and Supervision (whew) left from Montreal for Saigon (with Ernie on board). My turn came in early February when the 707 scooped up the second group for the long trek to Saigon via Elmendorf and Tokyo. Group two also had a short stop at Trenton thrown in as a bonus because of a bomb scare out of Montreal.

My job as Prisoner of War Exchange started shortly after the second contingent arrived. For the next month and a half, our time was to be spent observing on the release of POWs of the warring parties—North (NVA) and South Vietnam (SVN), the Viet Cong (VC or PRG), and the United States. It took us pretty well all over the country but not—repeat *not*—to any garden spots or spas. The whole VN experience was a lot of frustration interspersed with a few moments of exhilaration. Most of the latter came during the PW phase. Some fragmentary memories!

The first prisoner exchange I attended was in Loc Ninh about three miles from the Cambodian border. Nine hundred and four NVA/VC ladies were repatriated during a twelve-to-thirteen-hour activity that incorporated many delays, mostly due to the USAF Hercules blowing tires on the pierced steel planking (PSP) runway. During these delays, we wandered around the boundaries of the runway looking for nothing in particular until a land mine cooked off in the heat nearby and quenched these exploratory urges.

Later on, we had a pretty good view of a couple of SVN Skyraiders laying some bombs on a place called An Loc, a few klicks to the south of us. Yep, the war was over, all right. Still later, a U.S. major who was with the other long-named commission delegated to monitor the peace accords (4PJMC—see warring parties above) came over to me and asked that we stay until the SVN security force was ferried out because he was concerned that the VC, who owned that part of the world, might extract a little revenge for the bombing incident. This occasioned my first Huey ride at night. I sat in the gunner's position with the doors open and watched the odd green tracer as we rode back to Saigon. My lasting impression of Loc Ninh has to be the eerie feeling I experienced when, just before dusk, a large crowd of people came out of nowhere to watch the last Hercules load of females get their release. We virtually had not seen any locals all day and then suddenly they were there!

Of course, at that time, we were unaware of the underground complexes so laboriously and ingeniously constructed by the Vietnamese in those environs.

Another unforgettable tasking was one in late March to Hanoi when we observed the release of the last sixty-seven American POWs at the Cu Loc prison ("the Zoo") and the Gia Lam airport. We had a chance to go through the prisoners' quarters, and, although we were briefed not to engage them in conversation, I tried to convey the admiration I felt for them by saluting them as we passed. You've got to feel you are a part of history when you are sitting at a large conference table populated by high-ranking officers of the U.S. and NVA military, with Walter Cronkite standing across from you about six feet away observing the proceedings.

A little grimly humorous note: sixty-six of the U.S. personnel had been released and the North Vietnamese said, That's it—you've got them all, and there was one POW left standing there in his grey-blue windbreaker and blue pants and his dufflebag in hand. After a hurried little group conversation, number sixty-seven was released to U.S. authorities. By coincidence, his name happened to be Agnew—and Spiro T. Agnew just happened to be vice-president of the United States at that time. Who says the Communists don't have a sense of humour but lots of subtlety?

Between those two releases, there are some other impressions: the city of Quang Tri being completely levelled from the attacks in late '72; the city of Hue still badly damaged from the '68 Tet offensive; and the first trip to Thien Ngon when we had CBC reporter Don McNeill and his cameraman with us. I guess Norm Altenhoff, my co-team member, and I made the CBC national the following night. All I know is they shot miles of film and earned me a rebuke the next day from the VC camp commander for their intrusive activities during proceedings when we returned for the next day's scheduled releases.

Also, I must mention the Air Cav helicopter pilots who flew us on the missions before they left in late March and Air America took over. These guys didn't give a crap about anything and they did not—I repeat, *did not*—like their former enemies. They didn't think much of our mission either, referring to ICCS as Indo China Chicken Shit, or, alternatively, I Can't Control Shit; nor did they like our Polish and Hungarian Commission confreres. On one trip, after Canada had turned over chairmanship of the ICCS to the delegation from Hungary (it rotated in alphabetical order on a monthly basis), we were going to Thien Ngon. The Hungarian colonel directed the pilot to land (we'd been there before).

The pilot turned to the colonel and said, over the intercom that we all were plugged into, "I'm not taking orders from any Commie bastard." He then turned to me and said, "If you say to go down, we'll go." I told him to land and just looked at the colonel and shrugged.

The Cav always had M–16s with them, even though the Hueys were supposed to be completely devoid of weaponry. They were ready to use them, peace accords or not. They were all young, in their early twenties, veterans of the war; some had been shot down several times. They were completely irreverent and could they fly those Hueys—I loved every one of them!

On the downside, the loss of Capt. Chuck Laviolette in a helicopter shoot-down in early April has to rank as the low point of my tour. I had met Chuck in Phu Bai when we were billeted there on TD during the several days of the Quang Tri exchanges. We spoke several times, and he was distressed at the lack of mail from home. (His mail had been misdirected for awhile.) I met up with him again in Tan Son Nhut, and he used my room for keeping safe some items he was sending home; he was then in a much better frame of mind. Shortly after, his chopper was shot down on a recce mission to his port of entry team site at Lao Bac, near the Laotian border. When the PRG (VC) released the bodies of those killed in the crash, I somehow got the task of forming a pallbearer team to meet the incoming C–46. Although it was a grim and sad chore, I was gratified to be able to pay my final respects to him and the other American and Philippine crew members in that manner.

Once the American military left Vietnam, the urgency for activity went out of the peacemaking process, and our secondary mission of getting civilian detainees released just never happened. The remainder of my tour was spent as an ops officer for the ICCS Air services (read Air America), getting cargo and personnel around the country. And other than considering myself as a Green Beret Packer, nothing noteworthy was achieved. Once the powers that be realized we were just spinning our wheels, they brought us home at the end of July 1973.

Before we departed, however, Ernie, in from Phan Tiet, and I met up with Col. Perrin Gower, who had been a USAF exchange instructor at the Bagotville OTU. He was the Air Attaché in Saigon and invited us to the Embassy for a couple of parties; he also arranged a luncheon meeting with Sir Robert Thompson, well known for his counter-insurgency activity in Malaya, post-WW II. Perrin said Sir Robert wanted to meet somebody in the ICCS who had been out in the field, as it were. We had a very enjoyable lunch and managed to get Sir Robert to spend more time talking about his activities than interrogating us. On that pleasant note, my Vietnam experience ended.

Postscript: In addition to Ernie Poole, Joe Sosnkowski, and Lynn, AW types who participated in this ICCS exercise included Don Carney, Luc Caron, Danny Gagnon, Bill Marsh, Alex Saunders, and Gord Welsby.

Exchange excitement
Alex Saunders

When on exchange with 72 Squadron at RAF Leconfield (Javelins), I had a half-hour or so of deep concern during a night mission on October 18, 1960. My pilot (RCAF), F/L Gerry Smith, was suffering with a heavy cold and was off the available list. An RAF crew was short a navigator, so for that night's flying I was crewed up with an RAF pilot whose navigator was also "under the weather." We were scheduled and subsequently flew two missions that night, taking off at 1900 hours and, after turnaround, were airborne again at 2110 hours. Both missions were practising the same tactics: "OP2–T1," the meaning of which I do not recall after these many years.

The first mission was a "DCO," but the second was a "DNCO."

On the second mission, an incident developed while we were climbing through about 30,000 feet over the North Sea off Flamborough Head. As usual, in the "backseat" there was not an awful lot to do while under the control of GCI and being vectored toward the target area. I recall that as usual I was fiddling with the Gee, setting base coordinates, aligning with the runway at Leconfield, and fine-tuning the AI radar, while carrying out the usual back-to-front checks with the pilot. At about 32,000 feet, I was not getting any response from the pilot, and at the same time, I noticed that we were in a starboard turn — an orbit, actually — and gradually losing altitude. No instructions had come from GCI. I asked my pilot what was up. No response. There followed a continual one-way monologue: "Pete! Pete! Do you read me?" After slowly losing a couple of thousand feet, the light went on in my skull that "things were not normal at this particular time," which is a euphemism for "holy shit!"

Not pulling any punches, for the first time ever or since, I made a MAYDAY call to GCI, conveying my suspicion that the pilot was anoxic. So the drama ensued from that transmission. A bewildering array of concerned people got into the act. The first was a request for a course to steer to Leconfield. I recall an embarrassed response to the effect, "Right! Roger! You are a Javelin and you are in the backseat . . . understood!"

As I recall, a voice of authority came on and told me to report every 500 or 1,000 feet of descent and the cardinal (ninety-degree) points of the descending orbit. It was quite a lazy rate of descent, actually. So, from around 30,000 feet downward, this repetitive reporting went on and on . . . e.g., "Leaving 27,000 turning through 180 degrees . . . leaving 26,000 through 090 degrees," and on and on. At around 14,000 feet, I was advised that I should prepare to leave the aircraft. Not a really welcome suggestion, as we were out over the North Sea and it was mid-October! The monitoring became more and more intense from then on. In the meantime, I was repeatedly calling, "Pete! Peter! Pull the apple! Pete, do you read me?" At about 10,000 feet, I was given the instruction that I should leave the aircraft at about 8,000 feet if no response was forthcoming from the front seat.

A factor I was considering, apart from the cold waters of the North Sea, was that the orbit and descent was so very "lazy." It was going on forever! If it had been a dive, there would have been no question in my mind; but the fact is, the descent and orbit were so gentle! What surprised me was that the throttle seemed to have been brought back—but that, too, was reasonable because at around 30,000 to 32,000 feet, we would have been throttling back a bit anyway, awaiting an intercept vector. All the readings from the backseat were, "Yes, we sure had a problem, but it was not a rapidly unfolding problem."

We went down through 8,000 feet, as I recall, and because it was an orbit, we were still a ways out to sea. I started to cheat on my altitude reporting. Then, around 6,000 feet, I heard a "What the hell?" from Pete. "What the hell—what the hell?"

I said, urgently, "Pull the apple—pull the apple!" and followed with something like, "Pete! Pete! You are anoxic! Ease back on the stick and level your wings. Read your instruments!"

He reacted accordingly, and we simply flew straight and level and got our breathing and senses in order . . . then I reported to GCI and the master controller that everything was back to normal. We were vectored to RAF Leconfield and made a normal recovery and landing. The aircraft was impounded and our personnel safety equipment as well. The outcome was the discovery that the pilot's oxygen mask had malfunctioned from mucus causing valves to stick; his mask was overdue, as it turned out. I imagine Safety Equipment was pretty busy the next morning cleaning O2 masks for any guys whose due date was near.

It was a rather bizarre experience in that it unfolded so gradually after the initial realization that something was amiss. I realized that many chaps in similar situations had a helluva lot less time to sort things out.

Sea survival—Deci style

Doug Munro

It was 1970; ADC had been sending aircrew to Sardinia to go take the CF–104 water survival course until a similar school was set up in Comox. Ernie Poole and I were selected to attend the one for March 4–5 and, accordingly, we began to plan our activities in the most efficient manner in order to attend the course and still see a bit of Europe. Our first plan was to request a T–33 to fly there and back (much like a weekend request) and to that end spent a couple of Friday nights planning a route structure there and back. We didn't formalize the request because we were politely (or maybe it wasn't so politely—my memory is dim here) told to Forget It! As subsequent events would show, we probably should have asked for the T–Bird!

On a Saturday late in February, we boarded the eastbound sked to Trenton, after noting that the incoming flight the previous evening had brought in several candidates for the above-mentioned survival course in Comox. Little did we know that that was one of the last passenger manifests that our names would be on. Except for the return trip from Lahr to Deci in the middle of the following week, we had vanished as far as Air Movements were concerned. However, we did make it to Decimomannu and, along with several other stalwarts from other ADC units, went through the prescribed course curriculum.

I have to mention one extracurricular activity of that trip that may be of interest to readers. Although I had been to Sardinia many times during my tour with 423 Sqn, I had never toured the island. Part of the arrangements made by the school included such a tour. It was conducted by Pedro, a local DND employee, and he took us on a most enjoyable ride around the very scenic Sardinian landscape. It culminated with a dinner in a downtown Cagliari hotel. The food was good, the wine was flowing (as it had all day), and general good fellowship was being shared by all, when one of the waiters came up to Pedro and in a torrent of voluble Italian told him that one of our compatriots was up on the roof of the hotel. Does this sound a familiar note? I know I felt an immediate sense of déjà vu because I had been in Val–d'Or when the original peeing from the hotel roof incident occurred. It will come as no surprise that one of the perpetrators of that episode was also the star of this one, too! Pedro, using the skills of an ambassador, along with said star, returned to the table without further incident, keeping this one from becoming the three-ring circus that ensued from the previous one.

"Hurry up and wait" became the modus operandi for several days after our return to Lahr from our somewhat successful dunking in the Golfo de Cagliari. The Trenton–Lahr–Trenton express kept to its schedule, the other attendees returned home, and Ernie and I were still in AMU limbo. Finally, Ern was able to get through to our squadron commander, Hammy Hammond, who used the "priority" that he needed this experienced crew back for a Tac Eval that was looming on the horizon. That was the magic wand being rubbed—we got seats to Trenton—out of Gatwick! A now seasoned pair of travellers, we fought our way onto a trip to London and a trip back to Canada, bumping a pair of army majors in the process (that almost made all the "hurry up and wait" worthwhile). Ernie was about twenty-five pounds heavier because, impatient with currency exchange in the UK, he kept paying for things with pound notes and ending up with pockets full of coins.

The remainder of the trip was without incident, but there is a sequel. About eleven months later, I actually put what I had learned to good use when Doug Stuart and I had to depart an airplane and we landed in the Strait of Georgia.

Postscript: 409 Squadron must have had a rolling, permanent "Chair" on the Deci course. Phil Schreiner and I abandoned the flight simulator and attended a course immediately prior to Lynn and Ernie. We travelled to Deci, swam, and returned to Lahr without a hitch. There was a heartwarming moment on the Herc from Lahr to Deci. The Herc nav wanted to know why we were going to Sardinia. When he learned we were off to take a course that he was scheduled to take at Comox the following month, he nearly ate his nav bag.

The Lahr AMU knew we existed but regretted we weren't scheduled to Trenton for eight days. Aircrew are taught to suffer such pain! We caught a local sked to Gatwick, a train to London, a taxi to the Columbia Club (an American officers' club on Hyde Park), checked in, and repaired to the nearest pub. After seven days of trying to consume the CC's stock of Chateau Neuf du Pape, we journeyed to Gatwick to connect with the Lahr sked. A note at the Canadian Force departure desk advised that the sked was cancelled, as were all flights to the Continent. No problem: a bus to Heathrow, an East African Super VC–10 to Frankfurt, and a Budget Beetle to Lahr. I drove while that wretch Schreiner drank my bottle of Chivas and made the Trenton sked with an hour to spare.

Sardinia days
Al Chapman

A couple of incidents come to mind: On the day that the whole bunch went into Cagliari for a bit of R and R, we were on a military bus driven by an Italian private who was coming to the end of his compulsory military service. Unfortunately for us, his term expired just as we were leaving the Deci base, and he pulled over at the guardhouse and quit the army right on the spot. It took about a half hour to get another driver, and the bus was *hot*.

Don Little and I left the main group in the square in Cagliari and went by tramcar to the Maple Leaf Club on the beach a few miles away. We bought a bottle of scotch and sunned ourselves on the beach as we sipped and talked. After a blurry while, we decided that it was time to rejoin the guys so we went to the tramlines and stopped the next one by the simple expedient of lying on the tracks. The locals thought this was hilarious, especially when we passed the bottle around. We left a lot of new friends behind when we were finally ejected into the main square, where we joined up with the rest of the squadron, who were drinking in the cloisters on the edge of the square. We were feeling so good and full of bonhomie that we wound up leading a conga line of local street urchins along the tabletops until the local police decided that we were a bit too boisterous and asked our more sober friends to get us out of town before we were introduced to the local jail.

Finally, do you remember the time that we had a live scramble? When we were holding "Zulu," we could usually expect to be scrambled on a practice sortie, unless the weather was really bad. Practice scrambles were always initiated with a phone call from operations, whereas an actual scramble was signalled with a very loud bell. On this particular night, the weather was well below normal limits, so we relaxed, had a steak each, and went to sleep confident that we would not be called.

Sometime around midnight, we were rudely awakened by the BELL! Since the Canadians were about the third line of defence in the event of an attack from the east, it was obvious that World War III must be well underway. We were in the cockpit in record time, before being fully awake, and starting the engines while the ground crew were arming the rockets on the wing tips (which had never been called for on any of our previous Zulu launches). By now, we were convinced that we were embarking on what might well be our last night on earth as we nervously contacted the controllers for instructions. The reply was a puzzled, "Who scrambled you?"

We said, "You rang the bloody bell!"

To which they replied, "Oops . . . There are some techs working on the alert system and they must have done it by mistake."

Our great relief was somewhat spoiled by his next remark: "Since you're awake anyhow, you may as well go practise."

So we had to go flying in really s****y weather anyway, without the opportunity of venting our wrath on the bad guys. Probably just as well, in retrospect.

Naylor's farewell

Gary Naylor

In late August 1968, I was leaving Bagotville, where I had instructed on the Voodoo OTU (410 Squadron), to go to Moose Jaw. The mug-out for myself and probably others given the normal posting season, was a great rollicking, raucous, Friday night beer call. Everything went swimmingly until approximately seven a.m. on Saturday.

It was one fine party. Little did I realize that my fellow 410 instructor Ron Egli had organized a surprise for me.

About seven p.m., Ron, with enough accomplices to manhandle me with no chance of resistance, carried me off to the female officers' quarters (no co-ed accommodation in those days). En route from the mess, Ron and his team had laughingly told me I was destined to be left naked in the ladies' common room on the third floor.

Ho! Ho! Ho! thought I, but sonofabitch, that's exactly what they did. I was very soon absolutely bare-assed naked in the living room of the women's quarters—which was apparently completely empty. Egli and his co-conspirators had returned to the mess, and I was on my own!

Two entrances—"both doors locked and figure out how the heck to get out of this one!"

Sorry to disappoint everyone, but the first noise in the hall outside the locked room, I investigated by unlocking and partially opening one door, hiding behind it, and peeking out: and whom did I see but a lady who was a great friend of both my wife Bernice and me! Tastefully attired in a red barracks blanket, out the door I hustled to her car and got a ride home to the Naylor PMQ. Bernice was her usual, unflappable self!

Chatham daze

Gary Naylor

The place was Chatham, New Brunswick; the time, the winter of 1964/65. My next-door neighbour in PMQs was an RAF exchange officer on the CF–101 Voodoo. He was scheduled to return to England in the summer of 1965 and had recently purchased a beautiful, large, new, right-hand drive Pontiac to take with him on his return. It was his pride and joy and so it should have been.

USAF C–124 ("Old Shaky") delivering stuff to 447 Bomarc Sqn at La Macaza.

Leaving beer call one night to walk home, as I passed my neighbour's pride and joy in the mess parking lot, I suddenly recalled that he never locked his car doors and always left the keys in the ignition. Knowing that he had been drinking, I got in his car, drove it home, and parked it in his garage — thank God without incident.

An hour or so later, I awoke to the sound of a ruckus in the driveway between our homes. It was my neighbour and the Air Police discussing their next cunning move in the hunt for his stolen car. Sometime during the discussion, his garage door was opened. It immediately became apparent that the missing vehicle had been found. The Air Police assumed they were dealing with a fine young officer who had left his car at home rather than chance driving home from beer call. However, they seemed a bit perturbed that he had bothered them at all.

Postscript: There is no evidence that I, during Chatham's Survival '68, let the air out of all the tires in the parking lot and then threw all the mattresses and bedclothes out of the barracks and into the rain.

Editor's Note: Under no circumstances is Gary to be confused with his brother Bill, a proper gent hiding somewhere in Nova Scotia.

A Bomarc stands up to stretch.

447 (SAM) Squadron[16]

Bob Merrick

The RCAF entered the missile age in 1962, when it acquired two half-squadrons of Boeing's Michigan Air Research Centre (Bomarc) missiles. The missiles guarded Canadian and American industrial centres and Strategic Air Command bomber and ICBM sites from attacks by the nuclear-equipped Soviet long-range air force. The 446 Surface-to-Air Missile (SAM) Squadron, based near North Bay, Ontario, began its training first, followed by 447 (SAM) Squadron, based at RCAF Station La Macaza, Quebec. Four-forty-seven became the world's only self-sufficient Bomarc squadron, as all the others were adjuncts of various USAF or RCAF bases.

As did 446 Squadron, 447 began its training at Chanute Air Force Base, Illinois, then one of the USAF's primary technical training facilities. RCAF technicians, freshly posted from fighter squadrons, began their training in this strange new world with some trepidation, until they found that the Bomarc was just another aircraft. Better still, there were no pilots or navigators to make obscure L–14 entries, such as "engine missing," which required difficult technical responses such as "engine found on nose of aircraft." Although some Bomarc technology was a considerable jump from that of the Sabre and the Clunk, the technicians easily mastered it, and Canada's two Bomarc squadrons set enviable serviceability records during their ten years of air defence service.

True to form, the big thinkers in personnel thought that this would be a magnificent opportunity for tour-expired air defence aircrew to broaden their horizons by entering the missile age on the ground floor. The first CO at 447 was W/C Art Laflamme,

---

16 Permission granted by Larry Milberry.

a decorated WW II bomber pilot. He and the five operations officers also trained at Chanute.

Their training epitomized the "nice to know" teaching era. When he and his ops officers finished the course, they could have: (a) built a Bomarc; (b) built a Semi-Automatic Ground Environment (SAGE) direction centre; and (c) controlled an air battle encompassing the entire North American continent. These were all noble feats, but none of these officers would ever be called upon to do any of those things.

However, the technicians who were called upon to build Bomarcs demonstrated that they learned their craft well. There was a later course at Hurlburt Field, part of the Eglin AFB complex on the Florida panhandle. There, the technicians showed their skills by assembling a Bomarc, which was then launched by the SAGE direction centre at Gunter AFB, Alabama. Much to the USAF's dismay, 447's technicians had built a masterpiece that nailed a brand-new QB–47 right between the eyes.

In September 1962, W/C Laflamme led his band of warriors to their new home at RCAF Station La Macaza, where a mix of RCAF technicians, Boeing tech reps, and other contractors had built a snug little station. The missiles were housed in twenty-eight shelters that looked like largish garages.

The people were housed in 114 brand-new, double-trailer PMQs. For families with one or two children, the cozy little homes were just fine. For people who had large families, such as W/C Laflamme, the houses bordered on cruel and unusual punishment. As always, there were more families than there were PMQs. Off-base accommodation was sparse, distant, and not always of a high standard. A trailer park just off the base housed about twenty families.

Although Boeing, the other contractors, and the initial cadre under S/L Elmer McGinnis had accomplished much, a lot more was needed to get all twenty-eight Bomarcs up and serviceable. To their everlasting credit, the technicians, directed by S/L McGinnis, the other technical officers, and the many first-rate senior NCOs, such as Sgts Floyd Smith, Sonny Aumais, Len Goertzen, Don Hynes, and others, did it all in what seemed record time.

As noted, 447 SAM Squadron was a self-contained unit called RCAF Station La Macaza, with a station headquarters and other impedimenta of a full-fledged station. Flight Lieutenant Dick Taylor was the CAdO, while F/L Cam Fraser served as PAdO. Flight Lieutenant Jean Lapointe kept the finances straight, and F/O Lorna Kelly tended to those who fell ill. Sergeant Lloyd Scharfe kept the Orderly Room running efficiently. As 447 was going to have what the RCAF diffidently referred to as a "nuclear capability," security loomed large. The many people needed to keep any capabilities securely penned in were competently led by F/O John Grogan. Supplying the base was the province of the multi-talented F/L Mike Powell, while F/L Bruno Guay was the "sticks-and-bricks" wizard who solved the many construction problems inherent in a new station. These officers were carefully chosen for their competence in their chosen fields. They were also chosen for their ability to turn a collection of empty buildings into a vibrant, dynamic, air defence station.

They were not alone. The officers chosen to help S/L McGinnis also had the professional and personal attributes needed to breathe life into a new station. Flight Lieutenant Cal Calvert was a no-nonsense leader who earned great respect from his expert technicians. Flight Lieutenant Sugi Sugimoto thoroughly understood the Bomarc's systems, and the "work hard, play hard" ethic handed down to the RCAF by the RAF. Flying officers Jim Washington, Pete Berry, and Al Massey contributed much to getting the Bomarcs on line and to setting up the amenities to improve life at an outlying station. A bit later, they were joined by the nuclear safety officer, F/L

Lorne "Snuffy" Smith. His job was such that if wives did it, it would be called nagging.

Four-forty-seven Squadron's Bomarcs were controlled by the SAGE direction centre at North Bay, Ontario. An operations centre headed by F/L Terry Lyons tied the squadron to the SAGE centre. The ops centre was manned continuously by one of four operations officers: F/Os Merv Eagleson, Herb Karras, Gerry Maguire, and Bob Merrick. Each of them was somewhat overqualified for the job (see above), but like the other officers, each helped establish amenities to improve life for those at La Macaza.

Station life was richly enhanced by Boeing tech reps. Dick Shafer, Keith Svendby, Tom Russell, Ray Skoronski, and Dick Kachel were among many who added immeasurably to operational effectiveness and quality of station life.

In May 1963, W/C Joe Roussell, a decorated WW II Spitfire pilot and post-war Sabre pilot, succeeded W/C Laflamme as CO. It was a time when banning the bomb was a regular feature of Canadian life. As 447 Sqn was reputed to have "bombs," it was the target of activists who enjoyed camping on roads leading to ADC bases. W/C Roussell defused these situations without harming those who wanted Canada to lead the world in unilateral disarmament.

Shortly after Roussell arrived, so too did the "capability." This was, of course, very hush-hush, and no one was supposed to know what was going on. One morning, a USAF "Ole Shaky" C–124 landed smoothly on the runway adjacent to the station. An extensive convoy was there to greet it. Security was tight, and access to the station was temporarily denied to the butcher, the baker, the candlestick maker, and the many other itinerant merchants who brought base residents the necessities of life. So there they sat, on the road leading to the base, watching an aircraft that was considerably larger than most of the buildings for fifty miles around, while it disgorged "stuff" into a closely guarded convoy. Fortunately, most of them just put it down as one of those weird things that the military unaccountably does from time to time, and secrecy was maintained.

The "stuff" off the airplane became the province of a small detachment from the USAF's 425th Munitions Maintenance squadron, commanded by Major Dan Chisa. He was admirably supported by Captains Al Brock, Darrel Duncan, several NCOs, and numerous airmen. The vibrant American presence greatly enriched station life.

Security played an important role in squadron operations. Several security huts rimmed the perimeter of the missile compound. Intrusion alarms inhabited each missile shelter. These alarms were quite sensitive and susceptible to false alarms. Such alarms provided much training for the sabotage alert teams that always lurked nearby. Each night, they responded to many alerts caused by wind gusts and other phenomena. Sergeant Hank Pankratz oversaw such security operations, and no one ever succeeded in stealing a Bomarc.

Radical elements of Quebec's Separatist Movement caused occasional anxious moments. Some worried that the station's phone links to the outside world could be broken by dedicated zealots. The solution was to bring in a radio, apparently built by Marconi himself, to maintain a comm link with ADCHQ, then at RCAF Station St. Hubert. Each day, the duty ops officer fired up this antique, barked messages into a WW I mike, then listened to what sounded like a whole kitchen full of bacon frying over high heat, interspersed with what seemed to be obscene messages in an obscure Serbo-Croatian dialect. After several minutes of this esoteric sport, he nodded sagely, entered "Successful HF contact with ADCHQ" in the log, and went on to other things.

On November 29, 1963, a Trans-Canada Airlines DC–8 crashed at Ste. Thérèse, Quebec, killing all 118 on board. Shortly after, the ops phone rang. It was the *Montreal Star*. Had the station accidentally launched any of its Bomarcs? The ops officer assured the caller that twenty-eight soft white lights still glowed on his panel, indicating that all twenty-eight Bomarcs were still onsite. "Is it possible," the reporter asked, "that one of the missiles could launch without anyone noticing?" The reporter was assured that many alert military policemen guarded the Bomarcs, and that a launch, accidental or otherwise, would be noticed by anyone within a ten-mile range.

As noted, the Bomarcs were launched and controlled by North Bay SAGE. How did anyone know the system would work? The technicians maintained the missiles in accordance with master schedules in much the same way they would maintain any other aircraft. True, no one was flying the Bomarcs, but like other aircraft, they could develop snags. Between the scheduled maintenance and the unscheduled snags, maintenance crews were always busy.

Two major tests periodically provided assurance that the missiles would respond to SAGE commands. The first was the Partial Squadron Demonstration, or PSD. In this test, the SAGE controller, the squadron ops officer, and maintenance control coordinated activities that resulted in the SAGE controller's sending a launch message to the site. If all was in order, the Bomarc would leap smartly to attention, showing that it was ready for flight. The checklists included positive measures to disconnect the fuse to the solid-boost rocket that flung the Bomarc aloft.

The other—and more complicated—test required the use of a Mobile Inspection Unit (MIU). Again, the controller, the ops officer, and the maintainers coordinated activities that resulted in a launch message being sent to the Bomarc. However, for this test, the launch message was routed through the MIU, and technicians measured the missile's response to the various commands imbedded in the message.

For a time, the messages moved over ordinary phone lines. One weekend, a local sport was returning from a party when his vehicle slammed into a telephone pole that jumped into the middle of the road. After that incident, greater attention was paid to multi-path message routing.

The station took part in the many regional and NORAD exercises that ensured all elements of the air defence system functioned efficiently. Most of this participation was done through the ops centre, and generally involved nothing more than receiving telephone messages from North Bay SAGE. During exercises, the Bomarcs were simulated within the bowels of the SAGE computer at North Bay. They were launched as needed by an intercept director (IND).

Had war broken out, 447's ops centre had to take a few initial actions. After that, the IND's switch actions would cause the real thing to leap out of La Macaza powered by a solid rocket booster that lifted the missile to either 40,000 feet or 71,000 feet, depending on what the IND requested. During liftoff, two ramjets flashed up and accelerated the Bomarc to M 1.3 or 2.1, again depending on the IND's assessment of the threat. From there, the IND used a data link to control the Bomarc in much the same way he controlled the CF–101s from, say Bagotville, except that the Bomarc was less likely to respond with smart-aleck remarks. The Bomarc had a range of 400 nm, radar to acquire a target, and a proximity fuse to detonate the "capability."

Within about three years, personnel turbulence in the air defence world resulted in changes to the ops centre. In 1964, 500 aircrew officers were turned loose, and two air defence squadrons, 414 at North Bay and 410 at Ottawa, disbanded, resulting in a change in the ops centre manning level. Flight Lieutenants John Sullivan, Cliff Scott, and Bob Conn came on board, and the charter members of the missile squadron started to move on to other things.

It was nice to have entered the missile age "on the ground floor," but I did notice that we were still on the ground floor when we left, and we were all happy to return to a world where all the pilots weren't called Otto. Our various successors kept the Bomarcs in service until 1972, when higher authority determined that the threat from the Soviet long-range air forces had declined to the point where Voodoos alone could handle the threat. It was a short-lived introduction to the SAM world, but it must have worked. After all, how many Badgers, Bisons, and Bears did you see in Canadian airspace between 1962 and 1972?

Squadron picnic

John Wheeler

During the hot summer of 1965, Mike Colbert organized a beach party. The plan called for him to ferry men, women, and children in his boat to a small, uninhabited island in the middle of the Miramichi River. Once there, we would set up a table, light a fire, and consume vast quantities of alcohol aided by presence of a tame Brit-exchange officer who had a duty-free ration of twelve bottles a month. I remember the table had been set with cloth and cutlery when Pete Delong spotted a tiny black dot, seemingly skimming along the sea, coming toward us at horrendous speed.

"Run, run!" and we all scattered just as John Rose flashed across the beach and hit the burners, pulling into a vertical climb; end of table, food etc.! The coals did not catch, and we salvaged little food.

Mike thought it would be a good idea if I—the Brit—swam out to some lobster pots. I had never used a "tank" before, but the water was not too deep for someone on his first dive lugging a bottle of Seagram's. The idea was to exchange the whisky for the lobster, which I did. Somehow we all survived the picnic, and the Voodoo made it back to base.

I wonder what the fisherman thought when he hauled in his pots; did his story enter local legend? When I returned to Chatham on holiday in 1998, my wife and I enjoyed dinner at the Sea Shells Hotel Chatham, which had been the officers' mess. One of the staff rustled up his father, who had been the Station barber, but he had never heard of the story. I wrote an article about it for the local paper but never got a response. So we may never know.

Blue Four

Author Unknown

One of our members is routinely referred to as "Blue Four," but many are not aware of the reason he came to be bestowed with this prestigious handle. Many years later, and with admitted cloudy recollections, I'll try to put the story together with as much accuracy as can be mustered.

Four-twenty-five Squadron planned to do a sixteen-plane formation on February 6, 1970. The only reason I can recall for this great display was that it would help celebrate "Carnival" in the Saguenay Valley. In the cold winters, serviceability of that many aircraft could sometimes be problematic, so 416 Sqn ferried up a couple of spares we could use if necessary. This was looked upon with some dismay by our own technicians! Actually, they felt slighted.

On the day, Joe Couillard, our CO, briefed the mission. Four sections of four in box formations were to join up after launch to form one large box of four diamonds. The four boxes were comprised of Red in the lead, White on the right, Green on the left, and Blue in the trail position. The Sqn ops crew flew a seventeenth aircraft as a spare if needed and acted as spotter otherwise. Our maintenance crew really produced; we did not need the kind assistance of 416 Sqn.

After takeoff, the Alouettes penetrated a low cloud deck and were pretty well in formation by the time we passed over the first checkpoint at Jonquière at about 2,000 feet above ground. On that nice sunny day, the spotter looked the gaggle over and pronounced it to be pretty good. But to get it looking even better, the spotter suggested that "Blue Four move ahead two feet." Next checkpoint was Val-Jalbert on the south side of Lac St–Jean. The spotter checked them over and pronounced, "Alouettes, looking great. Blue Four, close up two feet." The next check was at Roberval on the west side of the lake, and not much had changed. Everyone was doing a super job, but Blue Four was still a bit of a laggard. "Blue Four, Move Ahead Two Feet!" Next checkpoint of Péribonka on the north side of the lake would let us see if Blue Four was getting the message.

Péribonka was quickly coming up, then Alma, and down the Saguenay to Chicoutimi, where it was important that Alouettes look their best. By Péribonka the same little correction was urged by the spotter, "Blue Four, Move Ahead Two Feet." As we passed Alma, it was obvious that another approach was needed. The exasperated spotter came on the air "Alouettes, you're looking good. Red Flight, White

Those burners certainly suck in your eyeballs . . .

Flight, Green Flight and Blue One, Two and Three, move it back two feet. *BLUE FOUR, HOLD YOUR POSITION.*"

Alouettes went by Chicoutimi in a perfect formation and soon after landed at BG without incident. It was a relief to see sixteen drag chutes on that landing. It was a good morning workout for the crews, and Blue Four is fondly remembered still. So next time you see Rennick, address him as Blue Four with a knowing smile . . .

PART THREE

THE CF–101 IN CANADIAN SKIES

Bob Merrick

A swelling roar. Two thunderous explosions, closely followed by intense, crackling thunder. Transfixed, watchers could see twin torches of flame disappearing into the night sky, visible evidence of the raw power that propelled the CF–101 Voodoo into Canadian skies. For almost a quarter of a century, Canadians who lived near the air force bases at Comox, British Columbia, Bagotville, Quebec, and Chatham, New Brunswick, were daily reminded that whatever it was that the McDonnell Aircraft Company set out to build in 1952, it certainly wasn't a stealth fighter.

From October 1961 until November 1984, the CF–101 patrolled Canadian skies, filling the interceptor role that was deemed to have died in February 1959 when the federal government cancelled all work on the Avro Arrow. However, the reports of the manned bombers' and manned interceptors' demises were quickly found to be exaggerated. The CF–100s that then equipped Canada's air defence squadrons were obsolete and unable to catch contemporary airliners. The Arrow was on its way into mythology. Attention quickly turned to the McDonnell F–101B, which had just entered service with the United States Air Force's Air Defense Command.

The 101, or Voodoo, as it was known, had two engines and carried a two-man crew; one to fly the beast, and one to wrestle with radar. In the bad old days before integrated flight management systems, the two-man crew solved many design problems, even if it doubled the wage bill. The Big Silver Jet, as many of its crews called it, was an impressive aircraft throughout its lifetime. More than seventy feet long, with a wing span of about thirty-nine feet, the Voodoo stood eighteen feet tall and dwarfed the CF–100s it had replaced. Empty, it weighed about 32,000 pounds. With two full external tanks, it burdened the runway with almost 52,000 pounds.

Now, did all that weight make it ponderous? Well, maybe, on a hot day coming out of Denver. But at one of its more usual locations (Bagotville), at a more usual temperature, the acceleration was truly neck-snapping, with or without the tanks. The two J–57s produced about 35,000 pounds of thrust and many more pounds of noise. Applying this much thrust to a 45,000-pound (the normal takeoff weight) aircraft meant that one did not linger on the runway. It also meant that one did not hesitate to raise the gear on takeoff, as the air loads imposed by the rapidly increasing airspeed made it all too easy to hang the forward retracting nose gear.

From a standing start, the CF–101 could climb to 35,000 feet in just two minutes. Even without the burners, it got to 35,000 feet in seven minutes. Its normal cruising speed was 480 knots true at 35,000 feet, but it readily accelerated to 700 knots, or Mach 1.73, if needed. For crews still holding alert in CF–100s, who were accustomed to falling behind contemporary airliners such as the Boeing 707 or the Douglas DC–8, the extra speed provided by the two big J–57s was a welcome change from the .85-limiting Mach of the venerable Clunk.

The Canadian CF–101 years began in 1961, when Wing Commander R.D. Schultz led a small band of pilots and navigators to the USAF's Otis Air Force Base in Massachusetts for the academic training needed to master the F–101. From there, this hardy band of pioneers did the Westward-ho bit to Hamilton Air Force Base, just north of San Francisco, to begin training on the Voodoo. Schultz was a veteran night-fighter pilot who had won two Distinguished Flying Crosses on Mosquito intruder operations in World War II and had been in at the start of the RCAF's Vampire and CF–100 operations in the early days of the Cold War. He immediately set to work moulding the cadre of Canadian aircrew who would introduce the rest of the air defence squadrons to the Voodoo. And, he had an impressive crowd of young, experienced aircrew to help him. They were pilots and navigators:

W/C R.D. Schultz with F/L J.L. Bradley
S/L H.S. Tetlock with S/L D.L. Munro
F/L J. Deacon with F/L K.A. Robinson
F/L J. Flannigan with F/O E.J. Poole
F/L R. Anslow with F/L D. Dumond
F/L P. Griffiths with F/O R.G. Chester
F/L E.M. Robinson with F/O L.G. Taylor
F/L D. Broadbent with F/L L. Raina
F/L D. Hook with F/O L. Jokinen

There was a lot to learn. The aircraft was in some ways more complicated than the CF–100 it replaced. And, once the burners were lit, the complications whizzed by more rapidly than they did in the Clunk. The Voodoo's high tail engendered some interesting manoeuvres if the pilot allowed the angle of attack to get too high, at night during a high-altitude attack, or even during a prosaic landing. The Voodoo flew like, well, a Voodoo, and it had to be flown as such with due regard for the numbers.

The backseat had its share of complications that kept the navigators hitting the books so that they could efficiently manage the electron flow. And the weapons. Unlike the CF–100—which carried fifty-eight rockets that either went or didn't, with little planning required—the Voodoo carried two types of weapons. The first was the AIR2A Genie rocket, which had what the RCAF and, later, the Canadian Forces, diffidently called a "nuclear capability." The AIR2A was a relatively uncomplicated rocket that was given precise guidance until launch time, when it accelerated away from the fighter at phenomenal speed. After a predetermined time, set according to such parameters as fighter speed and altitude, it made a satisfying "POP!" which cleansed Soviet long-range bombers from a large chunk of sky. On returning home, the fighter crew could be stood in hallways and used as night lights.

The other weapon, the AIM 4D, was designed to be used against aircraft that had mastered the art of electronic countermeasures, but had yet to master the art of flying with cold engines. It was a heat-seeker and was, in many ways, more complicated than the aircraft that carried it. It had a host of B times, D times,[17] and other occasions when things happened—or didn't happen. For some attacks, it required that the pilot be able to count to ten, which some people said was the main reason the navigator was brought along. In the hands of an experienced crew working against a non-manoeuvring target that obligingly stayed away from the sun, the AIM 4 could be a useful weapon. In other scenarios, it would probably have been less effective than the shotgun pattern produced by the Mick-oops-Mighty Mouse rockets it replaced.

---

17 These are events that occurred within the AIM–4 missile while it was preparing for launch. They were signals to the pilot to advance the process another step.

Big, fast, and noisy, the Voodoo was the most visible part of an air defence team built to thwart the manned bomber threat that peaked in the fifties and sixties. The air defence system was a sophisticated evolution of the basic system that had proven successful in the Battle of Britain. It required close coordination between controllers on—or in some cases, under—the ground who detected and classified targets, and aircrews far above the ground who intercepted and identified the targets.

An immutable feature of squadron life during the CF–100 and CF–101 years was something known variously as standby, alert, or the Q. Whatever it was called, it referred to two crews, two aircraft, and the requisite ground crew whose purpose in life was to get the aircraft airborne within five minutes when such action was deemed essential by the radar defence network. Generally, the aircrew, aircraft, and ground crew were in a special compound called the Quick Reaction Alert area, where they would normally spend twenty-four hours awaiting the raucous call of the klaxon that announced the scramble (as such sorties were called).

Upon taking over the alert duties, the aircrew completed the pre-flight inspection of the alert aircraft, installed their parachutes in the ejection seats, placed their Mae Wests and brain buckets in readily accessible locations, and set the cockpit switches to the pre-start settings. The ground crew readied the ground support equipment, checked power supplies, and ensured that all was ready for an immediate launch.

Then, everyone settled back to wait . . . and wait . . . and wait some more. Not that the time was wasted. Air and ground crews alike were awash with secondary duties that thoughtful commanders had laid on to combat terminal boredom, so there was always much catching up on administrative work, as well as ping-pong, knock rummy, and similar pursuits; all of them done with one ear to the horn, so to speak.

When the designer built the horn, he knew that he was working with people who spent too much time around jet engines without their ear defenders, so he designed a horn that made the walls vibrate and no doubt served as the inspiration for countless rock bands. When it went, it blotted out all other sounds, including those produced by adenoidal navigators in deep slumber.

A scramble horn going at zero-three double-dark produced some interesting moments. People who were sound asleep were lifted off their beds by a wall of sound. Shrugging into zoom bags and zipping up flying boots, the aircrews run to the aircraft to find the ground crew already there. Up the ladder, slide into the seat, a quick flurry of straps, buckles, hoses, and snaps, then slide a frozen brain bucket over your ears as the loud hiss of escaping air announces the starting of the first engine.

"Tower," you wheezingly intone, "Kilo November 04, taxi, scramble."

"Roger 04," she responds smoothly (she hasn't had to run anywhere), "it's off runway 29, climb the 020 radial to flight level 350 and contact Seeing Eye on designator 21."

By this time, the second engine is running, the ground crew are completing the pre-flight and post-start checks, the canopy is coming down, and it's time to run the challenge-and-response checklist that is a feature of CF–101 operations.

Halfway through the checks, the ground crew gives a thumbs-up. Once again, they've done a fine job. The aircraft starts to roll toward the runway button. The checks are completed just as the aircraft reaches the button. The tower controller, watching the lights, issues a takeoff clearance. Within seconds, four thunderous burner lights cause the neighbours to sing joyous odes to the sounds of freedom, or something. Elapsed time from blaaaaaaat to boom-boom? Just over four minutes.

Such vignettes were repeated countless times at the main and alternate bases that housed the CF–101s over the almost quarter century that Voodoos "stood on guard for thee." Initially, the aircraft were based at Comox, British Columbia, where 409 Squadron operated them from 1962 until 1984; North Bay, Ontario, where 414 Squadron defended the country from 1962 to 1964; Ottawa, Ontario, where 410 Squadron defended Parliament Hill from 1962 to 1964; Bagotville, Quebec, where 425 Squadron defended the Saguenay until 1984 and 3(AW)F OTU trained Voodoo crews until 1982 (in 1968, when the CF started hanging squadron numbers on any collection of aircraft greater than two, the OTU became 410 AW[OT] Squadron); and Chatham, New Brunswick, where 416 Squadron chased Soviet aircraft destined for the workers' paradise in Cuba. They clung to their chores until 1984, when the CF–101 was removed from the air defence role.

Voodoos also operated for many years from Val-d'Or, Quebec, and on and off from Goose Bay, Labrador, Gander, Newfoundland, and North Bay, Ontario, which was the home of the last two Canadian 101s, one an electronic warfare training aircraft that served Canada with 414 Squadron until 1987, and the other, 006, which was a dual-controlled pilot trainer.

But where was the first Canadian Voodoo operation set up? The answer is, none of the above. When W/C Schultz led the first contingent north from Hamilton AFB, he steered not for Comox, Bagotville, or Chatham, but for RCAF Station Namao, which had a runway that went forever, a salubrious climate, and a generous amount of relatively uncluttered airspace. Thus it was that Namao became, for a ten-month period, home to 425 AW(F) Squadron. At Namao, 425 was not primarily in the air defence role.

The squadron's task was to train the other squadrons that would, with 425 squadron, form the most visible part of Canada's air defence system.

By early November 1962, 425 Squadron was established at Namao and ready for business, the business being that of introducing the remaining air defence squadrons to the CF–101. The initial cadre of Canadian crews was bolstered by the arrival of a USAF exchange crew: Captains Perrin Gower and Ernie Throne, both of them well experienced on the Big Silver Jet.

The first crews through the training mill came from 410 Squadron, which was then employed in guarding the nation's capital. In slightly more than a month, 410 Squadron had learned some of the intricacies of the CF–101, and the crews were back home just in time to assume the alert commitment on Christmas Day of 1962.

Meanwhile, back in Namao, 425 Squadron was hosting 416 Squadron, which had re-formed one day earlier at RCAF Station Bagotville. The crews came mainly from the ranks of 432 and 413 squadrons, which, until then, had been defending the Saguenay with CF–100s. The new aggregation showed that they could learn just as quickly as those from 410. They were back in BG on February 1. But not for long. The BG runway was being resurfaced, so for five months, 416 squadron operated from RCAF Station Uplands.

Early in February 1963, 425 Squadron welcomed 409 Squadron to Namao, and to the world of supersonic flight. The conversion training for this squadron resulted in the first bent aircraft, when a returning Nighthawk—F/O Ray Rohr and his navigator, F/O Jim Shultz on their first solo—broke out of some low cloud and hit the runway hard enough to remove the starboard main gear from the aircraft.

F/O Rohr applied full power and went around for another approach, which was executed flawlessly.

Although the aircraft suffered considerable damage, it was soon repaired and served with 409 Squadron until it was destroyed in a mid-air collision not far from Comox in 1969.

The Nighthawks were as adept at adapting to the CF–101 as the squadrons that preceded them, and they were soon back in their West Coast wonderland, while the instructors of 425 Squadron welcomed 414 Squadron to the phantasmagoria of afterburners, horns, pushers, and pitch-up avoidance. By now, 425 Squadron pilots were adept at pitch-up avoidance, as F/Ls Hook and Deakin had, during an air test, gone searching for the horn and pusher, rather than accepting the fact that neither could be found at the posted numbers. The recovery from the ensuing pitch-up was smooth and professional.

This training, too, proceeded on schedule, as did the training of the next two courses, which included crews destined for all the squadrons, including 425. There was a definite need to augment 425 Squadron, since it was to assume an operational role as 425 Squadron and continue the training role as 3 AW(F) OTU. And just where would the OTU and 425 Squadron carry out their roles?

Why, at Bagotville, where the squadron would replace the doughty band of warriors from 416 Squadron, who would, in turn, move to RCAF Station Chatham. Thus, by mid-1963, the Canadian air defence alignment was virtually complete. The operational squadrons at Comox, Bagotville, and Chatham would remain in place for twenty-one years. Only the squadrons at North Bay and Ottawa were destined to be short-lived, lasting for but two years in the operational CF–101 role.

For 416 Squadron, the news of a permanent home at Chatham was a welcome end to a period of considerable instability. As earlier noted, the squadron had been melded largely of crews from 432 and 413 CF–100 squadrons at Bagotville. They had spent a month in Namao, then lived out of suitcases for five months at RCAF Station Uplands in Ottawa while the BG runways were removed and replaced.

The time at Uplands had been a useful experience for the crews, cementing the knowledge they had picked up during their abbreviated course and acquiring, through experience, more bits of knowledge that weren't on the course, such as the need to differentiate between the switch for the identification light and the canopy open/close switch during identification passes. Although opening the canopy in night flight does allow a closer look at a blacked-out target, the practice never really caught on.

Slowly, the squadron developed standard operating procedures for the CF–101 and shared them with the other squadrons, which were also adding to the lore they had gained from the short but effective course given by 425 Squadron. It is to the considerable credit of all those associated with the aircraft in the first few formative months, both in the air and on the ground, that their pioneering efforts stood the considerable tests of time and experience. Throughout the many years of the Voodoo reign, the procedures for flying, maintaining, controlling, and employing it evolved continuously, but it was always possible to discern the strong foundation erected by those who were there first.

And it was not only the aircrews who were pioneering. The efforts of those initially selected to service and maintain the Voodoo also stood the test of time. Certainly, they learned much from the Americans who were their initial instructors. Just as certainly, they improved on what they had been taught, adapting many procedures for use in the different conditions that existed in Canada.

Similarly, the air weapons controllers were compelled to make many changes to the control procedures they had perfected for the CF–100, although the CF–101, with its additional speed and acceleration, was in some ways more tolerant of control flexibility.

The RCAF started out with sixty-six Voodoos: fifty-six single-stick fighters and ten dual-stick fighters that could be used as pilot trainers when not needed for operations. But the total was not to remain at sixty-six for long. In August 1962, the RCAF suffered its first Voodoo loss when F/Ls Dave Broadbent and Vic Bartlett from 409 Squadron were compelled to do something about a double-engine flame out. With both engines gone, the hydraulics took the rest of the day off, making the aircraft uncontrollable.

The sudden silence was shattered by the sound of two ejection seats firing, and onlookers were treated to the sight of two parachutes descending into the mountains, whence the crew were plucked from the wilderness and returned to Comox by a U.S. Coast Guard helicopter, none the worse for their experience.

Another Voodoo was lost in October 1962. Flying officers Stu Whalley and Ray Jeffries, taking off from Bagotville, were horrified to see a TCA Viscount loom up in their path on the runway. Flying Officer Whalley hauled his aircraft off the ground in a desperate effort attempt to miss the airliner. He almost succeeded, but one of the CF–101's wheels hit the Viscount's roof. The stricken 101 staggered into the air, and Whalley and Jeffries ejected safely. Alas, on the Viscount, two died and eight others were injured.

November 1963 saw 416 Squadron move to Chatham on a day when the weather was at or near minimums, which prevented a formation arrival, but twelve aircraft landed in a nicely timed stream and settled in for the next twenty-one years. The year 1964 saw each of the squadrons comfortably ensconced in their home bases, perfecting the teamwork between themselves and the ground control environment, which is such an essential part of an air defence environment. Hitherto, the bulk of the con-

410 William Tell shoot team. Clockwise from left: Spieser and Gladders; Rose and Lauder; Hickman (USAF) and Helstrom (USAF); McCurdy and Wierelechyk.

trol had been exercised from individual radar sites at such idyllic locations as Mont Apica, St. Sylvestre, and other mosquito meccas. But the times, they were a'changing.

The Semi-Automatic Ground Environment (SAGE), which was basically a huge computer joined to a superb communications network, was poised to dramatically change the way in which interceptors were controlled. In Canada, the SAGE direction centre was located zillions of feet underground at North Bay, Ontario. There, controllers monitored almost half a continent of sky. Unlike their air traffic control counterparts, whose job consisted of keeping airplanes apart, these controllers were hired to bring airplanes together. Previously, this had been accomplished with considerable chatter. "Rhino 27, come left heading 270, attack vector, when steady, your target bears 315 for 35." Interspersed with the directives came a steady stream of breakaway headings, armament checks, and almost everything else except the latest Dow-Jones Averages (pilots being notoriously underpaid in those days).

With SAGE, all of that changed. SAGE (commonly called Clyde, for whatever reason) received information from all the radar sites in the region. The computer knew where the target was and what direction it was heading. It knew where the fighter was and what direction *it* was heading. Using its tubes, transistors, punched cards, and other ganglia, it could, under the guidance of a skilled controller, direct the interceptor to a position from which a tactically sound interception could be made. And, it could theoretically do it all without a word ever being exchanged between the controller and whoever in the airplane was answering messages that day. It did this through a system known as "datalink," which was developed to end the dependency on voice messages that are so susceptible to communications jamming.

How did the pilot know what direction to point his Voodoo? An electronic dot appeared on his weapon scope. If the dot was in the middle, the aircraft was on the right heading. If the dot moved either right or left, the pilot (or the autopilot) turned the aircraft to re-centre the dot. Target information appeared on dials that alternated between displaying target heading and altitude, and fighter commands, which commanded the pilot to fly at a specific speed and altitude.

And where on the scope would the navigator look for this elusive beast? Why, in the general area of the circle that the datalink had caused to appear on his scope. Using the information gleaned from the dials and the position displayed by the circle, the interceptor crew could develop an accurate picture of the attack geometry and determine how best to complete an identification or a firing pass, all without a word being exchanged between aircrew and controller. In theory. In day-to-day practice, a few words were mandatory. At initial check-in, for example, so that everyone knew the radios were working; or an armament safety check, just to keep the target happy. In peacetime, it was also mandatory to call the range and bearing of any target, so the controller could be sure that the navigator had not locked onto some sleek airliner rather than the T–Bird or Clunk that was the intended target. When it came time to return home, the aircrew or the controller would so state, and a centred steering dot would point the aircraft at its base, and the target marker circle on the nav's scope would be centred on the "home drome."

During 1963–64, the crews became better acquainted with the CF–101 and its flight characteristics. One particular characteristic that gained a lot of attention was known as pitch-up, which defined one corner of the flight envelope much as the stall defined that corner of the flight envelope in a more conventional aircraft. Although the pitch-up boundary was no more restrictive than a stall boundary, and did not prevent the Voodoo from accomplishing any of its tactical roles, the consequences of a pitch-up could include the creation of a smoking crater.

In the Voodoo, pitch-up was caused by an excessive angle of attack, and several gizmos that would remind the pilots when they were nearing a critical angle of attack had been designed into the aircraft. But, like all things electromechanical, the gizmos could be fooled, and, on occasion, could fail. So, it did not pay to put one's trust entirely in the system. And why the caution? Because it could take as much as 10,000 feet to recover from a pitch-up, which is not too hair-raising when starting from, say, 35,000 feet. When starting from 5,000 feet or some lower altitude, it was a different matter. The pitch-up recovery in such cases was to grab the ejection handles firmly and pull. This may not have done much for the aircraft, but it was a morale booster for the crew.

"How," you ask, "could a knowledgeable, experienced pilot, cosseted by myriad protective devices such as horns and pushers, possibly stick-handle his airplane into a pitch-up?"

"Easily," is the answer. Although pitch-ups were unlikely to occur in normal, unaccelerated, straight-and-level flight, the CF–101 was not really an airliner and was often called upon to do things that "you have not dreamed of," such as snap-up attacks on manoeuvring targets at night. Not that there's any less lift in the night sky. It just makes it sound better.

The fighter is committed against a supersonic, simulated hostile target at 60,000 feet. To complete the attack, the crew select an initial attack altitude of 45,000 feet. The target marker circle moves quickly down the navigator's scope.

Then, "Contact, 310 for 25."

"Your target."

"Judy."

The navigator then provides the pilot with terse descriptive and directive commentary while getting the radar to lock onto the target, and not some wretched chaff bundle. When the radar locks onto the target, the pilot's scope display changes. The steering dot now shows the direction to turn to complete a firing pass. In this case, it is a front snap-up attack, and the AIR2A switches are confirmed to be armed. Because it is a snap-up attack, the pilot maintains the assigned altitude of 45,000 feet, preserving manoeuvring energy so that, at the instant of weapons launch, the interceptor can be pointed at the correct angle to destroy the target.

Suddenly, the pilot's steering circle shrinks. This is his signal to centre the dot in elevation as well as azimuth. Back comes the stick. Up comes the nose. Down comes the airspeed. During snap-up attacks, the gospel according to Air Defence Command was a minimum airspeed of 230 knots and a maximum pitch angle of 30 degrees. But, a manoeuvring target could pull the dot out of the centre of the circle just before firing time, and it was easy indeed, when trying to re-centre it, to find both pitch angle and airspeed saying things that ADC didn't want to hear.

Would the airplane turn into a pumpkin? No, it was still an airplane, subject to aerodynamic laws. But quick actions to correct matters could induce pitch-up. In this condition, the downwash from the air flowing over the wings blanked out the tail, and there was insufficient airflow over the elevators to realign the aircraft with the relative wind. Aircraft in this condition could emulate a brick all the way to the ground. Fortunately, the designer had placed a drag chute in the Voodoo to shorten the landing roll and to save having to pave an entire province for it to land in. Popping the drag chute at the peak of the pitch-up would force the nose down and realign the aircraft with the relative wind. As it recovered, there was always the possibility that one wing would recover from the stall before the other one was ready to fly, resulting in some truly exhilarating snap rolls, which soon went away, and the aircraft was flying again.

Pilots who found themselves out of limits during snap-up attacks soon discovered that it need not always, or even often, result in pitch-up. Smoothly unloading the aircraft toward zero G and then smoothly rolling it over on its back and playing gently with the elevators commanded a ballistic trajectory that got the nose gingerly pointed into the relative wind, although it brought the crews a bit closer to any fall-out generated by the attack. The half-roll was, in any event, the recommended recovery from a snap-up attack, but it required smooth, precise control.

Pitch-up could also occur during afterburner climbs from takeoff to combat altitude. When starting such climbs, the drill was to let the speed increase to 400 KIAS (knots), then smoothly rotate to 30 degrees of pitch while maintaining 400 knots to the point where it intercepted .85 Mach, then climb at .85 Mach. In such a climb, it was possible to decrease the G loading to less than one and let the aircraft stray to an angle of attack that could mislead the various warning devices, and the pilot, too; the latter could find himself going down when he really wanted to go up. This gave rise to the unofficial operating instructions that said, "To make the airplane go up, pull back on the stick. To make it go down, pull back harder."

As noted earlier, 1964 was in some ways a transition year for the CF–101 alignment in Canada. The RCAF disbanded 410 and 414 squadrons. Some of the crews were dispatched to other squadrons, some of them disappeared in the notorious "500" list that pared the air force down to what was deemed to be an effective strength—although some of them were rapidly recalled to the colours, where they completed full careers—and the rest were absorbed by Bomarc squadrons and various mahogany bombers.

By now, the annual structure of events for the CF–101 squadrons was taking shape. The role of each squadron, and indeed the OTU under whichever title it bore, was to maintain the maximum possible number of combat-ready crews and aircraft for C-in-C NORAD's use in beating back the filthy Red aggressor. Each squadron vied with the others to be the best in the business, and they all sent glowing reports up the line. And were those reports believed? Well, maybe. But despite this tendency to believe, there were some sceptics. Thus it was that each squadron, each year, was evaluated by an endless stream of evaluators who poked, pried, prodded, and snooped into all aspects of squadron training to ensure that those who advertised themselves as being combat-ready were in fact qualified to counter the various threats then thought to exist.

The biggest annual event was the Tac-Eval (later called the Op Eval), which examined every aspect of a base's ability to fight a sustained war. For some days before the event, exercise intelligence summaries informed the base that the diplomatic crises were multiplying; that Fantasian forces were on "manoeuvres" near friendly NATO borders; that Badgers, Bisons, Bears, and other beasts had disappeared from the Soviet Long-Range Air Force Bases and could not be found. Eventually, they were discovered at northern deployment bases. It was all bad news.

Then, a C–130 Hercules, or some other form of commodious, luxury VIP transport would land at the Voodoo base and disgorge, no, not the Red Army, but an assault force that was almost as big: the Tac-Eval team. Promptly, at some unearthly hour the next morning, the base went on alert, as the Tac-Eval team chief put his script into play. Sirens wailed, phone lines buzzed, cars tore from sleepy suburb to sleepy suburb as the entire base turned out to ready all aircraft and facilities for . . . WAR!

The fighter bases were deemed to have a nuclear capability. Could they safely and quickly break the weapons out of secure storage, transport them securely to the flight line, sanitize and secure a loading area, safely load the weapons on the aircraft, and ensure that only authorized flight and ground crews got anywhere near the armed aircraft? Only one way to find out—do it. Almost as soon as the Voodoos appeared on the flight line, a cordon was thrown around them, security forces cleared the areas around the cordon, and the weapons trailers materialized from the predawn mists. Quickly the weapons loaders swarmed to their tasks, watched closely by beady-eyed inspectors looking for incorrect or unauthorized procedures.

During the weapons loading phase, intelligence reports continued flooding in. Our diplomats never succeeded in keeping the peace. The Badgers, Bisons, and Bears were seen to take off, ostensibly on routine manoeuvres and war games. Soviet submarines were tracked . . . in the Saguenay river. The situation was, like a pitched-up CF–101, definitely going downhill.

As quickly as they had arrived, the weapons were returned to storage and each Voodoo was loaded with at least one McDonnell Simulated Rocket (MSR), an evaluation device that was fitted to determine if a particular practice attack had resulted in a successful weapons launch. The weapons—er, pardon, capabilities—may have been back in storage, but the rest of the nuclear trappings remained. Could the base continue to provide security and whatnot for the simulated armed fleet? Again, legions of inspectors watched all the procedures used by the air and ground crews to ready the aircraft for flight.

And soon it came. The base is threatened by a possible attack. How soon can we get the aircraft off? As it turns out, there is a procedure known as a "Flush" designed to get all aircraft off the ground quickly, with ten or fifteen-second spacing. The first aircraft off turns right to a predetermined heading, and the second aircraft turns left, and they alternate from then on in a joyous maelstrom of booms, roars, dust, smoke, and power, which is a sight to behold and a sound show that defies description.

Initially, the crews use the aircraft radar to provide separation among the aircraft, but the Bisons, Badgers, etc., which took off a few paragraphs back are suddenly here, or at least close to here. SAGE assumes command of the interceptors and steers them toward the most likely bomber routes. Soon, a splendid air battle begins.

The Badgers, etc., now magically transformed into B–52s, CF–100s, T–33s, Arguses, Trackers, and other mock bombers flood through the regions. Aircraft turn. Jammers jam. Chaff beckons invitingly. Electronic countermeasures of all kinds paint beguiling pictures on scopes. Communications jammers obscure the airwaves. At last, a target. Declared hostile? Yes. Remember, we're carrying simulated nukes. Authenticate the launch command. Great—the authentication checks. And so, into the fray. Just before weapons launch, the gate stealer breaks the radar lock. A hard, breaking turn to break the collision. Let the nose fall to maintain manoeuvring energy. Now back the other way to get behind this dude. The Voodoo shudders in protest as the burners come in and the G goes on.

A little help from the controller? "Two-twenty for six." Ah yes, there he is, probably about 10,000 high by now. Crank up the radar antenna. Keep the burners in. Lock on. Centre the dot. Pull the trigger. Great. "Splash one B–52." And now, bingo fuel. Time to go home. You and the rest of the fleet. Between SAGE, terminal, and tower, the Voodoos land in a steady stream, scant seconds apart. As they taxi one by one into their assigned parking spots, fuel bowsers appear. Simultaneously, the safety systems truck pulls up behind the aircraft and replaces the drag chute. Other technicians replenish the oil, rearm the simulated rockets and missiles, and refill the oxygen in an exotic, graceful ballet of frenetic activity.

At one base, one year, the base information wallah obtained some sort of divine intervention to conduct a tour of high school guidance counsellors through the base during the evaluation. The counsellors were strategically placed in a high vantage point overlooking the flight line and fortified with several issues of squadron coffee, than which there is nothing coffier. One rather dour counsellor observed the haste, skill, and precision with which the ground crew prepared the returning aircraft for flight, and was visibly awed when the first two down were scrambled after about ten minutes on the ground. "My God," she said, "for years I've thought of the Forces as a last resort for my less capable people. Now I don't think too many of my people could cope with this."

You probably thought that last anecdote was tossed in there so that I could get out of telling you how, when the aircrews claimed a kill, the inspectors could tell if they were telling the truth. Each Voodoo contained a NADAR can,[18] which recorded the view of the pilot's scope after the navigator locked on to the target.

---

18 NADAR can is a recording device that, when examined after flight, can help assessors determine whether a particular attack would have resulted in a kill. NADAR cans and other devices had to be used to see if the system would work.

Watching a replay of this fancy tape, the inspectors could indeed determine if the dot was in the middle, as the pilot claimed, or if it was somewhere out in right field. They could also tell, by checking the overtake gap—which appeared in the perimeter of another circle on the pilot's scope—if the crew had actually zapped a target or if they had just wasted a warhead on a chaff bundle, which occasionally happened. And, if the navigator hadn't broken lock a split-second after the X appeared, they could tell if the pilot had done a real break turn, or if it had been a lazy pull-off, for which they would gleefully deduct points.

Even if the pilot, clever chap, did wrestle the acrobatic dot into the centre of the circle and by dint of Herculean effort hold it there, would the various gewgaws in the fire-control computer have sent the correct signals to the rocket? The McDonnell Simulated Rocket (MSR), which was a large part of all these evaluations, contained an automatic instant camera that snapped a picture of various switch settings at time of launch. Using this picture and the known target and interceptor speeds and altitudes, weapons officers and evaluators could determine if the aircraft was also combat-ready.

Similarly, the AIM 4 was evaluated by a Weapons System Evaluation Missile (WSEM), a device that had the same seeker head as the real missile, but back where the propellant and explosives would be on the real thing, there was a complex mess of wires, paper, and styli. During the attack, this contrivance recorded all the signals entering the missile, and showed whether or not the seeker head had acquired the target. Although it could not tell if the fighter had manoeuvred into the heart of the launch envelope, it could certainly tell if the missile had seen the target.

There were, in truth, few ways in which the inspectors could be outwitted. Before they would accept a claimed kill, they would review the NADAR, check the rocket or missile simulators, talk to the inspectors who were monitoring the exercise from the SAGE site, and discuss matters with the target crews. They almost wanted to see wreckage on the ground before they would reluctantly award a "kill."

Meantime, the war went on. Generally, our side was getting pushed back. Matters deteriorated. Radioactive fallout arrived. How did the crews cope with that? How did they cope with combat losses? How did they . . . ? How did they . . . ? How did they . . . ? You name it, and someone had thought of it and worked it into the script. Every aspect of the base's ability to support a sustained attack was evaluated. And not just on paper. The base was put to the test, and all members had to demonstrate the ability to perform wartime tasks. In particular, the technical organization was thoroughly wrung out. A tactical evaluation generated many more Voodoo missions in a shorter period than did routine operations. Not only did the ground crew have to deal with the routine servicing, but they had to clear the many snags that would occur as a result of the heightened pace. Invariably, they produced the airplanes for the crews to fly.

Another evaluation that kept the squadrons on their toes was the alert force capability test. Unlike the Tac-Eval, this was a no-notice operation and did not involve everyone on base. For this evaluation, the inspectors arrived in a couple of T–Birds and concentrated their efforts on the individuals and aircraft holding alert in the Q. The alert aircraft were armed only with secondary weapons, the AIM 4s. These live weapons were downloaded and replaced with simulated rockets and missiles. The crews were then sent aloft to do several firing passes to prove that they and their aircraft were capable of doing their air defence thing. Just to keep everyone on their toes, there was, as there was in Tac-Eval, a written exam designed to test the crews' knowledge of the aircraft, radar, tactics, airmanship, meteorology, and the other items featured in ADC ground schools.

Because the CF–101 squadrons had a nuclear capability, they were subject to — what else — capability inspections. These were examinations of the bases' ability to support nuclear weapons should such noisemakers ever appear on base strength. These, too, featured a written examination, and demonstrations of everything that could be done with a nuclear weapon, short of detonating it, which was considered to be overkill. Even accidents were considered, and in these, the firefighters, like the diplomats a few paragraphs back who never prevented a war, never put out the fire. In all of these evaluations, inspections, exercises, tests — or indeed, in routine operations — CF–101s were never sent aloft carrying nuclear weapons, had such things been part of the arsenal.

Tac-Evals, alert force capability tests, and capability inspections told C-in-C NORAD how well a particular base or squadron could fulfill its role in NORAD, which was probably comforting to him. But how well did the system work? To find out, the various NORAD regions staged regional exercises that required the regional SAGE direction centre to conduct an air battle that used all the air defence resources in the region. Such exercises normally took place during hours when no one else wanted to use the sky. The first scrambles would generally occur at about midnight, and the last would launch at about 0600. These exercises, too, would be invigilated by numerous inspectors, although they did not always deploy to the interceptor bases. There was, at each base, a trusted agent who provided the evaluators with an account of the squadron's participation, and who examined the NADAR replays to ensure that any claimed kills were just that and not figments of the pilot's imagination.

Throughout the year, each squadron developed its own exercises and inter-flight competitions to keep the air and ground crews lean and mean. The officers detailed to plan the exercises were chosen for their vivid imaginations, and the targets could include anything short of the real Badgers and Bears. These exercises and competitions often featured some of the most realistic situations the crews would encounter throughout the year, as some of the target crews considered the ADC evasive action limits to be unduly restrictive and went beyond the call of duty. Often the top crews of the squadron exercises would represent the squadron in the MacBrien Trophy Shoot, or in Callshot exercises that were held annually to determine the ADC top guns and top maintainers. The winners of this would represent the RCAF or CF at the USAF's William Tell intergalactic rocket meet and clambake held biennially at Tyndall AFB in Florida. In later years, a composite ADC team represented Canada.

Each year, each squadron formed an air show team that was tasked by NDHQ to show the flag at various such events in the local area. The Voodoo was a true crowd pleaser at air shows because it was big, noisy, and impressive. The hard lights of the afterburners were guaranteed to get the crowd oohing and aahing, and the tight formations, while tactically useless, showed spectators that the pilots had indeed mastered their aircraft.

Such displays were not without their hazards. In 1973, Captains John Pew and Gary Raindahl parachuted to safety when their Voodoo disintegrated during a series of vertical rolls at the Abbotsford air show.

As the annual succession of Tac-Evals, alert force capability tests, and so forth rolled by with all the inevitability of the seasons themselves, it became obvious that the original CF–101s lacked the capability to search out and destroy low-level targets, which were thought to be an increasing threat. When the Voodoo was first designed, it was meant to counter mostly high-level bombers; bombers that would have to remain at high altitude to have any chance of getting near their assigned targets. But time and technology fixed that. Improved engines, stand-off bombers, and cruise missiles radically altered the threat facing North America from exclusively high-level to an intriguing mix of high- and low-altitude targets. And, low level was just the area where the CF–101 was weakest.

And what brought about the weakness? The same radar that made it such a formidable foe at high altitudes. For its day, it was a truly remarkable radar that could see large aircraft forty or more miles away, tune away from jammers, identify chaff bundles, and do everything except balance cheque books. However, at low level, this magnificent radar had a disturbing tendency to make Mount Waddington look even bigger than it is. The first chap to shout, "Let there be light!" was probably thinking of the glow given off by a CF–101 radar painting the Rocky Mountains.

In such a sea of light, it was difficult to pick out airborne targets until quite close to them, regardless of how finely one tuned the scope. Mix in a couple of chaff bundles, and a crew could spend an entire trip without a glimpse of the target. Often, SAGE would not be tracking the target all that well, either, and the controller would be unable to give an accurate relative position.

The USAF recognized this problem and did something about it. That something was the addition of an Infra-Red Search and Track System (IRSTS) to the Voodoo. The sensor for this was mounted immediately in front of the pilot's cockpit, where it supplanted the refuelling system, which Canada, in the absence of tankers at that time, was unable to use in any event.

By 1971, the Canadian CF–101 strength had diminished to fifty-six from the original sixty-six. An exchange program called Operation Peace Wings saw the original CF–101s returned to the United States. They were replaced by sixty-six F–101s (ten of them dual stickers), which carried the IRSTS, but otherwise differed little from the original aircraft.

Helped by the OTU, each squadron quickly developed training programs to get up to speed on the complexities of the new toy. And complexities there were, albeit not insurmountable. The crew had to be aware of the mode being used, as it was possible to launch the AIM 4 missiles with no chance of their ever seeing the target; or not to launch them at all, which was equally embarrassing.

Soon the crews learned that the auditory warning provided by the IRSTS meant that the back-seater could join the pilot in a visual search for the intruder, knowing that his headset would tell him if a heat source was out there. Once the system beeped, it was head back inside, to get some idea of the target's bearing. When the telltale IR spike appeared among all the grass and whatnot on the scope, the navigator could lock the seeker head to the target in much the same way the radar locked onto the target. By then switching to a radar mode and locking onto the radar target, the likelihood of a kill was improved, as the radar provided better information to the missiles than did the IR information, although what the target was supposed to be doing during all this fiddling about was never clearly explained. Gradually, the crews mastered the intricacies of the new system, and the ground crew mastered the arcane art of troubleshooting the complex plumbing, hampered somewhat by laconic aircrew descriptions of what the problem really was.

But the CF–101 remained essentially unchanged from its introduction in 1961 to its phase-out from active interception service twenty-three years later. Many of the crews returned for second, third, or even fourth tours on air defence squadrons. This phenomenon provided squadron commanders with a solid nucleus of experienced veterans to guide the odd new lieutenant that providence would sometimes provide. But it had another side effect, which could be described as creeping unrealism. Tactics were occasionally based on obscure capabilities of the weapons system, rather than on tactically sound manoeuvres. Exam questions occasionally strayed to the esoteric, rather than the need to know. And, courses occasionally became painstaking journeys through the wiring diagram of some missile or other, while remaining relatively silent on the tactics, equipment, and doctrine of any potential adversary. Concentration on the night-fighter part of the role led more or less inevitably to reduced attention to the tactics that had been developed by people such as Barker, Collishaw, McCall, and MacClaren in WW I, and continued by Beurling, McLeod, Davoud, Bannock, and Braham in WW II. Because the Voodoo was expected to fight a radar war at night, little attention was paid to developing the instinct needed for those occasions when the target might be visible and might not have a strong death wish. Such preoccupation with technical, rather than tactical, skill spilled over to the ground side, where controllers attempting to upgrade from one category to another were expected to control four interceptors on one target, which, while challenging, was tactically useless.

Before this unrealistic slant could become too firmly entrenched, the new fighter mystique took over, and it did so many for many years before the first CF–18 took wing. Part of the return to reality was spurred by the CF–5 fighter lead-in training course, which *ab initio* fighter pilots destined for CF–101s had to complete from 1975 on. These pilots were taught to fly the CF–5 like, well, a fighter. The principle of maintaining manoeuvring energy so that one could point the nose of the CF–5 where one wanted was second nature to them.

Their scepticism caused others to reflect on the time-honoured realities of air fighting. Squadrons

"Hi, there. You look better at night, think I."

changed their training routines. Slowly, cautiously, basic fighter manoeuvres, air combat manoeuvring, and various combat formations were added to the Voodoo repertoire — not because the CF had given up the search for a new fighter and were about to hang a cannon on the Voodoo, but because the tactics would be extremely useful in a fight with a bomber pilot who was fighting not for godless communism, but for his life.

Thus it was that the CF–101s participated in Maple Flag exercises at Cold Lake, where they shared the sky with F–15s, F–16s, CF–5s, F–4s, and other charter members of the jowl-sagging, G-sucking, gun-toting set. In these exercises, as in so many others, the crew showed the skills and versatility needed to complete their assigned missions. Close-in day fighters the Voodoos were not, but given one good look at a target, the crews could use them to defend a base from a fighter-bomber attack against heavy odds.

At the same time, the crews maintained the classic night and all-weather interception skill needed to intercept the relatively steady flow of Bears that appeared off Canada's east coast, en route to Cuba, and many CF–101 crews gained considerable experience in flying loose formation on such intruders at night.

What with evaluations, exercises, inspections,

and other forms of aerial entertainment, squadron life must have been really exciting, right? Oddly enough, the answer is: Not particularly. The routine varied from squadron to squadron as dictated by operational commitments, desires of commanders and crews, and tradition. Each squadron had some system for alternating its crews between day and night activities, and for ensuring that alert duties were equitably shared among the crews.

On days when there were no exercises, evaluations, or other distractions, the daily flying program kicked off with a morning briefing that could include a few words from the squadron or flight commander, and would include a briefing from the duty weather-guesser covering the home air patch and whichever of the possible alternate airports was in use that day. Then the crews would be told their takeoff time, aircraft number, and control agency, and be given a brief description of the mission, including any necessary weapons evaluations needed to keep the aircraft categorized. The mission briefing was often followed by a pitch from the flight safety officer, or from the pilots or navigators who had been assigned duties such as intelligence, weapons, or engineering.

The crews detailed for the first launch would drift toward the aircraft, with the pilots conducting any necessary formation briefings en route to the flight line. Crews with later take-off times busied themselves with the various administrative tasks needed to keep the squadron running smoothly, until it was their turn to "slip the surly bonds of earth." To some, this pre-flight briefing routine may seem a bit casual. But these crews were expected to be capable of scrambling after an unknown target at any hour of the day or night without any previous briefing, barring the mandatory best guesses of the weather wizards. Thus, an extensive pre-flight briefing on the mission profiles, target parameters, and other minutiae would have been self-defeating.

The post-flight routine was somewhat more formal. The NADAR film was always viewed to ensure that the dot-steering prowess of individual pilots did not decline below perfection or such higher standards as pilots believed that they met. And there was also a post-flight call to the intercept director at SAGE, who had done his or her level best to get the Voodoo into the same air mass as its target. Any difficulties were thoroughly thrashed out so that they did not impair later operations. Witness the following debriefing between F/L Hammy Phistte, noted pilot, and F/L Chuck Blewitt, a SAGE controller:

"I would'a got him if you had put me over the right continent."

"Nonsense, I had him right on the line. What did you do? Centre the dot on your left wingtip?"

Such constructive feedback did much to improve a well-oiled, smooth-running air defence machine.

And stats. Each mission resulted in the generation of a humongous form that, joined with all its brethren, would reach some distance past the moon, and would provide ADC with more stats than those enjoyed by either the National or American baseball leagues. Crews soon became expert in completing this form and other locally generated forms that allowed the squadron hierarchy to determine that the training goals for simulated single-engine approaches, ILS approaches, AI approaches (these being approaches done by the navigator using the aircraft radar), and other training events were met each month. In addition to flying training, there was simulator training, which provided the crews with skills needed to cope with situations that could not always be practised in the air. Generally, the simulator crews made their missions as realistic as possible, albeit the trips were slanted toward emergency drills. However, years before line-oriented flight training became the norm with airlines, it was being practised in the Voodoo simulators and was instrumental in maintaining skills at a high level.

And such training paid dividends. Every so often, something whirring around in the engines would let loose from its moorings. If it let loose while it was travelling down, the crew got to practise a real single-engine approach. If it let loose when it was travelling up toward the fuel tanks that comprised most of the Voodoo's fuselage, the crew got to practise an emergency parachute descent. Although no simulator ever prepares a crew for an inflight explosion and bailout, the training was useful in helping them sort out return trips with various bits of ironmongery poking out of the engines.

As the '70s merged into the '80s and it was evident the Voodoos were heading for the big military museum in the sky, the crews were given greater opportunities to fire the weapons that the CF–101s carried. In earlier years, only those crews taking part in the William Tell rocket meet ever had the opportunity to fire either the AIR2A or the AIM 4. Toward the end, however, most crews made the trip to the air weapons range at Tyndall AFB, where, over the Gulf of Mexico, they experienced the considerable tumult that resulted from an AIR2A going noisily on its way. Needless to say, these weapons were warhead-free. For the crews, it was a welcome interlude in a procession of dry firing passes, and they made the most of it.

Gradually, the introduction of the CF–18 came closer, an event that greatly excited the pilots while engendering a sense of sadness among the navigators. Despite the CF–101's imminent phase-out, morale did not suffer. The crews approached their flying and alert commitments with the same dedicated professionalism that had always marked the Voodoo years.

In 1982, 410 Squadron quietly folded up its tent in Bagotville and moved to Cold Lake. That is, the artifacts, histories, and so forth moved to Cold Lake. The Voodoos and their crews dispersed to various other employments. In 1984, the remaining Voodoo squadrons traded in their aircraft for CF–18s, and Canada was almost out of the Voodoo business.

"Almost?" you say? "If all of your squadrons are flying something else, it sounds like you are entirely out of the Voodoo business." But not so. The double boom was still to be heard at North Bay, where 414 Squadron was operating an electronic warfare version of the CF–101 and one dual, which was used for pilot checkouts. These two aircraft soldiered on until April 1987, when the electronic warfare bird was returned to the USAF, and the dual was taken to CFB Cornwallis, where it went on display to remind Canadian Forces recruits of a proud chapter in Canadian aviation history.

Before we bid farewell to an aircraft that lasted for almost a quarter of a century in front-line service, let's take one last nostalgic trip. We'll do this one from Comox, so that you don't have to strap into an aircraft that has been sitting in minus forty-degree temperatures, and where it is a nice, sunny day. Climb the ladder and peer into the cockpit. Check that the seat pin is in, the gear handle is in the down position, the armament is safe, and the pitot heat and battery are both off. Then, throw the chute in, hook it up, come back down the ladder, and we'll do a walk-around.

The checklist identifies some thirty-eight items for us to check, but there is no need to list them here, since you're so familiar with them, but we'll collect the pins, covers, and so forth. Now it's back up the ladder to complete the strap-in ritual. Shrug into the chute harness, connect the Mae West, fasten the seat harness, and hook up the oxygen mask and telecom leads. Once the cockpit is in order and the ground crew are ready, select the combustion start, turn on the left engine master switch, and hit the start switch. As the fuel flow starts to move up, watch the acceleration and be ready to go to emergency fuel if the engine is slow to accelerate. As the RPM passes

35 percent, wave the ground crew away and return the fuel to normal. Before starting the right engine, check the hydraulic pressure and then repeat the starting procedure so that you can have a two-engine fighter. Once the engines are running smoothly, the before-taxi checks must be complete, which will require a little help from the ground crew. Then:

"Tower, Cudgel 17, taxi."

"Cudgel 17 tower, it's runway 11, altimeter 3006, surface wind calm. Taxi with caution; construction near runway."

En route to the runway, we'll pick up the IFR clearance and finish off the pre-takeoff and takeoff checks. Then:

"Tower, Cudgel 17, takeoff, requesting gate climb."

"Cudgel 17, change departure control frequency, monitor guard channel, surface winds light and variable, your gate climb approved, cleared for takeoff."

The engines run up to 80 percent, the maximum permitted with the brakes on. Temperatures and pressures are good. Release the brakes. Power to 100 percent. Slowly the Voodoo starts down the runway. A quick check of the dials. Everything okay. Move the throttles outboard. Boom-Boom. Both burners lit. Check the EPRs and EGT. Everything still okay. Now we're moving, really moving. Off the nose wheel steering and onto the rudder . . . 155 knots. Raise the nose to about six degrees of pitch . . . a blink . . . 175 knots. She comes unstuck. Another blink and a climb indication on the VSI. Get the gear and hope the nose gear doesn't hang. Thump, as the nose gear announces that it, too, is up and locked. Flaps complete their travel, and the aircraft continues its spectacular acceleration.

Within a few seconds, we're at 400 KIAS. Now, rotate to 30 degrees of pitch while still maintaining 400 knots. The 5,000-foot check is started on time and completed at about 12,000 feet. Start to change the altimeter to 29.92 and we're through 20,000 feet before it's reset. A few more seconds, and we're through flight level 310. Smoothly roll the aircraft over on its back and let the nose fall to the horizon. Roll it right side up, and there we are at flight level 350. The awesome splendour of the coast mountains unfolds underneath.

"Departure, Cudgel 17 level, flight level 350."

"Roger 17, contact Dustbowl on designator sixteen."

"Dustbowl, Cudgel 17, armament safety checks complete, ready to play."

"Roger 17, follow dolly." This last is an indication that further communication from the ground to the fighter will be via datalink.

A few seconds later, the datalink dials start getting excited. There is a target about fifty miles away. Shifty devil that he is, he has noticed that there is a fighter nearby, and he is evading. The target heading dial struggles to keep up.

Then, "Contact, 340 for 18."

"Roger, your target."

The intercept director has asked for an identification pass.

"Port hard forty, and down 5,000 feet," saith the navigator.

"Port hard forty and down 5,000," saith the pilot.

"It's now fifteen port, twelve miles, slightly low, overtake about 900 knots."

"Rog," says the pilot, "we've still got about 180 degrees to turn."

"Roger that, port hard."

"Port hard it is."

"Twenty port, ten miles still a bit low, harden up the turn."

"Roger, hardening up to hard as possible, height set."

"Range now six miles, ten port, level to slightly high, overtake about 500 knots. Burners."

"Roger, burners, about 90 degrees to turn."

"Okay, keep the turn going. We're about four miles, ten port, level to slightly high, overtake around 300 knots."

"Check, he's seen us and turning into us and he's confirmed (simulated) hostile. I'll start taking out the preps for the AIM 4's."

"You hold him visual, and I'll roll out of the turn and go high."

"Okay, he's now about ten o'clock low and starting to move away. Now, start your turn back to his deep six."

"Rog, the missiles are armed and the preps are out. Can you get a lock on him?"

"Rog, there's the lock; now can we get a little deeper into the heart of the envelope?"

After a few seconds of hiyawkas, twizzles, and alternating sky and mountains, it's, "Dustbowl, Cudgel 17, splash one Voodoo."

"Roger 17, turn starboard to 360 to set up your target run."

A few minutes later, it's time to begin the target run. Both pilot and nav scan the skies to spot the incoming interceptor.

Suddenly, "Tally, left, 9:30, slightly low, three or four miles. Sliding back and pointed right at us."

"Rog. Tally."

A sharp, descending turn into the oncoming interceptor. Watch his nose come up as he trades airspeed for altitude to manoeuvre out of our plane's ambit. "Now, reverse and pull up into him."

Slowly the fight deteriorates into a stalemate.

"Seventeen, knock it off."

The rules of engagement for the Voodoo are not quite those of the day-fighter crowd, and in any event, a continuous twisting, turning fight in a CF–101 is not a recipe for longevity.

The controller has heard the "Knock it off" call. "Ready for another set-up?" he asks.

"Negative, Dustbowl. Get us down out of the controlled airspace so we can cancel and return to Comox VFR."

Within seconds, the clearance comes through, and the two Voodoos, now in echelon formation, descend toward the Mount Waddington area, snaking their way through passes and gorges. Every day, the colour of these mountains is different. Look at the purplish hues as dusk gathers in the valleys. Lead wants the troops in line astern, loose line astern. A roll, just to keep things loose. Now one the other way. Now a few sinus-clearing turns to show the airplane who is boss. Now, back into echelon and continue the descent into the inlet below us, keeping a sharp watch for the light aircraft traffic that so changed the transportation picture of this area.

"Traffic, about ten o'clock, four miles, diverging." Even so, swing wide to give him plenty of room. Go peacefully on your way, little friend.

Clear now, of the mainland.

"Comox Tower, Cudgel 17 flight, ten north landing."

Tower responds with the required litany of information, and the two Voodoos swing onto final. Okay, look at the way the last of the sun is reflecting off the Comox glacier. How many people are lucky enough to see that?

"Tower, Cudgel 17 flight is three miles on initial for a formation break and landing." Of no tactical use, but it looks good. "Seventeen flight, number one, call the break."

About thirty seconds later, the two Voodoos bank smoothly into a steep 180-degree turn, 1,000 feet above the runway. As they roll out, the speed brakes come in, and the gear and flaps go down. Holding position perfectly, the two aircraft turn base, get landing clearance, and then roll smoothly onto short final, perfectly aligned with the runway. Now flare, and there is the shriek of protesting rubber as four tires hit the runway. "Two's got a chute," and lead pops his drag chute, allowing the two aircraft to decelerate as one. Two sets of nose wheels touch down simultaneously.

"Tower, 17 is clearing the active, going ground for [sob] ever."

So it was a lot of fun. But was it a good airplane? Well, it had its critics. And there were in fact things it wouldn't do. It wouldn't carry troops and it wouldn't seek out submarines far from home—or even close to home. Nor was it much use in the search-and-rescue role. As a day fighter, it had a number of shortcomings that would have permitted it a brief, but spectacular, career, although the armament it carried was responsible for at least some of the shortcomings.

But as an interceptor, which was what it was intended to be, it was superb. To combat Badgers, Bisons, Bears, Blinders, Backfires, and other beasts of contemporary mythology, the CF–101 had all the capability needed. From a pilot's perspective, it was an excellent instrument platform by the standards of the day. Pilots who had been accustomed to the somewhat random instrument placement in the CF–100 were delighted to have an aircraft that permitted a relatively easy instrument scan while rolling upside down in a dirty, black cloud.

Navigators, too, were quick to see the Voodoo's virtues. By almost any standard, the back cockpit was roomy. The chief attraction was the radar, and later, the IRSTS. The radar was a more powerful big brother of the radar the CF–100 had carried. This made it possible to see targets at greater distances, which meant a better chance of closing to a firing position quickly. And, the extra performance of the two J–57s meant that minor miscalculations of attack geometry did not result in the boring stern chases of yesteryear.

The radar contained a host of electronic counter-counter measures that remained effective to the end of the aircraft's life. Not, perhaps, 100 percent

CF–101 formation over Bagotville—including the "Hangar Queen" (count the shadows).

effective, but effective enough to make the aircraft tactically capable throughout its lifetime. The transmitter could tune away from a jammer faster than a campaigning politician could make promises, and even better than that, faster than the promises could be broken. The system featured measures that protected against angle deceivers, gate stealers, and the old standby, chaff. As an added attraction, navigators would occasionally be assigned a dual-controlled aircraft, which gave them the opportunity to make the sky and earth change position.

Perhaps the biggest drawback was the armament. The primary weapon, the AIR2A, required precise radar ranging if it was to achieve its potential. As jammers, etc., improved, there was an increasing likelihood that such ranging might not be available. The AIM 4's, being heat seekers, did not need precise guidance at launch. As they did not have proximity fuses, a one-inch miss was still a miss. Had the aircraft been fitted with a cannon or two, its combat capability would have been considerably enhanced.

Working in conjunction with SAGE, which was the relatively invisible part of the NORAD network, and supported by a host of dedicated, professional, ground crews who were second to none, the CF–101 and its crews provided Canada with topnotch air defence for more than two decades. Although it was never tested operationally, there is little doubt that it would have acquitted itself well against the threat it was designed to meet. For the crews who controlled, supported, and flew it, the CF–101 was respected, admired, and ultimately loved for its many honest qualities. As one pilot said, after landing from a trip that included a smidgen of everything the aircraft would do, "It's the most fun you can have with your clothes on."

Terrorism has supplanted bombing attacks as the threat of the day, but in the era when the Voodoo came to stay, and stay, then stay some more, air defence was an urgent concern. Canada's existing air defence aircraft, the CF–100, had slid into obsolescence, and the CF–101 filled the gap. It is a measure of the aircraft's excellence that it continued to do so, credibly, for more than twenty years.

The double-boom is heard no more in Canadian skies, but while it was there, it was an audible sound of freedom: a reminder that Canadian youth were still ready to defend their country. It was a tradition that started many years ago and continues today. The CF–101 years are a proud chapter in that history.

PART FOUR
SUPERSONIC YEARS

Creating the Voodoo[19]
Bob Merrick

From bomber buddy to bomber buster is one way to sum up the varied career of the aircraft that Canadians remember as the CF–101 Voodoo, which provided air defence for what seems like forever. But, when the McDonnell Aircraft Company sat down to design the aircraft that eventually became the Voodoo, it wasn't thinking of defence of the base. Rather, it had in mind a long-range escort fighter that would escort B–29s, B–50s, and B–36s that were supposed to make hash of someone else's base.

The U.S. Air Force, mindful of the carnage that German fighters had inflicted on unescorted B–17s and B–24s, obliged with a contract for some development, and on October 20, 1948, the XF–88 Voodoo took to the skies. Although the aircraft made a good impression on those who flew it, it could do little for the USAF that the F–84 and F–86, which were already in production, couldn't do. So, it was not then ordered into production. But, neither was it forgotten.

The Korean War showed the USAF that the long-range fighter was still an idea worth pursuing. McDonnell was asked to resurrect its XF–88, but with some upgrades—considerable upgrades. The F–88 was fifty-four feet long. The F–101A measured sixty-seven feet. The F–88's engines produced 3,000 pounds of thrust, the F–101A's engines 15,000 pounds of thrust, which was just as well, because the F–88 weighed 18,500 pounds; the F–101A weighed 48,000 pounds, or was, as one wag put it, "so heavy that in straight and level flight it sustained 2 G."

The first F–101A flew on September 29, 1954, but the Voodoo was not destined to enter Strategic Air Command until May 1957, following some testing difficulties that saw the entire program placed on hold for three months while the USAF reviewed the aircraft's flight characteristics. Two months after entering SAC service, the F–101As were transferred to Tactical Air Command, where they remained for twelve years.

But the Voodoo was not just a fighter. Equipped with a longer, flatter nose and a couple of cameras, it became an effective reconnaissance aircraft, the RF–101. The prototype of this version first flew on May 10, 1956. Thirty-five RF–101As were built, followed by 166 RF–101Cs. The C models were destined to become the primary recce aircraft during the early years in Vietnam. RF–101Cs also brought back the pictures that clearly showed the Soviet missile buildup in Cuba in 1962.

The interceptor version of the Voodoo was born in 1955, when the USAF recognized that the F–89 Scorpion, whose low-slung engines gave it the nickname "Ramp Sniffer," would not last forever, or even until the F–106 was ready for service. The USAF noticed that the Voodoo was capable of impressive speed, climb, and endurance and asked McDonnell to come up with an interceptor version that would fill a gap in the NORAD defences until the F–106 came on line.

---

19 Reprinted with permission of CAHS.

On March 27, 1957, two years after the contract was signed, the first F–101B roared aloft, propelled by about 35,000 pounds of thrust. The experience gained with the fighter and recce versions meant that there was little in the way of airframe and engines to worry about. The aircraft needed a couple of states to turn around in, and would not have fared too well against contemporary fighters. But who cared? It wasn't intended to do so.

However, because of initial radar and fire control system problems, it wouldn't have fared too well against contemporary bombers, either. Considerable work was needed, and it wasn't until early 1959 that the Voodoo started to serve with the USAF's Air Defense Command squadrons. The aircraft stayed in USAF service until 1971, and soldiered on with the Air National Guard until 1982.

In the fighter and reconnaissance roles, for which it was intended, the Voodoo had a relatively short career. As an interceptor, originally seen in a stop-gap role, the aircraft served well for more than twenty years.

Escort fighter, tactical fighter, recce-bird, interceptor . . . it just goes to show that when somebody asks, "What's that you've got on the drawing board (or, these days, the computer screen)?" a wise designer will say, "Oh, I don't know. What is it you need?"

425 (CF–101) Squadron formation

Les Taylor

In July 1961, while on staff at the OTU in Cold Lake, we heard that Canada had purchased the F–101 Voodoo from the United States. Shortly thereafter, I was informed that I had been selected to join the initial group to form 425 Squadron. After several false starts, we finally had a date in August to commence ground training at Otis AFB in Massachusetts for a week and then a week later to be at Hamilton AFB near San Francisco. Taking some leave, my wife and I drove east to Ontario and thence to Otis. There, the eight original crews would complete the ground phase and would be sorted into crews and assigned tasks to prepare our syllabus for Namao. Our drive from Otis to Hamilton in six days was swift and hot. August in the cornfields and Salt Lake area without air conditioning was not pleasant.

At Hamilton, the USAF was very good to those of us who had brought our families, finding accommodation in temporary quarters—or even houses. We were split between the two squadrons for training: the 83rd and 84th FIS[20]. Naturally, the pilots had more flying time, but the navs got enough to qualify. After seven flights that included five actual AI exercises, my pilot, E.M.W. Robinson (Robbie), and I were scheduled for our Tac Eval. During briefing, it was learned that a B–52 ECM flight was passing through. Our USAF crew was keen to engage, so en route to intercept, we completed our Tac Eval, were declared combat ready, and intercepted the B–52. We were possibly the first 425 Voodoo crew to do so. On landing, I had a total of eleven hours and thirty-five minutes on type.[21] In early October, we finished at Hamilton and departed for Namao to prepare for the conversion of the other squadrons.

Bagtown follies

Doug Brown

"It was a dark and stormy night" . . . actually, it was a nice fall evening.

The boys from the Bagotville Ghetto (the local French-Canadian neighbourhood that had been

---

20 Fighter Interceptor Squadron (U.S.).
21 "On type" denotes the number of hours a particular pilot or navigator has acquired on a particular aircraft; in this case, it means the writer has flown eleven hours, thirty-five minutes in the CF–101.

invaded by English-speaking military families) had convened at Mouldy Roy's for drinks and war stories this fine evening, having fired off Officer Brown's flintlock rifle in the backyard and terrorizing the locals. The "B" Flight crowd were out in full force: Officers Ruppel, McNamara, Brown, Mould, Mosher, and several of the other usual suspects. The only regular missing was Officer Lott, who was attending a dinner party at the flight commander's home.

After consuming several bottles of "Gros Cinquante" (really big bottles of beer), these intrepid aviators decided to check on their brethren in the QRA (five-minute alert, Quick Reaction Area). The QRA could be pretty boring unless there was an English movie to watch, an opportunity to bump heads (go flying), or the chance to play UFO with the ident light over the city of Chicoutimi. I recall knocking a generator off-line doing this one time, and while we were taxiing back off the ramp, Rupp shut off the good engine . . . talk about embarrassing . . . but I digress. There were lots of ways to excite the boys in the Q; for instance, you could get Irradiate (GCI controllers) to do a practice scramble, especially when one of the aircrew was in the shower. Anyway, on this quite inebriated evening, it was decided to mess with the boys in the Q.

Since Officer Brown had the best French accent — and it was agreed he sounded just like Lou, the NCO on duty at the CAC (Combat Alert Centre) — Brownie was chosen to do the deed. Calling from an outside line (Officer Mould's) to an outside line (this should have been a tipoff) in the QRA, in his best Frenglish, Officer Brown, speaking to Officer Larke, said, "Sir, we 'av an unknown in de see-stem — go RUNWAY ALERT."

This should have generated no more response than, "Screw off, we're watching *Caddy Shack*," but since the boys in the Q had been heavy into cutting cards for a buck, no one really noticed that it was not the phone it should have been for this type of an order. Before Officer Brown had a chance to say, "Ha Ha Ha it's just us," four J–57 P–55s were screaming to life. "Oh, shit!" was Officer Brown's response as he quickly dialled the CAC to try to end the joke.

"Lou, it's Officer Brown. Call the hot birds on UHF and tell them the Runway Alert is bogus."

"Authenticate Alpha Hotel" was his reply.

This was no longer funny, to say the least, but after several minutes of the alert birds' sitting at the end of the runway waiting for takeoff clearance, and all the jokers involved speaking to GCI and CAC to convince them this was a prank that had gotten out of hand, the issue was resolved and the two Voodoos taxied back to the Q. Unfortunately, this was not yet the end of the evening for the Boys of "B" Flight.

After a couple more hours of Gros Cinquantes and contemplating how much trouble they were in, they thought it might be prudent to call the new Sqn. CO, who also lived in the ghetto, and tell him they were coming over for a "Welcome to Bagtown — here we are for egg-in-the-hole."

I'm not exactly sure where the expression "Red Alert" originated, as it applies to warning someone that the whole flight is about to descend on them in the middle of the night and expect to be entertained, but that was the expression used by whoever made the call to the CO that evening.

As three or four cars full of happy fliers approached after making the two-block trek from Mouldy's, a man in a flying suit was seen emerging from the boss's residence.

"Hi, Colonel. Where are you going, sir?"

"I just got a Red Alert and initiated Base Recall." OOPS!

You can probably fill in the blanks after that.

The worse part was that the "B" Flight Commander and the Deputy Commander had to leave their dinner party, and around one a.m., Officer Munro requested the attention of two "B" Flight individuals, one pilot and one WSO (names protected here). The Mission: call everyone on "B" Flight and tell them there would be a flight meeting at the squadron at 6:00 a.m.

As you may have guessed, overcoming the credibility barrier was a challenge.

But we had the meeting, and the boss didn't string anybody up, and there was no lasting resentment.

'Nuff said.

"'Nuff said."

A tribute to Eric "Thumper" Matheson

Larry Lott

One anecdote that stands out in my mind occurred in October 1982 at the William Tell bi-national air-to-air weapons competition held at Tyndall AFB in Florida. As head honcho of the Canadian contingent, and based upon previous William Tell experience, I knew that a sound public relations man was mandatory. Without hesitation, I appointed Eric to this task for a myriad of reasons, the three main ones being that he had a fertile mind, was an excellent writer, and could always separate the wheat from the chaff when the task needed to get done.

Picture then the scenario: Eric and I attended an In-briefing for this event wherein the USAF major general in charge of the event (a pompous ass, to be sure) virtually read the riot act, carefully outlining what would and wouldn't be tolerated across the event spectrum. Central to this was his underscoring that all public relations would be handled by his office. Eric, comfortable with the relaxed yet professional manner in which we Comox flyers conducted business, was astounded. Similarly, the Air National Guardsmen in the audience were more than a little dismayed at what they heard.

Eric decided that the vibes were just all wrong and set about to change the mood. He produced the first copy of his "underground" newspaper entitled *The No-Shit Bingo News* (for you non-aviators, "Bingo" is a term meaning "I must terminate my flight due to fuel-remaining considerations." Because the Bingo fuel amount was generally conservative, the no-shit Bingo level was not and represented the bottom line!) under the byline of "Thumper." In his six-page newspaper, Eric concocted all sorts of aviation stories relating to the event—bogus in the main—to create some rapport, camaraderie, and spirit among the competitors. It was an instant hit with all but the major general!

Before the general's team of sycophants could determine who this "Thumper" guy was, Eric had produced a second, third, and fourth edition. When I was finally called to the general's office and told emphatically "that's it," the general's deputy, possessing a keen sense of humour, walked me out of the building and, while he was expressing his regrets over the cease and desist decision, as soon as we were outside, he whispered that he had missed the third edition and could I get a copy to him on the QT?

Bear intercept — 1978

John "Bosco" Haazen

It was December 16, 1978; the height of the Cold War. At 2249 hours, the phone rang. As the AFC (Alert Force Commander), I pick it up. "Okay, cool. Hey, guys, suit up — we've got trade!" There's an instant jumble of activity, and in a few minutes, Tom Sabean and I are taking the runway with Bill Boucher and Michel Caron (his 'gator) right behind. I read back the clearance: "GN 01 flight, Profile 1, FL330, direct Gander." Someone means business tonight.

As soon as we break ground, Mike calls, "Two's locked, rolling," meaning he's got us on radar and will keep Bill clear of us in the climb. Two minutes after brake release, we're level and on our way to Gander. (I never got over that the old girl just climbed like a homesick angel.) A little over an hour later, we're in Gander, getting briefed by "Sidecar." Two Bear D intelligence-gathering aircraft are on their way down the coast to Cuba for what we derisively refer to as their "dirty weekend." Our mission tonight is to intercept them and make sure they don't enter Canadian airspace.

Once we get them on radar, it's obvious they're quite far out, and it's going to be a long tail chase, but the point is to let them know we're there so they don't decide to take a detour. We close in "buster," but the old Tupolev cruises amazingly quickly for a turboprop. Just when I can hear (or is that just my imagination?) those four big, counter-rotating props beating the air into submission, Tom announces that we're "bingo" (minimum fuel). No up-close-and-personal-encounters-of-the-Soviet-kind tonight; flight safety is, after all, paramount. It's a long haul back home, and I give Tom the gears because we get there with a few hundred pounds more than we absolutely need because of slightly more favourable winds. I'm disappointed, but I know we did the right thing.

But now it's been over twenty hours since we took over Alert, and I am beat, but North Bay won't hear of leaving their armed alert birds in Gander overnight. I check the others. "Okay, guys; if you're all good to go, we'll press on home . . ."

We ask Gander for another Profile 1 (because we can). "Roger GN 01, cleared [with the unspoken words "I guess" hanging in the air] — call through 5,000 feet."

"We're already through ten."

"Okay, call through FL230."

"Through 230."

"Roger, switch centre, advise them level."

"Centre, GN 01, level FL350."

God, I just love this machine! Centre hands us off to Sidecar for flight following on the way home. Now, it is a little-known fact that the Voodoo had data link long before "Aviation Leak and Spy Technology" made such a big fuss about JTIDS. Well, at FL350, the sun is just starting to come up and a warm, fuzzy glow fills the cockpit . . . and man, am I still tired. The soft fuzz around "the muff" beckons, and when I regain consciousness, North Bay is calling to give us our clearance into Chatham. I kick "the tit" (the transmit switch under my right foot), mutter "Stand by," and, stumble, stumble, crash, crash, am all knees and elbows as I shake myself awake and scramble for a pen. As I read it back, from the front seat I hear . . . stumble, stumble, crash, crash. This can't be good.

"Ah, Tom, were you asleep?"

"Ah, yeah, were you, too?"

"Ah, yeah. Let's not tell anybody, okay?"

"Yeah, good idea."

It seems that with the autopilot "coupled to Dolly" (data link), the Voodoo was doing such a good job of taking us back to Chatham that Tom got bored, and the long day (and night) took its toll on him, too.

Maple flag — 1979

John "Bosco" Haazen

It is November 8, 1979, and we're into the second week of Maple Flag IV. The tactical war has been scrubbed because of weather, and we're just sitting down to lunch when the SAC liaison guy comes rushing up to our table. "Hey, are you guys going to go out and intercept the B-52s that are coming through the range this afternoon?"

"We didn't think they'd still come."

"Well, they left long before we decided to cancel up here, so they still plan to meet their TOTs."[22]

We look at each other and quickly decide who wants to go flying while everyone else goes to the bar. Since I'm the Det OpsO, I haven't done a lot of flying yet this Flag, so I'm in. Mike Spooner (Spike Mooner) who's in from Group HQ in North Bay, says he's game, too. Another pilot and nav pair off down the table and I race to a phone and call the ground crew. "Hey, Warrant, don't put those birds to bed yet, there are B-52s coming down the range!"

We inhale our lunches and scramble for the flight line, where the Warrant has two big silver jets ready for us. We launch into the murk and find a clear layer above MSA (IFR minimum safe altitude). This is going to be a challenge; the old MG-13 isn't terribly good down this low, and the B-52s fly so low they have to climb to make a turn. We set up our CAP along their ingress route. Spike is keeping us safe while I'm peaking and tweaking the radar, looking for anything that might resemble a target amid the ground clutter.

And then . . . "Spike, I've got chaff."

"You sure it's chaff?"

"Yeah, a line of it, stand by." I take "half action" on the trigger on the hand controller and force the radar into "super search." Suddenly, a line appears across the entire width of the scope. It's an "inverse gain jammer" designed to deny the azimuth of the target, but, with the trail of chaff, this one forms a perfect inverted "T."

"O . . . kay, Spike, I know where he is. Six miles on the nose; can you get down below this?"

Spike transmits "Going down" as he rolls the big jet over, and we slice down through an opening in the clouds, our number two hot in pursuit. Now, the ground returns are even worse, so it's time to haul another tool out of the bag of tricks: IRSTS. RDR PASS mode[23] lets me search in IR without alerting him to the fact we've spotted him. Ping, ping, ping, ping! The IR audio reports multiple heat sources in front of us—but then, the B-52 does have eight of them. Okay, lock up the left, inboard, IR source and go RDR SLVD,[24] so the radar looks where the IR points. Some more tweaking, and there he is! "Two miles, Spike!"

Then: "Tally . . . holy shit, the trees are swaying in this guy's wake!"

Then, "Fox 2!"

So far, so good, but there are three of them, and we had just used our only IR weapon. This can only get better. Back on CAP, there's more chaff, but the half-action trick doesn't work; this time, we "convert" on the leading edge of the chaff trail. The IR once again finds eight heat sources, but we're going to need a radar lock this time to properly fire the "blivit."[25] IR-RDR SLVD again; there he is! Lock, break lock, another lock, another break lock. That's

---

22 TOT means time on target and is used under some circumstances to tell interceptor or fighter crews what time they might expect hostile targets in the vicinity.

23 RDR PASS mode means that the aircraft's radar is not transmitting, but is in a passive listening mode.
24 RDR SLVD means that the radar is slaved to the infrared receiver.
25 The blivit was the AIR2A rocket that was the primary weapon carried by the CF-101.

not the ground returns; the B–52's EWO is using his gate stealer.

"Tally, Bosco, can you get a lock?"

"He's breaking it, Spike."

"We'll shoot manually—what's the range?"

"Two miles. Just one more try, Spike. Stand by . . . ROT, DROT, shoot!"

"Fox three!"

"All right!"

The third guy got lucky. Near as we could figure, we got out there after he'd already gone by. By the time we got back to the mess, the lesser mortal, day-fighter types were well into their cups, but we didn't mind being late for this party. It was especially satisfying because, even though it was the first time the new whiz-bang F–15s played in Flag, it was the old AW(F) guys who went out and got the job done when the weather was too bad for everyone else to fly.

RAF cross country

John Wheeler, RAF exchange navigator, 416 Sqn

In looking through my short history with the RCAF, I came across a memorable gaffe. On Friday, August 13, 1965, S/L Dave Blucke and I flew from RCAF Chatham to Ernest Harmon AFB, Newfoundland. The mandate of the base was to maintain a KC–97 tanker alert force to refuel B–52s. Dave was after some golf clubs from the PX that he had been unable to get at Goose. The sight of a couple of RAF fighter jocks at beer call caused a bit of a stir, as you can imagine, particularly as we proceeded to get hammered and to win at crud. They were very interested to know all about us and where we were headed for the next day. Utter amazement followed when we said we had yet to decide.

Indeed, this was still under discussion in the flight planning room the next day. You can imagine the scene: a number of select star crews wearing white scarves with little blue stars strutting their stuff and pretending not to notice the two Brits trying to fill in their DOD flight plan (this had always been a bit of a mystery to us).

"Let's go to Summerside," said Dave. "How long will it take?"

So I put my chart on the floor and stood on it to measure the track against my shoe, which I knew was about an hour and a half long in cold power. Fine!

The ops clerk says, "Sir, I cannot accept this because you have filed the same time for your endurance."

"Okay," says Dave, "we'll make it an hour twenty and just go faster."

You could hear a pin drop as we sauntered out and off to the bird. Usually, the navigator handled the radios, so I let them know we were ready to go. (No, we couldn't be bothered with an engine start request.) As we lined up on zero nine, the tower came out with some horrendous list of instructions that involved climbing to 1,500 feet and then doing this and that at various NDBs.

"Roger that, but we are requesting a burner takeoff through vertical for a back climb on 270."

After a pause while they worked that out, we got "takeoff approved." Whereupon I felt the double thump in my back and checked to see the needle rushing over 150 kts within fifteen seconds; all was well, and Dave held her down until the 5G pull-up at the end. As she eased through Mach one at 5,000 feet, we rolled out on heading, and the altimeter gave a little jump to read the correct height—it only worked properly when supersonic. There then followed some R/T that I lost interest in and changed frequency to monitor guard. Not long after, we got that sinking feeling.

"Air Force 476—Summerside on Guard."

"Go ahead."

"Sir, we have been NOTAMed shut for three months while we have the runway fixed. What are your intentions?"

Answer: "Divert to Chatham." (And just hope we never meet up with any of those SAC guys again.)

Scramble
John Wheeler

S/L Dave Blucke and I became combat ready on 414 Squadron, North Bay, in January 1964. I suppose we practised scrambling against the "Bell," but I don't remember. When 414 was disbanded, we moved to 416 Squadron at RCAF Chatham. Perhaps we were briefed on operational scrambles, but I doubt it.

On November 29, 1964, we, and the other alert crew, were all sound asleep in the Alert Shack. The alert area was surrounded by heavy barbed wire and attendant armed guards. We were manning a conventionally armed aircraft. At precisely 0646 hours, the "Bells Went Off," and we are all out of bed and legging it to the aircraft in a flash. Dave stops for a pee, but I am in the back seat working the radios. "Chatham, 01 Scrambling." The hangar doors fly open to reveal the outside gloom, as the security lights pick out the blowing snow. Dave hits the double start buttons, and I am vaguely aware that our Number Two is having problems as we start to move.

"01 — Chatham, I have nothing for you; the active R/W is straight ahead; we have zero cloud base, in snow."

As we scoot through the only exit of the complex, I am aware of a fire truck going in the opposite direction to us and having great difficulty staying upright. Very soon afterward, I feel the welcome kick in the back as the burners light: the airspeed needle moves past 150 kts in about ten seconds, telling me all is well.

At 0650 hours precisely, CF–101B 463 comes unstuck and heads into the night. Taking off to the east, Dave pulls 5G as we rotate and back climb to meet the "threat." Going through the vertical at 5,000 feet, we become supersonic. Still nothing on the radio. To hell with it. Punching the Guard button, I announce, "Stargazer, Stargazer, Air Force 01, on Guard, scrambling out of Chatham, passing FL200 Mach 1.1; data link unlocked, demanding max alt and speed."

"Roger 01, Moncton Centre, stand by."

Although I was in bed asleep a little over six minutes ago, we are now passing 36,000 feet doing Mach 1.3; we are still only twelve miles away from base, but the fuel flow is phenomenal. I ask Dave if he had seen the fire truck that came a bit close as we rocketed through the horseshoe gate.

"No," he says, but he immediately unplugs the burners, and we level out at 40,000 feet! Then, on Guard, and for the world to hear, including the Russian Picket ship off the coast, "Air Force 01, Moncton Centre on Guard: we have the story if you are ready to copy."

"Go ahead."

"Roger, sir. You scrambled on the Fire Bells; Chatham is reporting half a mile in blowing snow with GCA on thirty minutes; there are no diversions. What are your intentions?"

Dave says to me, "Tell them we will do an internal aids letdown."

This is all very well, but I am one of those guys who has never actually been able to distinguish the Alert Shack from the end of the runway on my radar. Never mind; we will have a good go at getting the thing back on the ground.

In the event, GCA "woke up" when were at about five miles finals, and we touched down just forty-five minutes after liftoff.

No one had told us Chatham used a "Scramble Horn." Teleprinters all over Eastern Canada started to

"A bit late to be out and about, don't you think?"

chatter and record a "Broken Arrow" when overheat in the shower block set off the Fire Bells. That is how we later knew the precise timings of our four-minute rush into the night sky. Our number two failed to start, and the nuclear shack never even got unlocked before the penny dropped to other would-be heroes.

Postscript: S/L David Blucke and F/L John Wheeler were RAF Exchange Officers at 414 Squadron and, later, 416 Squadron, from January 1964 to December 1965. Never one to hide his light under a bush, John returned to Jolly Olde with a spanking new, blue, right-hand drive Pontiac. Tragically, in August 1974, Dave, then a G/C and CO of RAF Coningsby, was killed when the F–4 Phantom he was flying on a low-level route collided with a light aircraft.

My first scramble

Jim Gregory

Soviet Bear aircraft were beginning to fly from Russia to support their stronghold in Castro's Cuba. The year was 1968. In the history of NORAD, this was the first time that Russian bomber aircraft would come so close to the CADIZ and ADIZ. The bomber flight crossed the North Atlantic, where American forces in Iceland would intercept the Soviets and provide warning to North American defence force, such as 416 Squadron at Chatham. These bombers would approach the CADIZ and initially turn back. The NORAD system would, of course, have advanced knowledge of the approaching bombers via the Icelandic intercept. It would take a few hours for the bombers to approach the CADIZ from Iceland, allowing the NORAD system to adequately respond to this impending intrusion. Four-one-six Sqn was located on the easternmost point of the North American continent and closest to the Russian threat. However, we could not effectively initiate an intercept from our home base at CFB Chatham, New Brunswick, so the two alert CF–101s would be scrambled to Gander, Newfoundland, refuel, and meet the threat off the eastern coast of Newfoundland.

On July 12, 1968, I was on alert with my navigator, F/L Don Langille, and another crew when the ops phone rang. We answered and learned that we were to deploy to Gander forthwith, as Soviet Bears had just been identified flying by Iceland. They didn't, after being identified, perform the usual manoeuvre of a U-turn back to their Soviet base. Were they the forerunners of an attacking force?

Our task was to get airborne immediately, fly to Gander, the hold alert there, in case the Soviets continued into Canadian airspace. It wasn't a scramble in the usual sense, but the need to get to Gander and set up for further action was urgent.

We arrived in Gander, and our ground crew immediately had the aircraft set up on five. The Soviets continued on. Was this the real thing?

No, it wasn't. Not long after we landed, the Bears turned around. Was this a feint? Apparently not, as the people in Iceland saw them on track to their base in the Soviet Union. Then we prepared to return to Chatham. Shortly before we were ready to go, an unknown individual climbed the ladder to my cockpit and explained that he was an aide-de-camp to the Governor-General, who was also visiting Gander. The G-G had heard the commotion of our arrival and was, apparently, wondering what all the fuss was about. He wished to meet the Voodoo crews who were defending Canada.

We ceased our preparations to return to Chatham, followed the aide into the hangar, and were introduced to Governor-General Roland Michener, a trim, pleasant man who was well briefed on our operation. It's nice to have the Commander-in-Chief aware of your activities.

W/C J D "Red" Sommerville, DSO, DFC

Doug Munro

In 1965, 409 Squadron held one of its periodic reunions. "Red" Sommerville, one of 409's WW II commanding officers, graced the gathering with his presence. The reunion committee elected to present "Red" with a memento of his tenure as "Nighthawk" boss. Nighthawks aren't all that easy to obtain, so the committee decided a large White Leghorn rooster would be an ideal substitute.

After a tasteful speech, "Red" was handed the rooster. He grasped the chicken's legs with one hand and its neck with the other. The mixed audience of three or four hundred held their collective breath, for it appeared that the "gift" was bound for chicken heaven. "Red" gently tucked the rooster's head under its wing and, taking the chicken in both hands, proceeded to move it gently in circles. After a couple of minutes, he stood the chicken on the table and released it. Despite thunderous applause that damned chicken never budged—it apparently had concluded that it was bedtime.

The Ukrainian aerobatic team

Doug Munro

When one receives an invitation to an Oktoberfest party, it is polite to accept—even if the locale is Mountain Home AFB, Idaho. The USAF, desperate to add some much-needed class to their 1969 Harvest Fest, had Major Jim Hood contact 409 Squadron's social secretary and beg him to provide a few aviators laden with charm and wit. A three-plane formation was pressed into service.

Captain Ernie Poole led the gaggle, with Lt. Gord Saunders on one wing and Lt. Phil Schreiner on the other. Each of their rear cockpits was filled with a navigator—whose identities will remain secret to save their mothers undue angst.

Upon arrival, the Nighthawks were delighted to learn that the local weather was ideal for a vertically challenged arrival show—solid overcast at 300 feet and thirty miles' visibility. As soon as the threesome broke cloud, Ernie cancelled IFR and requested a low pass down the active runway. Granted! No one else seemed to be flying (it was later learned that the base was holding an "everyone be there" Flight Safety meeting; the Canadian air show provided an additional topic for their agenda).

"That pass went well; how about one down the ramp?" Granted! The navs in number two and number three noticed a bit of high-speed whimpering from their front offices, depending on where their aircraft was during a turn; two aircraft in the clear (the lower one scaring the prairie dogs), and the other in cloud. After a few more creative manoeuvres, the three-plane pitched and landed.

All went swimmingly until the wheels hit the concrete. Gord, landing third in the stream, elected to land without using his drag chute so as to avoid forcing the USAF to repack it! Unable to decelerate as quickly as his mates, he slalomed between number two and number one and skilfully assumed the lead. One of the navs was heard to mutter, "Geez, when I called us the Ukrainian Aerobatic Team before take-off at Comox I really didn't mean it . . . then!"

A large contingent of USAF aircrew met the visitors and forced them to immediately attend at the officer's club to replenish their fluids — flying formation with a couple of hundred feet of free board is sweaty business. The navs had avoided excessive anxiety by putting their hard hat bags over their heads.

The party was a roaring success. The tallest and most noticeable Canadian nav set the standard for *savoir faire*. The minute he entered the club, he made a beeline for the bar, reached over the bartender's shoulder, ran the TV through the channels, then turned and discovered a garbage bag full of popcorn, which he immediately appropriated, and turned to the nearest USAF type and said, "I suppose you heard about our pay raise?" The success of this comment apparently entitled him to segue into a critique of the U.S. involvement in Vietnam. Fortunately for him, Idaho no longer favoured the death penalty. Strange as it may seem, 409's invitation to the 1970 Fest apparently went astray. Those were moments to remember.

"C'mon, ice cream!"

Kent Smerdon

At Tyndall AFB, Florida, during William Tell '76, the clan gathered at the favourite off-base watering hole, an establishment known as Dee's Oyster Bar. Many such gatherings occurred there, but this one was memorable.

Despite the upmarket name, Dee's was literally a concrete-block house with a neon sign, a door, a bar, a can, a kitchen, and high-school-auditorium tables and chairs; a flat roof was held up with those adjustable steel poles you see in unfinished basements. It served draft beer, raw oysters, and Mexican food — in other words . . . it was perfect.

The whole team was there, plus a few visitors. It seemed rather hazy at the time, as I recall, and thirty-odd years has not clarified it overly. If I've missed a few, I apologize: Sundance, Angus, Snake, Kid Comotis, L'Homme Plastique, OB, Mongo, Master Captain Bill "Charlie" Gladders, Officer Butters, Sir Sydney, Haggis, Bill Books, Butch, one Rhinehart Koehn, and other n'er-do-wells and layabouts. Rarely has there gathered a more disparate group of desperados.

Mucho pitchers of draft washed down fiery Mexican food. The burners, so to speak, were being lit. More beer, more noise; Foster made a brief appearance, and the party began to accelerate. The other patrons, not being able to follow our Northern Yankee accents, found our entertainment value wanting and vacated in a huff.

The party reached a rousing crescendo when Rhiney climbed on a table and dropped trousers to pull his socks up from the inside. That caused Mr. Dee, a paragon of patience and indulgence up to this point, to explode in a torrent of rapid and loud Spanglish. We immediately sensed a certain displeasure in his tone; I believe that the drift of it was: "Get the @#$%&*! out of my bar!"

We sheepishly paid the tabs, spilled noisily into the parking lot, and piled into three vehicles. We stopped at a Dairy Queen for some ice cream to cool our innards. Someone asked if they served egg-in-the-hole. It was not pretty.

On the way back to the base, our three designated drivers (?) began passing each other in turns. This, *bien sur*, started a "mooning duel" between vehicles. Several "Vis ID passes" resulted in reasonable moons of above average quality, but the master was waiting to get the kiddies off the street. The contest was absolutely slam-dunk finished when, realizing that the base gates were nearing, a certain officer hung a moon so aggressive, so penetrating, so diabolical that the man's ordinance was seen swaying on its hard point in the rushing night air! This, dear readers, was no ordinary moon. This was a championship, jaw-dropping, eye-popping, show-stopping, lose-control-drive-in-the-ditch offering, the likes of which we never saw again. The other contestants could only bow down in defeat or double over in convulsive laughter. This man became an instant celebrity around the briefing rooms on the base.

We adjourned to the O Club for a final "debriefing." The remainder of the night and its festivities escape me. All I remember from the next morning is hearing Mongo (or it might have been Lowell) sitting on the can moaning, "C'mon, ice cream!"

I remember him well

Doug Munro

During my twenty-seven years in the air force, I served with eleven different squadron commanders. Of them, the most revered and respected was W/C Dean Kelly. During 6,100 flying hours, I flew with many fine pilots; none were more skilled than Dean. He could fly the narrow edge of an aircraft's flight envelope with seeming ease. He was a kind, modest, and self-effacing man; a unique and unorthodox leader. The members of 416 Squadron had every confidence that he could walk on water. He led—we followed.

Was Dean perfect? Well, not exactly, but any defects were minor. First of all, he was very hard of hearing. Apparently, his annual medical was conducted by the fighter pilot's tooth fairy. Second, he was slightly bereft of sartorial elegance (his lovely and charming wife Charmain possessed enough elegance for both of them). And, third, he was painfully shy: when addressing a group of people—even when everyone present was a friend and silently cheering for him—he clearly found the process to be a major effort.

When I arrived at 416 Squadron in February 1963, I received a short, sharp, "in briefing" from the navigation leader, S/L Merv Reid. Included in his pearls of wisdom was the suggestion that, if I was flying with W/C Kelly and wanted an external performed, I'd best do it myself. That was sound advice.

The first time I was scheduled to fly with the boss, I wandered out to our Voodoo about fifteen minutes before the scheduled takeoff time, performed a splendid pre-flight, climbed into the rear cockpit, strapped on my chute, plugged in, donned my hard hat, and sat and waited. About five minutes before launch, around the port wing tip came Dean. Tastefully attired in a faded WW II trench coat, a wedge hat that had survived Malta, and his chute (firmly buckled up), he ambled up the ladder, and, as his trailing leg entered the cockpit, both engines spooled up and down came the canopy. Ten seconds later, we were taxiing, and a minute or so after, with both burners plugged in, we launched. (A few trips later, I asked Dean why he refused to conduct an external. He stated that it kept the ground crew on their toes. They knew he wasn't going to pre-flight his aircraft, so they busted their backsides to ensure that everything was first cabin.[26] He was correct: I flew with him on a number of occasions and never found the tiniest snag!)

One of my most memorable trips with Dean took place in August 1964. He was being transferred to 25th NORAD Region, McChord AFB, Tacoma, Washington. I overheard him muse that he just might take a Voodoo to McChord to look over his new domain.

---

26 This phrase is borrowed from the Royal Navy; used to describe a well-respected individual to indicate that he or she belonged in the first cabin—a mark of respect.

Always one to volunteer for unpleasant and onerous duties, I suggested that I'd be honoured to accompany him. The subsequent trip, in a double-tanked Voodoo, had its moments.

The first leg was routine — RCAF Chatham to K.I. Sawyer AFB in upstate Michigan. Over Montreal, I remarked how surprised I was that Air Defence Headquarters had approved the trip. Dean responded that he hadn't asked permission — no point giving them a chance to refuse.

We encountered a minor hiccup on the second leg. We'd filed Glasgow AFB, Montana, as our destination. Over Grand Forks, Minneapolis Center called and asked if we were aware that Glasgow had been closed for six months. Dean allowed as how we probably should have checked NOTAMS and accepted my best guess that we'd enough fuel to reach Malmstrom AFB, Great Falls, Minnesota. And we did! The leg from Malmstrom to McChord was a snap.

After much gracious wining and dining by our hosts, Bev and Syd Burrows, it was time to head for the Miramichi. At flight planning, the boss asked me what route I'd like to take home. I'd never been to Las Vegas, so . . . !

We were abeam Portland, Oregon at 35,000 feet when Seattle Center notified us that McChord Tower had called and asked if we'd like to return and pick up our luggage. (Before luggage racks that attached to the inside of the armament door were available, personal belongings were loosely stowed by "cracking" the door and inserting golf clubs, short downhill skis, and other critical items.) It seems that the door rotated shortly after lift-off and dumped all our gear on the McChord runway at a couple of hundred knots.

Dean never dropped a stitch. "Roger Center, cancelling IFR, going tower." (Regulation addicts may argue that cancelling IFR at 35,000, in the high level structure, is a no-no.) He immediately switched frequencies, turned hard starboard, popped the speed brakes, plugged in the afterburners and started to descend. It was a glorious, clear day over Puget Sound, and shortly thereafter we advised McChord Tower that we were five miles back, from the active runway, and would like to land.

My luggage bag looked like a medium-sized elephant had jumped on it. What was left of my clothes reeked of Old Spice aftershave. We were understandably reluctant to submit what was left of our kit to the rotary door. No problem is too difficult for experienced aviators to solve. I climbed in the back, strapped in, put all the switches where they'd likely do the most good, and in came the luggage. I could just see the back of Dean's hard hat over the dirty laundry. Remember — always travel light!

The Lido show at the Stardust made all our troubles seem worthwhile. We were having a wee dram in the lounge. A long line of people wound its way through the tables and disappeared around a corner. Dean wanted to know where they were going. I opined they were lining up for the supper show in the main dining room. Dean suggested we attend. He disappeared around the corner and a few minutes later reappeared and told me to join him. We were seated right on the edge of the stage. (It seems he obtained this splendid location by tipping the head waiter five dollars.)(?) He should have received a medal — we were nearly in the chorus line. ("What a neat place for a tattoo!")

On a hot and dusty Sunday morning, after a fine evening spreading charm and goodwill the length of the Strip, we returned to Nellis AFB, and flight-planned for Richards–Gebaur (Kansas City, Missouri).

Everything had been going much too smoothly. The Voodoo's engines required high-pressure air to start (in addition to two internal bottles, each with 3,000 pounds of air, there was usually a high-pressure cart available). No high-pressure cart—just a low-pressure Joy compressor. Our "start crew" was comprised of a young USAF airman 3rd who had apparently never seen a CF–101, so I had the pleasure of babysitting him.

Dean decided that he was going to try a double start using the bottles. I modestly suggested I didn't think that would work. Being a GIB (the Guy In Back), my well-meaning advice was occasionally ignored. Neither engine started. The bottles were now empty (once airborne, air in the bottles was available to lower the undercarriage in an emergency situation). Forty-five minutes later, after using the Joy to recharge the bottles, both engines were finally lit. The bottles were empty, but when last did anyone have to carry out an emergency gear-lowering? It was about 125 degrees F on the ramp, and the boss was looking a bit flushed, so let's launch.

Twenty minutes west of Kansas City, St. Louis Center called us and advised that, unless we had Prior Permission, we wouldn't be welcome at Richards–Gebaur. Apparently not a problem. "Roger Center, cancelling IFR, going tower." Followed by a channel change, a turn to a southerly heading, and a leisurely descent.

Always the curious one, I said: "Mind telling me where we're going, sir? I believe I've a right to know! I *am* the navigator."

"No sweat, Doug—we'll go to McConnell AFB, at Wichita. I used to fly out of there."

We weren't incarcerated, but nothing gets a Strategic Air Command base's attention quite as quickly as arriving in a strange aircraft—unannounced. As we rolled to a stop on the active, I noticed, on our port side, jeeps at every cut-off, apparently armed with .50 calibre machine guns and manned by remarkably mean-looking air force policemen. We skillfully avoided this band of apparent well-wishers by turning starboard and parking on the Tactical Air Command side of the field.

The last two legs—from McConnell to Lockbourne AFB and Lockbourne to Chatham—were conducted with our usual consummate skill.

An otherwise uneventful trip was marred, upon our arrival at Chatham, by a minor tragedy: while unloading our gear, Dean dropped, and broke, his forty-ounce vat of snake killer.

Postscript: Dean has recently passed away. His friends and colleagues will never forget him.

Cold shaft
Jack Partington

People who live on air force bases are constantly subjected to aircraft noises: starting, taxiing, take-off, landing, engine run-ups. Some call it "the sound of freedom," much like those living downwind from a pulp mill call the prevailing fragrance "the smell of money." Either way, you get used to it and often you don't even notice it. But with aircraft, the noise is its unique signature, and after a while most of the neighbourhood can identify the kind of aircraft, what it is doing, and whether the engine is performing normally. If the noise suddenly quits, for example, it gets everybody's attention.

So when a Harvard pilot running up his 600 hp Pratt and Whitney R–1340 Wasp radial engine in Penhold moves the pitch lever through full coarse and full fine, the tips of the props approach—and then fade away from—the speed of sound, resulting in the most delightful and reassuring noise. Or when a T–Bird pitches out over the runway at Gimli, throttles back to 80 percent, 60 degree bank turn, pops the speed brakes, and pulls a two and one-half-G, 180-degree turn, you can almost hear the sigh from the aircraft and the pilot that they have to land —so soon.

Eager to launch, the CF–104 Starfighter J–79 howls like the furies when run up on the button in Zweibrucken: the engine check at full throttle, back to 80 percent; check the compressor guidevane scheduling, chop to idle, back up to 100 percent, and then light the burner for that extra 6,000 pounds of thrust. For its takeoff, the CF–101 Voodoo's pair of J–57s roar away at full throttle while the pilot stands on the brakes. At a nod from the wingman, he signals, releases the brakes, clicks the throttles outboard to select afterburners, and pushes them full forward. The raw fuel spraying into the tailpipe explodes with a vengeance, banging open the burner eyelids and creating the most spectacular booms — often you can count four booms, since the burners of a two-plane section rarely light-off together. In Chatham, New Brunswick, on January 21, 1981, at 0200 hours, this could only mean one thing: Cold Shaft! And the alert birds were airborne.

Even from the depths of a deep sleep, I had heard the Voodoos launch, registered the event, and was wide awake in an instant. Four-one-six All Weather Fighter Squadron maintained two armed Voodoos on Quick Reaction Alert (QRA) around the clock, one of the three squadrons responsible for Canadian air sovereignty and security as part of NORAD — the North American Aerospace Defence alliance with the United States. Scrambles to intercept intruders in our airspace, hijackings, lost aircraft, and hazards to air navigation were our operational bread and butter. Lately, the short winter days and stormy weather had provided us ideal conditions to practise our night and all-weather intercept procedures. Tonight's mission would prove the value of that training.

I dressed quickly in the dark: cotton long johns, white long-sleeved turtleneck, grey wool socks — layers that aren't supposed to melt in the event of a fire. Flying suit, zipper pockets weighted down with maps, local flip charts, hunting knife, flashlight, checklist; then the boots, zippers in front and an ankle strap with buckle so they don't fall off on ejection or the shock of the parachute's opening. Getting dressed in flying kit was almost a sacred ritual; I reminded myself, again, that this would not last forever and cherished the moment.

A kiss for my wife, a look-in on the kids, jacket, gloves, wedge cap, pass, keys, and out the door. Later, another of the squadron wives would tell me that she, too, had wakened with the sound of the Voodoos and then heard my car going down the street. She knew that something big was up and was concerned; her husband was one of the two pilots on QRA that night. Many of the other neighbours had probably awakened as well, listening, wondering, worrying.

Like most of the Chatham team living in the permanent married quarters (PMQs), I usually walked to work. I suppose it was a continuation of the dressing routine, something to be savoured, not to be counted on forever. I looked forward to passing through the gates to the base, stopping to chat with the commissionaires on duty — one of my friends on the gate was a gentle and decent man who tied salmon flies and was forever giving me his latest concoction to try out. My fishing buddies once laughed with glee at a large "Black Ghost" that he had tied — and then had to swallow their mirth a few minutes later when I landed a twelve-pound salmon with it.

But tonight I drove in, thinking of the mission and the four young men speeding through the night en route to Goose Bay, Labrador, "*Ad Saltum Paratus*" — 416 Squadron's Motto, "Ready for the Leap." At the Goose, they would refuel and set up an alert posture in the resident Air Force Search and Rescue Detachment building, waiting to scramble to their Strategic Orbit Point (STOP). And this was the essence of Cold Shaft: the forward defence of North American airspace against the threat of the Soviet strategic bomber forces.

Although it was peacetime, the Soviets conducted probes of our airspace, tested our defences, eavesdropped on our alert warning systems and communications, and, given the opportunity, violated our defined sovereign airspace. Under command of NORAD, and within the northeast sector of the 22nd NORAD Region, 416 Squadron was trained, equipped, and poised to counter these offences. And tonight we would be tested.

The duty crew in the Combat Operations Centre at the squadron had things well in hand. The call had come in from North Bay. The alert crews had been scrambled and were airborne within the five-minute criteria, and the aircraft were already well out over the Gulf of St. Lawrence. I wondered if they had been commanded to "Buster," that is, to continue to climb in full afterburner to cruise altitude, which would leave them tight on fuel at the other end. Or if the canopy pressurization seal had failed going through 15,000 feet, as it often did, causing the crew to stuff pieces of sponge carried for that purpose into the leaks to avoid having to abort the mission. Sometimes we used our leather gloves and helmet bags when the sponges ran out; all of this stuff dropped back into the cockpit on descent. I wondered if the "Tiddle" Time Division Data Link connection of the Senior Weapons Director in North Bay had commanded a supersonic transit silently through to the instruments in the front cockpit. If so, I could expect a nasty letter in a week or so from some citizen whose beauty sleep had been interrupted by the passage of two supersonic Voodoos "dropping booms"—the trailing edge of the shock wave—on his home. He would write a letter to the Minister complaining about the noise that had caused several deaths or miscarriages among his prize cattle/minks/turkeys—pick one—another claim against the Crown. However, this time the climb had been "Gate," with afterburner out when safely airborne,

a cruise climb, and a comfortable Mach .86 transit. The Instrument Landing System (ILS) approach and landing at Goose Bay had been uneventful.

But the Goose could be treacherous, especially in winter. The runway could be slick and icy, and the crosswinds fierce. I landed there once with several inches of hard rime ice projecting from the unheated parts of the aircraft, and we hadn't even been in cloud that much. Ice added to the weight of the aircraft, at the same time destroying the aerodynamic performance of critical surfaces. It could be deadly. And a soft drizzle could coat the aircraft with an icy glaze without your noticing, as you taxi out for take-off. Or the engines could suck in foreign material left lying unnoticed on the tarmac, such as chunks of concrete or nuts and bolts that chewed the brittle engine compressor blades to pieces and spit them back into the turbine. Or moose on the runway, or bird strikes from migrating geese. These were a few of the challenges to all-weather fighter operations. There were some psychological ones, too.

There had been a long-standing resistance to wearing immersion suits, for example, on long and fuel-consuming overwater flights such as Cold Shaft. Some felt that a bailout over the North Atlantic in winter—or summer, for that matter—was a forgone conclusion. You were a goner. Others felt that the "poopie" suit gave you at least a fighting chance. Aviation pioneers Antoine St. Exupéry, who had crash-landed in the Sahara Desert several times and survived, or his friend, Guillaumet, who walked through the Andes in winter after running into a mountain, would have been scandalized. And we were much better trained and equipped in the eighties than they were in the twenties. The attitude toward survival measures had to be corrected.

So we had increased our in-pool training in immersion suits to ensure that everybody was drilled in water entry and getting into the dinghy as quickly as possible. The Safety Equipment techs had provided everything we needed, and more, in a neat package we sat on in the ejection seat. We plotted the positions of the few oil rigs with helicopter landing pads on the Grand Banks and registered these and our STOPs with the Search and Rescue teams at Goose and Gander. The thinking here was that the rescue choppers could land and refuel on the rig and keep up the search if the worst happened.

I thought this put the "overwater" issue to bed. Then it became, "Well, what if you land in the bush in your poopie suit and freeze to death?" So a short winter survival exercise was organized, dropping folks off with the base rescue chopper to spend a cold but bearable weekend in the bush, poopie suits and all. Maybe not everyone was convinced that the immersion suit was the greatest thing since sliced bread, but wearing it became standing operating procedure (SOP) for the squadron, and that was that. Attitudes toward survival improved along with the overall confidence to reach out over the North Atlantic and take on the elements—as well as the opposition.

The Soviet Bears had taken off from a base in northern Russia and were planning to fly an electronic surveillance mission against North America and land in Cuba, the only Communist client state in the Western Hemisphere. Their flight profile mirrored that which could be flown by their strategic bomber force. But the Soviets rarely sent their strategic weapons and cruise missile carriers; doing so could quickly heat up the Cold War. So they would send their reconnaissance Bear Deltas to skirt the coast of Norway and fly through the Greenland/Iceland/UK Gap, snooping. They would be intercepted in turn by the Royal Norwegian Air Force, the Brits, and the USAF fighters based in Iceland, and carry on to North America. NATO would thus be able to alert the Canadian and U.S. NORAD alliance that a flight of Bears was headed our way and provide an indication of the time we should expect them to penetrate our airspace.

The Soviet aircrew would approach the Canadian ADIZ—our Air Defence Identification Zone—in the middle of the night, since they preferred to land in Cuba during daylight hours. The challenge was to figure out where they would penetrate the ADIZ and intercept them, employ internationally recognized signals to warn them of their violation, and escort them away from our sovereign airspace. This would deny them the intelligence coup they sought, while sending Soviet High Command the message that NORAD was, as always, on guard. Such was the constant "push" of the Soviet forces wherever in the world they were deployed; where they found weaknesses, they oozed their way in. But they needed to understand that if "push came to shove," there was no way we in the West were coming in second. It would take over seventy years for them to get the message.

To intercept a flight of bombers in such a huge chunk of airspace was easier said than done. It required astute positioning of the strategic orbit point, based on the analyses of our defence scientists. Once the STOP had been decided, it required intricate figure-eight manoeuvres by the Voodoos to ensure that at least one of their airborne intercept radars was sweeping the sky in the expected direction of the Bear approach. Flying STOPs was carried out at maximum endurance settings to conserve fuel, but at this low speed and high altitude, aircraft handling was critical. The aircraft required a delicate touch on the controls—overreaction could exceed critical angles and cause a pitch-up. A pitch-up, or a high-performance aerodynamic stall in which elevator authority was totally lost, was to be avoided at all costs; there was not much in the pilot's bag of tricks to recover from it.

The navigators had other things on their minds: controlling the timing and shape of the figure eight and using the radar to maximum advantage in its limited search time. A "tallyho" radar contact on the inbound Bears meant the navs had to make a rapid analysis to determine the best attack geometry for an identification procedure; by this time, the Bears would have the Voodoos on their own radars, know that they had been caught, and would probably take evasive action. While figuring all this out and keeping out of each other's way, the navs would guide the Voodoos into a stern position on each Bear and talk the pilot in to carry out a visual identification. This was a hands-on, not an automated, procedure; an unintended "lock" on the target by the Voodoo radar might convey the impression, electronically, that the Bears were under attack, and cause a defensive reaction by their tail gunners. So the navs had to be very delicate, too, in the handling of their equipment.

This was the set-up: the lead Voodoo would cautiously move in between the two Bears, and Voodoo number two would stay well back to cover the three aircraft ahead of it. The Voodoos carried two AIM–4D heat-seeking missiles — each one with 4.5 pounds of high explosives, and they could only be fired in a salvo. Not much in the way of deterrent, but especially effective from the stern on a hot target like the four Bear contra-rotating turboprops — and the Bears knew it. The Voodoos were also capable of carrying nuclear-tipped Genie rockets when more serious defence conditions were required and authorized — the Bears knew that, too.

The idea was for the nav to talk the pilot into a position 400 feet back from the target, 200 feet right and 200 feet low — the ideal ID slot. Close in, he would be working his target in the bottom quarter-inch of the glowing radar screen — not much to go on, and no room for error at 350 knots. When the team was satisfied that they were in the slot, the pilot would call for the nav to switch on a 20,000-candlepower spotlight fixed to the side of the Voodoo, aimed up and to the left of where the tail of the Bear should be. The sky suddenly would become much brighter, and in cloud the effect was almost blinding. The pilot would make a rapid transition from instrument to visual cues, while the nav picked up his camera and started photographing the lead Bear. The Red Star on the tail was always a big attention-getter.

The pilot would then fly close formation on the Bear, illuminating its various features. Caught like a deer in the headlights, the Bear pilot usually held a very steady course with the fighter tucked in so close beside him. Both Voodoo pilot and nav would note the type of antennae protruding from the belly of the Bear; both would try not to take too much notice of the twin 50-calibre machine guns in the tail that followed every move. Then out around the wing and in to inspect the weapons bay, the radar bulges, the nose of the aircraft, and the number below the cockpit.

The second Voodoo would then move in on the number two Bear and repeat the procedure while the lead Voodoo circled back to cover the activity. All of this was being orchestrated in the dark, maybe in cloud, on instruments and radar, 200 miles or more off the coast of Newfoundland and Labrador. And all the time, the Bears were turning away from the protected airspace, away from the land and back out over the ocean.

Sometimes the second Bear moved forward to squeeze the lead Voodoo while it was carrying out its identification procedure. This would add an element of risk to the operation: the risk of a mid-air collision, perhaps, or causing the lead to break down and away and losing the opportunity to complete the mission. Or spatial disorientation leading to pitch-up. Or the dreaded overwater bailout.

However, the Cold Shaft of January 1981 followed pretty much the textbook procedure. And while the lead Bear slowly changed its heading to depart Canadian airspace and incidentally to take the Voodoos even farther offshore, the second Bear sensibly held well back.

Given the time on STOP, there would not be enough fuel to set up the complete identification on the second Bear. This gave the number two Voodoo the rare chance to dash forward and take photos of the lead in the process of the intercept, prior to both aircraft's knocking it off and returning to base. This was the first time that a night intercept of a Soviet Bear bomber had been captured on film; mission accomplished, and then some, for 416 Squadron's alert crews.

Imagine the excitement in the squadron as we gathered around to listen to the cockpit recorder tapes of this particular Cold Shaft. Such coolness; professionals at work — best in the world! And always hints of the gallows humour typical of this kind of work.

After the Voodoos had broken off, reformed, and headed west with minimum fuel for recovery (bingo), there had been a great outbreak of relief in the cockpits, a release of incredible tension, pride in mission accomplishment, joy. All recorded. Then the inevitable "Where in hell are we?" discussion.

Long pause. Pilot to nav: "Okay. Now switch that scope on to max range and find me some land."

Longer pause. Nav to pilot: "There is no land . . ."

So there they were, well past bingo fuel by now, on a dark night somewhere out over the ocean — having the greatest time of their lives. As dawn started to appear behind them, the coast of Newfoundland began to paint on the radar scope, and they recovered safely in Goose Bay. After refuelling and a quick pit stop, they decided to launch for Chatham, get their photos developed, debrief, go to the mess, relive the event over and over, and celebrate. They might even have something to eat other than the peanut butter crackers and instant coffee they'd filched from the Search and Rescue kitchen — but probably not, after the first round.

By the time they recovered in Chatham, they had been at it for about fifteen hours. They logged almost half of that time harnessed into the ejection seat of an all-weather jet fighter aircraft, experiencing and controlling the incredible stresses of high-performance flight. The rest of the time had been devoted to planning, briefing, reporting, aircraft and weapons inspections before and after flights, up the ladder, down the ladder, strapping in, unstrapping, checks, checks, and more checks. They had flown far out over some of the coldest and most treacherous waters in the world, over desolate, uninhabited landscapes, wearing rubberized canvas immersion suits, Mae Wests, parachutes, six-pound helmets and oxygen masks. They had gone eye-to-eye with a Cold War enemy, five miles up in the sky, at night, and he had blinked.

Probably those who had heard the scramble in the middle of the night hadn't paid much attention to the pair of 101s that came steaming in over the runway later that afternoon, pitched out, downwind, dropped the landing gear, flaps, turned final, and landed. That happened every day. Or saw the puff of white smoke and heard the squeal of the tires on touchdown, the snap of the drag chute deploying. Few heard the burst of the engines when they released their chutes and blew them halfway across the infield. Only those of us who waited on the tarmac to greet the Cold Shaft crews heard the last shot of power from the J–57s as the Voodoos pulled into the line, the abrupt chop to idle and throttle cut-off, the last of the unburned fuel splashing into the drip pans, the rattle of the ladders against the cockpit rail, the exuberant young voices drifting down the line.

The sounds of freedom.

The keys
Pete Armour

In the Quick Reaction Area (often abbreviated to "the Q"), there were thought to be nuclear weapons stored or uploaded for training on an aircraft in the two outside hangars or bays. Several armed guards—MPs—in small, glass-windowed huts guarded this highly fenced compound. We knew the Sten guns they carried were loaded; periodically, we heard of an MP being injured in an accident. Access to these two bays was very strictly controlled through the use of codes. It was a serious business for obvious reasons.

The nuclear weapons, if any were there, would never have been flown, and we were told they were not even real. However, procedurally, we treated them as if they were real. The Americans owned them, shared custody of them with us, and did all the maintenance on them. There were two keys: one was held by an American, the American Duty Officer (ADO) specifically assigned for that duty. The other was in the hands of a Canadian aircrew squadron member, the Duty Alert Officer (DAO). These two officers were in addition to the normal five-minute crews in residence for their twenty-four-hour stint in the Q.

One day, when it was my turn as the DAO, we received proper notification that some maintenance was required on items in the structure. The ADO and DAO would each set up his own separate code on the phone with access control before going out to one of the outboard weapons bays. Once there, each of us plugged in a phone jack and spoke with Access Control to verify the opening of the bay with the codes established earlier. This day, the ADO went first and spoke with them at Control. Then he unplugged abruptly and spun around facing me.

It was readily apparent that something was amiss. "You pooched the code, didn't you," I said. It seemed he was still nodding his head when the area around us erupted and filled up with armed MPs pointing their weapons at us. It took some time as they went through the procedures with us until they were happy we were who we were supposed to be. Although they were certainly doing their jobs professionally, I steeled myself to slow movement and careful speech. I can tell you that, for me, when a loaded Sten gun is pointed at my forehead, it itches intensely.

Buzzer... Stream... Evasive... What else might he do?
Bob Merrick

It was another humdrum morning on alert. But not for long. Twenty-fifth NORAD Region had discerned some airborne interloper approaching Canada's west coast on a path that might take it to the Seattle area. The civil control agencies knew nothing about it. So Topsoil, as they were then called—intrepid call signs were not their forte—decided to scramble the alerts at Comox. Our wing man's aircraft didn't like the idea and retired for the day.

Our aircraft, however, wanted to fly, and we were soon airborne, heading for the Pacific Ocean. Our controller, from the sound of things, was a young lad who had been in the service all day, and thought that the air force was just great. The ground control network was working well, our CF–101 was working well, and it looked like another ho-hum ID of an elderly piston-popper from who knows where.

After a while, the target appeared on my scope, about where the datalink said it would be. My practice was to do these intercepts without touching the hand control, reasoning that there was no point in telling a possible opponent that I'd seen him. But suddenly, there wasn't one target, there were several. And my scope was lighting up in ways I hadn't thought possible.

Well, let's share that information. "Topsoil," I said, "Buzzer, stream."

There was a silence. After a while, the young controller responded, "Hotel Golf 25, say again."

I repeated the message while continuing to direct my pilot, Dale Northrop, toward the unknown — and now possibly hostile — intruders, who were likely enmeshed in the same clouds that enclosed us. Throughout the chase, Topsoil kept using increasingly senior voices to find out what was happening with this suspicious target or targets.

Yes, there was no question but that these intruders were larking about, using ECM and generally being uncooperative. They were heading generally for the Victoria area and descending. We continued to shadow them until we popped out of cloud in the descent. There, about half a mile ahead of us, were two USN ERA–3Bs in a loose combat spread. They had flown from a carrier still a long way from the coast of Vancouver Island, and were heading for their base at Whidbey Island, not far from Bremerton, Washington.

We later heard that the exercise had been planned, sort of, but various messages that should have been sent never reached those who needed them. But it was certainly interesting to hear the increasing seniority of the voices as the situation progressed. I think the next one would have been C-in-C NORAD himself. Fortunately, the quite realistic "enemy" emerged from cloud, was identified as a "friendly," and all concerned breathed a sigh of relief and got back to work. On our way back, even our young controller sounded older. Well he might!

Col. Pat and the cable

Pete Armour

I remembered this episode because of LCol Patterson (then CO of 409 Squadron) and have often thought of it as the years went by.

The arrestor cable was a cable stretched across the runway supported by round "pucks" so as to be above the runway for the aircraft's arresting hook to snag or "pick up the cable." It was intended for emergency purposes such as brake failure on landing. When all else failed on landing, you could extend the arrestor hook and take the cable to stop on the runway. Yes, it could be used for an "approach end engagement," but we had decided long ago that hurling self and craft at the runway while depending on a cable to arrest your near-suicidal landing was something better left to the navy. Only at times of extreme duress was such an approach worth contemplating.

These cables were usually in place at about 1,500 feet from the far end of the runway in use. But it was not unusual to have both "up." Aircraft movement over the cables was limited to low speed. We had been warned that our own nose wheel could set the cable bouncing on the pucks and snag the front of our underslung external fuel tanks when fitted to the aircraft or could snag the nose wheel of the number two aircraft on a formation takeoff run. Approach end cables were part of the morning's briefing, so we were always advised.

One day, Bob Barr was scheduled to lead me for a formation takeoff. Everything was fine as we started, taxied, and lined up on the runway. He led us to position on the runway, we held our brakes on while he gave the signal for engine windup to 80 percent, brake release, and the call for burners to be selected; then we were on our way. Out of the corner of my eye, I saw the approach end cable rush past underneath and muttered an earnest, "Oh, dear!" into my mask. Okay, I cannot remember exactly what expletive I used, but it was over in a blink without incident, and we conducted our flights, with me leading for the return to base.

After we landed and signed in our aircraft, I checked with Bob: "You saw the cable?"

"Yeah, but what the hell could we do then?"

"Well, it was no big deal," I replied.

Upstairs, after we had signed in our times, the operations officer on duty advised us we were to report "to the boss's office—with your hats." Well, it was a big deal now. Bring your hats was emphasis to salute on entering the CO's office—something you would do anyway, but it meant stuff was gonna fly!

LCol Patterson was a legend known to us as "The Silver Fox." He had lots of experience on fighters, and we all had great respect for his flying ability and were grateful to be living this good life under his wonderful leadership. Some may be born to lead and some develop it, but "Col. Pat" was someone we considered had both. You wanted to please. The best definition I had heard of leadership was, "Getting others to do what you want them to do—willingly." This was the essence of our CO. Nobody on the squadron wanted to let him down, and, if you did, it was the ultimate disappointment.

He started in to Bob and berated him for having missed the cable set-ups at briefing and for being a bad form lead. He never raised his voice; it would have been easier if he had. It went on for no more than a very short time but seemed interminable; and then he turned to me, "And don't think you're off the hook on this, mister. You've got a damn radio. Why can't you pass information on it? There are good wingmen, too, y'know! Now get out of my office and you both owe me a beer."

We saluted and retreated. We never did it again and no one else ever did, either. Oh, and we each bought him a beer without his even mentioning the offence.

Brodeur #1
Don Brodeur

In September of 1979, I was lucky enough to fly in the CNE Air Show with the Warlocks—425 Squadron's formation team. I was flying with JP Paquette, and our fearless leader was Romeo Lalonde. On the ground, "observing," was 425's CO, Rhiney Koehn. The show, like most Voodoo displays, always ended with the four aircraft going by low and fast in half-mile trail as close as possible to Mach 1.0, followed by an aggressive pull to the vertical and hopefully out of sight.

We flew a normal four-day CNE show. On the final day, being twenty-eight and full of p. and vinegar and overconfidence, my pull to the vertical was very aggressive. So much so, in fact, that as I approached about 60 degrees nose up and smoothly pushed the stick forward, absolutely nothing happened! Being very experienced and professional, I calmly smashed the stick into the instrument panel with all my strength! The nose of the aircraft, being both more experienced and probably older than I, deigned to continue with no response. By now, the adrenalin was flowing almost as quickly through my veins as the beer had down my throat the night before. Time had expanded sufficiently that, to this day, the moment that probably lasted three or four seconds seemed like an hour. To JP in the back, I am sure it felt like two hours . . . I was just beginning to wonder whether the board would spell "pitch-up," with or without a hyphen, when the nose slowly stopped at about 100 degrees nose up. Despite my ham fisting, the poor airframe and crew had survived. The adrenalin blew out of my skin as sweat, leaving a musk in the cockpit. By the time we got back on the ground, both JP and I had a beer-low-level light on.

That evening, happy that I had "gotten away with it," not only with the flying gods but also with the powers that be on earth, JP and I were replacing the Molson in our systems when Rhiney K. came up and casually said: "That was an interesting last pass today, Brode."

"Yes, sir," I replied with all the panache of a first-tour pilot.

"The LJM was quite well done," he stated.

At first, to my relief, all I heard was, "well done"; then I decided that as long as I had "done well," I might as well admit I was not familiar with an LJM.

"An LJM, sir?"

From his answer, it is obvious that Rhiney, who flew one of the best solo Voodoo shows I have ever witnessed, knew exactly what JP and I had experienced that day.

"An LJM is a Little Jesus Manoeuvre . . . when you do one, it makes you say, 'JESUS!'"

I learned a few things from that experience:

1. There is nothing new you can do with an airplane.
2. You can't fool your CO if he is a good pilot.
3. If you are a good leader, as a CO, you can put a first-tour pilot firmly in place without crushing his enthusiasm.
4. Never pull the stick back that hard in a Voodoo!
5. Your backseater on his second Voodoo tour will forgive you when you do something stupid—but only if you buy him LOTS of beer!

Don Parker's AFC[27]
Author Unknown

On the morning of April 10, 1963, F/O Parker was the navigator on a CF–101B aircraft of 416 All-Weather Fighter Squadron, participating in a tactical exercise. During the second mission in which he and his pilot participated, while making an attack on a target aircraft at 20,000 feet, F/O Parker was surprised to observe his aircraft turning in the wrong direction for the intercept manoeuvre that was underway. Upon querying the pilot, F/O Parker deduced from the replies that the pilot was in difficulty and suspected that a malfunction of oxygen equipment was the cause. He calmly, but emphatically, directed the pilot to descend and follow emergency oxygen procedures. When this action produced no tangible results, and from further remarks made by the pilot, F/O Parker realized that the pilot was seriously ill. He then commenced to direct the pilot to return to base and prepare to land the aircraft.

Although the situation was obviously hazardous, F/O Parker did not even declare an emergency in his radio transmissions, since he had reasoned that this would unnerve the pilot completely. Nevertheless, he elected to remain with the aircraft and to attempt to save it and the pilot. Handling all radio transmissions himself, he soothed, persuaded, and encouraged the pilot through the approach and landing in less than ideal weather conditions, despite the pilot's uncertain and often incorrect reactions that caused the aircraft to repeatedly approach critical performance limits.

Following the landing, the pilot collapsed and was helpless. F/O Parker climbed forward to shut down the engines and assisted the ground crew and

---

27 Air Force Cross, a medal awarded for feats of derring-do while *not* under enemy fire.

medical personnel in removing the almost unconscious pilot from the cockpit.

Throughout a dangerous situation, F/O Parker demonstrated exceptional courage, devotion to duty, and loyalty to his pilot, in hazarding his own life when he might have safely ejected from the aircraft. His cool and skilful direction, which made full use of the pilot's severely limited ability, was instrumental in saving both their lives and a valuable aircraft.

George Rawson's memories

George Rawson

My career, as carefully recalled by a non-drinking, non-smoking, air navigator, George Rawson, CD2!

Sept. 24, 1954, I joined the RCAF. Selected for navigator training at PSU(O), RCAF Stn. London, Ontario.

Feb. 22, 1955, first AI trip, on Dak 345 with F/O Clarke for three hours at RCAF Stn. Winnipeg, Manitoba.

Sept. 16, 1955, first CF–100 trip in #174 with F/L Lee for 0.45 hours at RCAF Stn. Cold Lake, Alberta.

Nov. 1955, crewed with F/L Cec Moore on Course 24 at #3 OTU Cold Lake.

Feb. 2, 1956, I passed out after night takeoff in CF–100 #174 with F/L Cec Moore for 0.20 hours at Cold Lake. I remained unconscious for twelve hours. Cec saved my life with less than two minutes left without oxygen, as I had thrown up in my mask. I was CT'd (Cease Training) for AIM check. Found nothing. Returned to flying with Course 28 and crewed up with F/O Lloyd Currier. I said I was a teetotaller to Lloyd at the crewing party, and he said, "That's great — I love Black Label beer." A perfect match! Sent to 432 Sqn.

Mar 19, 1957 (my birthday), on air test with F/O Lloyd Currier in CF–100 #539 on 413 Sqn. at RCAF Stn. Bagotville, Quebec. Set an unofficial endurance flight of 3.0 hours day, with Mark V with no tanks. Ordered to land by the flight commander. We could have made 3.30 hours. Flew a total of five hours that day.

May 17, 1957, flew from BG, PQ, to Torbay, Newfoundland, for static display at air show with F/O Lloyd Currier. Lloyd was wounded in the leg by the canopy explosive charge as he stood on the fuselage when a kid in the cockpit flicked the canopy release switch. Purple Cross candidate!

Sept. 2, 1957, we attempted flight from Vancouver to Cold Lake in CF–100 #643 with S/L Campbell. With great skill and dexterity, we ended up near Great Falls, Montana, before discovering the "navigator's" variation error. We managed to land at Cold Lake after 1.45 hours with very little fuel. We took part in the first annual rocket meet in Cold Lake.

Dec. 16, 1958, my last 413 Sqn. CF–100 flight with Lloyd Currier in #649. One-hour-night against B–52.

Jan. 24, 1962, getting my quarterly twenty-five hours' flying time (out of RCAF Stn. Edgar) in the VIP C–5 No.10,000 at OW [Ottawa]. Two hours of "circuits and bumps."

Nov. 1963, crewed with F/L Andy Anderson at BG OTU. He said he drinks beer. I don't. Another perfect match!

Jan. 22, 1964, last CF–100 trip. At #3 OTU Bagotville in #497, and F/L Andy Anderson doing low level sterns. 1.10 night.

Feb. 25, 1964, first CF–101 Voodoo trip. In #399 with Andy Anderson. 1.25 hours day.

July 9, 1964, 409 Sqn. deployed to Paine AFB, Washington. BIG party following Exercise Chinook Knife Golf Zot. In wee hours, while "boys" were attempting a steal of rival McChord FIS gun mascot from fenced and armed guard-protected QRA, S/L

Patterson ordered F/L Anderson over the fence. At the top of the wire, Andy heard a cocking sound from below where a big, black, MP was. Andy beat a hasty, ripped retreat, with apologies to the "Grey Fox"! "MI"!

Dec. 5, 1964, at 409 Sqn, Comox, British Columbia. Hairy flight out of McChord AFB, Washington, in WOXOF[28] conditions with "Super Sid" Popham at the controls and a formation wing man desperately hanging on.

On takeoff, Sid's orders were: "George, keep an eye on runway lights; Number Two, don't lose me!"

Tower's instructions were: "You are cleared for takeoff, wherever you are!" We made it. 0.45 minutes day.

Feb. 26, 1965, at 409 Sqn. in CF–101 #445 with Andy Anderson. Scramble—a CL–44 with an emergency; 1.15 hours night.

Sept. 1965, at 409 Sqn. Andy Anderson came in to 0700 hours briefing hung over. The "Grey Fox" came into briefing also hung over. After briefing, Andy and Gerry got into a very heated, highly vocal, very visible, uncharacteristic screaming match for five full minutes. Exhausted, each looked at the other, shook hands, and said to each other, "Have a nice day!" Hangover cured!

May 6, 1966, in CF–101 #475 with F/O Stoss on exercise "Top Rung." Nailed a B–58 Hustler; 1.40 hours night.

May 10, 1966, in CF–101 #411 with F/O Stoss out of Kingsley AFB. "MA" on a U–2, HL Snap;[29] 0.45 hours night.

Oct. 1966, following a mug-out for Andy Anderson—Andy was told to follow George home to Andy's house. George arrived. No Andy! He was seeing two centre lines on Anderton Road and took the right-hand line, wiping out two wooden ditch approaches, and ended up in the ditch unable to move.

Jan. 19, 1967, in CF–101 #440 with S/L Patterson, the Grey Fox. Last flight of 409 Sqn tour. HL AI; 2.0 hours day.

Mar. 23, 1970, in CF–101 #441 with Capt. Earl McCurdy at #410 OTS Bagotville. Voodoo refresher. Mission #11, sterns;[30] 1.25 hours day.

Apr. 10, 1970, in T–33 #607 with Major Stroud. Conjugal visit from BG to LaMacaza. 1.10 hours day and plenty of night!

May 2, 1970, in CF–101 #393 with Major Stroud flying from CH to BG low level. Another George variation error. Ended up in Maine, USA, briefly. Low on fuel returning. Fudges 1.0 hours day.

May 26, 1970, in CF–101 #463 with Capt. Clay. First flight at 416 Sqn, Chatham. FSRA[31] & Stern at HL. 1.3 hrs day.

Mar. 23, 1971, at 416 Sqn, Chatham. All CF–101s grounded due to engine failures.

Apr. 27, 1971, in CF–101 #403 with Major B.K. Doyle. Operation Peace Wings (trading old Voodoos for new IIP). Flew to WG [Winnipeg]; 3.5 hours day.

June 17, 1971, in CF–101 #408 with Capt. John Mulvihill. Last flight in original Voodoos. Super and FSRA snaps HL; 1.7 hours night.

Aug. 11, 1971, flew first trip in new IIP Voodoo with Capt. Wilson on an air test, 1.0 hours day.

Aug. 24–25, 1971, Capt. Mike Blair and George Rawson flew T–33 #3508 to Seymour Johnston and flew a mission on a B–52 #0258 for 7.5 hours night and 3.5 hours day. Sang "Oh Canada" over the North Pole.

Oct. 7, 1971, near-collision on runway after FSRA on CF–100 with Capt Blair; 1.4 hours day.

Oct. 15, 1971, Diverted to BG after windshield cracked. Capt. Dixon and I flew 1.3 hours day.

---

28   Weather and ceiling both zero, and no one should be flying in such conditions.
29   HL = high-level; Snap = snap-up attack.
30   Devoted to attacks from the stern.
31   Front/stern re-attacks.

Jan. 26, 1972, Lt. O'Shea and George picked up #016, new IIP from Donaldson Centre; 2.7 hours day.

Feb. 26, 1973, in CF–101 #029 with Capt. Blair. My 1,000 Voodoo hours. Mission FSRA Snaps and CO; 1.2 hours day.

Apr. 30, 1973, took a CH–118 (Huey) to CFB Gagetown for three-day vasectomy operation!

June 13, 1973, in CF–101 #029 with new 416 Sqn CO, LCol Super Sid Popham, on his first AI flight on Sqn. Flew against B–52; 1.5 hours day.

June 20, 1973, with Lt. Charlton in CF–047. Ferry flight from Bristol in WG to Chatham; 2.8 hours day, 0.6 hours night. Last flight with 416 Sqn.

Feb. 21, 1977, transferred to OTU — 410 Sqn.

Postscript: A brief overview of the career of a great guy.

A trip to Colorado

Jim Gregory

In February 1970, I was part of a two-Voodoo formation that flew from CFB Chatham to Colorado Springs for a familiarization visit to NORAD HQ, and to visit a colleague then working there. The first leg, to Griffiss AFB, Rome, New York, where we remained overnight, was uneventful.

The next day, we were to stage through Richards–Gebaur AFB for a refuelling stop. However, strong winds meant weak fuel reserves, so we found another destination: Whiteman AFB, which apparently had the equipment needed to turn us around, so we diverted there. The approach and landing were uneventful, but as we taxied in, we noted there were no other aircraft on the ramp.

There were many problems with the refuelling truck, the air compressor, and the other equipment needed to refuel two CF–101s, with the result that

Impressing the French ambassador, Bagotville. Dick Lidstone in the box (getting close to Jesus).

the planned one-hour turnaround took four hours.

We eventually departed for Peterson Field. As we were approaching Denver, Denver Center asked about our destination. When told, they helpfully said, "Peterson Field is NOTAMed closed for a major parade for CinC NORAD's retirement."

"Denver," we said, "we'll divert to Buckley."

"Roger that," said Denver. "We'll need your prior permission required number for Buckley."

We didn't, of course, have one, but fuel considerations meant that we had to land at Buckley. They relented, and we were soon on a two-mile run-in for an overhead break, which we announced, to which the tower replied, "We don't have you in sight." There was a reason for that. We had lined up with Denver Centennial Airport.

On touchdown at Buckley, a "follow me" truck guided us to a very crowded ramp, where we were met by the ultimate in crabby base operations officers. He loudly shared his opinions of pilots who considered it unnecessary to perform such plebeian tasks as checking NOTAMs.

Following that inauspicious start, our colleague from NORAD HQ arrived to treat us to a splendid weekend of skiing and dining after we had completed our NORAD orientation.

On Sunday, we departed Buckley for YCH, with a planned refuelling stop at Wright–Patterson AFB. We planned a formation departure from Buckley without considering Buckley's elevation of 6,000 feet above sea level. The aircraft performance was anemic. Just as we were getting airborne, Buckley tower called, "Golf November 04, your number two's drag chute is deployed." It was too late to abort, but fortunately the drag chute hadn't deployed. It had merely fallen away from the airplane.

The remaining legs of the trip unrolled without any untoward incidents and we returned home a much wiser group than we had been.

So young — so innocent

Jim Gregory

I had just graduated from 3 All Weather (Operational Training Unit) at CFB Bagotville in October 1966, having completed about sixty hours of CF–101 Voodoo flying. My course navigator, F/L RAD Arthur (a CF–100 all weather navigator from previous days), and I had been transferred to 416 All Weather Fighter Squadron at CFB Chatham, New Brunswick. RAD was the "ole pro" kind of guy who had taken me under his wing. He had been to Chatham before and knew the route to drive from Bagotville to Chatham. Since I didn't own a vehicle at that time, I accompanied F/O Dave Wilson (another young pilot who had graduated from pilot training at Gimli, Manitoba, and was on the same CF–101 course as RAD and I) in his vehicle to Chatham. We were to follow RAD.

We departed Bagotville taking Route 170 from La Baie to Saint–Siméon, Quebec. Arriving at the ferry at Saint–Siméon, we had to wait about half an hour before we boarded the boat. The late October skies were beginning to get dark as we began our ferry trip from Saint–Siméon to Rivière–du–Loup on the eastern shore of the St. Lawrence River. The drive from Rivière–du–Loup to Grand Falls, New Brunswick, was uneventful. RAD had told Dave and me about this road called "The Plaster Rock Highway," which was a "shortcut" across the province of New Brunswick to get to Chatham. Dave and I had no idea where we were going—all we knew was that RAD "knew" where he was going, and we were following.

It was very dark by the time we arrived in Grand Falls. We continued to follow RAD's vehicle through what seemed to be a back-country dirt road. Where in the world were we going? The road became very narrow, winding, changing from gravel to rock to dirt and back, and had vegetation encroaching on the very edges of the road and in some cases overhanging the road itself. I thought to myself, what in the world did I get myself into by being transferred to this place called Chatham?

The Plaster Rock Highway (Route 108) was primarily built as a logging truck road. The road was simply cut out of the woods without the traditional ditches or elevated roadway. At points along the road, huge boulders protruded through the road surface. You had to steer your vehicle around these boulders in order to avoid seriously damaging your car. At one point, Dave drove over one of these boulders and managed to damage the tire, which immediately went flat. As we stopped, we could see the tail lights of RAD's car disappearing along the road ahead. Dave and I got out the materials to change the tire, and about fifteen minutes later, we could see a vehicle's headlights approaching ahead. It was RAD. He finally noticed that we were no longer following him and he turned around to check on us. We continued to follow RAD all the way to Chatham. Unbeknownst to me at that time, I would come to know the Plaster Rock Highway intimately by travelling it on numerous occasions.

Dave Wilson and I had gotten our "local checkout" on the T–33 and CF–101 and we began flying regular interceptor missions. As a normal procedure, any new pilot was crewed up with an "experienced" airborne interceptor navigator for the first few missions before we were permitted to fly with our navigator. In conversation with our squadron colleagues, Dave and I discovered that it was possible to ask for an aircraft to fly away to some exotic location for a weekend.

WOW! You mean that we could actually put a request for an aircraft in to the boss and, if approved, we could fly away for the weekend? Yep!

Dave and I immediately put in a request for the only CF–101F on the squadron (a dual-control version of the CF–101B single-pilot control aircraft) for the weekend of December 3, 1966. Where should we go? Why not New York City! The justification? High-density air traffic training and exposure!

So on Saturday, December 3, 1966, Dave Wilson and I (with about 100 hours' total time each on the CF–101) climbed into the massive Voodoo CF–101F #17400 and headed off to Suffolk County (KFOK) Air National Guard Base on Long Island, New York. Dave was in the front seat and I occupied the back seat. The ANG squadron at KFOK also operated the F–101 Voodoo in the airborne interceptor role, so they would be looking after our aircraft after we landed.

The weather was clear when we arrived after our one hour and thirty-five-minute flight to KFOK. After landing, the ANG ground crew expertly attended to our aircraft. One of the ANG squadron pilots met Dave and me as we dismounted the CF–101 and offered to take us to their squadron operations. There, we met the ANG squadron commander, and he invited us to have lunch with him and some of the other squadron aircrew. We graciously accepted. During lunch, the squadron commander asked Dave and me what our plans were for the night. We quickly replied, "We are off to see the Big City!"

"And how are you guys planning to get there?" asked the squadron commander.

Suffolk County was a good one-and-a-half-hour drive to the city. We hadn't thought about *how* we were going to get there. It was just a minor detail that we thought we would address when the time came to address it. The squadron commander motioned to one of the other pilots nearby, saying, "Call motor pool and get a staff car for our Canadian friends."

Wow, that simple! I thought.

"And have you guys thought of where you will be staying in New York?" asked the squadron commander.

Heck, just another detail that we figured we would address when the time came. The squadron commander motioned to another person, "Call the New Yorker Hotel in Manhattan and book a couple of rooms for our young Canadian friends—and make sure they get the military rate for the rooms."

Gosh, Dave and I thought, that was easy!

Dave and I left the squadron operations center and climbed into the USAF dark blue military staff car that was waiting for us outside. Not only was there a car for us, but there was also a driver, who, we found out later, was tasked to look after us.

"Don't worry about your aircraft," said the squadron commander as he wished us a great time in the Big Apple, "we will look after it." Hell, this is going better than Dave and I could have ever planned.

The drive to downtown New York City was uneventful, I recall. Can you imagine me, from the backwoods of Saskatchewan, being chauffeured to the Big Apple?

The staff car stopped in front of the New Yorker Hotel. Before the driver departed, we asked him if it would be possible for him to meet us right here tomorrow (Sunday) at 1000 hours for a ride back to the base. "No problem, sir," he replied. Dave and I were off to see the City!

As it turned out, Dave and I met up with two of our squadron colleagues, Lou Glussich and Doug

Clark, who had landed in Suffolk County for the night on their flight back from Tyndall AFB, near Panama City, Florida. They also were staying at the New Yorker Hotel, so we toured the big city as a group. Greenwich Village in the late 1960s was a sight to see.

Sunday morning arrived, and sure enough, promptly at 1000 hours our staff car and driver were waiting to drive us back to the base. Lou and Doug drove back with Dave and me, as it was their plan to fly back to Chatham at the same time. A quick detour through the John F. Kennedy airport allowed us to see this huge complex. We arrived back at our respective aircraft and planned to fly back in formation with Lou leading. I climbed into the front seat for the trip back, and Dave occupied the rear seat. The USAF ground crew had readied our aircraft, and we were soon airborne en route to CFB Chatham. The sun was setting as we approached New Brunswick, so by the time we arrived at Chatham in the traffic pattern, it was very dark. This was my very first time flying in close formation at night, and it was a rewarding experience. The approach and landing were uneventful.

So ended our excursion to the Big Apple. I still have this underlying feeling that somehow the events that unfolded when we arrived at Suffolk County Base didn't just "happen." I suspect that our flight commander, S/L Sam Miller, called the squadron commander at Suffolk County to ensure that we were "looked after"! I never did ask Miller about this, but I would like to think that it happened this way!

Heading south

Ron Egli

In the early to mid-sixties, there existed, at least in the Bagotville area, something called the "Boom Line," which defined the area where transonic/supersonic flight was permitted. This "line" ran more or less east-west north of Bagotville. North of the line, supersonic flight was allowed on a northerly heading at a minimum altitude of 30,000 feet in a level or nose up attitude, while south of the line it was a no-go. It was required to log the particulars of each supersonic event (position, time, heading, and altitude of commencement and termination of each event).

On April 14, 1965, 425 AWF Squadron was engaged in exercise Naskapi Feather. This exercise included the five-minute alert crews from Val–d'Or, who, I understand, had downloaded their weapons and were flying "cold" aircraft. Upon termination of the exercise ("Fade Out"), my pilot, Andy Kennedy, and I were assigned to leave our parachutes and hard hats in aircraft #482 and to hold "cold" alert until the Val–d'Or crews were ready to take over.

We were just checking in on the radio when we were scrambled. We were ordered to take off and do an afterburner climb to 35,000 feet, but, instead of going north where one would expect a bogey to be, the combat heading was southwest. It was soon established that the scramble order had been late and that we were ten to fifteen miles behind the target, which was in a gentle descent. We requested "supersonic," and the request was immediately approved.

We had the Voodoo cooking nicely and caught the bogey as we descended through 26,000 feet doing Mach 1.45, and pointing directly at a town that I believe was La Tuque. As one might expect, given the recent "fade-out" and the back scramble, it was a target from the exercise—a CF–100 from the Electronic Warfare Unit based in St. Hubert, heading home. Somewhere in the system, an "eyes only" or "trusted agent" probably had a lot of explaining to do. But, at the time, Cold War tensions were pretty high, and we took the job very seriously. Besides, we got to go "super" below the "boom line," heading south and descending.

Queen's colours
Author Unknown

After twenty-five years of active service in the RCAF and Canadian Forces, squadrons are eligible to receive the Queen's Colour and Battle Honours; 410 (AW) OTS was awarded the honour on June 12, 1976, at CFB Bagotville, Quebec. As an adjunct to this commemoration, Captains Dick Walker and Denis Bouchard flew an envelope on a supersonic training mission in excess of 50,000 feet at a speed of Mach 1.2. The Commemorative of 410 Squadron reads:

> 410 Cougar Squadron began at Ayr, Scotland, on June 30, 1941, as a night-fighter unit involved in the defence of Great Britain. Flying single-engined Defiants, the Squadron was operationally ready in August and immediately moved to Drem, near the Firth of Forth. In April 1942, the Defiants were exchanged for radar-equipped Beaufighters. On completion of conversion training, the Squadron went to Scorton, Yorkshire in September, where a 410 crew brought the Squadron its first wartime success. In October, 410 moved to Acklington, where it received Mosquito night fighters and won its first confirmed kill. In February 1943, the Squadron moved to Colby Grange, Lincolnshire; where, in addition to normal night defence duties, it undertook offensive missions into enemy-held territory by day and night; attacking trains, vehicles, canal shipping, airfields and aircraft. In October 1943, the Squadron moved to south-eastern England, where it was attached to No. 11 Group and primarily involved in the defence of Great Britain. In September 1944, with 50 3/4 confirmed kills, the Squadron moved to Glisy, near Amiens, and remained in France until the spring of 1945. The last wartime move was to Gilge-Ryen in the Netherlands, where it remained until the end of hostilities.
>
> 410 Squadron personnel won 41 awards, including 19 DFC's. On the Roll of Honour were the names of 62 officers and airmen, of whom 30 were killed or presumed dead on operations against the enemy. The Squadron badge, approved by His Majesty, King George VI in May 1945, depicts a cougar's head superimposed on a crescent moon. "Noctivaga" (wandering by night) refers to the Squadron's wartime role as a night-fighter unit. The Squadron was disbanded on June 9, 1945.
>
> Reforming in December 1948 at St. Hubert, Que., 410 became the first fighter squadron in the post-war Regular Force. Flying Vampires in a day-interceptor role, the Squadron was part of the RCAF's Air Defence Group.
>
> 410 was the first RCAF Squadron to receive F-86 Sabres shortly before moving to North Luffenham, England, in November 1951. 410 also became Canada's first day-fighter squadron to participate in the NATO alliance. In November 1954, the Squadron moved to Baden Baden, Germany, and then on to Marville, France, in early 1955 and was disbanded in October 1956.
>
> Reformed again in November 1956 at Uplands airport, Ottawa, the Squadron was equipped with the CF–100 Canuck. In 1962, the Squadron converted to the CF–101 Voodoo and continued to operate in the defence of North America until March 31, 1964, when it was disbanded.

In April 1968, 3 All Weather Operational Training Unit of Canadian Forces Base Bagotville was re-designated 410 All Weather Operational Training Squadron. At present, 410 is responsible for the training of aircrew for the other three interceptor squadrons of Air Defence Group. The Squadron also gives an annual Air Weapons Instructor's Course to squadron weapons crews.

410 is now able to look back upon 25 years of active service with the RCAF and the Canadian Forces. It is with great pride that the Cougar Squadron received its Queen's Colours on the 12th day of June, 1976.

Rendezvous over the Miramichi

Les Hare

One beautiful Friday in 1966, excellent flying missions were completed by 416 (AW) Fighter Squadron and the Sabre Transition Unit (the STU) at RCAF Station Chatham, New Brunswick.

Following their flights, the crews repaired to the officers' mess for Beer Call and full and descriptive debriefings.

Two "Maritime boys" were joined in spirited and animated conversation! An intrepid STU instructor, F/O John Yerxa, call sign "Eagle," regaled us with tales of bold and fearless skilled flight in their F–86 "Swords." The missions were preparing young airmen for their future advancement to the CF–104 "Starfighter," then on to Europe as low-level strike pilots.

Yours truly, having now spent over a year flying the Voodoo, was up to the task of defending the question at hand: "Who had the better aircraft?" Studies must be completed! Right! While enjoying "adult beverages," cunning plans took place.

The following Monday, after speaking to Eagle at his office, further plans were completed.

"Check your six after you leave the range,"[32] said I; and ascertained his mission frequency for our "meeting" somewhere over the Miramichi. F/L Ron Elliot, my nav (from whom I learned a lot), and I launched for a high-level Sqn. mission early in the afternoon. Monitoring my Timex closely, I called "R.T.B." after three quick runs and then positioned ourselves on CAP over the Tracadie range.

"Three targets—twelve o'clock, range ten miles," Ron instructed, "low."

No doubt; we lurked overhead at 10,000 feet.

"Range five miles, closing," called Ron.

"Contact," I acknowledged.

"Let's go get 'em!"

It wasn't long before we were five miles in stern, closing! The Eagle had called his formation into "vic"; I had them two miles ahead.

"Keep it tight," called the lead.

"Range one-half mile," Ron chuckled.

"Time for a vis-ident," said I; Ron agreed. Snuggling the Voodoo into position, the best place would be the "slot" to view the targets. Two clicks of my mike button, and the Eagle knew I was in position.

"Check our six!" called the Eagle. Numbers two and three both complied. They looked hard left and right, and—"Yikes, where did he come from?"

"Tuck it in, Eagles!" lead called. After a few seconds of "aileron flutter," Eagles two and three moved back in, allowing Eagle four to *fill* the diamond.

"Eagles, go tower!"

"Chatham Tower, Eagle plus three; five miles

---

32   This is fighter pilot talk for "Pay particular attention to your vulnerable six-o'clock position" after leaving the range that is set aside for the Sabres. It is the area directly behind the Sabre, in this case, and if the Sabre pilot is not wary, he could be "shot down."

back, request low and over."

"Roger, Eagle, cleared," duty controller Mac McDonald calmly responded. "Confirm Eagle plus three?"

"Rog, we have a stray," replied the lead.

After a pass down the taxiway, formation changed to echelon right, positioned for a fighter break, and landed. The three Sabres dispersed to their hangar area, and I parked in front of the squadron hangar. Mission complete!

Off to the mess for a full debriefing with the Eagle plus two. Naturally! As all were enjoying refreshing "suds," John informs the gathered troops that he has landed "in the glue" with his boss! It seems the squadron leader was not impressed with this "unauthorized flying" and rewarded the Eagle with a few days' Orderly Officer.

"What about you, Les, anything said at 416?" asked John.

"Yep," I answered. "My flight commander had something to say, for sure."

"Was that you in the 'box' with those Swords?" asked S/L Fred Tupling, a glint in his eye.

"Yes, sir," I answered, without hesitation.

"Next time, tighten it up, okay?"

"Yes, sir!"

Wonderful days on the Miramichi!

[P.S. I volunteered to share the O.O. duties with the Eagle.]

SARAH II

Ron Egli

At noon on Easter Sunday, March 29, 1970, my wife was about to serve Easter dinner to our family of six. Our four sons were aged three to twelve years, so an early dinner made for an easier day for Mom and Dad. My sons and I were seated at the table, and my wife was bringing in the turkey platter when the phone rang. I was to report to base immediately to go on a SARAH search for a missing aircraft. The search was to be out of Val-d'Or about 285 nautical miles west of home base.

As a nav on 410 AW(F) OTS in Bagotville, I had received some training on an airborne search device called SARAH (Search And Rescue And Homing) that could be mounted in a T-33. SARAH was operated from the backseat. It was designed to pick up radio signals on the emergency frequency. The trick then was for the nav to detect the signal and direct the pilot to fly to its source using procedures to determine its exact location.

My wife was not the happiest camper in the Saguenay Valley, but away I went. I arrived at the squadron to meet Dave Speiser, the 410 staff driver who had been designated to fly the search. We understood it was to be a one-shot mission: fly to VO,[33] fly one search, and fly home. We took T-33 #176 to Val-d'Or, briefed, and took off again for James Bay. By this time it was getting well on into the afternoon. We flew over Fort George then to Bear Island, where the missing aircraft was thought to be down. We went as low and stayed as long as fuel would possibly allow, but I could pick up no signal. This was pretty disheartening to both Dave and me. I had been quite successful with this procedure during training exercises, and the thought of some poor fellow down, possibly injured and freezing, made me feel pretty damned useless. We got back to VO in the dark with not a lot of fuel remaining.

On arrival, we were told we were to stay overnight and try again the next day. I called home and told Leslie the story, and like all good service wives, when told the reasons she was fine about it all.

The next day, we flew over Twin Islands, Grey Goose Island, and Bear Island . . . still no joy. Again

---

33 Val-d'Or.

we limped back to VO feeling rather down but knowing we'd given it our best shot. We were then advised our part was over and we were to return to BG. So, washed but unshaven, we headed home.

On Tuesday morning at the squadron we were told the missing pilot had been found alive and uninjured in the area we had searched. He'd been on a flight in a helicopter doing a polar bear census when, for whatever reason, he'd been forced to set down on the ice and wait for help. When told that a search had been conducted on Sunday and Monday and that no emergency locator beacon had been picked up, he said that he did not turn his beacon on until Tuesday because he did not think anyone would be searching for him on the long Easter Weekend!

Pre-OTU training

Pete Armour

One of the interesting facets of the air defence world was the training of "sprog" pilots. These were the ones who had just had wings bestowed upon them. To hold alert in the system, a pilot had to be able to fly in weather down to a ceiling of 200 feet and visibility of half a mile. These were "green ticket" (instrument rating) limits. Upon graduation, a sprog had "white ticket" limits of 400 feet and one mile. The requisite increase in flying instrument skills was deemed to have occurred at 500 total flying hours (newly graduated pilots had some 270 hours).

The additional hours were obtained at an Operational Training Unit (OTU), flying the Silver Star T–Bird or T–33 on a twenty-week, 200 flying hour course led by qualified flying instructors. By the end of the Voodoo course, a new pilot would have 500 hours and could be tested for upgrading to the required green ticket. Before my time in 1967, the extra time was gathered by flying the CF–100.

It was a busy time. Ted Kasprzak and I arrived at the Bagotville OTU in late April 1967. After a unit checkout and some local training, we were off with the instructors on a long-range target assignment. On May 5, Syd Rennick and I departed for Gander, getting there in just under two hours. Ted was on our wing with Don Elphick. We were introduced to Screech in the mess and learned that, if you fiddled in idle curiosity with the Connie wheel (from a Super Constellation transport aircraft) attached to the bar, you could end up having to buy a round after one of the buttons you pushed on the control yoke sounded throughout the building. (From the number of people who showed up, I was sure it had sounded through the entire STATION!)

We departed for Chatham, New Brunswick, in the early morning (around 0200) of May 5 in thick, swirling snow that brought the visibility down to one mile, and maybe less. There was a huge weather system over the region, and for part of our target run, we were an "unsafe target" because we were in cloud. Soon we were in the clear on top. Our flight plan was on an "airspace reservation" that had been pre-coordinated with Air Traffic Control (ATC) for the Exercise. I recall an American voice lamenting from time to time that he was still in cloud at his assigned altitude and, thus, unsafe. The Ground Control Interceptor (GCI) controller acknowledged calmly each time.

Finally, the pilot came on the air stating he had climbed 4,000 feet to flight level (FL) 350 (35,000 feet) and was now clear of cloud — was that okay?

The GCI controller calmly replied, "It's okay with me but I don't know about ATC."

After several seconds of silence, we heard the same pilot's voice: "Level at flight level FL 310."

We landed, refuelled, had breakfast, and proceeded to Goose Bay, Newfoundland. In the early hours of May 6, we repeated a similar target flight to Shearwater, the naval station at Halifax. After a long delay to refuel (they were not expecting us, they said), we went to the wardroom for breakfast. I recall we caused quite a stir because flight suits were not allowed in the wardroom. Finally, the rule was waived so we could eat and return to Bagtown. I was fine until taxiing in to Bagotville. I remember the meltdown. I was tired. We had just flown nine hours and five minutes in four days and it was 0930 in the morning.

Canada's Centennial Year was 1967, and we flew nearly every day. In addition to flying routine target missions, for OTU student training during the week, we frequently flew on the weekend in an air display led by one of the instructors, at places all over Quebec. If someone was going on a course, we flew him there. If someone had to go to Edmonton, we flew him there! I flew some 250 hours throughout Canada and some trips into the States, from late April to early September, when we began on the Voodoo OTU. Ted's time was comparable, and we loved every minute of it!

Snyder stories

Lloyd Snyder

I did only one tour on Voodoos but I garnered some interesting experiences. My first squadron checkout was with LCol Ron Hayman. The clear hood stuff went well[34] and the high TACAN was on target so we embarked on a radar square. Halfway around the pattern, he asked, "Have you ever had a single engine in this aircraft, Lloyd?" to which I stupidly replied, "no." He responded, "You do now," and he shut down the left engine. Quick as a wink, nothing happened! Practice single engines involved boards and rudder. Real ones involved power on the good engine. If there was any rudder required, I missed it.

We have all done something stupid in our lives and lived. What farm lad has not peed on an electric fence? Mine was a little more exciting. I was holding alert in Val–d'Or when the radar on our bird decided to take a vacation. We called Bagotville Voodoo control and requested a new aircraft, which they said they would supply.

We set off for Bagtown. It was a beautiful Sunday morning in July, and my intrepid navigator, Mike Faucher, and I decided to request a supersonic transit. North Bay obliged, and we scooted up to 45,000 feet and were soon cooking along at about twelve miles a minute, when I had a brain fart. "Let's see how high this thing will go," I said, and Fauch said, "Why not?" I pulled the nose up about forty-five degrees and headed for the realm of the angels. At about 55,000, I rolled inverted to get ready for the recovery, and somewhere over 60,000 (63,700, I think), I realized that I had miscalculated the recovery somewhat, as the Alpha wand tried to cross the RLS boundary marker, and the indicated air speed hit ZERO!

With the nose still about ten degrees above the horizon, hanging in the straps and trying to keep those damned wands from doing the tango, I remember thinking, "If one of those engines quits we're dead!" Well, the engines worked just fine, the nose fell through the horizon, the airspeed picked up, and we levelled at 45,000 and about Mach 1.2. I think Mike enjoyed the ride, and I learned a lot about flying, so I guess it all turned out okay.

Another incident that sticks out in my mind was Tactical Evaluation 1973. We were on five[35] when the horn blew, so we got to go chase the bad guys and then write the exam. Just to make my life interesting, we were paired on a high-level supersonic target at

---

34 The portions of the exercise that did not require reference to the flight instruments were satisfactorily completed to established standards.

35 "We were on [or set up on] five" means that they were at a state of readiness that would allow them to become airborne within five minutes.

409 Nighthawk Squadron and their nearly new CF–101: "The Painted Lady."

takeoff, but that was changed to a low-level intruder shortly after takeoff. We were down in the weeds looking for the target—with the controller telling us we were merged with the target—when I saw a flash of motion out of the corner of my left eye. Sure enough, there was a Clunk intent on blowing up the beautiful Saguenay Valley. For a second I considered letting him do it, but duty prevailed and I plugged in the burners and started after him, calling out the clock position to the nav in hopes of a lock on and secondary armament kill. About halfway around the corner, I saw another flash of motion, this time out of my right eye, as the altimeter climbed about 3,000 feet to signal that we were now travelling at the speed the Voodoo was built to travel—Mach one plus! At about 1,000 feet, we were considerably below the supersonic clearance altitude, so I slowed down, we shot down the Clunk, the Saguenay Valley was saved, a bunch of bunny rabbits learned how high they could jump, and we said nothing to anyone! Gulp!

It was February and we were having one of what seemed to be endless NORAD exercises. The aircraft were all lined up in front of the hangar, and we were set up on five. Ops was receiving the scramble orders and relaying them over the squadron PA to the intrepid airmen playing acey ducey and drinking coffee interspersed with various lies and war stories when "Kilo November 6" came up. "That's us!" I said to my nav, and we raced off. The temperature was plus one, so we could use the afterburners. We were paired on a high-level supersonic target, so it was a profile one climb. Cleared onto the runway, I stood on the brakes and ran the engines up to full military and let them "cook" for a few seconds. I released the brakes, punched the clock and lit the burners. We were going 500 Kts TAS as we passed over the end of the runway. Forty degrees nose up and hang on (I may have cheated a little here), inverted as we passed through 30,000, level at 35,000, and punch the clock. One minute thirty-six seconds from brake release to level, and the base was six miles directly below us.

Another Sunday morning in Val–d'Or, Jim Denovan and I were the alert pilots, and I organized a practice scramble. All went well, and we spent an hour bumping heads. The weather was a little grungy, so we elected to do individual recoveries, with me going down the chute first. As I was parking, the crash bells went off, and all hell broke loose. I scrambled to the ops desk, as I was the Alert Force commander. As I arrived at the desk, the corporal said, "He's down okay."

It turned out that when he lowered the gear on final, the right engine blew up. The blast blew off the right engine door and the right flap, and he did a rapid roll. He recovered control of the aircraft, declared an emergency, and landed. Afterward, we found out that the engine casing had been incorrectly installed with the weld at the eight o'clock position (aimed at the engine door) instead of the two o'clock position (aimed at the #2 feed tank). Improperly installed, the weld failure always resulted in the loss of the aircraft and more than once the crew. It turns out that the USAF had had a similar problem and had gone to a seamless casing several years previously, but some engineer in NDHQ had decided that the fix was too expensive and/or unnecessary. Tell Doug Stuart and Lynn Wagar that!

They say that memory is the second thing to go. I can't recall the first, but I believe these tales to be fairly accurate. As you know, the older we get the better we used to be.

Some stories you should chase down:

1. The day Jimmie Speiser taking off with double jugs full and returning with half of one tank on sideways and no drag chute. When asked what happened, he said, "Nothin'."
2. Judge Wenham arriving at the Bangor clam bake a little hot around the corner so he deployed the drag chute just prior to getting lined up with the runway.
3. The day someone escorted two sweet young things (exotic dancers) into the Q in Val–d'Or for a tour, and the B Flight commander and his deputy strapped them into the back seat of the two birds not on alert and gave them an afterburner jaunt down the runway and back.
4. Bob Smith's last trip with 425 Sqn when he did a four-plane roll over the runway during his cleared low approach (Joe Couillard was the squad boss, and I am sure he remembers that day well).

More *Totem Times*
CFB Comox, Thursday, October 31, 1968

The following excerpts are from one of the best base papers in the RCAF/CAF during the sixties and seventies.

Cudgel Capers II, Again

Recently a group of 409 Squadron officers gathered to draw up a set of timed inputs for an exercise. This exercise was scheduled to simulate a Tactical Evaluation of the Base, and, to a great extent, the posture the base would assume during an actual combat situation.

Primarily they were interested in exercising all the different levels of air defence readiness and our procedures and capabilities for the combat turnaround of aircraft. Other objectives included the completion of a maximum flying schedule in a short period of time and operating under nuclear fallout conditions.

During the exercise, these officers acted as an observer team. Their duty was to scrutinize the phases of operation for mistakes and erroneous procedures and submit a rating for the phases.

The initial call out of personnel started at 5:00 a.m. Monday last. While the levels of readiness rose, ground crews were busy towing out the aircraft, inspecting them, and preparing them for flight. High winds and rain hampered them continually. However, they still managed to have the required aircraft ready to go and accepted by the aircrews before the flying phase was scheduled to commence.

Once flying started, it continued steadily into the afternoon. Each flight was assessed after landing. This plus other procedures involved in the exercise assured little idle time being spent on the ground between flights.

Later in the morning, a fallout situation was simulated. Time spent outside necessarily became less and less. Still, the jobs had to be done, just as thoroughly but faster. The decontamination of everyone and everything coming inside was paramount. Never did the operation come to a standstill — it just took more time.

The possibility of infiltrators was always a problem. Security of personnel, sites, and equipment were most stringent. Food was screened to ensure it wasn't poisoned. Fuel dumps and bowsers were scrutinized to prevent contamination.

Safety was an overriding factor in any operation attempted. Due to the high winds and rain, some of the outdoor phases became shortened or were eliminated from the schedule.

By mid-afternoon, the exercise was completed. Probably the staff of the CAC felt more relief than anyone else when the announcement was made. They had been in the thick of things continually from the outset and performed most admirably.

Within the hour a debriefing of the squadron aircrew was held. Indeed, the team did find mistakes, but none that required much time to correct. Overall, the results were satisfactory.

Now all that remained was to correct mistakes and start plans for the next operation.

Night Hawk's Nest — 409

A new crew has entered our nest. They were Captains Don Elphick and Bob Merrick. Bob and Barb Merrick are familiar faces around the squadron, since they came to us from the EWU detachment that was once based at Comox. Don and Ann Elphick arrived from CFB Bagotville, where Don was the flight commander of the T–33 flight.

Welcome to the squadron, y'all, and may your stay be most enjoyable.

Truth is indeed stranger than fiction. Captain Laurie Bastie started the latest cycle with his unique method of catching a cold. To further illustrate this statement, read this excerpt from a conversation that took place at the Base Hospital. The scene is set. It's about nine-thirty p.m. on a weekend night. A squadron member limps into the doctor's office . . .

M.D. – "Come in, Captain Northrup. Sit down and tell me what happened to your foot."

D.S.N. – "Well, Doc, Marilyn and I invited some of the squadron for a cocktail party before coming out to the Fall Formal tonight. I was just getting dressed before anyone arrived and when I put on my right shoe, I felt something snap. During the party, my foot got sore and started to swell. One of my guests pushed something back in place, but it's still swelling up on me."

M.D. – "Problems putting on shoes, eh. Are you a pilot?"

D.S.N. – "Why, yes. How did you guess?"

M.D. – "It's not a guess, really. We doctors learn to make a correct diagnosis from the smallest bits of information. No doubt you feel a bit foolish over such a silly little accident. Just remember, people can become preoccupied with things and put shoes on with laces done up and while forcing them on, you can easily snap a bone or cartilage out of place."

D.S.N. – "But these aren't really shoes — they are Wellingtons. They don't have laces and slip on like slippers."

M.D. – "You wouldn't also be an Instrument Check Pilot, would you?"

D.S.N. – "Why, yes — is that one of your correct diagnoses again?"

M.D. – "No, that was just a lucky guess. Let me check your boots. Some people end up buying two left shoes."

D.S.N. – I never bothered to check them myself, but they are for different feet, aren't they?"

M.D. – "You're okay in that department. Let me look at your feet. Sometimes people have two le—. No, that's a right foot, all right."

D.S.N. – "You had me worried for a minute."

M.D. – "My inspection shows that everything is back in place and the swelling should go down soon. Keep your boot and weight off the foot, and it should be as good as new in the morning."

D.S.N – "That means I can't dance tonight. Would you mind explaining that to my wife? Just so she doesn't think I'm pulling a fast one."

M.D. – "Certainly, and here—take this cane along to help you walk. If no one believes your story, it can be used to beat them off."

D.S.N. – "You might say I could raise a bit of cane."

On that bit of humour, the consultation ended. Dale and Marilyn eventually hopped to the mess, where he resisted all attempts to get on the dance floor. This plus the pain killer he consumed did wonders, and he recovered within the next few days. So successful was the recovery that on Tuesday he was in the Alberta marshes, where he bagged several ducks.

In case you wondered, it was Captain Beatle MacLeod's healing hands that performed the miracle on the foot.

There was talk of an arrest for practising medicine without a licence, but it stopped when Beatle explained in all modesty that any other minor hockey coach could do the same.

You just have to ask the right questions . . .

Bob Merrick

This happened back in the late '60s or early '70s, when the Soviet long-range air force was an aging, but according to conventional wisdom, still potent bogeyman. The officers and gentlemen of 409 Squadron were preparing for the annual extravaganza known as Tac Eval, or, later, as Op Eval, which poked into all aspects of the squadron's ability to make war, not love.

Part of the preparation was a series of exercises known as Cudgel Capers, which were modelled on the evaluations conducted by higher authority. They featured exams, mass loads, simulated nukes, simulated fallout, and virtually everything short of the care and feeding of Soviet prisoners whose parachutes had wafted them onto the base.

A large part of the exercise was the target force that was assembled to give the SAGE controllers and aircrew alike a good workout. Usually these folks and their aircraft would arrive at CFB Comox the night before the exercise then start their target runs fairly early the next morning.

For this time around, the exercise planners had cast their nets far and wide. There was an Argus from the other side of our hangar. There was a Tracker from down island. There was an imposing collection of CF–100s and T–33s, along with some USAF B–57s, bolstered by B–52s and ERA–3Bs, aircraft that neither took off nor landed from Comox.

At about 0330 on the Monday morning of the exercise, 407 Squadron's dedicated ground crew began preparing the Argus for flight, an event that seemed to take forever until all the spark plugs started firing reliably. For those of you who may have forgotten, an Argus during run-up was about as noisy as four Harvards, and one Harvard, as you know, makes all the noise in the world.

Eventually, all was right with the Argus, and it went to full power for takeoff, with a roar that awakened all those who had slept during the run-up. Moments later, the Tracker began preparing to "slip the surly bonds of earth." As it had only half as many engines, it only made three-quarters as much noise.

At intervals thereafter, the Clunks, T–Birds, and

B–57s thundered off the runway, just to ensure that those jolted into wakefulness stayed that way. There was a momentary calm, broken only by the unique clattering roar of one of 442 Squadron's Labradors trying to shake itself into little pieces.

Meanwhile, how was the target force doing? Those aircraft had reached the northern limit of their target runs, and were now revealed to the SAGE controllers as elements of an attacking force. How do I know that? Because now, all the Voodoos were flushed, an event that called for the fighter force to vacate the base. This meant a takeoff every fifteen seconds. Such takeoffs were marked by resounding booms, followed by a resounding roar that would get them expelled from any civil airport in the world today.

On this day, I was part of the exercise as a fighter-gator with 409 Squadron, where I, like the rest of the squadron, was poked, pried, and prodded by a group of ersatz evaluators from the squadron trying to see how we responded to all-out war. But I was also the acting PR guy, as the real one was away on course.

The PR problems started early, but they were initially handled by MCpl Paul Jacquard in the squadron's combat alert centre. An infuriated caller was truly upset by the noise and was threatening to call the Minister of National Defence if it didn't cease forthwith. As the exercise progressed, she became even more furious and demanded to speak to someone higher in the food chain. That someone was me, but because the exercise was so well planned, I wasn't able to break away from the flight line, as we were scrambled as soon as we were turned around.

Finally, MCpl Jacquard said to me, "Look, I'm the trusted agent for this exercise, and I know you won't get another sortie. Please come and deal with this woman." This wasn't an unusual exercise. Nothing had changed from previous exercises dating back to 1954. What could be the difference?

She was on the phone when I walked into the alert centre. Well, let's find out where she's calling from. "Kye Bay," she said. For those of you unfamiliar with the Comox layout, Kye bay is, or was in my time, a small, idyllic beach community that could almost serve as the basement for the CFB Comox control tower. It was accessible to residents by a road that wound all the way around the base, then descended a fairly steep hill to a rustic little settlement right on the beach.

I asked her when she first moved in.

"Yesterday," she said.

"Did you not notice the large airport you had to drive around to get to your house?" I asked?

"Yes," she said, "the real estate agent told me that Pacific Western Airlines was in and out twice a day, and that some smaller carriers also provided us with excellent connections. We can go anywhere in the world from here."

So far as I know, she never phoned the defence minister, but I do wish I had heard her follow-up conversation with the real estate agent.

Gear down and locked?

Keith Bottoms

It was a pleasant day for flying in Val–d'Or, and we had scheduled a normal two-plane sortie, with one aircraft acting as target while the other was the defending fighter. We, as the one-hour alert crews, were permitted to fly training sorties while the two five-minute crews held down primary alert duties. The four aircraft and four crews at Val–d'Or were a 24/7 commitment by 425 Squadron at Bagotville, which was in addition to alert duties at our home base.

The QRA (Quick Reaction Area), known affectionately as the "Q," was home to us for up to a week at a time every three weeks. The "Q" was fully equipped with four alert hangars near the end of the main north/south runway at Val–d'Or. Crew accommodation consisted of sleeping quarters for eight plus a staffed kitchen and a briefing or ops room, which was also used for entertainment that included bridge playing and magazine reading (in particular, the one published by Hugh Hefner).

"Time to go flying," says our detachment commander, forcing us to put down our magazines and interrupt the bridge game. For this particular sortie, I, as navigator, was flying with Mel Branter, pilot, while John McLellan was piloting the other Voodoo. I do not recall who his navigator was that day. We got airborne without any difficulty and flew a successful exercise, taking turns as target.

For reasons I have forgotten, we decided to return to base a bit early, a decision that turned out to be fortunate indeed. Mel and I were the lead aircraft on the descent, with John following in loose formation. Everything was quite hunky-dory as we descended from the north and lined up for our approach to Runway 18. We reached circuit height and slowed down as we approached the glide slope in preparation for the landing check. Mel selected gear down, and all of a sudden things were not at all hunky-dory. We should have had three greens for the undercarriage down and locked. Instead, we had port gear "green," nose gear "green," and the starboard gear "red." No problem, says we; just do a recycle. Mel did this, and we still had the starboard gear showing an unsafe "red." By now, of course, our Voodoo with an approach speed of 185 knots was fast approaching the airport. Mel went into overshoot mode while I was reading the checklists like crazy to confirm our choices, which did not look good. You could not attempt to land a Voodoo with an unsafe main gear. The choices boiled down to two: a gear-up belly landing on a foamed runway, or bail out.

At this stage, we asked our buddy, John McLellan, to fly by and visually check the condition of the starboard undercarriage. John confirmed our worst fears; the starboard gear was only partway down and in no condition to permit a landing. The control tower also confirmed that the wheel was unsafe. All this time, of course, we were burning fuel, which the Voodoo did quite happily, especially at low level. We had enough fuel for one more circuit and a trip to a bailout area.

While we were turning for downwind, I suggested to Mel we give the gear one more try at maximum gear down speed so that we could pull all available "G" at the same time as we selected the gear down. Mel readily agreed, as neither of us wanted to leave our nice, warm cockpit. Mel accelerated to 280 knots, which those in the know will recognize as being above the maximum gear-down speed of 250 knots, and simultaneously pulled all available "G" while selecting gear down.

There was joy in Mudville and Val–d'Or as Mel said, "We have three greens!"

We were still concerned that the gear might not be safe, so the emergency reception committee was out in full force to welcome us. We landed without further incident and taxied to the "Q" for shutdown. I climbed down the ladder and assumed the push-up position, explaining to the ground crew that I was kissing the ground and not doing calisthenics. Mel and I were quite happy to be able to return to earth in the normal manner rather than via the big silk umbrellas.

An inspection of the undercarriage revealed that a small bolt had been left in the knuckle part of the starboard gear, and our application of the force of gravity plus the 3,000 pounds per square inch from our hydraulic system was enough to dislodge it and allow the gear to come down normally.

In my nearly 1,000 hours on the Voodoo, this was the only time I had to give serious consideration to bailing out. She was big and she was hard on gas, but you could always count on those big engines to run. With the help of some very fine pilots, she brought me back safely every time. I will always have a soft spot for the old Voodoo. May she rest in peace in aircraft heaven.

Up and down do make a difference in a J–57

Doug Munro and Bob Merrick

It was a crisp, sunny, Comox winter morning. The air patch was abuzz with a variety of aeronautical activity. A 407 Squadron Argus was, with one of its interminable run-ups, vibrating all the walls in PMQs. The crew of a 442 Squadron Labrador was just finishing the pre-flight preps before departing for a training exercise on fabled Denman Island. And, a pair of CF–101s from 409 Squadron headed toward the runway as part of an air defence exercise.

The Lab departed. A couple of minutes later, the CF–101s started their takeoff roll. They didn't do so in formation. To fill squares on some board, they did an "in-trail departure," where the lead aircraft, flown by Capt. Doug Stuart, with Capt. Lynn Wagar in the backseat, thundered off alone. Thirty seconds later, the number two aircraft, flown by Capt. Mike Pollard, with me in the back seat, followed, the idea being that I would maintain position on lead using the radar that the McDonnell Aircraft Company had thoughtfully placed in the Voodoo's nose.

Sure enough, just as we broke ground, the lead aircraft emerged from the ground clutter. Seconds later, Mike said, "Hey, look at the fire."

I looked at the ground, expecting to see one of the old wooden homes blazing fiercely. No luck. "Where?" I said.

"Doug's airplane," Mike said.

As I shifted my gaze, the thin stream of flame following Doug's aircraft suddenly became a massive fireball, and the aircraft disintegrated in a fine rain of confetti. By this time, it was almost exactly abeam—although somewhat above—the Lab, which was on course for its Denman Island exercise. Capt. Bill Charland, who, like most helicopter pilots, never trusted the boom-boom go-fast guys to ever do anything right, had been monitoring the 101's progress when it suddenly blew up beside him. His first thought? "My God, these air defence exercises are getting realistic!"

That thought lasted for a microsecond or two before he had the Lab smoothly banked into a turn that would take it to the two parachutes that emerged from the smoke and flames. Within seconds, he was over the first man in the water, but before they could do anything, the SAR tech, who had switched automatically into the lifesaving mode, noticed that the other survivor was still struggling in the very cool saltchuck.

Quickly, he directed Charland to the position and lowered the Billy Pugh net into the water. He was just in the proverbial nick of time. Wagar had had a rougher ride through the fireball than did Stuart. The shock and the burns hampered his efforts to dump the chute and clamber into the dinghy. His strength was ebbing fast but he had just enough left to take a death grip on the Billy Pugh net—a sort of hockey goal with pretensions—and was hoisted into the chopper. Then they picked up Stuart, who was comfortably (?) bobbing about in his dinghy. The entire episode took less than ten minutes from "b-boom, BOOM!" to having everyone safely back on the ground.

The 442 Search and Rescue Squadron Labrador crew that plucked Lynn and Doug from Georgia Strait were Captain Bill Charland, Captain Barry Farnham, and Corporals Lew Ervin, Bill Munden, Bob Perrier, Ken Hogg, and Sonny Fullbrook.

Excerpts from the Wednesday 24, 1971, edition of the *Comox District Free Press* captures the trauma of the ejection and the timely and professional response of the rescue helicopter crew.

Stuart and Wagar had taken off from the base on a routine training flight. The first indication that something was wrong was when a series of "five or six thumps" occurred.

"I didn't know what they were . . . we had no indication that the plane was on fire," said Stuart. He said that he saw the tachometer winding down and seconds before they both ejected a fire warning light went on.

"I knew it wasn't a malfunction on the instrument panel because the plane was hard to control."

Wagar, who was behind Stuart in the navigator's cockpit, also felt the "thumps," which may have been explosions.

"We both noticed it and thought it was the engine stalling," he said. "We were going to transmit and tell Departure Centre we had a problem. Then there was another series of thumps."

Then Stuart told Wagar: "We have a steady fire warning light on the left engine. Eject! Eject!"

Wagar described the next three seconds—the time it took to be ejected from the plane to the moment their parachutes opened.

"There is a handle on either side of you. When you pull it up it pulls you back into the seat and jettisons the canopy. Once the canopy is off you can't see anything . . . the dust on the floor and the wind blast . . . you close your eyes."

The plane was travelling at 325 m.p.h. when they ejected.

Wagar thought he got burned when the canopy jettisoned . . . When they hit the water Wagar found himself in trouble. He had difficulty with his safety equipment and was being dragged through the water by the parachute driven by a 20 knot wind.

"My head was in the water for a good portion of the time," he said.

And in Lynn's own words some thirty-four years later: "No SAR tech had to go into the water; apparently they were prepared to, but I was able to roll into the Billy Pugh rescue basket and they hauled me up in it. I flamed out on the trip up and I was told they had to practically break my hand to get me to release my grip on the basket. I remember they dropped it very close to me so it was easy to reach, which was a good thing because I was at the end of my strength (except for my "death grip" on the basket). This little narrative is confirmed by the Flight Comment story on the bailout/rescue, which I retained and just reread.

"Two of the SAR techs I remember from later were Pinky Hogg and Sonny Fullbrook (whom I'd played hockey with on the 423 Sqn team in 2 Wing) (and who didn't recognize me, by the way—I guess I was all bloated and bluish-black by that time). They didn't know I'd survived until later in the day when they were told I'd recovered consciousness in the base hospital."

Commentary: When the Lab crew delivered Lynn to the base hospital, he received instant and expert lifesaving medical attention from Major Bob Thatcher, the base surgeon. Bob was very familiar with the hazards of flying high-performance jets—prior to attending medical school, he was a combat-ready navigator on 409.

425 Emergency
Bob Merrick

A few years later, I was with 410 Squadron at Bagotville, where we shared the field, and the Voodoos, with 425 Squadron. On this particular day, Les Alouettes were happily engaged in an exercise that included CF–5s, T–Birds, CF–100s, Trackers, and everything short of Badgers and Bears as targets. As 410 Squadron weren't likely to get their hands on the 101s for some time, I took the opportunity to go for a run along the perimeter road.

I was about half a mile west of the tower when I heard the familiar b-boom sound of two J–57s getting serious about flying that day. Within seconds, the aircraft was abreast of me and I heard kind of a funny "blap" sound and watched with very wide eyes as an undisciplined rabble of spare parts descended from the aircraft's belly. Much as Bill Charland had thought a few years earlier, I thought: "Man, this is a pretty realistic exercise!" That thought quickly gave way to utter astonishment as the aircraft continued merrily on its way. It wasn't trailing smoke, nor was it showing any signs of distress. I glanced back at the tower. Some of the controllers were by now out on the walkway. They had seen the debris fall and notified the departure controller who was then working the aircraft. He was having some difficulty persuading the pilot, Captain Rick Galashan, whose engine instruments told him that everything was just fine, that he should RTB quickly, as important bits of the Voodoo's engine were even then being swept from the runway so that he could land on it.

The controller must have been persuasive; at about the eight-mile arc, the aircraft began a gentle turn to bring it back to Runway 29 for the high-speed approach—around 250 knots—recommended for a Voodoo still loaded with about 12,000 pounds of fuel. It's an operation that gives drag-bags and brakes—not to mention pilots—something to think about. The manoeuvre ended successfully, and Galashan and his navigator, Lt. Paul Peloquin, were soon back in the hangar polishing up their war stories.

So what had gone wrong with these two airplanes? In Stuart's aircraft, one of the turbine blades whirring around at full takeoff thrust got the idea that it was too hot and left its cozy nest on the turbine wheel, going straight up where it could get a cooling bath in the 12,000 or so pounds of fuel remaining. Outraged by this, the fuel exploded and destroyed the aircraft.

In Galashan's aircraft, a similar blade did a similar thing, but it figured that a good blast of Saguenay air would be the quickest way to cool off. Thus, it went straight out the bottom of the aircraft, doing little damage to the airframe or any of the major systems. It did, however, do a lot of damage to flying time over the next few months, as the fleet was largely grounded until a fix was found. Up? Down? In a J–57 at takeoff thrust, it was almost a life and death matter.

William Tell 1970
Doug Munro and Bob Merrick

For Canadian air defence squadrons, in the sixties, seventies, and eighties, "Callshot" was the All-Canadian competition that selected a Voodoo team to take part in "William Tell," an international rocket meet periodically held at Tyndall Air Force Base, Panama City, Florida.

Herein lies the tale of one such rocket meet.

Callshot was not held in 1969 but the Nighthawks managed to carry their winning formula over to the 1970 competition and once again emerged victorious with 8,825 points out of a possible 10,000. Team members Captains Ernie Poole and Brodie Templeton were winners of the Vincent Trophy for having obtained a perfect score. Major "Moe" Morrison, Captains Doug Munro, Doug Stuart, Pete Dunda (USAF exchange officer), George McAffer, Fred Williams, Rhiney Koehn, and Don Marion were the remaining team members. This team, less Templeton, McAffer, and Williams, and including Captains Lynn Wagar, Bob Merrick, and Lieutenant Pete Armour, proceeded to Tyndall AFB to compete in William Tell, a live weapons competition . . .[36]

Came the morning of October 20, the Nighthawks launched for Hill AFB, Ogden, Utah—the first stop on their pilgrimage to Tyndall. A quiet evening with a therapeutic visit to the Christian Science Reading Room and early beddy-bye found the team splendidly prepared for the second leg of the journey to Perrin AFB, near Sherman, Texas. Unfortunately, the launch was delayed slightly when the USAF ground crew inadvertently closed a canopy on Pete Dunda's helmet (fortunately it wasn't on his head at the time), damaging the canopy seal and the canopy telescope tube plus totalling said headpiece. In addition to this slight error, the same aircraft had experienced oil pressure problems en route to Hill, and a precautionary engine shutdown was accomplished prior to landing.

Keeping everyone in the picture was a must, so Doug Stuart left explicit instructions for the USAF maintainers not to run up his aircraft, as Canadian ground crew would arrive by Hercules the next day and fix a broken oil line. The outgoing crew briefed the incoming crew but omitted the word "not." Later in the evening, Doug was advised that the run-up had been completed, and there was no oil pressure in the engine. More calls to Comox: bring an engine as well as canopy parts as previously ordered.

A sunny and very hot East Texas afternoon greeted the team as they touched down at Perrin. As they rolled to a stop, all suffering from a severe liquid deficiency, up went the canopies, on went the ladders, and before anyone could exit their aircraft, hands came over the edge of all cockpits clutching tins of ice-cold beer. It was love at first sight! Their saviours, and soon-to-be eternal buddies, were members of the Happy Hooligans, the Fargo, North Dakota Air National Guard, and their main competition at Tyndall. The Nighthawks and Hooligans immediately repaired to the officers' club for modest refreshment and much lie telling!

Major Moe and Colonel (later Major General) Alexander Macdonald, head Hooligan, during the course of the evening discovered that each team had six Voodoos, which, when aircraft are flying in four planes, leaves the possibility of a third four plane. Alex and Moe immediately cobbled together an International Flight that included two Nighthawks and two Hooligans, ably led by our Major Arnie Leiter. This gaggle launched next morning to the immortal words: "International Flight, Speed Brakes, Speed Brakes, oops, as you were, Burners, Burners, go!"

It was a beautiful day when the two Willy Tell teams arrived at Tyndall a few moments apart. Team members were milling around when what to the wondering eyes of assorted USAF senior brass should appear but the International Flight, making its entrance. After a very skilled box formation pass, the Flight executed a perfect three-second break and performed four "greasers." It was evident from the puzzled looks of the USAF bigwigs that they suspected they had just witnessed some heinous crime—but couldn't quite identify what it was. They turned a blind eye, which was probably wise because the Hoo-

---

36 Mike Mahon, editor-in-chief, *Nighthawk! A History of 409 Night Fighter Squadron* (Courtenay, B.C.: E.W. Bickle Pub. Co.), p. 63.

ligans were the Governor of North Dakota's private air force, and the Canadians weren't liable to be listening!

The rocket meet consisted of four missions: a supersonic front snap with a target at 50,000 feet, a supersonic stern co-altitude with the target at 45,000, a run against an electronic countermeasure aircraft, and, last but far from least, a low-level stern. On the first and second missions, the fighters were armed with an AIR–2A Genie, minus warhead. They were unarmed on the third mission, and on the fourth carried two live AIM–4D infrared Falcon missiles. The second and third missions went smooth as silk. The first mission had its moments.

How all were to behave during the competition was assured, as the USAF conducted a pre-meet briefing for all nine squadrons—three each F–102s, F–106s and F–101s (Voodoos). To say the briefing was thorough is damning it with faint praise. It was of the "I'll tell you the time, but first here's how you build a watch" genre. It doesn't seem possible they overlooked any points, no matter how picayune. But they did, and it wasn't insignificant. They didn't mention what would happen if you were forced to abort a mission with a serviceable aircraft for problems beyond the crew's control. Would the crew get a re-fly? Would the crew be penalized?

First mission day, the Nighthawks launched, climbed to 35,000 feet over the Gulf of Mexico, and went into a holding pattern. They were being controlled by Data-Link (by electronic inputs with penalties for breaking radio silence). Around and around they went. They were advised by the Meet referee that their target had gone unserviceable. Around and around they went. A second target went unserviceable. Around and around . . . !

Eons later, the third target was—wait for it—serviceable. The crews were committed. Moe Morrison had approximately 5,000 pounds of fuel on board, and his three teammates had similar amounts. The target was at 50,000 feet, and the fighters were required to go flat out to perform the snap-up manoeuvre. Full afterburner . . . locate the target . . . arm up . . . lock-on and climb . . . centre the dot . . . squeeze the trigger . . . the door rotates and the weapon (an MB1) launches . . . out of afterburner and throttles to idle . . . check the fuel—1,800 pounds—set up the shallowest possible rate of descent and head for the Intial Approach Fix for Tyndall's main runway. "What did the briefer say? A twenty-five point penalty for missing the estimated time of arrival at the Fix? Can't have that." They all made their ETAs. Moe landed with about 1,000 pounds of fuel, each of the others with less, and Rhiney and Don (number four) refused to discuss the matter. Put the rosaries away. Repair to the officers' club. Start breathing again!

Up until the last day, the scores showed that, after three missions were completed, the Nighthawks had opened a nearly insurmountable lead over their two competitors. One successful IR weapon launch during Mission number four, and the Meet was theirs, along with a probable Top Gun for the highest score by a crew. Kicking up their heels in the officer's club that evening was *verboten*. The Hawks were going to be on their best behaviour, even though the last mission couldn't have been simpler: a low-level, moderate speed target, no evasive action, no ECM, great weather, and no radar ground clutter.

Could this be their year? Everyone was brimming with confidence. All were ready.

Then things just happened. Morrison and Munro experienced a weapons malfunction. Score zero. Poole and Wagar's weapon launched and immediately made for the Gulf of Mexico, hitting a shark right behind its ear. Score zero. Then their Ground Control Intercept controller came unglued. The Weapons Range is a fixed-area rectangle within which the intercept had to be completed. The controller paired

Stuart and Dunda on an aircraft flying parallel to and outside the Range. Rather than kill a couple of innocent bystanders, the referee terminated the mission. Score zero. Last, Koehn and Marion were paired on the real target well down the Range (which the crew had no way of knowing). The controller was either unaware of his faux pas or forgot how to order an increase in fighter speed — or had just dozed off. The fighter ran out of range — another zero. But wait, the team didn't finish empty-handed. The ground crew, whose dedication, expertise, and hard work were instrumental in 409's Callshot victory, came up with their own victory in William Tell. The load crew, M/Cpl Norm Black and Cpls Russ Andrews, Graham Ellis, and Claude Jacques, hung the weapons fast and flawlessly to capture the weapons loading competition.

Kicking and bitching was not on, and, in true Nighthawk fashion, they congratulated the Hooligans for a job well done and repaired to the flight line to watch a wonderful air show. Bob Hoover put on an outstanding display in his P–51 Mustang and his Aero Commander. The closing manoeuvres in the AC didn't seem possible. He approached the front of the crowd from right to left, at about fifty feet from the ground, and did a loop. On the backside of the loop, he feathered an engine and did another loop. On the backside of *that* loop he feathered the *other* engine and did a third loop. As he glided by, he raised the nose a bit and did a 180-degree turn and touched down on the parallel taxi-way on one main gear, then the other, then both. Dead quiet, he did a 90-degree turn onto another taxi-way and rolled to a gentle stop a few yards from the grandstand.

Earl McCurdy's "Blunderturds," 410 AW (F) Squadron's Aerial Demonstration Team, followed. LCol Hal Pike with Captain John "Hooter" Houghton in the rear seat provided a stellar solo show, which culminated with a heart-stopping inverted low pass at a couple of hundred feet, the length of the Tyndall main runway. Colonel Poole, boss of the 318th Fighter Squadron from McChord AFB (an F–106 unit), summed up everyone's thoughts on the closing pass: "I didn't know a Voodoo could be flown like that!" Major Earl McCurdy and Captain Alex "Chuck" Wierelejchyk led the four plane. The other members were Captains Dave Hickman and Doug Hillstrom (both USAF exchange officers) as number two, Jim Speiser and Bill Gladders as number three, and John Rose and Jim Lauder as number four.

Their takeoff was unique. Numbers one and two rolled down the runway in military power. Shortly thereafter, three and four plugged in the burners in very hot pursuit. As one and two were coming airborne, three and four came out of burner and slid into position, forming a very neat "finger four" right. Following an exemplary series of formation changes and a pair of formation landings, the four plane parked line abreast in front of the crowd and deployed their Voodoo's refuelling probes (a sight not unlike a group of young lads exposing themselves to a gathering of old friends).[37]

Did it end there? No, in addition to the above, the USAF Thunderbirds, flying F–4 Phantoms, put on their usual spectacular display. They ended their show with a missing man formation.

USAF, National Guard, and Canadian participants (and a massive gathering of freeloaders) were treated to a fine banquet, the highlight of which was a comic, introduced as Air Commodore Chumley of the Royal Indian Air Force, who delivered a splendid, if apparently inebriated, speech. In real life he was Foster Brooks.

Perfect weather greeted the Nighthawks as they departed Tyndall and headed for home. The tone of

---

37 Tragically, Dave Hickman and Jim Lauder were killed in a Voodoo crash less than a month later during a low-level mission out of Bagotville.

the Meet was succinctly summarized when Morrison and Munro landed at Davis–Monthan AFB, Tucson, Arizona. As their aircraft rolled to a stop at the end of the runway, they were met by a "follow-me" jeep. They followed the "follow-me." Suddenly it became apparent where they were to be parked in the "Bone Yard"—the final resting place for thousands of "beyond their best date" aircraft.

Note (Pete Armour): Shortly after returning to Comox, the Nighthawks received the following message:

> FM 119 FTRGP HECTOR FIELD FARGO ND
> TO 409SQ COMOX
> UNCLAS 119CCR. PERSONAL — NIGHTHAWKS FROM HOOLIGANS. MAY YOUR SKIES BE CLEAR, YOUR WINDS BE TAILWINDS, YOUR LANDINGS BE SMOOTH AND YOUR GLASSES BE FULL. OUR LAND IS YOURS AND A NIGHTHAWK WILL ALWAYS BE AN HONORARY HOOLIGAN WHENEVER AND WHEREVER WE MEET. YOUR SQUADRON CREST WILL OCCUPY AN HONOURED SPOT IN OUR TROPHY CASE, BUT MOST IMPORTANT, YOUR FRIENDSHIP WAS THE GREATEST EXPERIENCE OF OUR TRIP. FARGO LOOKS FORWARD TO YOUR VISITS. PERSONAL — MACDONALD TO MORRISON — MAJ MO, YOU SHOULD BE THE PROUDEST GUY IN THE WORLD.

Postscript (Ernie Poole): Remember the last practice day we had at Willy Tell when Officer Koehn asked me what we were going to do on our return to Tyndall? I said I would wait for him, and we could do a low pass down the flight line. As it turned out, we ended up short of fuel, and I couldn't wait for him. At the last minute, I asked for a "low and over on the inner runway with a closed pattern full stop on the outer." It was approved, and as I was doing a very low pass down the ramp, I heard Rhiney say, "I'll take one of those, too." As you remember, after Major Mo picked himself off the ramp, he sent us to apologize to the dreaded General Price (USAF). His only comment was, "That's okay, boys—ONCE." For the rest of the meet, I returned via a coupled ILS.[38]

Chatham scramble

Don Harrington

It was the dead of winter. I was on alert with my pilot. The bells went off for real at two a.m. In those days, we wore the old, grey flying suits that had bunny pants and the winter flying jacket plus mukluks. The leg zippers in the bunny pants needed to be done up tight, otherwise all your checklists and letdown plates would fall out. I was in a deep sleep when the scramble bell sounded.

Out of bed and into my flying gear. Crap! The pilot had already left. Started running down the hall to the hangar, pubs (inflight publications) falling out of all my pockets that I had forgotten to zip up. Picked up the pubs, scrambled up the ladder. The pilot had the engines running. Jumped into the cockpit and started to strap in. The aircraft was now taxiing. I was still strapping in when the aircraft was lifting off the runway. Ninety seconds later, we were at 35,000 feet screaming toward our target.

Oops! I was so far behind the eight-ball strapping in that the radar hadn't been turned on, and it required a two-to-three-minute warm-up. By the time the radar blossomed up, the intercept had been cancelled, and we spent the rest of the mission bumping heads. The time from a dead sleep to 35,000 feet was about five minutes, and I was so far behind the power curve, all I could think of was: "This is Canada's finest in action!" I improved with practice on later scrambles.

---

38 Instrument landing system, which allows a pilot to conduct an approach to a runway that is shrouded in fog. Although newer systems are in use, ILS is still widely used.

Aborted scramble

Two young pilots arrived on squadron, and shortly after there was a night exercise. "B" flight was on duty, and the exercise was flown out of the squadron. After the initial briefing, there was the usual wait until the war started. All the aircraft were parked directly in front of the squadron, and you prepared your aircraft for immediate takeoff by putting all your gear in the cockpit and laying all your straps out for a quick strap-in.

There was sort of an unofficial game that went on with the crews to see who could start taxiing the fastest once you got the airborne order. We did have one experienced pilot on squadron — Les Hare — who was the fastest. His record was ninety seconds from order to taxi.

The young pilot got his order, rushed to his airplane, and was airborne with a full load of fuel (two jugs[39]). Three minutes later, he called, stating that he had to return to base. Evidently, once airborne, he heard flapping and banging on the canopy. He realized he had not done up his shoulder straps but had left them hanging outside the canopy when he strapped in. A very embarrassed pilot returned to a very annoyed squadron commander. He had to dump a full load of fuel and scrap the mission.

The Voodoo was supposed to land with a minimum of 3,000 pounds of fuel. The squadron was deploying to Dow AFB, Bangor, Maine, while the Chatham runways were being resurfaced. We were to take off in intervals and fly in pairs to Dow. We got airborne with four aircraft ahead of us. The weather at destination was reported to be good, but it was very hazy, and the visibility looking into the sun was one to two miles. You could see the ground fine, but forward visibility was poor. When we arrived for our approach, we were told to hold. We held! We discovered that the radar facilities at Bangor were unserviceable, with only one procedural approach being approved within a twenty-mile radius. Once one pair had landed, the next pair was cleared in. Our fuel was getting low when we were finally cleared for our approach. We were Number two in the formation on the right wing of our lead. The lead couldn't find the runway and missed the approach! By this time, we were below 3,000 pounds of fuel and could not divert to another field. The lead told us to take the lead, as he either didn't have serviceable navigation, or he was all screwed up.

So there we were, getting really low on fuel, unsure of our position, and couldn't see the field. My pilot oriented himself, and we landed safely. I think we shut down with 1,200 pounds of fuel. Ground never felt soooo good!

Short snappers

Then there was the Bagotville OTU instructor who signed out one aircraft and flew another off the line that had not been refuelled. He got airborne with 3,000 pounds of fuel instead of 13,000 pounds. A very embarrassed pilot landed very quickly when the low fuel light came on shortly after takeoff.

A Saint Bernard puppy flew in a T–33 from Montreal to Chatham. I asked the pilot how he fared for oxygen, and he said he did just fine. He flew at 10,000 feet cabin altitude.

We were bumping heads one night in two Voodoos when the pilot of the other Voodoo asked radar if he had a target at two o'clock in his vicinity. Radar came back with a negative reply. The pilot then said: "I would like to report a UFO." There was a long silence from radar. We never did see the alleged UFO.

The squadron was on deployment at Bangor, Maine. We were hosted by an American F–89 squadron, and I remember a big mob on the ramp drinking a few

---

39 A jug is an underwing fuel tank and contains roughly 3,000 pounds of jet fuel.

Bud and having a great time. A B–52 came taxiing by the group. Understand, there was always friendly rivalry between SAC and Air Defense. One of the American aircrew turned, took out his wanker, and proceeded to give the B–52 a urinary salute as he taxied by. To the B–52's credit, he acknowledged it by swinging the aircraft 30 degrees and, running up the outboard engine, blew us all away.

A section of four Voodoos was landing on the runway from an overhead pitch. One, two, and three landed fine, but four was hot. All we heard over the radio was: "Coming through." The aerodynamic braking of a Voodoo slowed it down immediately after landing. The pilot kept the nose up until thirty to forty knots had bled off. The first three aircraft had done their aerodynamic braking and had lowered their noses. Number four had his nose up when he passed Number three on the runway. Their wings overlapped by five feet. Because Number four had his nose up, the wings did not touch. I don't think that incident was even reported to flight safety.

One day, a pilot lined up his Voodoo for takeoff. At the same time, another aircraft called initial for a full stop. He was cleared Number one on the premise that the aircraft on the runway would be rolling when he was about to land. The aircraft on the runway started his takeoff roll. Imagine his surprise when he saw the Voodoo landing on the other end of the runway. The aircraft taking off was able to rotate and lift off before reaching the landing aircraft. The landing pilot was 180 degrees out of phase!

The squadron had a family day, and someone thought it would be a nice idea to let a few of the wives strap into the Voodoo, taxi out to the runway, start a mini-takeoff, abort, and taxi back to the line. It worked fine for two runs. On the third run with the same aircraft, the wheels melted, and all the tires blew. Evidently, no one thought how much heat is generated flexing the tires over five miles of taxiing for each ride.

A Voodoo was refilled with liquid nitrogen instead of liquid oxygen. It was fortunate that a crew didn't get airborne with the bird. N_2 is odourless and deadly.

425 tales

Don McCaul

I did three stints with AWF on Voodoos, first as a flight commander with 425, second as squadron commander of 416, and third as head of the Tac Eval Team.

At 425, Hal Pike was the CO and Bob Flynn was Ops O; I had A Flight. I believe Al Sundvall had B Flight and Ron Poole had C Flight. Memories include an alert at Val–d'Or, parties in the mess, one of our pilots making a move on the wife of our Brit exchange nav, and my pitch-up with Don Parker.

My pitch-up

We were flying with Jack Desbrisay and commenced a formation join-up after some intercepts. You may recall that one of the checklist items in those days was to turn off the Pusher before joining. Don and I had accomplished that. We were at about 35,000 feet. Joining on the left wing, we completed a "nice" turn and rolled into position wings level. The aircraft began to do its own thing. Jack said he never saw us arrive or depart. The pitch-up was very tame because of our altitude, very much like a slow spin, perhaps a touch flatter than a T–Bird spin. At any rate, I tried about three times to get the bird out by using full forward stick, all to no avail (all this against the advice of my nav, who said I should simply pull the drag chute and face the music back home).

Well, the chute was pulled, the nose went down, the chute separated at about 300 knots, and the rest was history, though the aircraft was handled very gently on final. I mention the incident because it was

Massive gaggle of CF–101s on Bagotville flight line, including USAF F–4 helper bees.

claimed by some that my subsequent briefing to 425 on the matter was the only reason I was promoted to the command of 416.

416 memories

I was the CO at 416 after Sam Millar and before Lew Tremblay. I believe that John Houghton was either my XO or the Ops O; B.K. Doyle had A Flight and Russ Bennett had B Flight. Five memories stand out: Callshot; the Toronto Air Show Team; survival parties and my own experience in the bush with matches; the international accident; and the transition to the IIP Voodoos.

1970 Callshot

Regarding Callshot, I had two related memories. The first was the major disconnect I had with my majors. I had reasonably assumed that one of them would be placed in charge of the Callshot team and the other would get the Toronto Air Show. Being a new lieutenant colonel full of democratic fervour, I decided to announce my choice of trainer/leader at a squadron briefing before informing the majors and picked a particularly capable captain. On hearing this, and understanding that I would lose a lot of face by changing my mind, one of my majors agreed to step away from the team and gave his place to me as "the new guy." I learned a lot about military democracy from that one!

During the competition itself, I learned a lesson that Lorne Bermel had tried to teach me during our graduation exercise at 410: a "peek" is way better than lock-on, and a pilot looks away from a target (a CF–100 at that time) at his peril. During the Callshot high-speed disadvantage mission, the one with the beam attack and a supersonic Voodoo at low level as target (flown by Col. Dooher), we descended right on the money, but all iced up because I had not bothered to put on the windshield de-icing blower. My nav at the time was the late Les Cox, who got a momentary lock at about the same time I saw the target through a small hole in the ice. Needless to say, I looked away in all the confusion of reverting to a stern chase, going supersonic ourselves, watching the altimeter jump, and all that stuff! And we never saw him again, radar or visual; and lost the competition. On a side note from another squadron, one of the more famous pilots was almost punched out by his nav for landing on fumes from the same mission before us!

CNE Air Show

At the Toronto Air Show, it was 416's turn to show off, so I selected B.K. Doyle to train and lead the team. I ended up as the solo, since my formation was not as great as that of the other members, and Dave Lennox agreed to be my nav. My job was to keep the audience entertained while the team came by in various formations. One of the manoeuvres attempted at low level was the high-speed turn. The air show coordinator had had the temerity to single me out on the practice run and stated that I had gone "out of bounds" over the big smokestacks to the west while during said turn. I made a mental note that I would really pull it tight the next time and that we would be well inside the stacks. During the show that afternoon, we pulled hard enough to be well inside the stacks, but it was getting a little grey outside. My nav, Dave, smartened me up by suggesting I roll off some bank because we were losing altitude and making a few power boats in the bay nervous! Thanks, David!

Survival

At the survival party of 1970 (I think), I failed to learn the true value of teamwork by falling for the old ploy of trying (twice) to catch a glass of beer, held on the ceiling by a broom handle. The key is to have your squadron mates climb up and rescue the beer for you!

The other survival story involves the 416 strategy of grabbing unsuspecting crews returning from missions and taking them out in the bush for some winter bush survival training. Being the boss, I took the first shift and made the mistake of putting the waterproof match striker in the same pocket of my flying suit that the matches were in. Have you ever tried to get through three layers of clothing to put out a small but painful fire?

International air-to-air collision

The international accident occurred on a night exercise when the Voodoo flown by our RAF exchange pilot and a pipeline Canadian navigator had a mid-air collision with a Brit-designed but U.S.-made B-57 Canberra, flown by a U.S. ANG pilot, and under the close control of a U.S. exchange controller in St. Margaret's. Fortunately, both aircraft returned safely and an International Board of Inquiry was set up to determine the cause. (Contributed by Don McCaul.)

It turned out that "Close Control" is always a few moments back, the Voodoo radar was in and out of proper operation but semi-usable, and the rules stated that running intercepts on unserviceable radars was verboten. The bottom line was that the entire squadron supported our crew, who were exonerated, and I received a huge blast from the commander of ADC for my part in this debacle. It could not have been too bad for my record, since I was selected to be the follow-on head of the Tac Eval team by the guy who wrote the draft letter (Gerry Patterson).

William Tell 1965

In 1965, the RCAF was invited to enter a team in the USAF William Tell competition. This would be the first time that a non-USAF team would participate. To select the representative Voodoo squadron team, ADCHQ Ops devised a tournament nicknamed "Street Fight," which was based on the four missions flown on William Tell. RCAF Stn Bagotville hosted the exercise, and the home squadron, 425, won it by a narrow margin. Fortunately for me, I had been internally transferred to 425 from Base Test Flight the previous year and had been selected as a member of the team to fly with a young "hot-shot" pilot and one of the best, Pete "Julie" Dzulinsky. As to the list of aircrew at WT, I don't recall that Jim Seel and Boots McIntosh were there. It may have been Ross Buskard and Bernie McComskey as our briefing/co-coordinating crew.

Postscript: 425's 1965 William Tell aircrew team was led by W/C Mike Dooher. The other team members were Pete Boyle, Nick Chester, Len Couture, Pete Dzulinsky, Ron Egli, Don Kidd, Gerry Langen, "Boots" McIntosh, and Jim Seel. The 425 history book recalls their performance: "Undoubtedly being selected to represent the RCAF at William Tell at Tyndall AFB in Florida contributed, in no small way, to being named the finest in ADC. The Alouette team led by W/C Dooher came through with an excellent showing of fourth place in this highly competitive and prestigious event."

The magic duct tape
Bill Gladders

One day in October 1976, five Voodoos deployed from CFB Chatham, New Brunswick, to Tyndall AFB, Florida, to participate in the William Tell Rocket Meet. The team included one crew from each line squadron and two crews from the operational training squadron, led by the CO of 416 Squadron.

The second leg was from Griffiss AFB, New York. To comply with FAA regulations, the two OTS aircraft went first, followed ten minutes later by the others. Just before the second group began the descent into Robbins, one of the navs checked the grey book for pertinent notes on Robbins. There was one. It said: "On approach to Robbins AFB rwy 18, do not mistake Middle Georgia Regional Airport 3.3 miles NW for Robbins."

That the first section had not seen the note was made clear when the radio silence was broken by someone, probably the Middle Georgia controller, shouting, "You're on the wrong runway; overshoot, overshoot!" Presumably, they did.

When we landed at Robbins in the rain, the OTS crews were not there to help us shut down. They had already gone to the club. We were delayed somewhat, as one of our navs wanted to duct tape the radar cooling ducts so that the rain would not seep into the radar's innards and thus spoil our chances in the forthcoming rocket meet. An observant U.S. airman remarked that the tape would only come off in the rain. The navigator informed the airman that this was special tape that only worked in the rain. A relatively brief discussion persuaded the airman that this was indeed magic tape.

Shortly, we finished tending to the aircraft and repaired to the visiting officers' quarters, where we changed for dinner. We met the OTS crews in the bar, along with a well-dressed gentleman who was, for some reason, buying our beer. We inquired. He was, it turned out, the commander of the wing at Robbins. He wanted to know, "Who landed at Middle Georgia Regional?" Six pairs of eyes turned in the appropriate direction, and the mystery was solved. There were no serious repercussions.

Well, there was one follow-on phone call. A few days later, the aeronautical engineering officer at Comox fielded a phone call from Robbins AFB, asking for the NATO stock number of the magic duct tape that only worked in the rain.

A piece of cake
Doug Munro

August 11, 1970, was a typically lovely West Coast night. The citizens of the Comox Valley were sleeping soundly, content in the knowledge that their air force was burning many pounds of JP–4 in their defence—409 AW (F) Squadron were up to their cockpits in Exercise Felix Brave, a max-effort war game.

Voodoo #17400 was in the capable hands of a famous naval aviator, Captain Hughie "The Big Silver Jet Is Just Putty in My Hands" Fischer. His GIB (Guy in the Back), in a burst of rare modesty, chooses to remain anonymous. On their last mission of the exercise, with dawn breaking in the east, these warriors found themselves up the stern of an EA–6B, a U.S. Navy electronic counter measure (ECM) aircraft that was usually a real pain in the hemorrhoids. It was evident that, unless the Voodoo crew were innovative, they were never going to complete their simulated firing pass. Fischer came to the rescue. Switching his UHF radio to 243.0 (International Distress), Hughie advised the target that, if he didn't shut his ECM off, they'd ram.

The GIB's scope was suddenly clear. Arm FCS manual. Lock on. Centre the dot. Squeeze the trigger. Mike Alpha (mission accomplished)—"Let's go home."

Identify one radar anomaly
Bob Merrick

No, that transmission never came from a CF–101, but it could have. The SAGE direction centre at McChord Air Force Base near Tacoma, Washington, had found a target behaving strangely. One moment it was nearly supersonic. The next moment, it was in the auto-plod mode. And, its behaviour was erratic. There didn't seem to be any specific track or destination. As they had no reasonable explanation for this phenomenon, they launched the alert birds from Comox.

This time there was none of that razzle-dazzle climb to 35,000 feet stuff. No sir, our target was at 5,000 feet, roughly. Sometimes we were commanded to go supersonic; other times we had to remind the controller that we'd stall—well, all right, pitch up—at the requested speed. Despite the controller's best efforts, he couldn't seem to get us in the same air mass with this UFO.

Our wing-man fared no better. He was at the other end of the area of interest and he, too, flew many headings and many airspeeds. Eventually, fuel considerations dictated an RTB, and the target obligingly disappeared.

What really happened that morning? According to the story we were told, two radar sites—the USAF one at Neah Bay, Washington, and the Canadian one at CFS Holberg, British Columbia—were painting the same target, a prosaic Beaver that was happily going about its assigned role of supplying remote, isolated communities. However, that radar info was massaged by the humongous computer that had been developed to solve air defence problems. Somehow, the two bits of information arrived at the computer "out of phase." No, I don't know what that means, either, but on this day it resulted in erroneous supersonic readings, erratic tracking, and, for us, a truly unusual flight on a lovely B.C. morning. But we learned that it's really hard to identify "a radar anomaly."

Hawk 1 tour
George Herbert

One night after flying, a group was sitting in the Snakepit at Comox discussing suitable projects for the upcoming 409 colours and reunion. Among others present were Russ Hellberg and Rick St. Germaine. They happened on the idea of painting an aircraft, and Rick came up with the design, which was eventually used. The next day, they came to me with the idea, and I agreed it was a fitting project.

However, we needed approval, so I set about obtaining same from various technical sources. None were willing to support the idea, so we resorted to a more subtle approach. We put a copy of Rick's drawing in colour in our guest book and when CINC NORAD visited, we had it on the page facing the one commemorating his visit. Naturally, he inquired about the sketch. We repeated the same tactic when the commander of Air Command, Lt.-General Carr, came to visit and when Barney Danson, Minister of National Defence, visited. All were intrigued by the idea, and no one said no. I then got on to Tom Potter, who was the test pilot at Bristol, and asked if he could get Bristol to confirm that there would be no additional cost to repainting the aircraft. This he did, whereupon we set to work painting the aircraft. The first obstacle to overcome was choosing an aircraft. If we took one of our best, squadron maintenance stats would suffer. Hence, we took our hangar queen, #101012.

Initially, this was to be an aircrew project, but soon everyone on the squadron was involved in one way or another. The first task was to sand the whole aircraft with wet emery paper to roughen the surface. It was impossible to see the result of the sanding until the aircraft dried. When it was dry, the surface was just as shiny as before. A second dry sanding was then accomplished with much better results. Comox paint shop had a special paint gun that set up a charge differential between the a/c and the paint gun, thus causing the paint to adhere extremely well. Most of the final job was supervised by George Kulka. When the job was complete, Rick and George did the test flight. Before flying, a new weight and balance was required, and it is interesting to note that 250 pounds of paint was used to achieve the end result. During subsequent flights, the only problem we encountered was a tendency for the paint to peel off the horizontal stabilizer at high speed.

Shortly thereafter (commencing June 10, 1977), Russ Hellberg and I took "Hawk 1 Canada" on a North American round trip, stopping at a host of Air Defence bases (Great Falls, Colorado Springs, Fargo, Niagara, Chatham, Bagotville, North Bay, Winnipeg, Moose Jaw, Cold Lake, and Comox). We worked our way around all three of the other Air Defence Group bases. Out of Chatham, we were accompanied by Al Sundvall in a double-jugger as we flew to BG. On arrival in BG, we were met by the COs of 425 and 410 with clean birds, and I led a flypast over the field. Afterwards, an unbiased observer was heard to remark in the mess that the formation proved one thing: "There isn't a follower in the bunch."

After leaving BG, we went to OW where we picked up the 409 colours. In OW, we were greeted by the base commander, Col. Chuck Gauthier, and other dignitaries. We then flew on to YB, where, as luck would have it, the vice-chief of the RAF was visiting, so we gave him a quick tour and briefing on the a/c. Next, we were off to WG, where we were fortunate enough to meet up with Barney Danson and his entourage, who were heading to Moose Jaw for their air show. We had some photos taken, and Barney was quite impressed by the bird; he remembered seeing the sketch and knew the background as to why it was painted.

We were bound for Moose Jaw as well, but we arranged to leave WG after the MND. When we arrived in Moose Jaw we expected there would be a lot of activity, but all was quiet as the base was stood-down for the arrival of the MND. Since they were not flying, I requested a flypast on my arrival. Moose Jaw approved, and we tried to arrive as the MND was greeted by the base commander. Our timing was just a little off in that we arrived just as the base commander gave the general salute. Dave Tate was the base commander at the time, and I knew Dave from our time in AETE. After we landed, he remarked, "You sure screwed up a good parade. Half the Honour Guard were watching you and half were listening to the commands." But Dave was very good about the whole thing, I think because the MND was watching us as well, and I don't think he even noticed the ragged "Present Arms."

The next day, during the air show, Ron Coleman was scheduled to do his aerial demo in one of our 101s. Just before the show, he discovered that his aircraft was unserviceable, and he asked to use Hawk 1. I agreed, and his show went on as planned, with Hawk 1 complete, with the Squadron Colours in the travel pod. The next day, we returned to QQ, and from that time on, Ron used Hawk 1 for all his aerial demos. Hawk 1 flew regular squadron sorties as well. (With all the publicity we had received during our trip, no one was about to chastise us for unauthorized painting of an aircraft. Even General Carr was impressed, but he did say that had we requested approval, he would have said no.)

On August 10, I was scheduled to take Hawk 1 to Tyndall during William Tell. Unfortunately, Hawk 1 had just had an engine change, and during the first leg of our flight, I experienced fluctuating oil pressure. I returned to QQ and had to leave the aircraft behind and take another. Ordinarily I would have waited, but we had had a change of command parade that day as Col. Bruce Burgess took over command of the base. Our departure was delayed until after the parade, so it was already late when we set out for Tyndall.

That flight was the only one that our "Hangar Queen" missed during the entire time she was painted. On September 13, I flew Hawk 1 to Bristol to be repainted. Although I do not remember doing so, my logbook indicates that I flew her solo to WG.

Just a footnote: Bristol had to apply two coats of stripper to remove all the paint. The first just turned the whole a/c a purple colour.

One-nighter

Turbo Tarling

One of our least favourite exercises was the one-nighter. Why? Because you came in for half a day to do whatever and then went home to "get some rest," which translated into cutting the grass, helping with chores, etc. After supper, you tried to grab a few hours' sleep, which was difficult while the rest of the world was cutting grass, their new gas mowers giving off an annoying putt-putt-putt. Then, shortly before 2300, you got up (feeling not too bad since you hadn't been tired in the first place), attended "briefing" just before midnight, then sat around drinking coffee. This coffee, by the way, usually accompanied us on our flights unless you had been clever enough to sneak in a "nervous one" before the scramble order came.

This particular night had been going fairly well, and my nav, Captain Harry Redden of the wry, dry wit, and I had already completed one mission and were in descent at the completion of yet another suc-

Two CF-101s take the scenic route back to Comox after a practice mission.

cessful mission. Harry seemed to be content to let me do the driving and was just sitting back, obviously enjoying the ride. As the approach lights came into view, Harry piped up with, "Hey! You awake up there?"

"Yeah, Harry—why?"

"Jesus," says Harry, "I fell asleep back here!"

I allowed myself a little chuckle, since that meant that Harry was (a) very relaxed and confident with my flying, (b) lulled to sleep with my silky-smooth descent and approach, (c) totally bored with the whole exercise, (d) very tired, or (e) all of the above. After a barely audible "squeak" (the tires touching the runway), a slight "tug" (the drag chute deploying and doing what it was supposed to do), and a gentle "whiiiirrr" (the canopy opening), we climbed out and prepared to eat some more and drink some more coffee.

By the way, the Voodoo did have a relief tube, but it was seldom used—too little suction and you were in trouble; too much suction and you could be in big trouble! "Just right" only happened in *Goldilocks and the Three Bears*. I solved the problem by keeping my legs crossed, which only became a problem during the landing and rollout as my feet tried to figure out which pedal they were supposed to be pushing.

Back to the story. After just forty minutes on the ground, we're scorching down the runway into the black night on our third scramble, with full jugs (18,500 pounds of JP–4 or two- to two-and-a-half-hours' worth of boring holes in the sky, fun, and noise).

I contact GCI with a cheery, "Golf November 03 is with you . . ." immediately followed by GCI's equally cheery, "Roger, 03, we have no trade (targets/work) for you; looks like we'll be having fade-out (end of the exercise) pretty soon."

Me: "03 checks. Oh well, it's a nice night for flying, anyway."

GCI: "Yeah, I guess every night is a nice night for flying for you guys, eh?"

Harry, in a plaintive voice: "Hey, do I get a vote in this?"

And to think they actually paid us to do this!

The ghost plane episode
Turbo Tarling

The first operational mission was launched from the Quick Reaction Area (Bagotville QRA) on the night of December 10, 1962. Turbo and Flying Officer Pat Clancy, already airborne in the area, had insufficient fuel to intercept the "unknown." Within minutes, the No. 1 QRA crew, Flight Lieutenant Ron Jensen and Flying Officer Jerry Walker, were airborne heading southeast and climbing under the direction of Ground Control Interception (GCI), Call Sign "Scabbard" (RCAF Stn, Mont Apica), with orders to identify the "bogey." With this guidance, they soon made contact with their AI radar and, despite heavy snow, acquired their target visually at half a mile: a KC–97 tanker flying out of Plattsburgh AFB at 7,000 feet and "lit up like a Christmas tree." But this was not the end of the story. Drawing alongside the big aircraft, the Voodoo crew could see that all the interior lights were on, but the plane seemed totally deserted—and Ron Jensen reported as much to Scabbard.

This unlikely story was relayed to Bagotville, where on landing, the crews were pledged to secrecy; but it was too late. When Turbo arrived home, a mere thirty minutes later, his wife, Claire, immediately asked, "What's the word on the KC–97?"

In fact, the crew of the tanker had believed that an electrical fire on board was out of control and bailed out, leaving the aircraft to wend its way north on autopilot—to where, nobody knew. For their skill and perseverance, it was congratulations all round for the 425 Squadron crew, with commendations from their Deputy Air Officer Commanding and NORAD Headquarters, and an interview with NBC to follow.

Topless Voodoo
John Cucheran

November 14, 1964, started no differently than any other fall day in the Maritimes. I was scheduled to fly as Captain "Kip" Chaput's air intercept navigator in a CF–101 Voodoo—an all-weather jet fighter.

Kip and I were stationed at CFB Chatham, New Brunswick, as members of 416 All Weather Fighter Squadron. We were scheduled to take part in a high-level exercise and anxiously awaited a "scramble" in the squadron crew room. The scramble horn blew. We grabbed our parachutes, dashed to our waiting Voodoo, climbed the ladders to our respective cockpits, strapped in, fired up both engines, and taxied to the runway button. Our scramble orders were straightforward: identify a target above 40,000 feet, heading 230 degrees magnetic. Cleared for take-off, "Kip" plugged in both afterburners. The aircraft roared down Runway 29 and leapt into the air in a few seconds.

Minutes later, we levelled off at 37,000 feet. The radar was unserviceable and refused to function despite all my efforts. "Kip" and I opted for a visual intercept. Our ground controller advised that the target was in our four o'clock position at seventy nautical miles. "Kip" opened the throttles and commenced a hard starboard turn. We were pulling four G's at 570 knots when the aircraft shuddered, and the pusher—a safety feature designed to prevent a high-speed stall—engaged, bunting the nose down so violently that we went from four positive to four negative G's.

The negative G threw me upwards in the back seat. My wristwatch caught the ejection seat handle and pulled it up, ejecting the canopy. I was hanging by my shoulder straps in the slipstream above the Plexiglas between the seats. Fortunately, my shoulder straps held me in or I'd have been thrown clear out of the cockpit. Both "Kip" and Mike Colbert, in a neighbouring aircraft, thought I'd ejected. "Kip" pulled back on the control column, sucking me into my seat. The fog from the explosive decompression cleared, and I saw the ejection handle in the full up position. I gingerly pushed the yellow ejection handle down, realizing that a squeeze of the trigger would eject the seat with me in it!

All my maps and checklists had been sucked from my pockets. "Kip" was unaware what had happened. At 37,000 feet with what was a *de facto* 570-knot wind blowing, the absence of a canopy made inter-cockpit communication difficult, if not impossible. With no canopy, we automatically enjoyed pressure breathing—100 percent oxygen forced into our lungs.

With the aircraft now under complete control, we terminated our mission and returned, safe and sound, to base.

Luke Air Force Day
Doug Munro

In 1969, a very courageous coordinator at Luke AFB invited 409 Squadron to provide a couple of Voodoos to grace their flight line during Luke's Air Force Day. The Canadian presence would serve two purposes: first, it would provide a sample of an aircraft of some historical significance; and second, it would relieve the USAF from having to borrow a 101 from the Davis-Monthan AFB "boneyard."

Always willing to tackle a difficult assignment, Hughie Fischer, Lynn Wagar, Doug Stuart, and Doug Munro bravely volunteered to undertake this onerous mission. On the morning of November 28, two double-tanked Voodoos launched from Comox—destination Hill AFB, Ogden, Utah; 1.7 hours later, they arrived at Hill. After a questionable lunch, the crews attended Flight Planning. The en-route weather from Hill to Luke was "severe clear" (but they decided to press on regardless). A creative thinker in the group had an inspiration: why not go low-level VFR. No sooner said than done. Airborne at 1230 local, they gave Salt Lake City a wide berth and headed southwest. Cruising sedately at 300 or so knots, and avoiding all built-up areas, they enjoyed an all-expense-paid tour of some of the most beautiful and spectacular parts of the southwest, including Bryce Canyon National Park, Zion National Park, Monument Valley, and the Grand Canyon! At 1400 hours, the Canadians arrived at Luke AFB. They looked forward to an evening of gentle respite and a much-needed rest to prepare for the morrow's static display.

Always cognizant of their role as international goodwill ambassadors, they repaired to the Luke officers' mess to meet and charm their hosts. Entering a very busy lounge, they spotted the pilots from the USAF Aerobatic Team, the world-famous Thunderbirds resplendent in their gaudy flying suits (a bit of envy there). In an instant, an informal, international, lie-telling contest ensued—fuelled by the World's Largest Margaritas and other indigenous beverages. It was a long evening but it passed in a blur. Sometime before midnight, Hughie, who shall forever remain infamous, with a name that will live on in infamy, stood on a chair, attracted the attention of a couple of hundred locals, and proposed a toast "To that Grand Old Man, Ho Ho Ho Chi Minh." It is fortunate that keelhauling (Hughie was a naval person) is no longer legal in the great State of Arizona. Two of the Thunderbirds who demonstrated significant staying power were Stan Musser (No. four in their four plane), and Mac Angel, one of the Solos and latterly Aide to General Wade, the USAF vice-chief.

The air show, on the 29th, had its moments. The Thunderbirds, because of a cloud layer at 6,000 feet, were forced to perform their "low-level show." The closing manoeuvre and pièce de résistance was the Bomb Burst—in this instance, a flat four-plane, mid-show line crossover! Lead and Two met at show centre. Looking to the right, the crowd was greeted with No. three approaching stage centre at a crawl (full flaps and nose high). Looking left, here came Stan—in full afterburner and just subsonic. Neat crossover!

At the post-show debriefing, Stan suggested that the Canadians were partly responsible for the crossover hiccup. Not possible—they had never budged from the static display area. Rather than overstay their welcome, the 409ers headed for Comox as speedily as dignity allowed.

PART FIVE
THE 1981 WARLOCKS FROM 425 SQUADRON

Jim Gregory

The CF–101 was fast, noisy, and powerful. With its "hard" afterburner lights, it thrilled millions of Canadians at air displays across the country from 1962 through 1984, when it was replaced by the CF–18. Each of Canada's CF–101 squadrons, over the years, formed air demonstration teams that would "show the flag" in major Canadian air shows. This story describes part of one year in the life of one such team: the 1981 Warlocks of 425 Squadron.

Partway through that season, I was selected to command the team, which already had a crowd-pleasing routine developed by my predecessor, Major Keith Coulter. The show included a nice mix of four-ship passes, solo acts, and a dramatic finish with four CF–101s passing the crowd at near-supersonic speed.

When the lead changed, the team was comfortable with the routine, but I wasn't. I had to ensure that I was comfortable with lead's manoeuvres, along with those of everybody else. My first practice was disappointing. After a relatively complex series of manoeuvres, I lost my situational awareness, couldn't see an aircraft that was head-on to me, and broke off, telling the team the practice was over.

After landing, I explained why I discontinued the practice, gained the team's support, and, about a week later, we made another attempt. I retained my situational awareness throughout, and we scheduled another practice the next day, this time over the Bagotville airfield. This one went flawlessly. We were about ready to take the show on the road. But, just before we embarked, I wanted one more practice, this one over Lac St. Jean, so that we would be ready for the limited horizon at our first gig: the Toronto International Airshow. What a venue, and what a time. We were in a hurry to get there.

We needn't have hurried. The Toronto weather delayed our departure from Bagotville by a day, and created a two-day delay in the air show. That was a good thing for us, as one of our aircraft contracted some foreign-object damage in one of its engines. It required an engine change, which was done overnight by our small ground crew contingent, who worked overnight to have the aircraft ready for 0900 the following day, just in time to hear the decision that the air show that day was cancelled.

On day three, the weather improved sufficiently to fly the show, although we had to devise a novel way to get the four aircraft into box formation before penetrating some low-lying cloud just off the departure end of the runway. We flew to our holding area with some guidance from Toronto centre and our own airborne radar, then ducked under some more low-lying cloud, descended to show altitude . . . and we were onstage, on time. The show, with some revisions, went off well under the relatively hazy conditions, which kept the navigators monitoring their altimeters, and we were soon on the ground preparing for the air show party.

While there, I met a man from Kitchener–Waterloo who was trying to tap into the Toronto air show resources for a display they hoped to have the following day. "Could the Warlocks help?" Without making any promises, I said that such a thing was possible, provided that the weather was good, the fuel consumption wasn't too high, and air traffic control had no objections, and left it at that.

On the next afternoon, the weather was good, our show was on time, our fuel consumption was less than usual, and we were able to shake a couple of aircraft loose for some high-speed, burner-assisted flypasts of K–W to make even more friends for the air force.

The next weekend, we had not one but two air shows, which sounds simple enough, but they were at two different bases. One was the Quinte Air Show at CFB Trenton, which always attracted thousands of aerofans. The other was the CF–100 retirement ceremony, where a large crowd was expected to say farewell to this vintage interceptor. Doing both of them at the posted times meant that many things had to go perfectly. (Which is normal for military operations. Isn't it?)

The first show was at North Bay, where the weather was good, and hundreds of old vets showed up to bid their long-ago steed goodbye and, incidentally, to cast beady eyes on the formation skills of their successors. While returning to the Bay for refuelling before embarking on the Trenton odyssey, I felt a slight yaw when I popped the speed brakes momentarily, but it went away, and I thought nothing of it — that is, until my wingman told me that my speed brake appeared to be damaged. My aircraft was out of commission. Fortunately, there was another 425 Squadron CF–101 sitting on the ramp. In short order,

CF–18 and Russian Bear.
(Master Corporal Andrew Collins/DND)

it was ready for an air show in Trenton.

After a quick turnaround, the Warlocks were back in the air, heading for the Quinte air show. We hit our holding point smack on time and, under ideal conditions, gave the thousands of patrons full value for their money. Then, we landed at Trenton, where the wheels fell off the wagon. The servicing arrangements had not been fully communicated to all who needed to know them, and there were some delays, along with some dissatisfaction. But, the important thing is that both air show commitments had been met, and thousands of aeronuts went home happy.

The next show with the Warlocks was in London, Ontario, and was memorable for all the wrong reasons. The first was the weather. It was terrible, with steady rain, so the first show was cancelled. The second day was marginally better, but our show needed some modifications and a a great deal of coordination with Toronto centre to do our vertical departure from the show, then fall into place in the queue of aircraft returning to land in London in the prevailing cruddy conditions. Adding to the problem was the somewhat limited navigation system in the Voodoo, and the problems compounded quickly. Fuel was becoming a major concern, but we landed before it ran out.

The Bagotville air show of June 25, 1982, was my last flight with the Warlocks, and also in the CF–101. It was also the Warlocks' last flight, as the CF–101 world was winding down in preparation for the CF–18, which is still our first line of defence. There was, a bit later, one more four-Voodoo formation, when four of them, all duded up in the colours of their respective squadrons, took to the air for one last hurrah.

The Warlock experience was, for me, a thrilling one. I can now say, "I've been there, I've done that, I've got the T-shirt."

Those who were with me and also got the T-shirt were:

Pilots—Captains Doug McClennan, Daniel Pelletier, and Chuck McCrea

Navigators—Major Joe Sharpe, Captain Denys Guerin, Lts Gerry Lalonde, Rene Cousineau and Michel Latouche.

Thanks, guys.

APPENDIX A
The names inscribed on the AWF Memorial Cairn

Capt.	R.R. Abbott	416 Squadron
F/O	S.J. Allen	423 Squadron
F/O	M.C. Anderson	410 Squadron
Cpl.	P.J. Ardley	RCAF Station North Bay
F/O	J.M. Arsenault	423 Squadron
F/O	R.A. Ashmore	445 Squadron
F/O	J.R. Baer	3 AW(F) OTU
Capt.	L.E. Bastie	409 Squadron
F/O	D.G. Bate	433 Squadron
F/O	R.C. Bedard	3 AW(F) OTU
F/O	R.J. Bentley	423 Squadron
F/O	J.L.P.W. Berrigan	CEPE
F/O	E.N. Bilton	414 Squadron
F/L	R.W. Bogle	ADCHQ
S/L	L.A. Bolin	432 Squadron
Capt.	R.J. Borland	425 Squadron
F/L	H.H. Bouius	425 Squadron
F/O	J.A.F.G Boutin	433 Squadron
Capt.	P.M. Bow	410 Squadron
F/O	L.J.E. Buckman	433 Squadron
Capt.	T.M. Campbell	414 Squadron
F/O	D.G. Carter	423 Squadron
F/O	E.A. Charles	3 AW(F) OTU
F/O	D.R. Clark	416 Squadron
F/O	G.A. Cooling	423 Squadron
Capt.	L.J. Cox	409 Squadron
F/O	S.W. Cratchley	409 Squadron
F/L	J.R. Curtis	CEPE
F/O	F.M. Dakin	3 AW(F) OTU
F/O	J.G.G.G. Dallaire	414 Squadron
F/O	G.M. Davis	409 Squadron
F/O	J.M. Dawson	414 Squadron
Lt. (USAF)	R.A. De Genova	438th FIS
F/O	J.R.R.G. Desrochers	3 AW(F) OTU
F/O	G.A. Donald	419 Squadron
F/O	R.B. Donald	440 Squadron
F/O	R.C. Dougall	432 Squadron
Capt.	J.A. Emon	409 Squadron
F/L	K.M. Eyolfson	445 Squadron
F/L	J.S.N. Findlay	3 AW(F) OTU
F/L	H.A.K. Fisher	3 AW(F) OTU
F/O	P.A. Flannery	433 Squadron
F/O	R.R. Fletcher	414 Squadron
F/O	S.S. Franko	445 Squadron
F/O	D.J. Freckleton	3 AW(F) OTU
F/O	R.H. Frost-Hunt	3 AW(F) OTU
F/O	D.J.L. Graham	440 Squadron
F/O	F.A.S. Grant	445 Squadron
F/L	R.M. Grant	416 Squadron
F/O	J.A. Hardy	CEPE
W/C	C.E.L. Hare	414 Squadron
F/O	K.G. Heather	419 Squadron
F/L	W.C. Henderson	EWU
F/O	S.A. Henry	410 Squadron
Capt. (USAF)	D.I. Hickman	410 Squadron
Mr.	J. Hieber	Avro Canada
F/O	D.S. Hirst	440 Squadron
F/O	R.F. Holland	3 AW(F) OTU
F/O	J.O.J.Y. Houde	419 Squadron
Capt.	G.J. Hunt	414 Squadron
F/L	J.G. Keith	EWU

F/L	E. Keller	ADCHQ		F/O	J.A.S. Plante	419 Squadron
F/O	J.H. Kerr	129 A&FF		F/O	K.G. Presnell	419 Squadron
F/O	B. Kirkham	423 Squadron		F/O	G.R.B. Rayment	423 Squadron
F/O	R.W. Komar	423 Squadron		F/O	J.S. Read	428 Squadron
Capt.	J.D. Lauder	410 Squadron		Mr.	J. Rivett	314 TSU
F/O	A.N. Leaf	433 Squadron		P/O	J.Y.J.M. Roberge	3 AW(F) OTU
F/O	B.G.P. Leon	428 Squadron		F/L	H.J. Robertson	CEPE
P/O	B.I. Luck	3 AW(F) OTU		Capt.	R.E.J. Robichaud	425 Squadron
Mr.	G.J. Lynes	Avro Canada		F/O	A.R. Schellongovsky	423 Squadron
F/O	A.K. Mackenzie	432 Squadron		F/O	W.J. Schmidt	445 Squadron
F/O	B.D. Mackenzie	EWU		F/O	B. Shaw	409 Squadron
S/L	A. MacMillan	3 AW(F) OTU		F/O	D.A. Sheffield	433 Squadron
F/L	S.A. Marshall	428 Squadron		F/L	W.H. Siegel	ADCHQ
F/O	J.E. McCarthy	428 Squadron		Capt.	R.J. Smith	409 Squadron
F/O	E.R. McCoy	419 Squadron		F/O	L.E.V. Sparrow	433 Squadron
F/O	J. McLaren	409 Squadron		F/O	L.A. Strasser	433 Squadron
F/O	M.L. McLean	428 Squadron		F/O	G.S. Stubbs	409 Squadron
W/C	W.A.G. McLeish	440 Squadron		F/O	J.Y. Theriault	425 Squadron
F/L	K.P. McNulty	419 Squadron		F/O	H. Thiessen	445 Squadron
P/O	A. Miles	423 Squadron		F/O	K.D. Thomas	445 Squadron
F/O	J.E.A. Miller	409 Squadron		F/O	L.L. Tidball	129 A&FF
F/L	H.W. Mitchell	3 AW(F) OTU		P/O	J.M.Y. Turpin	3 AW(F) OTU
P/O	C.E. Ness	3 AW(F) OTU		F/O	J. Walton	440 Squadron
F/O	W.D. Ness	440 Squadron		F/L	B. Warren	Avro Canada
F/O	J. Nestoruk	425 Squadron		F/O	J.W. Wilding	419 Squadron
F/O	L.B. Neumeyer	3 AW(F) OTU		F/L	S.K. Woolley	ADCHQ
W/C	G.E. Nickerson	445 Squadron		F/O	A.D. Wright	423 Squadron
W/C	H.R. Norris	432 Squadron		F/O	C.R. Wright	425 Squadron
F/O	L.H. Ollenberger	423 Squadron		F/O	M.G. Wright	425 Squadron
Capt.	A. Oostenburg	416 Squadron		S/L	G.J. Zaleschuk	423 Squadron
F/O	G.R. Ormiston	3 AW(F) OTU		F/O	M.J. Zimmer	423 Squadron
Mr.	R.G. Ostrander	Avro Canada				
F/L	R.J. Palmer	EWU				
F/O	K.S. Partington	445 Squadron				
F/O	R.D. Perrie	3 AW(F) OTU				

Glossary

A/C	Aircraft	CO	Commanding Officer
ADC	Air Defence Command	Crud	A game played on a pool table
ADCHQ	Air Defence Command Headquarters	DAO	Duty Alert Officer
ADF	Automatic Direction Finding	DCO	Duty Carried Out
ADIZ	Air Defence Identification Zone	DNCO	Duty Not Carried Out
ADO	American Duty Officer	DOD	Department of Defence
AETE	Aeronautical Experimental and Test Establishment	ECCM	Electronic counter-countermeasures
		ECM	Electronic countermeasures
AI	Airborne Interception; Airborne Indicator (referring to navigators)	EWO	Electronic Warfare Officer
		EWU	Electronic Warfare Unit
AIM	Airborne interceptor missiles carried by the CF–101	FFAR	Folding Fin Aerial Rockets—carried by the CF–100
Air Cav	Air Cavalry—Vietnam helicopter units	F/L	Flight Lieutenant
AMU	Air Movement's Unit	F/O	Flying Officer
ANG	Air National Guard (USAF)	FOD	Foreign Object Disposal
AOA	Angle of attack	G/C	Group Captain
AOC	Air Officer Commanding	GCA	Ground Controlled Approach
APG	Air pulse gunnery (normally used to describe a gunnery computer)	GCI	Ground Control Intercept
		GEE	An RAF fixing aide
ATC	Air Traffic Control	Herc	A Hercules transport aircraft
AVM	Air Vice-Marshal	Hootch	A man-made hut in Vietnam
AWF	All-Weather Fighter	Huey	A helicopter—much used in Vietnam
Bagtown	Bagotville	ICCS	International Commission for Control and Supervision
BComd	Base Commander		
BG	Airport identifier for Bagotville	IIP	Improved Interceptor Program
BX	Base Exchange (or PX—Post Exchange)	IFF	(World War II) Identification, friend or foe
CAC	Combat Alert Centre	IFR	Instrument Flight Rules (applies to flights conducted through clouds, when the pilot can no longer see the ground)
CADIZ	Canadian Air Defence Identification Zone		
CAdO	Chief Administrative Officer		
CB	Cumulonimbus cloud formation		
Chaff	Strips of metal foil released in the air to obstruct radar detection	ILS	Instrument Landing System
		IR	Infrared
Clunk	Nickname for the CF–100	IRSTS	Infrared Search and Track System

JTIDS	Joint Tactical Information Display System	**Radar**	Instrument for airborne detection of speed and position (**Ra**dio **D**etection **a**nd **R**anging)
Klicks	Kilometres	**RAF**	Royal Air Force
Kts	Knots—nautical miles per hour	**RCAF**	Royal Canadian Air Force
LCC	Lead Collision Course—a firing pass for a Clunk	**RDR**	Radar
MA	Mission Accomplished	**R/T**	Radio Telegraphy
MAYDAY	An International Defence emergency call	**SAR**	Search and Rescue
MI	Missed Intercept	**SARAH**	Search and Rescue and Homing
MND	Minister of National Defence	**Sked**	A scheduled flight
NATO	North Atlantic Treaty Organization	**S/L**	Squadron Leader
Nav	Navigator; navigation	**Sqn**	Squadron
NDBs	Non-Directional Beacons	**TACAN**	The navigation system used in the CF–101
NORAD	Northern American Aerospace Command	**Tac Eval**	Tactical Evaluation
NOTAMs	A document entitled *Notices to Airmen*	**TAS**	True Air Speed
O₂	Oxygen	**TOT**	Time on target
OTS	Operational Training Squadron	**U/C**	Undercarriage
OTU	Operational Training Unit	**UFO**	Unidentified Flying Object
PAdO	Personnel Administrative Officer	**U/S**	Unserviceable
PMQ	Permanent Married Quarters	**USAF**	United States Air Force
PPI	Plan position indicator; the radar scope used in ground-based radar sites that track enemy bombers	**VFR**	Visual flight rules (less restrictive than IFR)
PSI	Pounds per square inch	**W/C**	Wing Commander
Q	Short form of QRA	**WSO**	Weapons System Operator
QQ	Airport identifier for Comox	**XO**	Executive Officer
QRA	Quick Reaction Area—area where interceptors held alert		

About the Editors

John Eggenberger

After high school, John Eggenberger worked for the next five years as a roughneck in the oil fields of Alberta. In 1955, the "oil patch" was in a bust cycle, which led John to join the RCAF and eventually the 409 AWF Sqn at Comox, BC. At the end of his 409 tour in 1959, John won one of three RCAF highly prized postings: a DEW Line tour at PIN, Cape Parry. On surviving this idyllic, year-long tour, John was reintroduced to the CF–100 at the OTU at Cold Lake, and this time lucked out with a posting to 445 AWF Sqn, located at 1 Wing, Marville, France. When the CF–100 was removed from fighter squadron status, John was transferred to 2 Wing, Gros Tenquin, France, as the Wing Intelligence Officer. However, the arrival of the CF–104 into RCAF NATO operations changed the landscape, and John was assigned as the senior project officer of the recently formed Radar Prediction Unit at 2 Wing. However, after Charles DeGaulle kicked NATO out of France, the RPU, along with John, was moved to 3 Wing, and shortly thereafter to 4 Wing in Baden Soellingen, Germany.

After a couple of years in 4 Wing, in 1965 John resigned in order to go back to school in Calgary. Upon being invited to rejoin the RCAF two years later, John returned to flying as a radar/inertial navigation instructor at the CF–104, 6 Strike/Reconnaissance OTU, Cold Lake. During the next five years John toiled at Cold Lake and the University of Calgary. Thereafter, John got lost in a maze of staff jobs here and there, retiring from the Armed Forces in 1981 to a job as VP Human Resources with the Pulp and Paper Research Institute in Point Claire, PQ.

John left the workforce in 1995 and moved to Elliot Lake, Ontario, and, after living contentedly in Victoria, BC, from 2000 to 2010, now lives in Ottawa with his wife and camp follower, Mary, who, as John's schoolmate in Grade 1 in Northern Alberta, and many, many years later in Comox, has shown that she is really tougher than tough.

Bob Merrick

Bob Merrick joined the RCAF in 1956, trained as an air intercept navigator, and was posted to 432 Squadron flying CF–100s at RCAF Station Bagotville. After that tour, he was moved to Test flight, also at BG. From there, he was moved to 447 (SAM) Squadron at RCAF Station La Macaza, where he babysat Bomarcs. His next posting was to the EWU detachment at RCAF Station Comox, and when that detachment folded, he was moved to 409 Squadron, also at Comox. From there, he went to 58th Tac Training Wing, instructing on F–4s at Luke Air Force Base. The payback for that was another tour at Bagotville, this time to 410 OTS, instructing on the CF–101. From there, he was posted to NDHQ, where he finished his air force career. He then went with Transport Canada, mostly in Aviation Safety Programs, for twelve years. He and his wife Barb now live in Orleans, Ontario.

Doug Munro

Doug Munro joined the RCAF in 1951. He was commissioned and received his nav wings in November 1952. His flying career was, if not unique, certainly unusual. He graduated from seven Operational Training Units (OTUs).

First came the Maritime OTU on Lancasters at RCAF Station Greenwood, NS, followed by a Lanc tour at 407 Squadron, Comox, BC (QQ). Next to the AW(F) OTU on CF–100s at RCAF Station Cold Lake, AB, and then to 409 Squadron on CF–100s at QQ. Next he completed the CF 100 OTU again—this time at Bagotville, QC (BG), only to have the great good fortune to have his posting to Europe cancelled. As a reward, he then completed the CF–101 OTU at BG, followed by a tour on CF–101s at 416 Squadron, Chatham, NB. A tour at the Air Navigation School, RCAF Winnipeg, MB, wedged its way between squadron tours. Then, in rapid succession, to the CF–101 OTU, followed a tour at 409 Squadron, QQ, and once more to the CF–101 OTU and a tour at 425 Squadron, Bagotville, BG. Now, for something a bit different, he completed the Hercules OTU at CFB Trenton and a posting to the Air Navigation School at CFB Winnipeg.

All was not fun and games. In 1958, he was posted to a darling little radar base in Northern Quebec (Mont Apica) as a GCI controller. Training for this position entailed a sixteen-week course at Tyndall AFB, Panama City, Florida. A candidate with Doug's background should have been able to ace the course in four or five weeks. This posting was twelve months long. His next base was RCAF Base Falconbridge, ON. He had struck gold. The base nursing sister swept Doug off his feet. Forty-eight years have passed and counting.

In 1971, Doug was the recipient of a mixed blessing. He lost thirteen years' seniority, received a ten-dollar raise, was promoted to major, and was posted to a year at DEW Line Station Dyer (on Baffin Island). In 1972, he was posted to the Canadian Embassy in Washington, D.C. as Staff Officer Training and Visits. It almost made up for Cape Dyer.

Rather than risk another OTU, Doug took early retirement. In 1982, Doug was called to the Manitoba Bar. He retired from the practice of law in 1997—a pleasant way to say adieu.

TO ORDER MORE COPIES:

GENERAL STORE PUBLISHING HOUSE

499 O'Brien Road, Box 415, Renfrew, Ontario, Canada K7V 4A6

Tel 1.800.465.6072 • Fax 1.613.432.7184

www.gsph.com